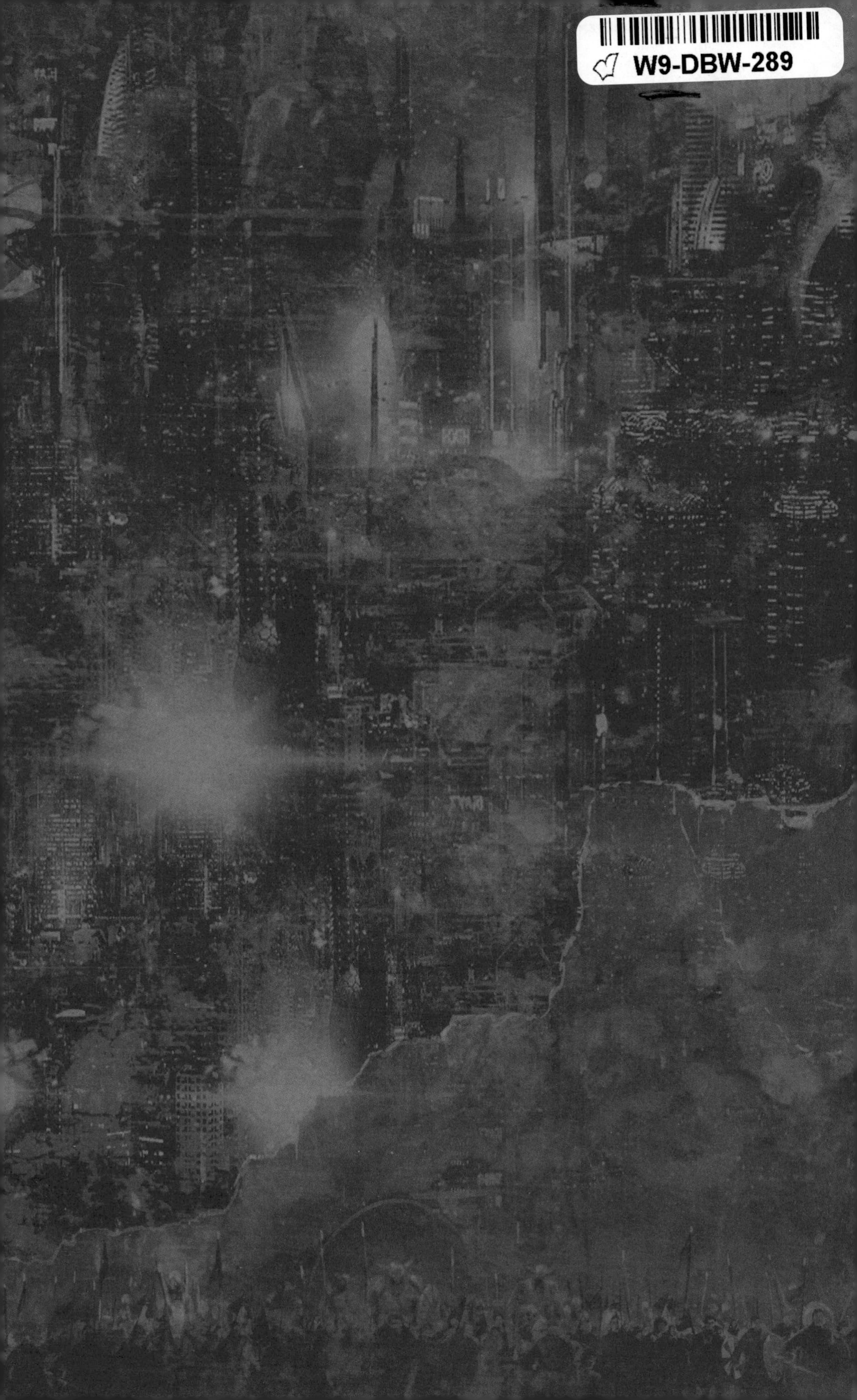

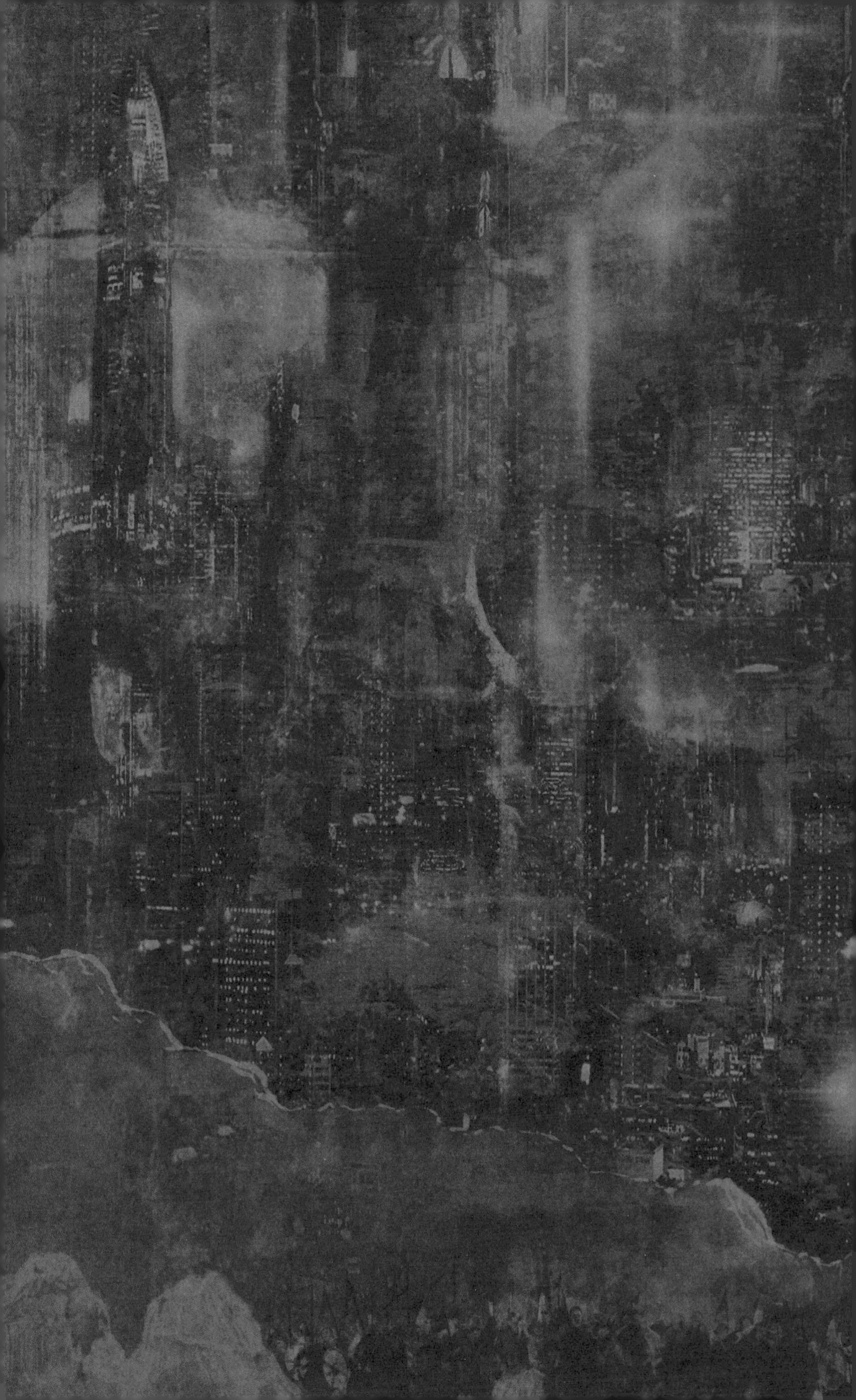

THE GREEN LANTERN

SEASON TWO

VOL. 2

THE GREEN LANTERN SEASON TWO

LANTERN

VOL. 2

GRANT MORRISON writer

LIAM SHARP artist

STEVE OLIFF and **LIAM SHARP** colorists

TOM ORZECHOWSKI and **STEVE WANDS** letterers

LIAM SHARP collection cover artist

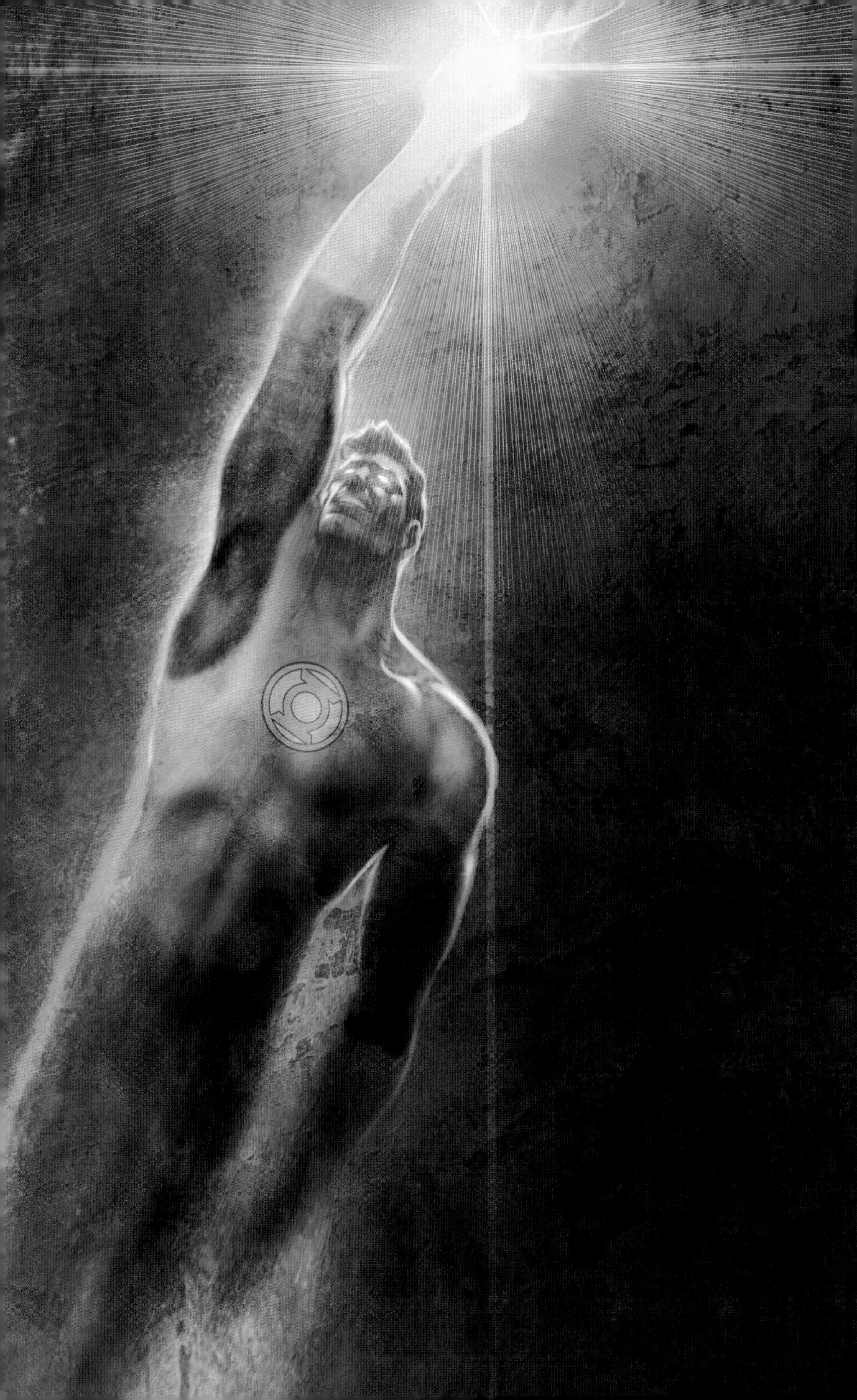

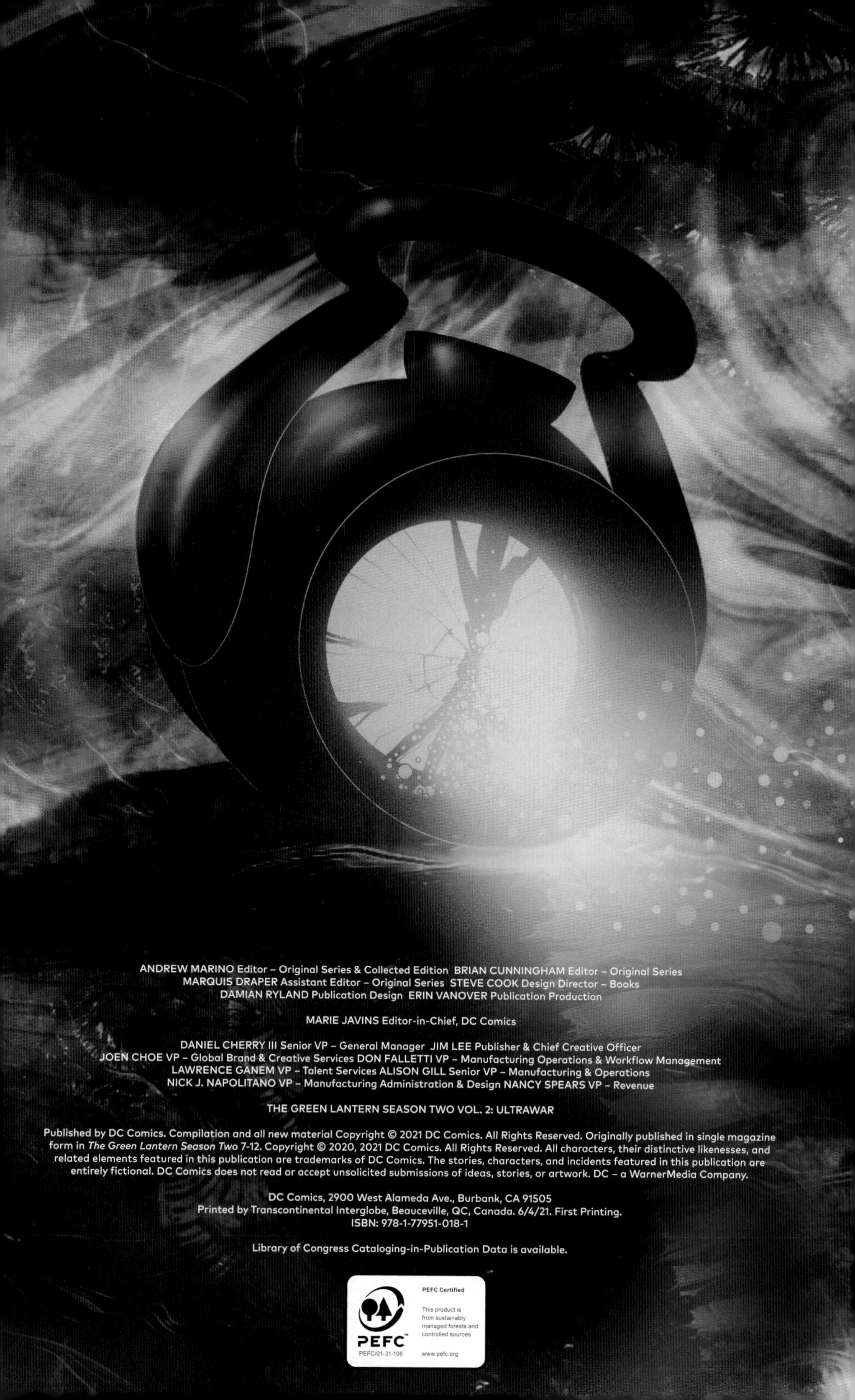

ANDREW MARINO Editor – Original Series & Collected Edition BRIAN CUNNINGHAM Editor – Original Series
MARQUIS DRAPER Assistant Editor – Original Series STEVE COOK Design Director – Books
DAMIAN RYLAND Publication Design ERIN VANOVER Publication Production

MARIE JAVINS Editor-in-Chief, DC Comics

DANIEL CHERRY III Senior VP – General Manager JIM LEE Publisher & Chief Creative Officer
JOEN CHOE VP – Global Brand & Creative Services DON FALLETTI VP – Manufacturing Operations & Workflow Management
LAWRENCE GANEM VP – Talent Services ALISON GILL Senior VP – Manufacturing & Operations
NICK J. NAPOLITANO VP – Manufacturing Administration & Design NANCY SPEARS VP – Revenue

THE GREEN LANTERN SEASON TWO VOL. 2: ULTRAWAR

DC Comics, 2900 West Alameda Ave., Burbank, CA 91505
Printed by Transcontinental Interglobe, Beauceville, QC, Canada. 6/4/21. First Printing.
ISBN: 978-1-77951-018-1

Library of Congress Cataloging-in-Publication Data is available.

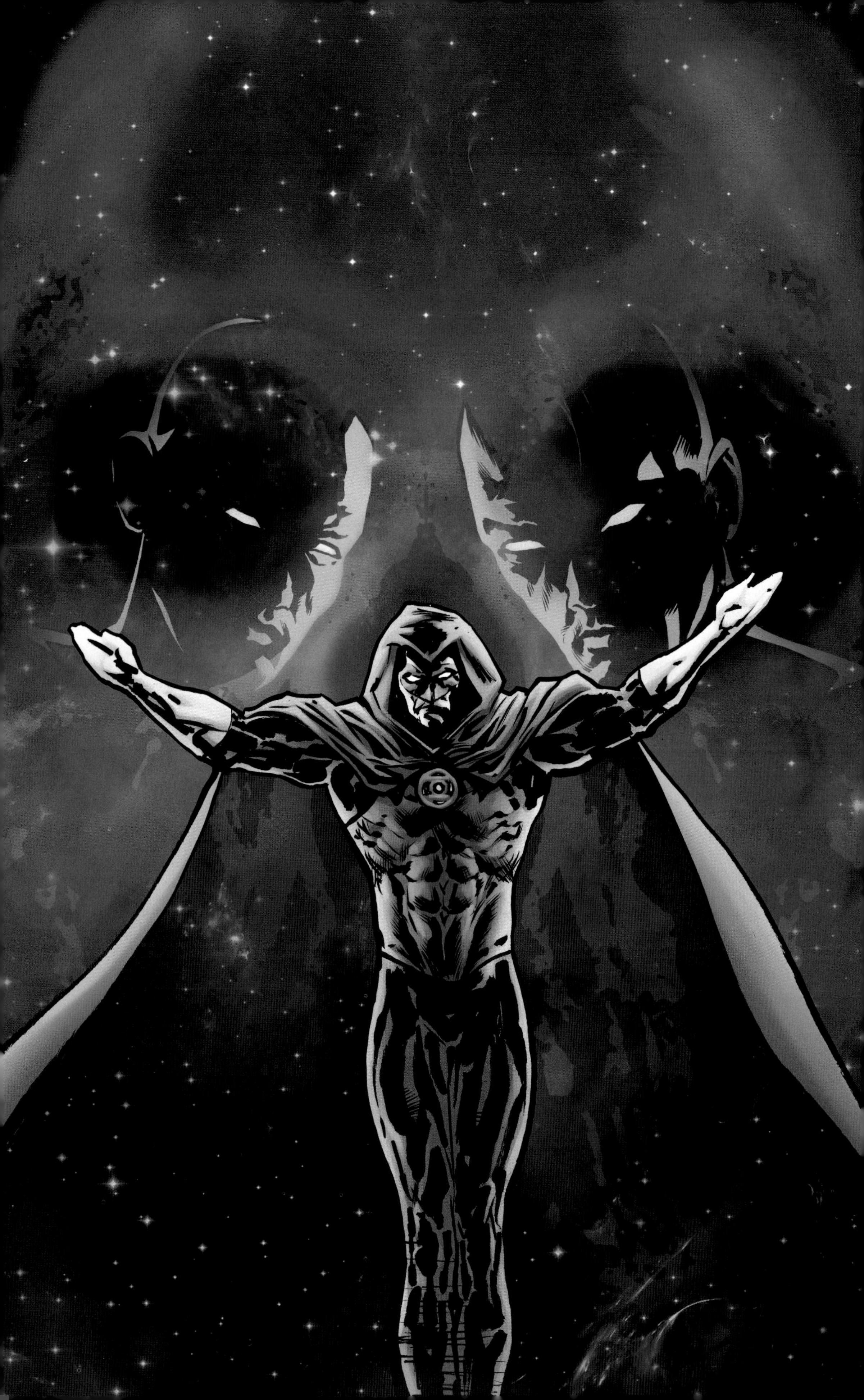

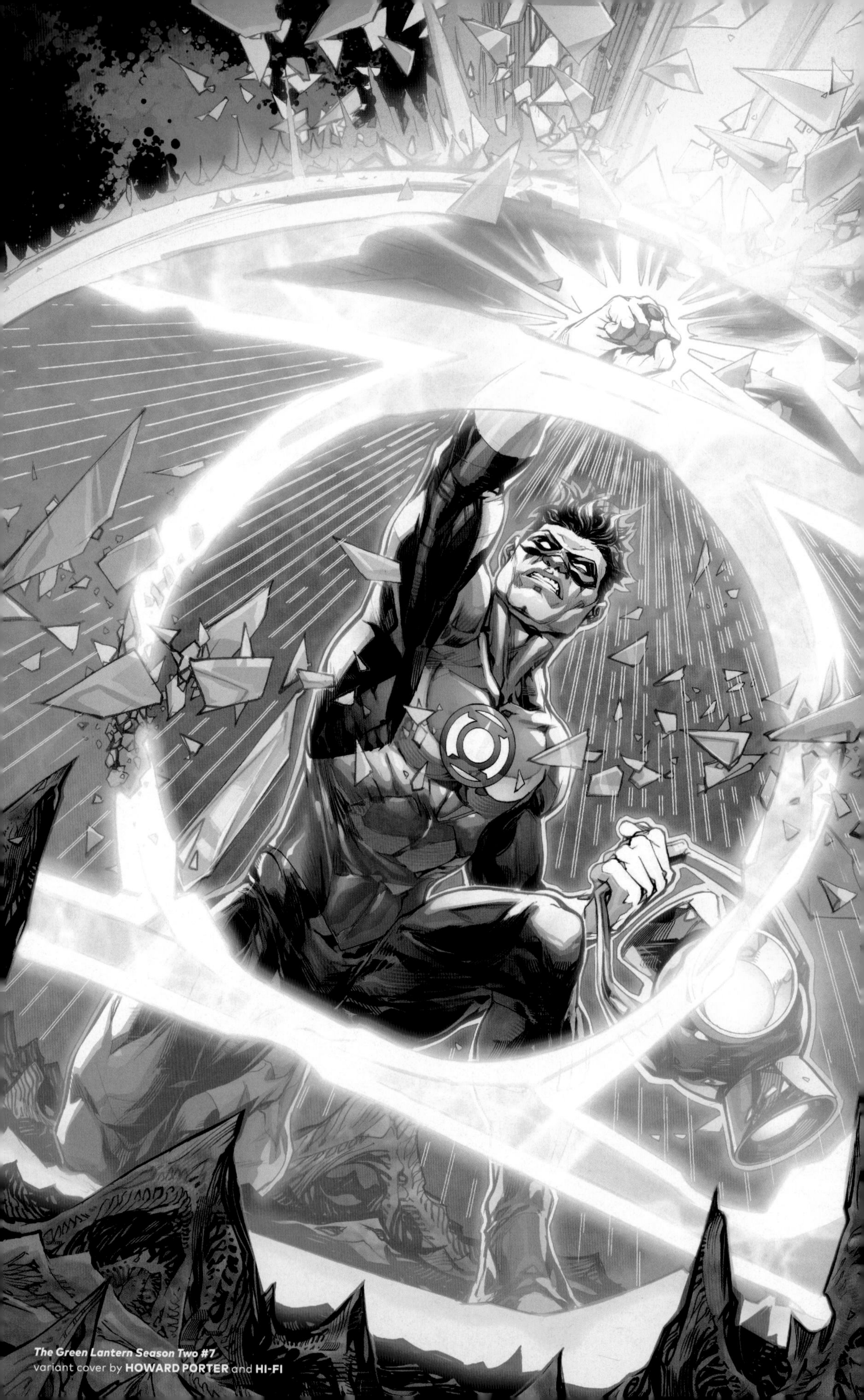

The Green Lantern Season Two #7
variant cover by **HOWARD PORTER** and **HI-FI**

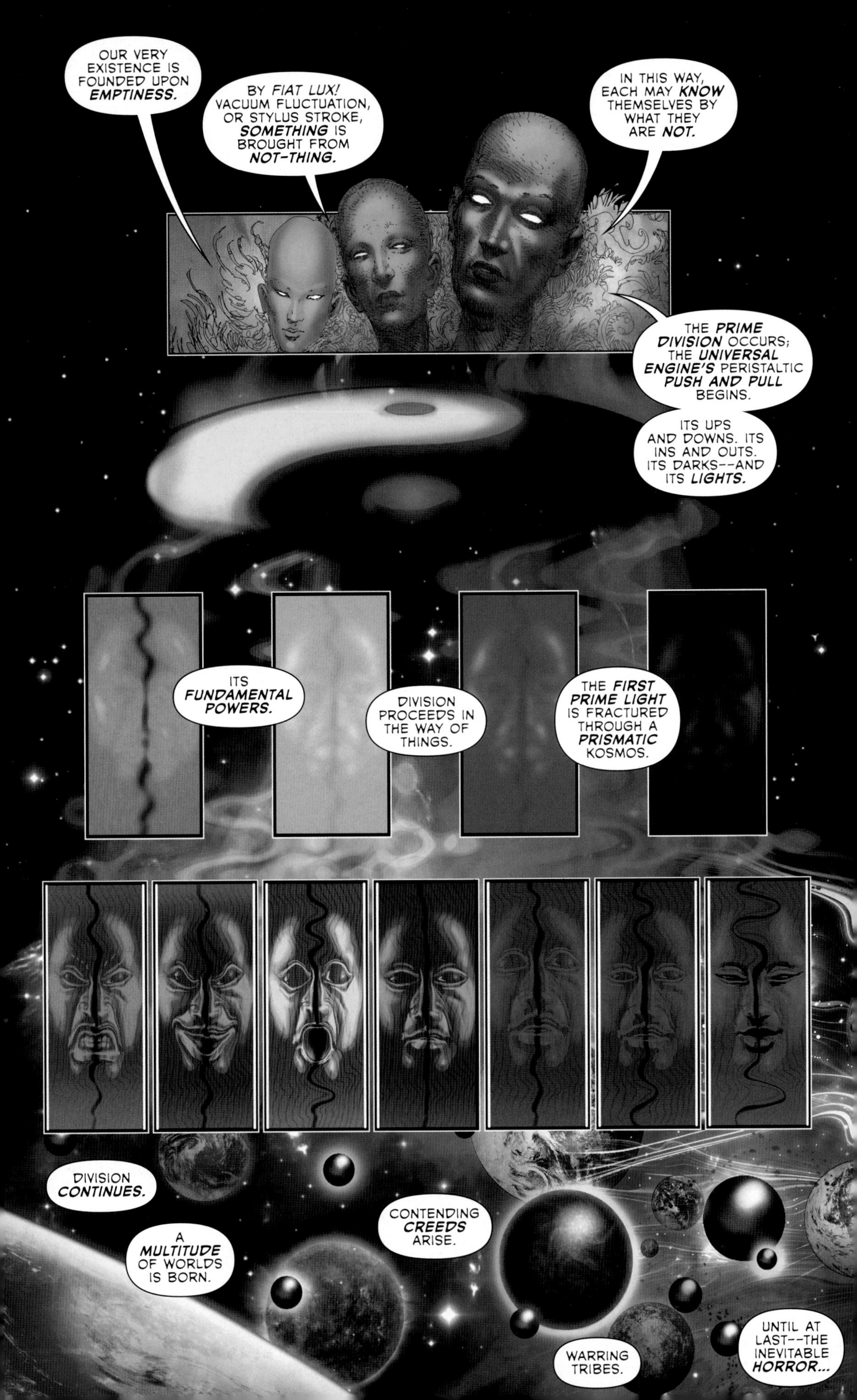
OUR VERY EXISTENCE IS FOUNDED UPON *EMPTINESS.*
BY *FIAT LUX!* VACUUM FLUCTUATION, OR STYLUS STROKE, ***SOMETHING*** IS BROUGHT FROM ***NOT-THING.***
IN THIS WAY, EACH MAY ***KNOW*** THEMSELVES BY WHAT THEY ARE ***NOT.***
THE ***PRIME DIVISION*** OCCURS; THE ***UNIVERSAL ENGINE'S*** PERISTALTIC ***PUSH AND PULL*** BEGINS.
ITS UPS AND DOWNS. ITS INS AND OUTS. ITS DARKS--AND ITS ***LIGHTS.***
ITS ***FUNDAMENTAL POWERS.***
DIVISION PROCEEDS IN THE WAY OF THINGS.
THE ***FIRST PRIME LIGHT*** IS FRACTURED THROUGH A ***PRISMATIC*** KOSMOS.
DIVISION ***CONTINUES.***
A ***MULTITUDE*** OF WORLDS IS BORN.
CONTENDING ***CREEDS*** ARISE.
WARRING TRIBES.
UNTIL AT LAST--THE INEVITABLE ***HORROR...***

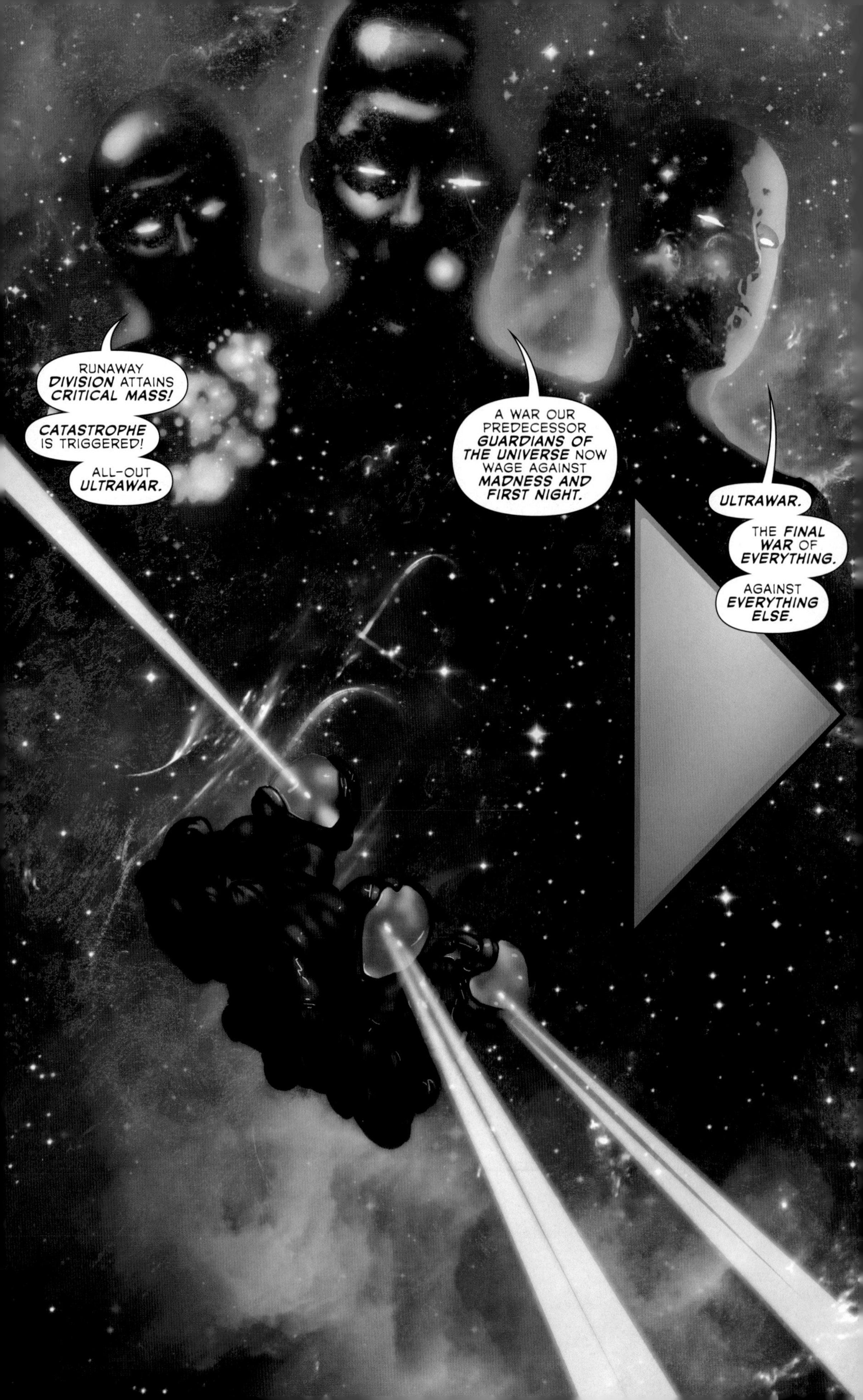
RUNAWAY DIVISION ATTAINS CRITICAL MASS!
CATASTROPHE IS TRIGGERED!
ALL-OUT ULTRAWAR.
A WAR OUR PREDECESSOR GUARDIANS OF THE UNIVERSE NOW WAGE AGAINST MADNESS AND FIRST NIGHT.
ULTRAWAR.
THE FINAL WAR OF EVERYTHING.
AGAINST EVERYTHING ELSE.

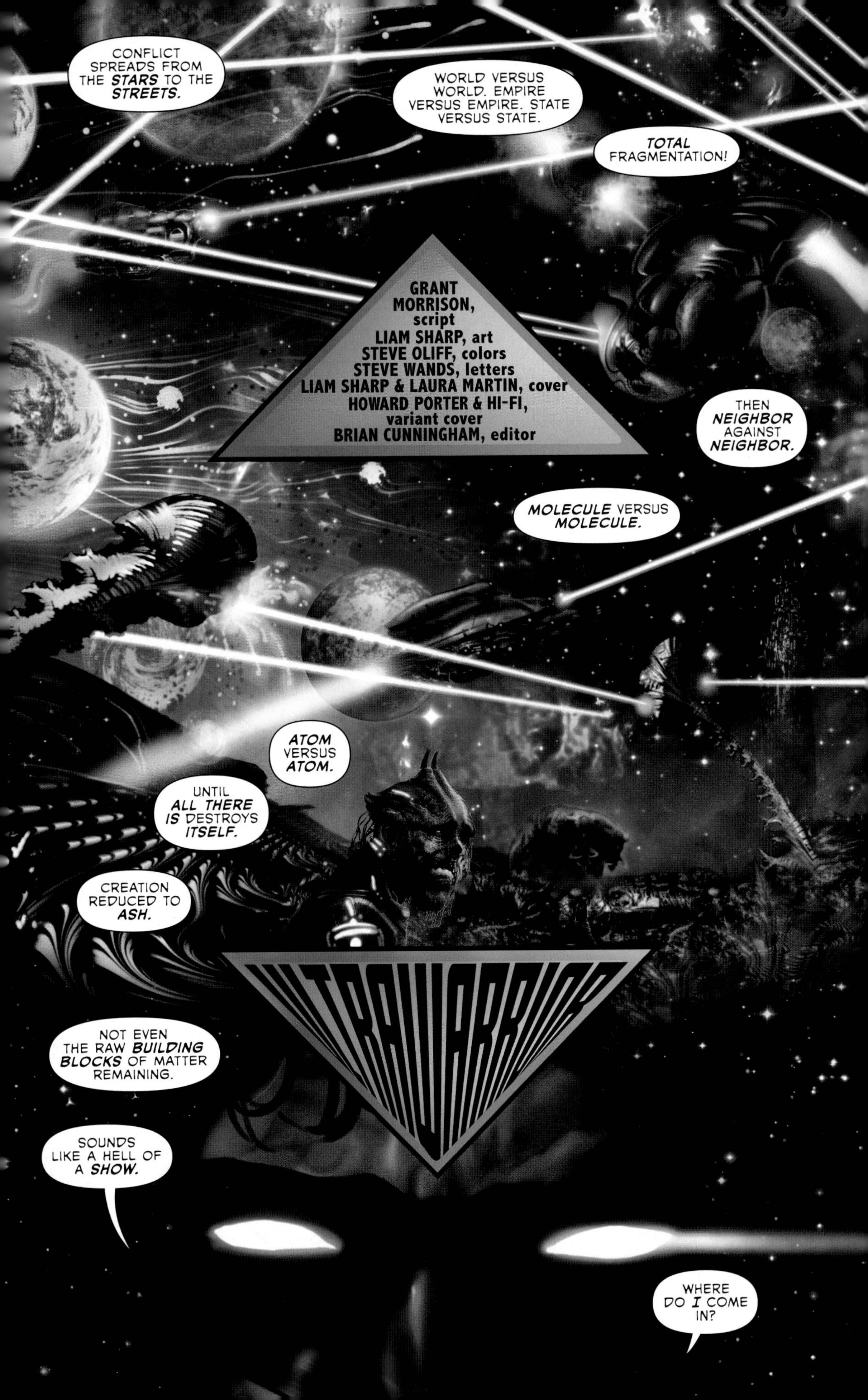

CONFLICT SPREADS FROM THE STARS TO THE STREETS.
WORLD VERSUS WORLD. EMPIRE VERSUS EMPIRE. STATE VERSUS STATE.
TOTAL FRAGMENTATION!
GRANT MORRISON, script
LIAM SHARP, art
STEVE OLIFF, colors
STEVE WANDS, letters
LIAM SHARP & LAURA MARTIN, cover
HOWARD PORTER & HI-FI, variant cover
BRIAN CUNNINGHAM, editor
THEN NEIGHBOR AGAINST NEIGHBOR.
MOLECULE VERSUS MOLECULE.
ATOM VERSUS ATOM.
UNTIL ALL THERE IS DESTROYS ITSELF.
CREATION REDUCED TO ASH.
ULTRAWARRIOR
NOT EVEN THE RAW BUILDING BLOCKS OF MATTER REMAINING.
SOUNDS LIKE A HELL OF A SHOW.
WHERE DO I COME IN?

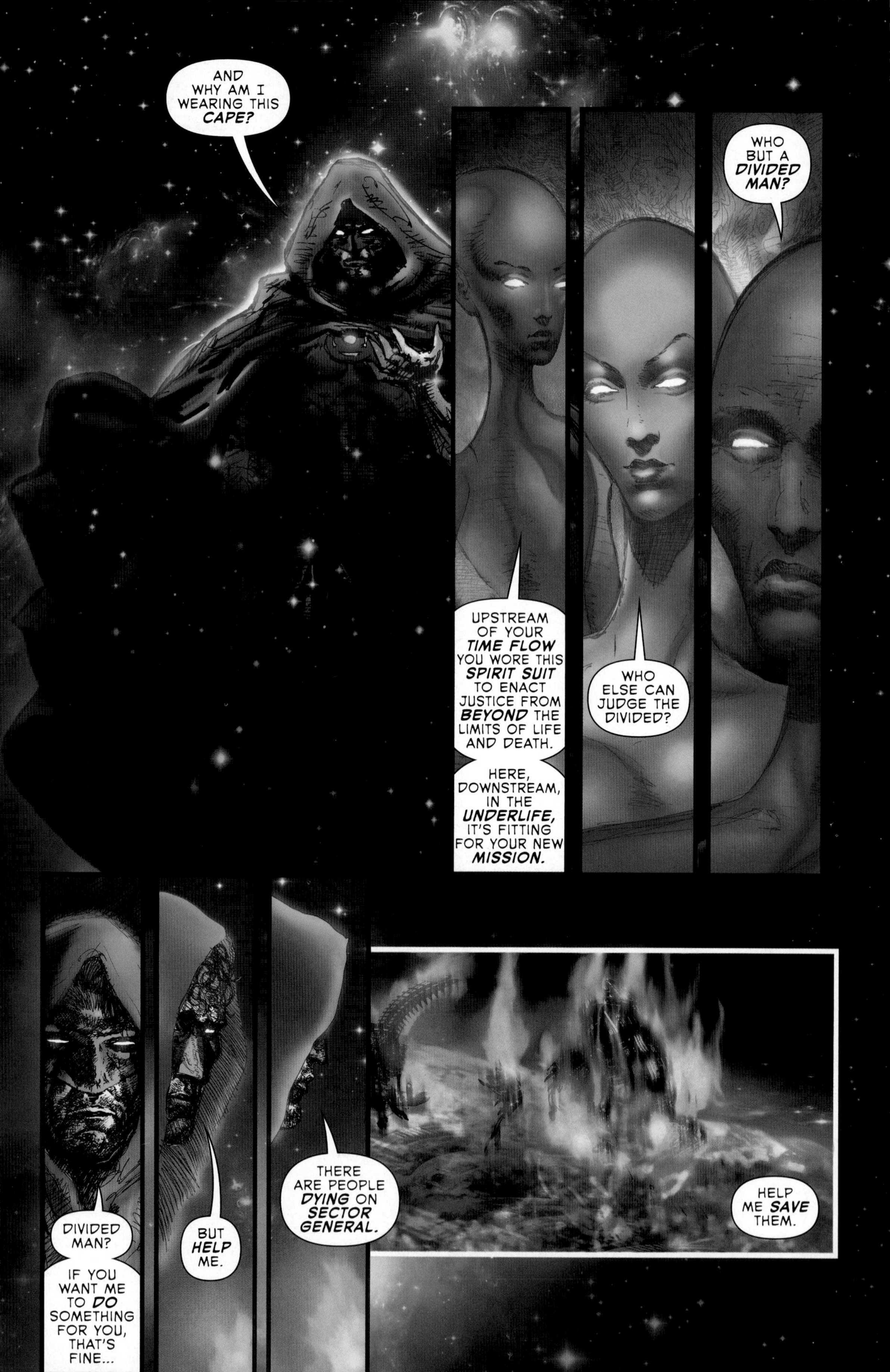
AND WHY AM I WEARING THIS CAPE?
WHO BUT A DIVIDED MAN?
UPSTREAM OF YOUR TIME FLOW YOU WORE THIS SPIRIT SUIT TO ENACT JUSTICE FROM BEYOND THE LIMITS OF LIFE AND DEATH.
HERE, DOWNSTREAM, IN THE UNDERLIFE, IT'S FITTING FOR YOUR NEW MISSION.
WHO ELSE CAN JUDGE THE DIVIDED?
DIVIDED MAN?
IF YOU WANT ME TO DO SOMETHING FOR YOU, THAT'S FINE...
BUT HELP ME.
THERE ARE PEOPLE DYING ON SECTOR GENERAL.
HELP ME SAVE THEM.

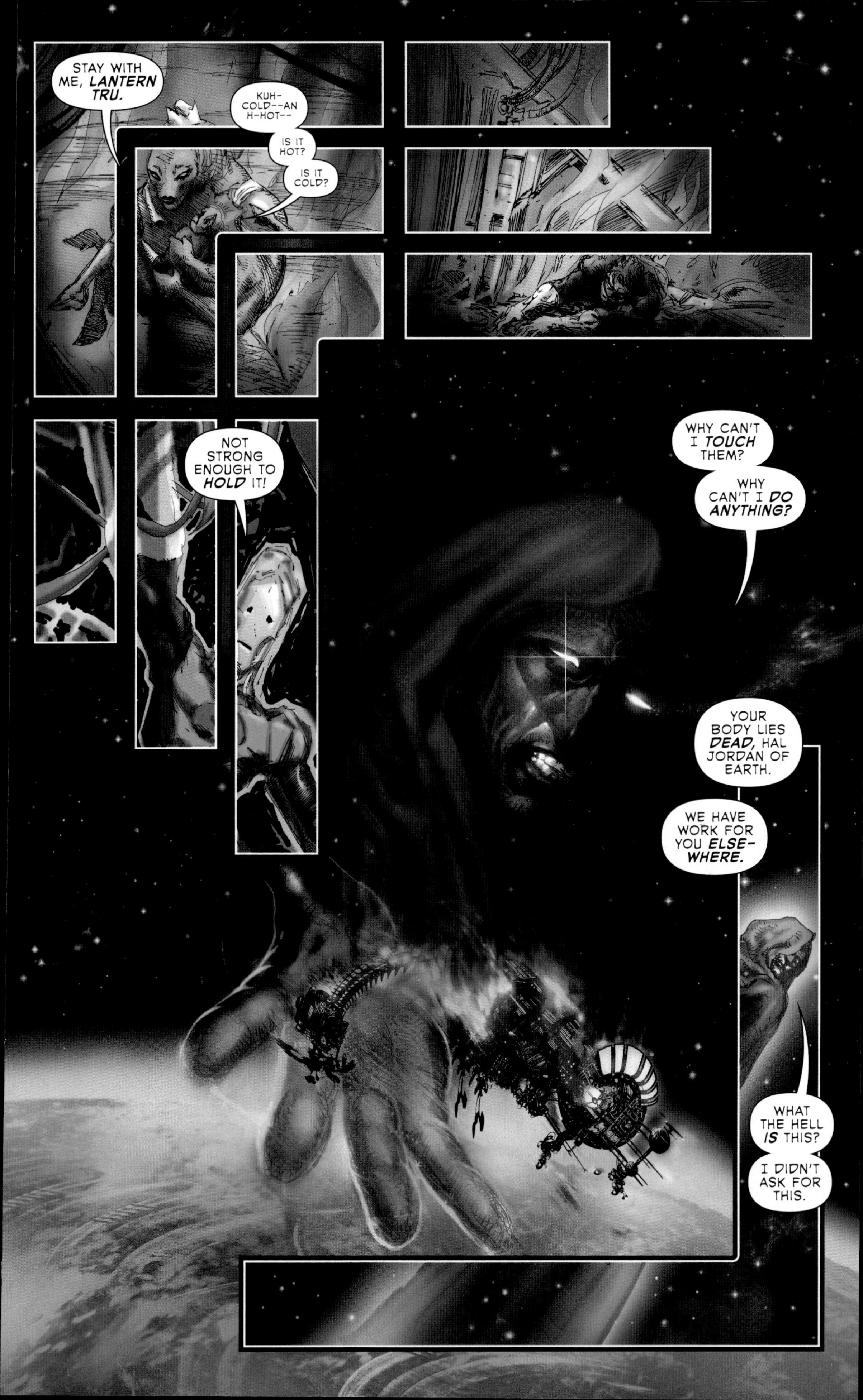
STAY WITH ME, *LANTERN TRU.*
KUH-COLD--AN H-HOT--
IS IT HOT?
IS IT COLD?
NOT STRONG ENOUGH TO *HOLD* IT!
WHY CAN'T I *TOUCH* THEM?
WHY CAN'T I *DO ANYTHING?*
YOUR BODY LIES *DEAD,* HAL JORDAN OF EARTH.
WE HAVE WORK FOR YOU *ELSE-WHERE.*
WHAT THE HELL *IS* THIS?
I DIDN'T ASK FOR THIS.

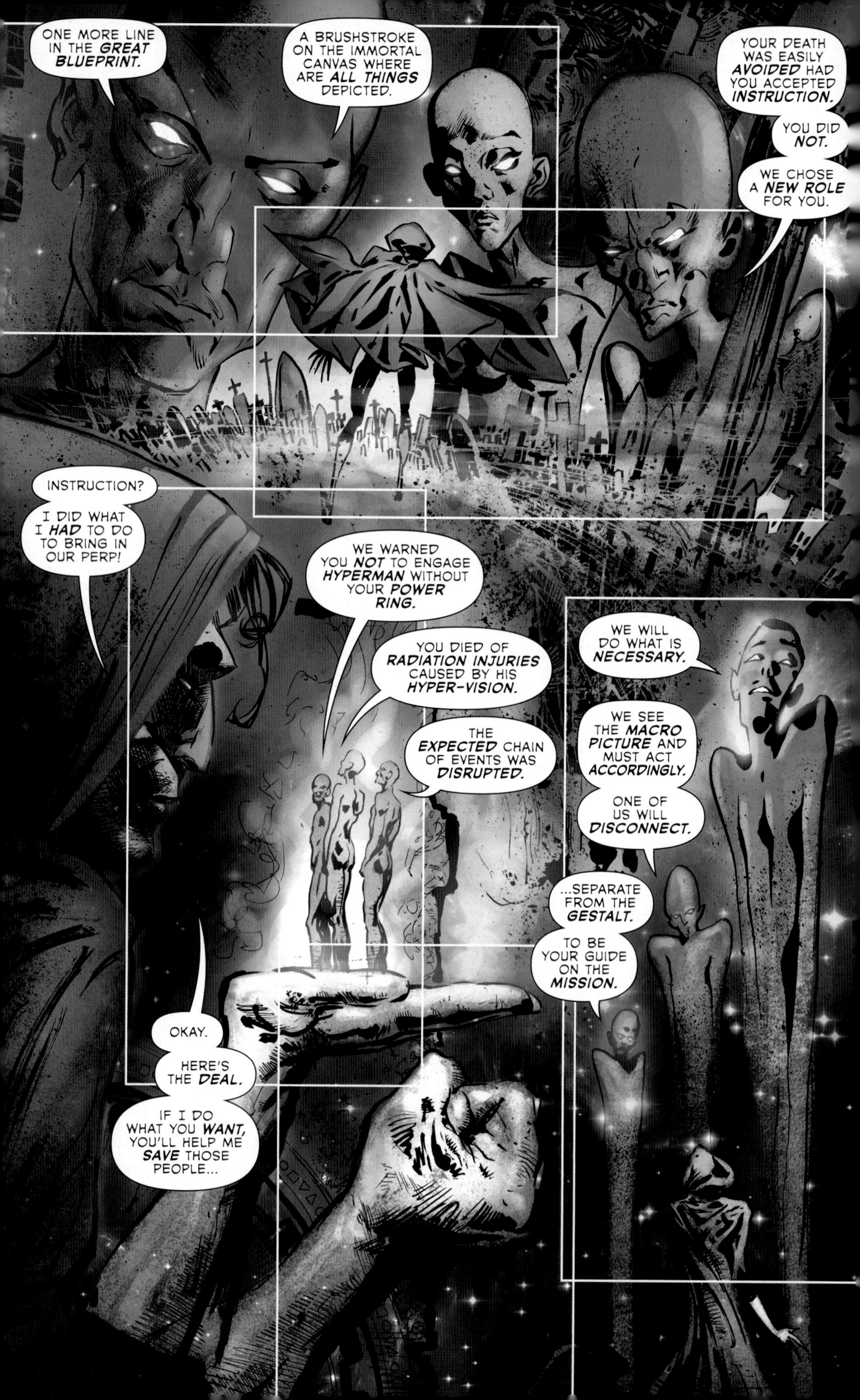
ONE MORE LINE IN THE *GREAT BLUEPRINT.*
A BRUSHSTROKE ON THE IMMORTAL CANVAS WHERE ARE *ALL THINGS* DEPICTED.
YOUR DEATH WAS EASILY *AVOIDED* HAD YOU ACCEPTED *INSTRUCTION.*
YOU DID *NOT.*
WE CHOSE A *NEW ROLE* FOR YOU.
INSTRUCTION?
I DID WHAT I *HAD* TO DO TO BRING IN OUR PERP!
WE WARNED YOU *NOT* TO ENGAGE *HYPERMAN* WITHOUT YOUR *POWER RING.*
YOU DIED OF *RADIATION INJURIES* CAUSED BY HIS *HYPER-VISION.*
THE *EXPECTED* CHAIN OF EVENTS WAS *DISRUPTED.*
WE WILL DO WHAT IS *NECESSARY.*
WE SEE THE *MACRO PICTURE* AND MUST ACT *ACCORDINGLY.*
ONE OF US WILL *DISCONNECT.*
...SEPARATE FROM THE *GESTALT.*
TO BE YOUR GUIDE ON THE *MISSION.*
OKAY.
HERE'S THE *DEAL.*
IF I DO WHAT YOU *WANT,* YOU'LL HELP ME *SAVE* THOSE PEOPLE...

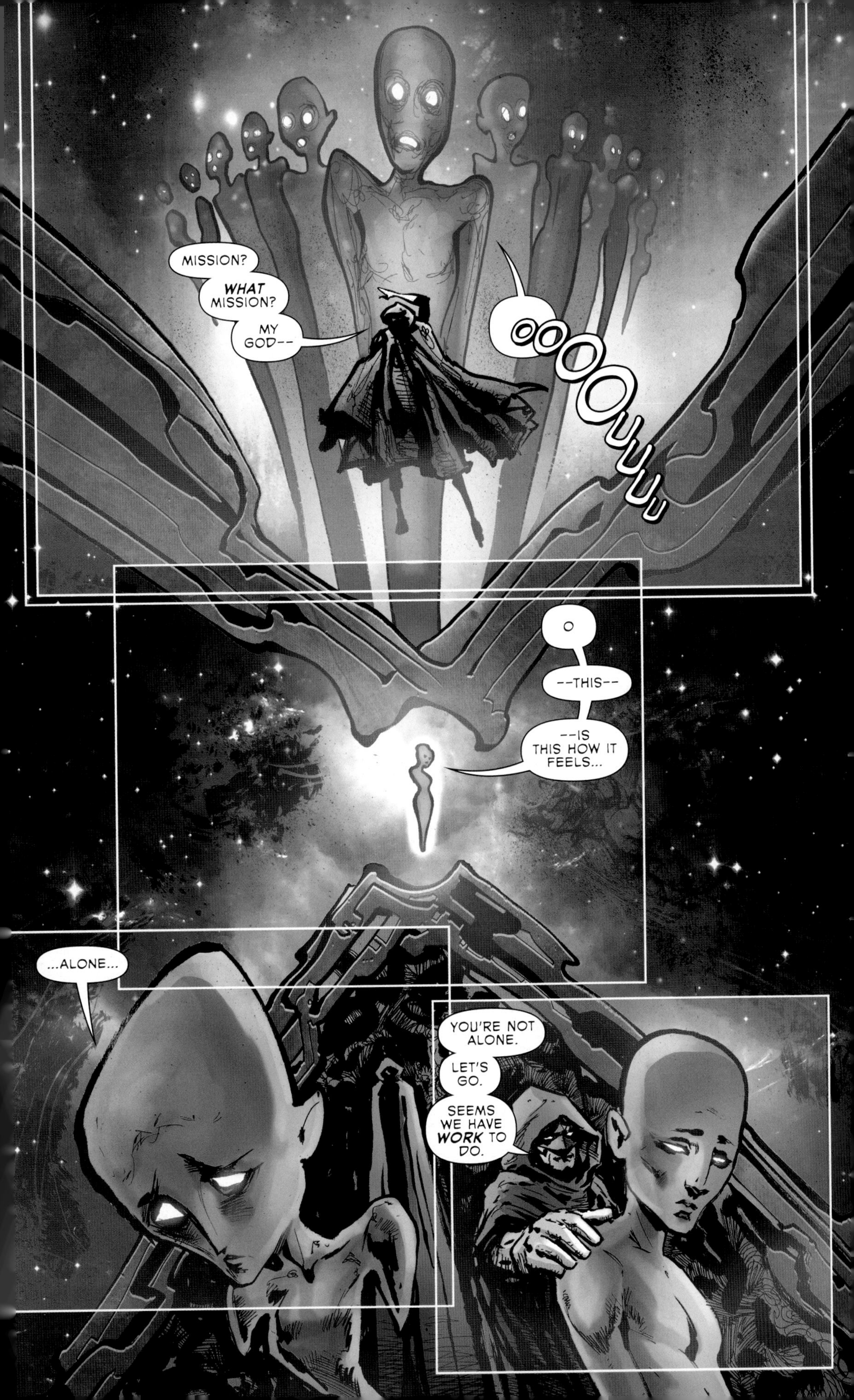

MISSION?
WHAT MISSION?
MY GOD--
OOOOOuuuu
O
--THIS--
--IS THIS HOW IT FEELS...
...ALONE...
YOU'RE NOT ALONE.
LET'S GO.
SEEMS WE HAVE WORK TO DO.

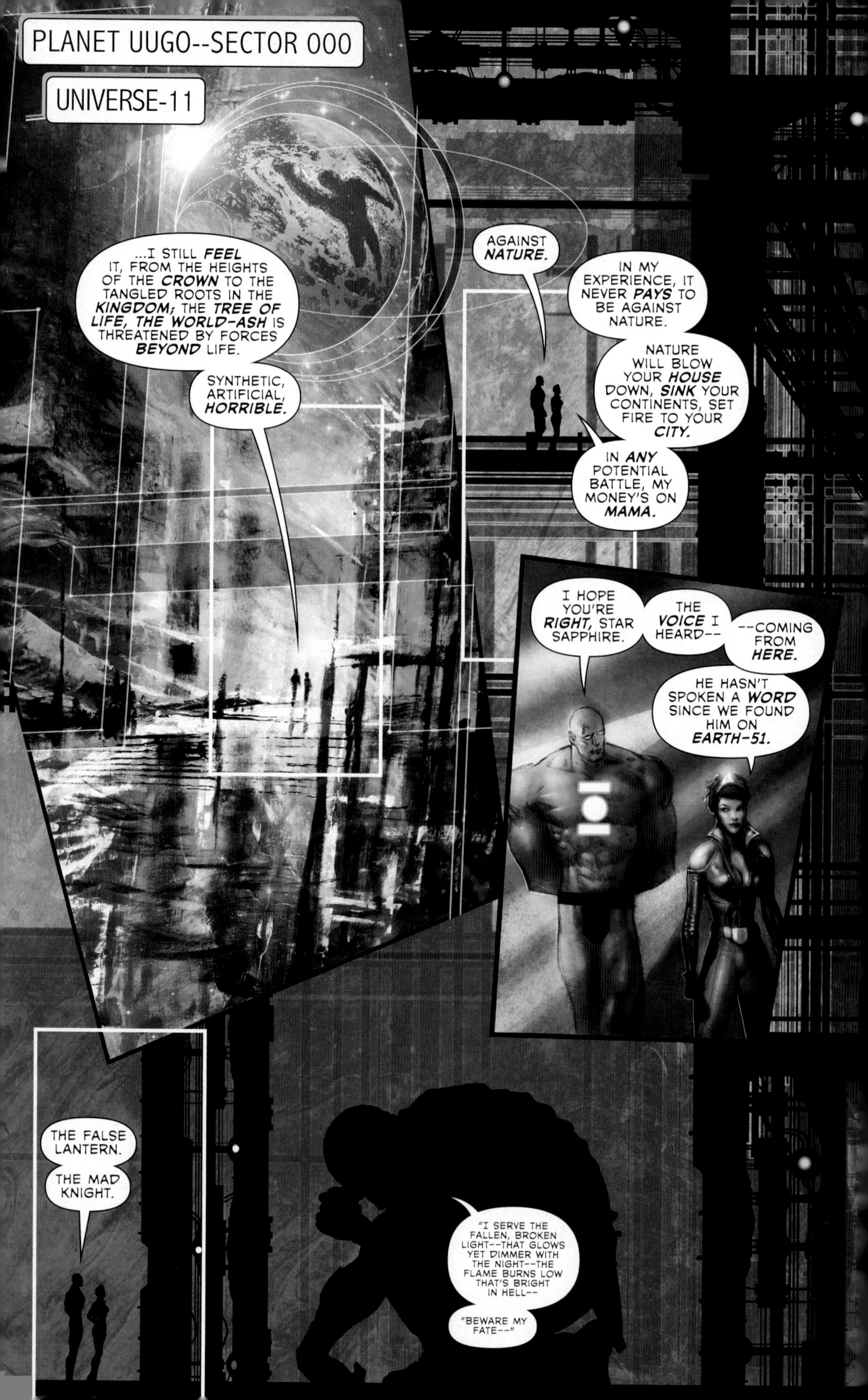
PLANET UUGO--SECTOR 000
UNIVERSE-11
...I STILL FEEL IT, FROM THE HEIGHTS OF THE CROWN TO THE TANGLED ROOTS IN THE KINGDOM; THE TREE OF LIFE, THE WORLD-ASH IS THREATENED BY FORCES BEYOND LIFE.
SYNTHETIC, ARTIFICIAL, HORRIBLE.
AGAINST NATURE.
IN MY EXPERIENCE, IT NEVER PAYS TO BE AGAINST NATURE.
NATURE WILL BLOW YOUR HOUSE DOWN, SINK YOUR CONTINENTS, SET FIRE TO YOUR CITY.
IN ANY POTENTIAL BATTLE, MY MONEY'S ON MAMA.
I HOPE YOU'RE RIGHT, STAR SAPPHIRE.
THE VOICE I HEARD--
--COMING FROM HERE.
HE HASN'T SPOKEN A WORD SINCE WE FOUND HIM ON EARTH-51.
THE FALSE LANTERN.
THE MAD KNIGHT.
"I SERVE THE FALLEN, BROKEN LIGHT--THAT GLOWS YET DIMMER WITH THE NIGHT--THE FLAME BURNS LOW THAT'S BRIGHT IN HELL--
"BEWARE MY FATE--"

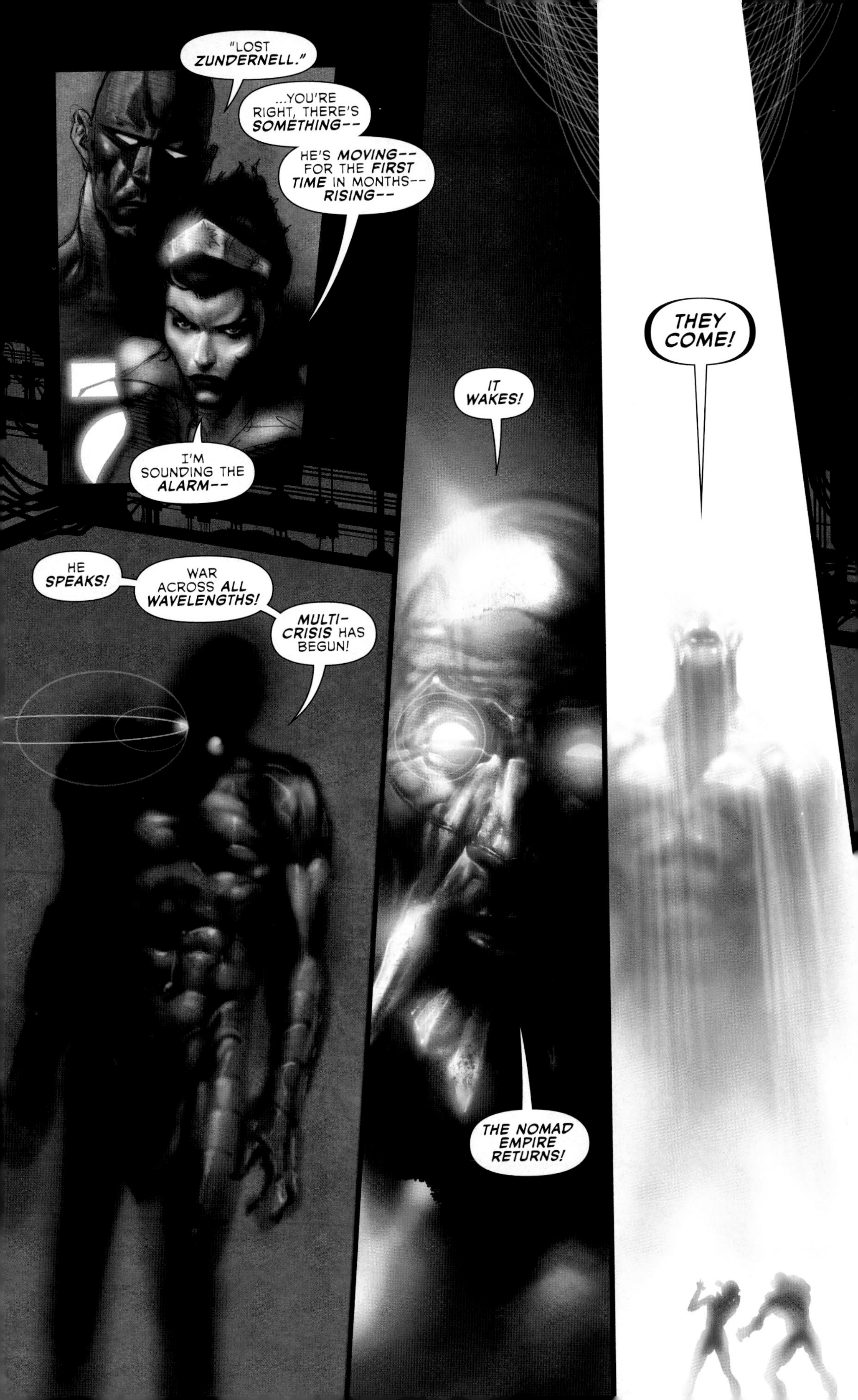
"LOST ZUNDERNELL."
...YOU'RE RIGHT, THERE'S SOMETHING--
HE'S MOVING-- FOR THE FIRST TIME IN MONTHS-- RISING--
I'M SOUNDING THE ALARM--
HE SPEAKS!
WAR ACROSS ALL WAVELENGTHS!
MULTI-CRISIS HAS BEGUN!
IT WAKES!
THE NOMAD EMPIRE RETURNS!
THEY COME!

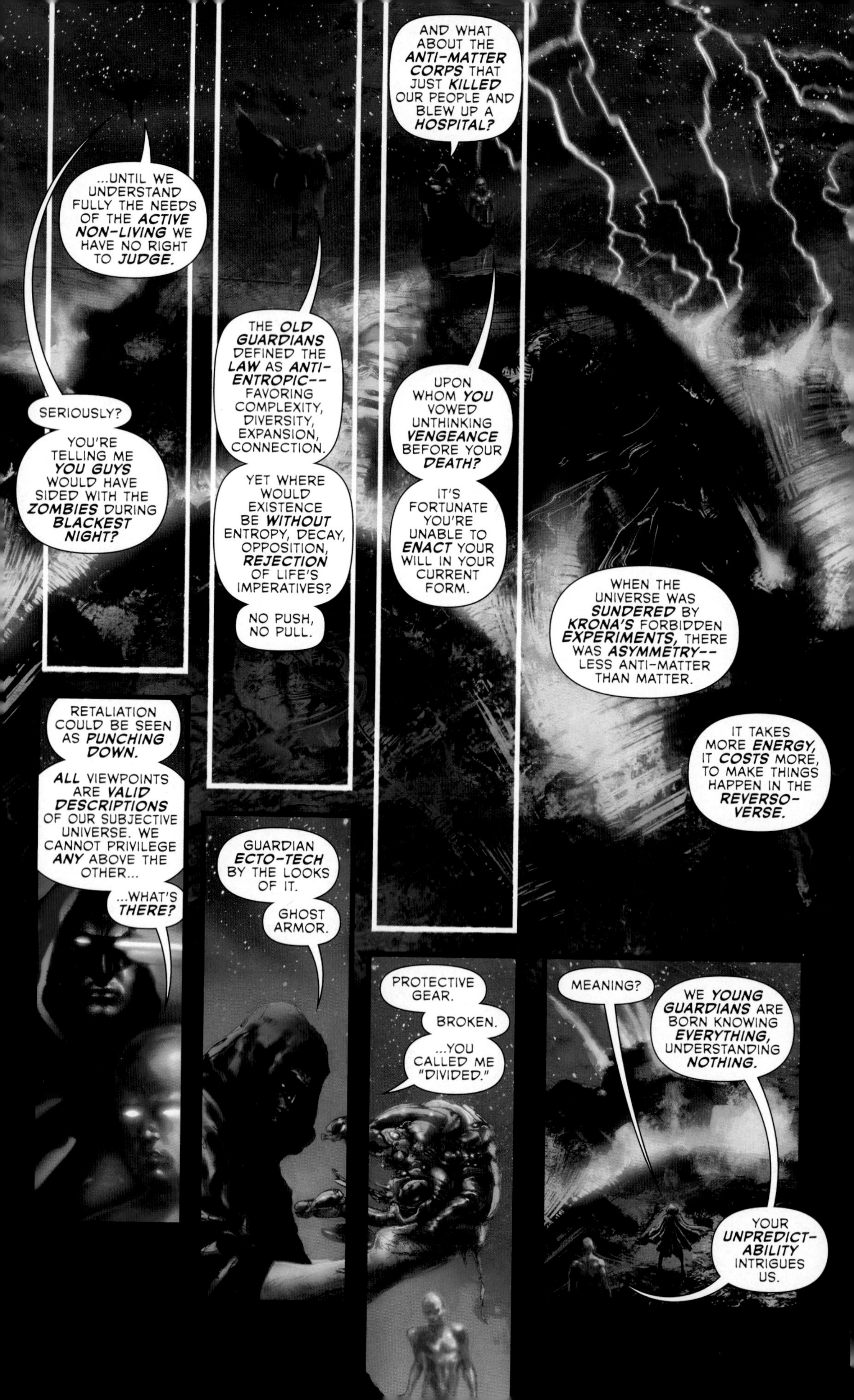
...UNTIL WE UNDERSTAND FULLY THE NEEDS OF THE ACTIVE NON-LIVING WE HAVE NO RIGHT TO JUDGE.
SERIOUSLY?
YOU'RE TELLING ME YOU GUYS WOULD HAVE SIDED WITH THE ZOMBIES DURING BLACKEST NIGHT?
THE OLD GUARDIANS DEFINED THE LAW AS ANTI-ENTROPIC-- FAVORING COMPLEXITY, DIVERSITY, EXPANSION, CONNECTION.
YET WHERE WOULD EXISTENCE BE WITHOUT ENTROPY, DECAY, OPPOSITION, REJECTION OF LIFE'S IMPERATIVES?
NO PUSH, NO PULL.
AND WHAT ABOUT THE ANTI-MATTER CORPS THAT JUST KILLED OUR PEOPLE AND BLEW UP A HOSPITAL?
UPON WHOM YOU VOWED UNTHINKING VENGEANCE BEFORE YOUR DEATH?
IT'S FORTUNATE YOU'RE UNABLE TO ENACT YOUR WILL IN YOUR CURRENT FORM.
WHEN THE UNIVERSE WAS SUNDERED BY KRONA'S FORBIDDEN EXPERIMENTS, THERE WAS ASYMMETRY-- LESS ANTI-MATTER THAN MATTER.
IT TAKES MORE ENERGY, IT COSTS MORE, TO MAKE THINGS HAPPEN IN THE REVERSO-VERSE.
RETALIATION COULD BE SEEN AS PUNCHING DOWN.
ALL VIEWPOINTS ARE VALID DESCRIPTIONS OF OUR SUBJECTIVE UNIVERSE. WE CANNOT PRIVILEGE ANY ABOVE THE OTHER...
...WHAT'S THERE?
GUARDIAN ECTO-TECH BY THE LOOKS OF IT.
GHOST ARMOR.
PROTECTIVE GEAR.
BROKEN.
...YOU CALLED ME "DIVIDED."
MEANING?
WE YOUNG GUARDIANS ARE BORN KNOWING EVERYTHING, UNDERSTANDING NOTHING.
YOUR UNPREDICTABILITY INTRIGUES US.

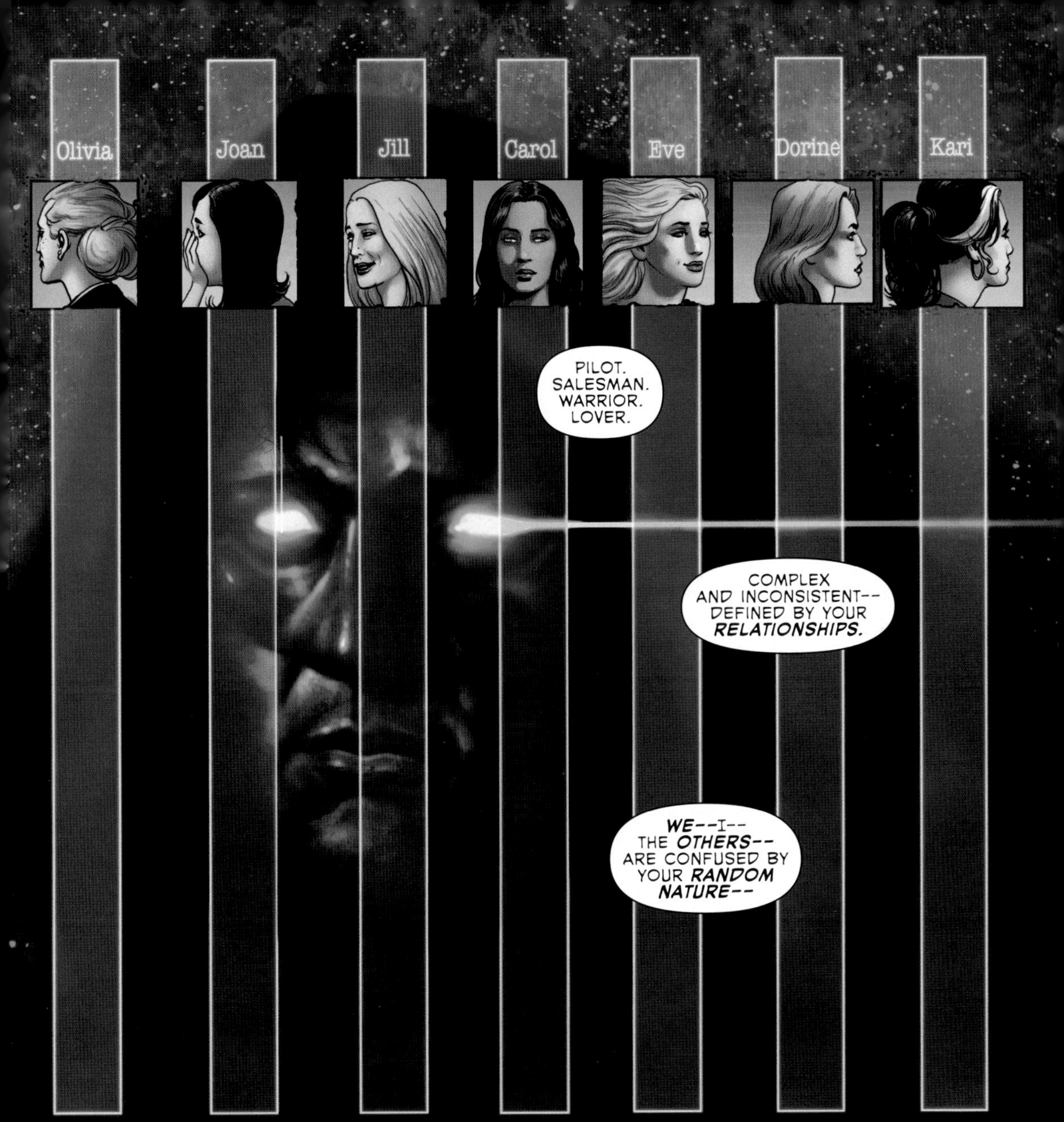
Olivia
Joan
Jill
Carol
Eve
Dorine
Kari
PILOT. SALESMAN. WARRIOR. LOVER.
COMPLEX AND INCONSISTENT--DEFINED BY YOUR RELATIONSHIPS.
WE--I--THE OTHERS--ARE CONFUSED BY YOUR RANDOM NATURE--

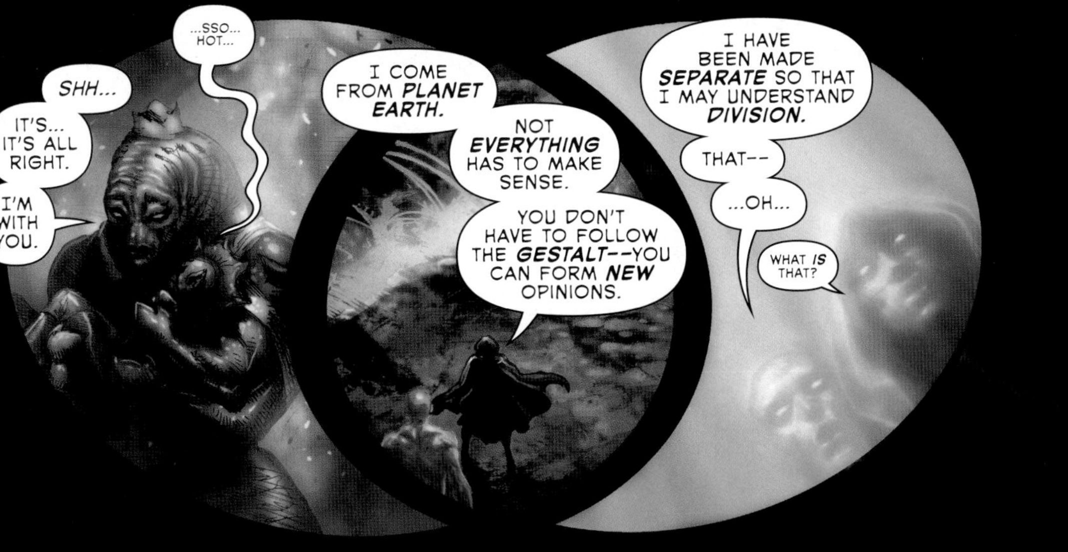
...SSO... HOT...
SHH...
IT'S... IT'S ALL RIGHT.
I'M WITH YOU.
I COME FROM PLANET EARTH.
NOT EVERYTHING HAS TO MAKE SENSE.
YOU DON'T HAVE TO FOLLOW THE GESTALT--YOU CAN FORM NEW OPINIONS.
I HAVE BEEN MADE SEPARATE SO THAT I MAY UNDERSTAND DIVISION.
THAT--
...OH...
WHAT IS THAT?

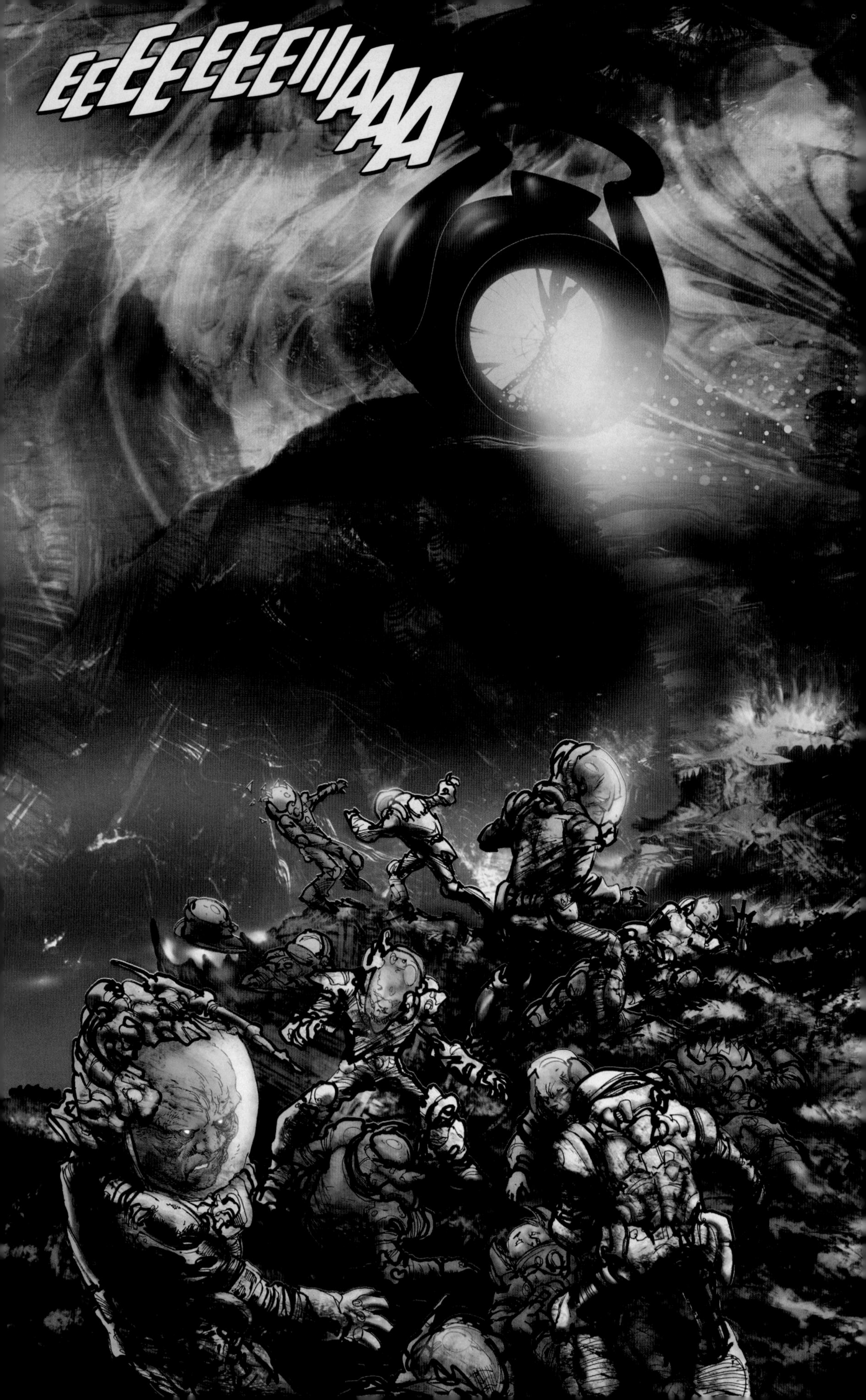
EEEEEEEEIIIAAA

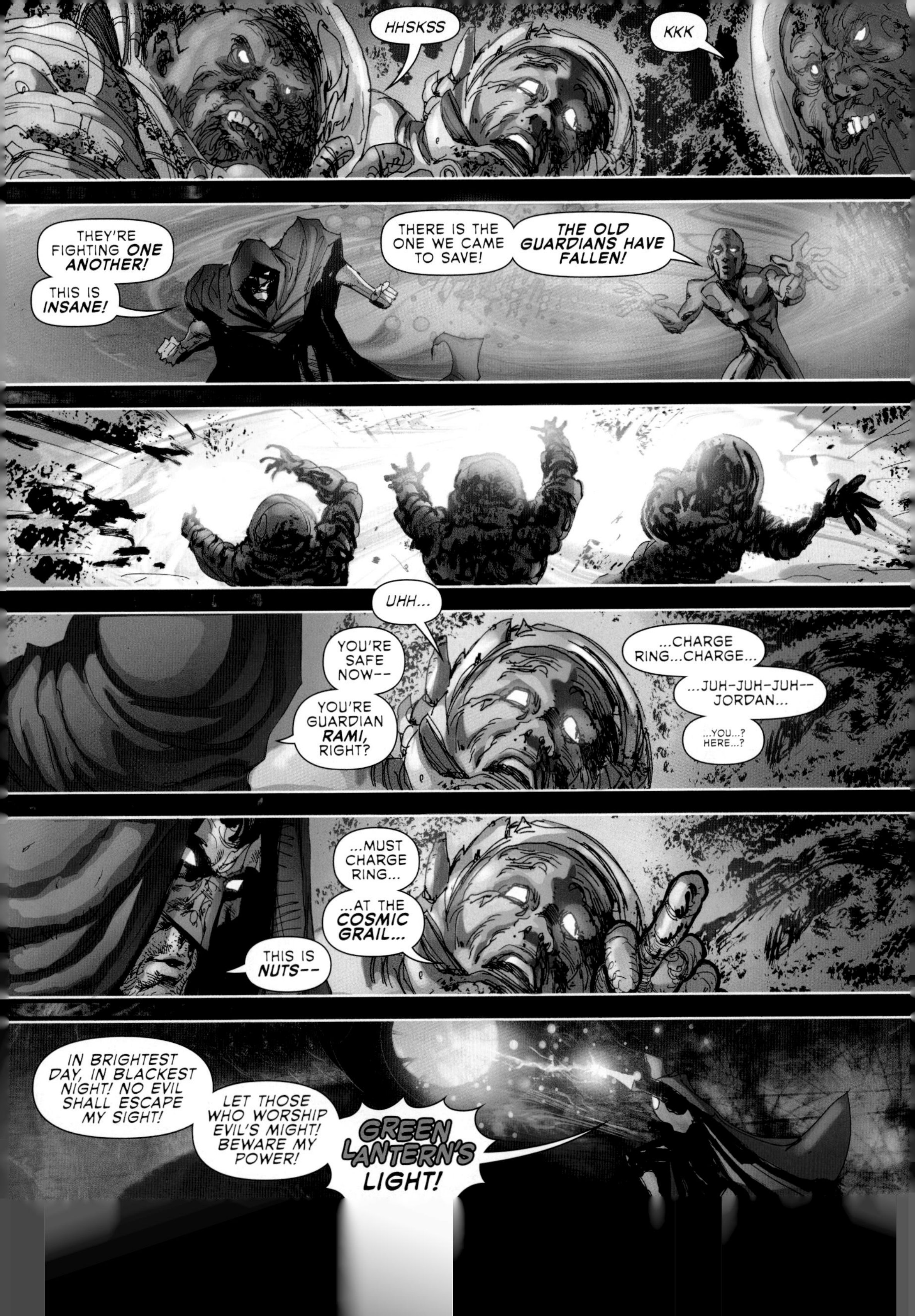
HHSKSS
KKK
THEY'RE FIGHTING ONE ANOTHER!
THIS IS INSANE!
THERE IS THE ONE WE CAME TO SAVE!
THE OLD GUARDIANS HAVE FALLEN!
UHH...
YOU'RE SAFE NOW--
YOU'RE GUARDIAN RAMI, RIGHT?
...CHARGE RING...CHARGE...
...JUH-JUH-JUH-- JORDAN...
...YOU...? HERE...?
...MUST CHARGE RING...
...AT THE COSMIC GRAIL...
THIS IS NUTS--
IN BRIGHTEST DAY, IN BLACKEST NIGHT! NO EVIL SHALL ESCAPE MY SIGHT!
LET THOSE WHO WORSHIP EVIL'S MIGHT! BEWARE MY POWER!
GREEN LANTERN'S LIGHT!

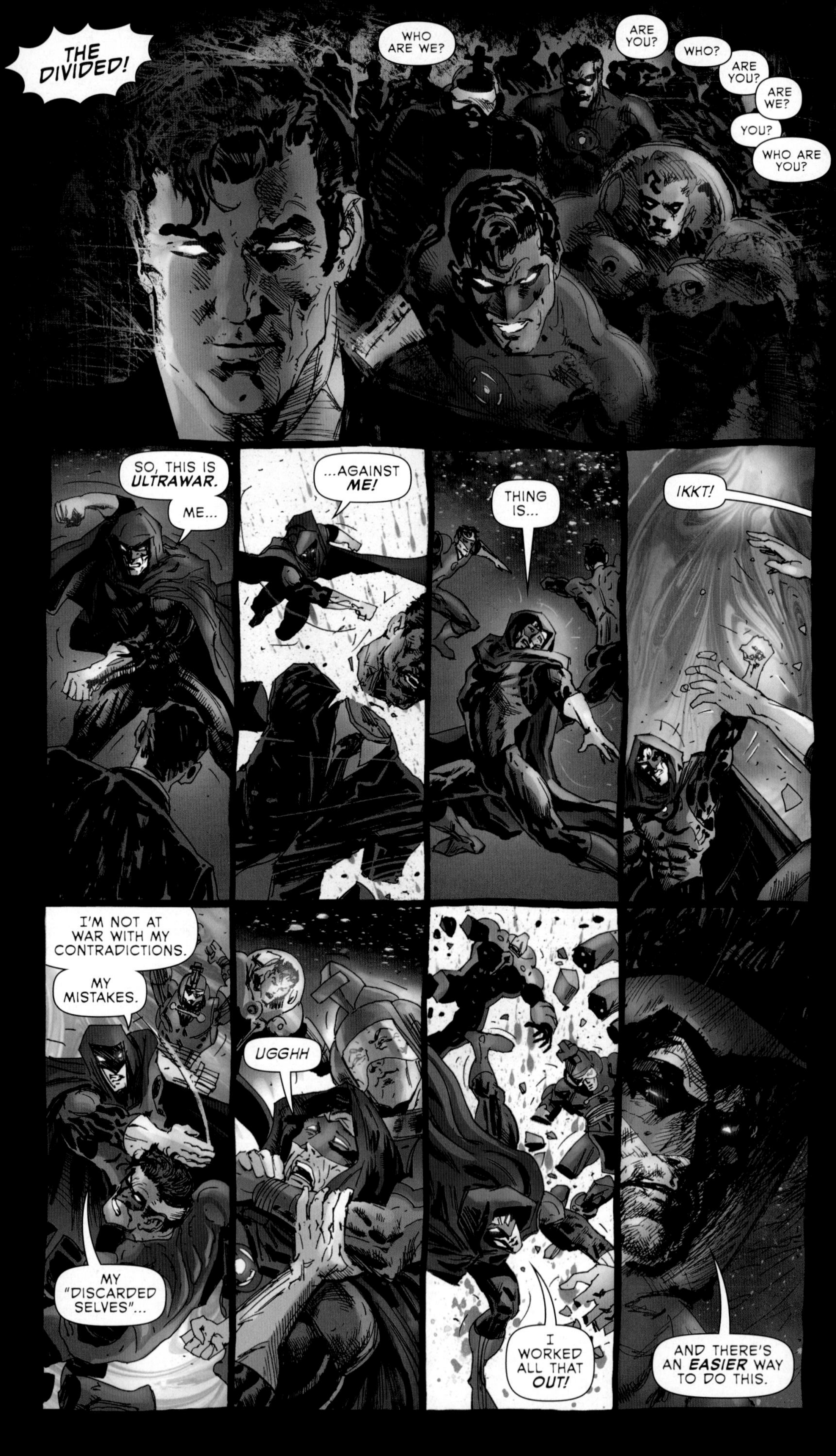
THE DIVIDED!
WHO ARE WE?
ARE YOU?
WHO?
ARE YOU?
ARE WE?
YOU?
WHO ARE YOU?
SO, THIS IS ULTRAWAR.
ME...
...AGAINST ME!
THING IS...
IKKT!
I'M NOT AT WAR WITH MY CONTRADICTIONS.
MY MISTAKES.
MY "DISCARDED SELVES"...
UGGHH
I WORKED ALL THAT OUT!
AND THERE'S AN EASIER WAY TO DO THIS.

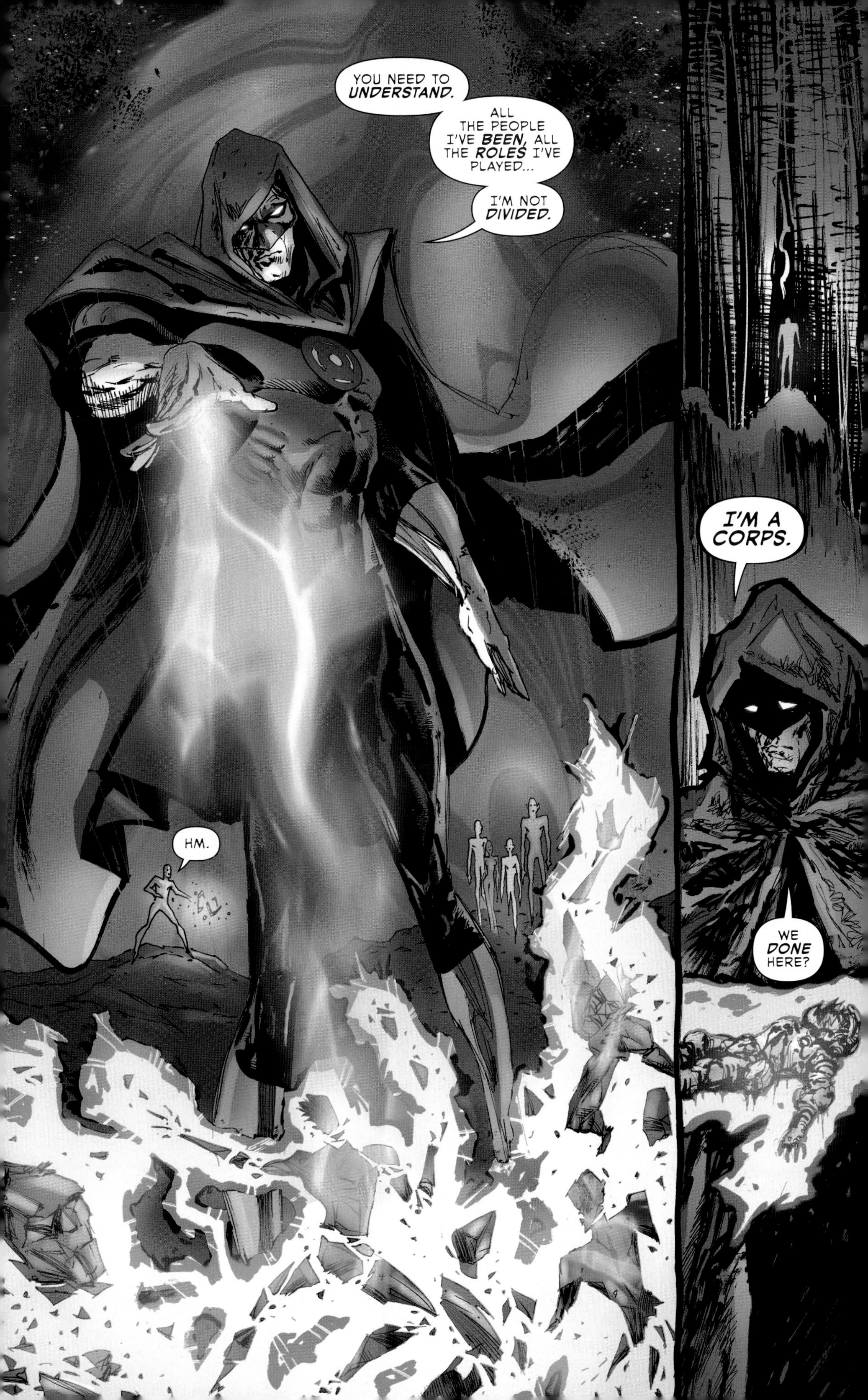
YOU NEED TO UNDERSTAND.
ALL THE PEOPLE I'VE BEEN, ALL THE ROLES I'VE PLAYED...
I'M NOT DIVIDED.
HM.
I'M A CORPS.
WE DONE HERE?

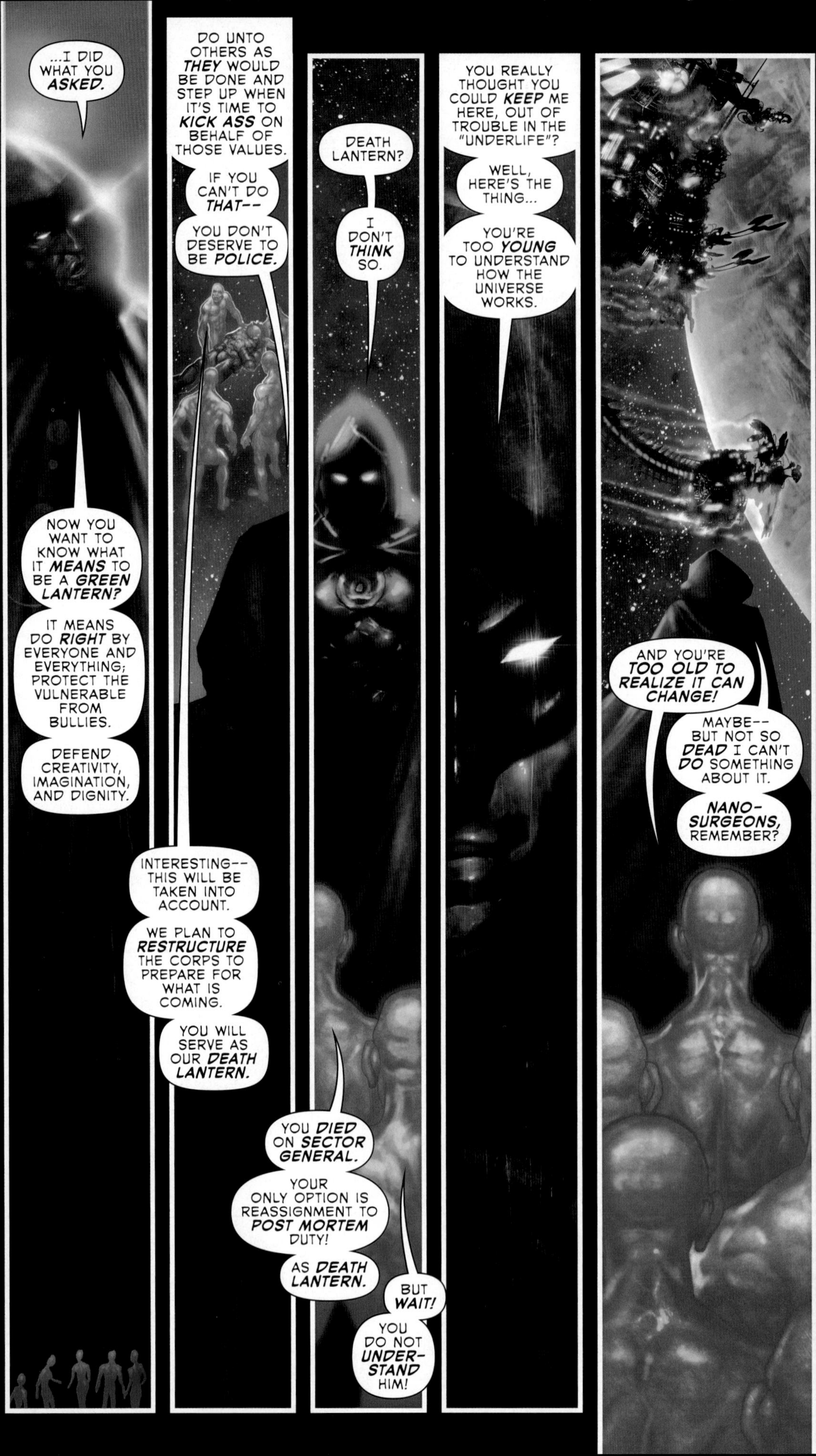
...I DID WHAT YOU ASKED.
NOW YOU WANT TO KNOW WHAT IT MEANS TO BE A GREEN LANTERN?
IT MEANS DO RIGHT BY EVERYONE AND EVERYTHING; PROTECT THE VULNERABLE FROM BULLIES.
DEFEND CREATIVITY, IMAGINATION, AND DIGNITY.
DO UNTO OTHERS AS THEY WOULD BE DONE AND STEP UP WHEN IT'S TIME TO KICK ASS ON BEHALF OF THOSE VALUES.
IF YOU CAN'T DO THAT--
YOU DON'T DESERVE TO BE POLICE.
INTERESTING-- THIS WILL BE TAKEN INTO ACCOUNT.
WE PLAN TO RESTRUCTURE THE CORPS TO PREPARE FOR WHAT IS COMING.
YOU WILL SERVE AS OUR DEATH LANTERN.
DEATH LANTERN?
I DON'T THINK SO.
YOU DIED ON SECTOR GENERAL.
YOUR ONLY OPTION IS REASSIGNMENT TO POST MORTEM DUTY!
AS DEATH LANTERN.
BUT WAIT!
YOU DO NOT UNDER-STAND HIM!
YOU REALLY THOUGHT YOU COULD KEEP ME HERE, OUT OF TROUBLE IN THE "UNDERLIFE"?
WELL, HERE'S THE THING...
YOU'RE TOO YOUNG TO UNDERSTAND HOW THE UNIVERSE WORKS.
AND YOU'RE TOO OLD TO REALIZE IT CAN CHANGE!
MAYBE-- BUT NOT SO DEAD I CAN'T DO SOMETHING ABOUT IT.
NANO-SURGEONS, REMEMBER?

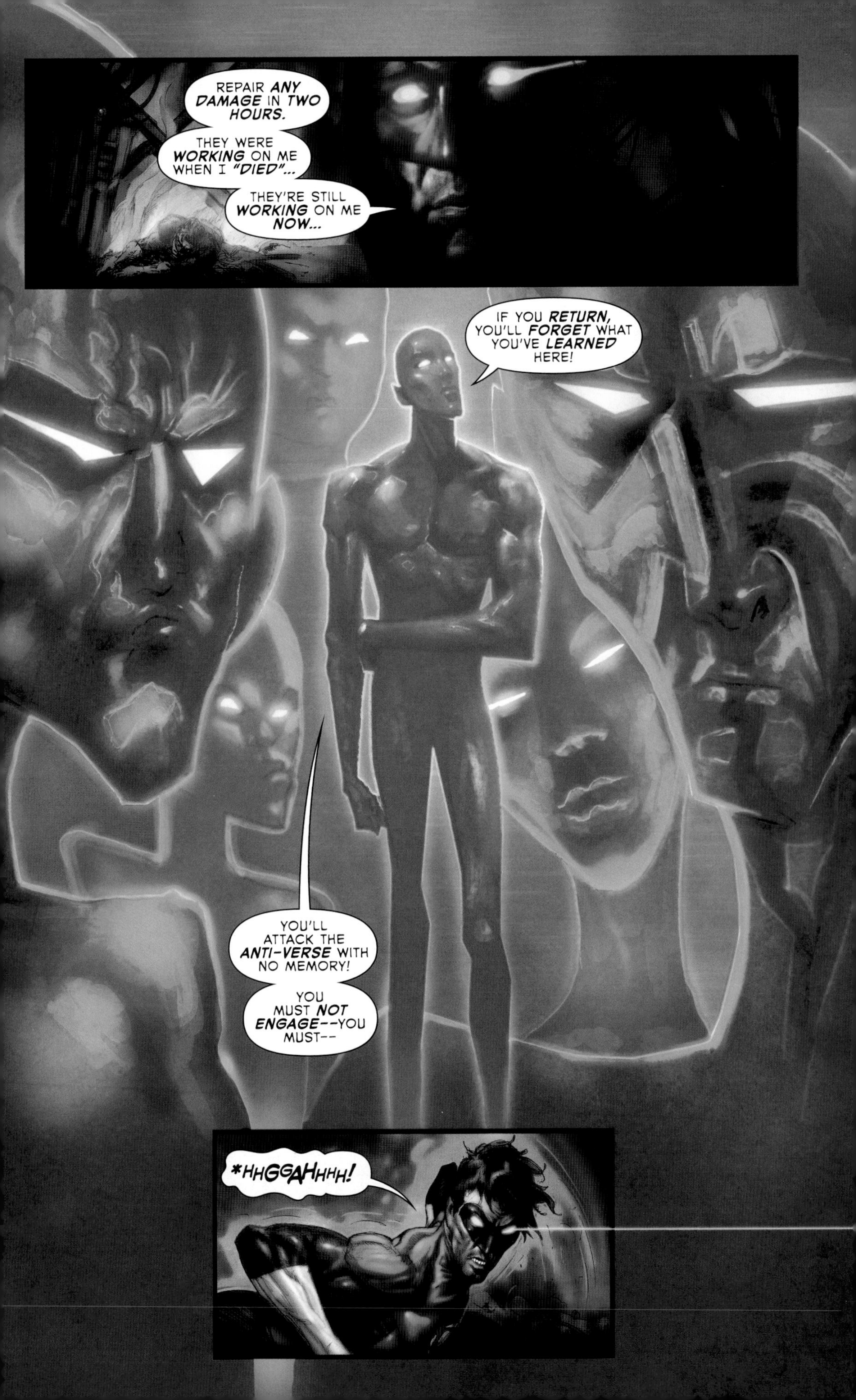
REPAIR ANY DAMAGE IN TWO HOURS.
THEY WERE WORKING ON ME WHEN I "DIED"...
THEY'RE STILL WORKING ON ME NOW...
IF YOU RETURN, YOU'LL FORGET WHAT YOU'VE LEARNED HERE!
YOU'LL ATTACK THE ANTI-VERSE WITH NO MEMORY!
YOU MUST NOT ENGAGE--YOU MUST--
*HHGGAHHHH!

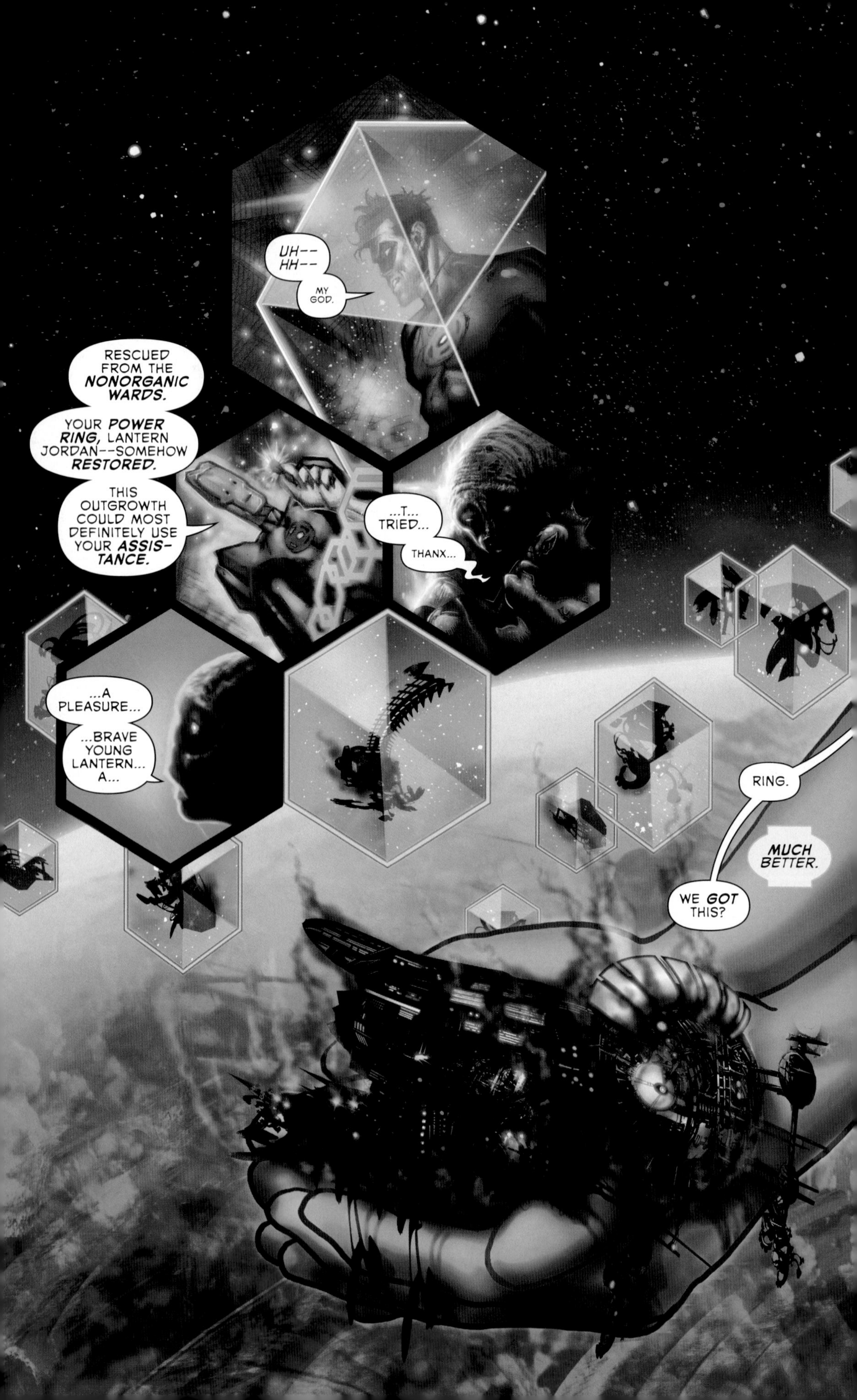
UH-- HH--
MY GOD.
RESCUED FROM THE NONORGANIC WARDS.
YOUR POWER RING, LANTERN JORDAN--SOMEHOW RESTORED.
THIS OUTGROWTH COULD MOST DEFINITELY USE YOUR ASSIS-TANCE.
...T... TRIED...
THANX...
...A PLEASURE...
...BRAVE YOUNG LANTERN... A...
RING.
MUCH BETTER.
WE GOT THIS?

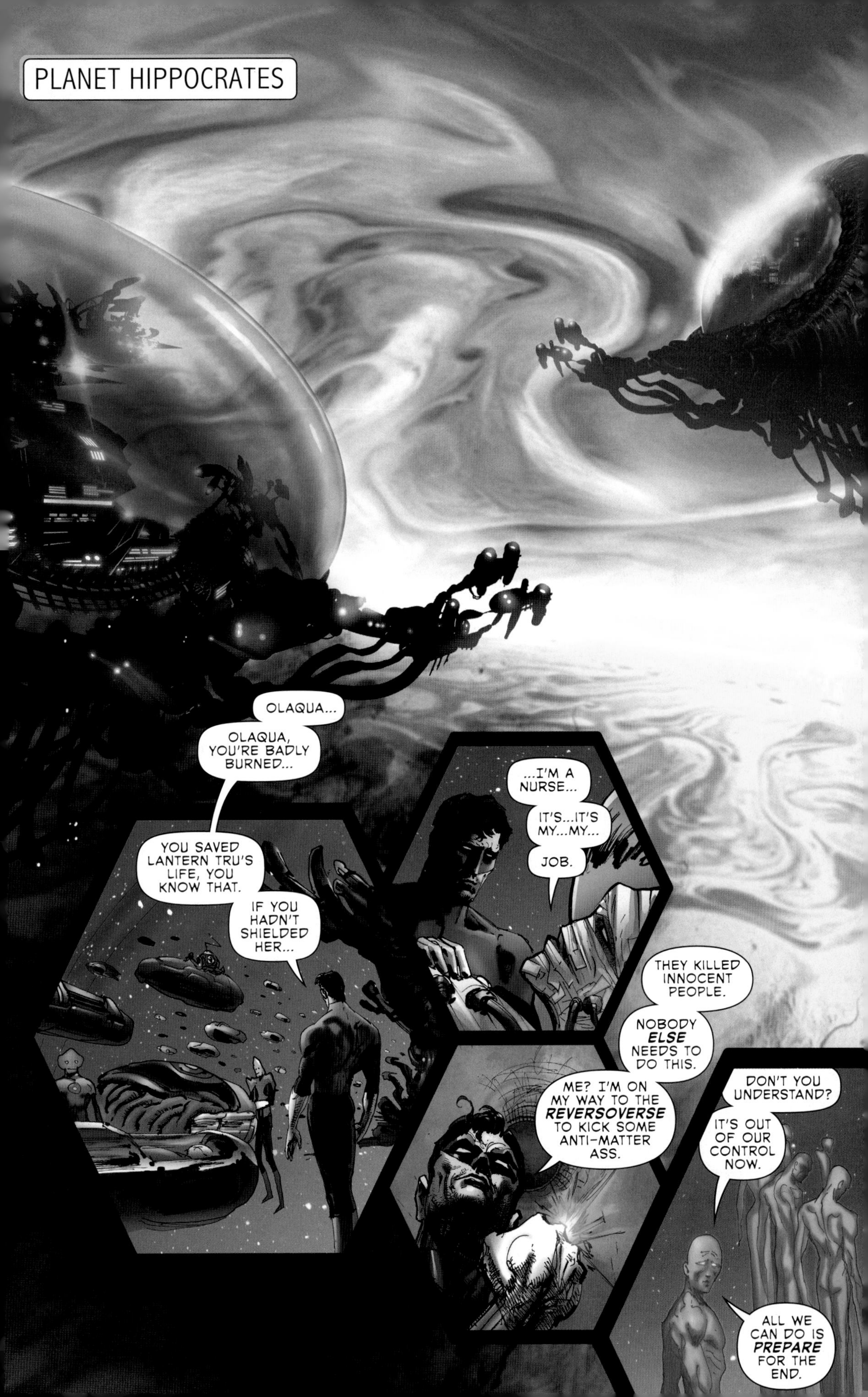

PLANET HIPPOCRATES
OLAQUA...
OLAQUA, YOU'RE BADLY BURNED...
...I'M A NURSE...
IT'S...IT'S MY...MY...
JOB.
YOU SAVED LANTERN TRU'S LIFE, YOU KNOW THAT.
IF YOU HADN'T SHIELDED HER...
THEY KILLED INNOCENT PEOPLE.
NOBODY ELSE NEEDS TO DO THIS.
ME? I'M ON MY WAY TO THE REVERSOVERSE TO KICK SOME ANTI-MATTER ASS.
DON'T YOU UNDERSTAND?
IT'S OUT OF OUR CONTROL NOW.
ALL WE CAN DO IS PREPARE FOR THE END.

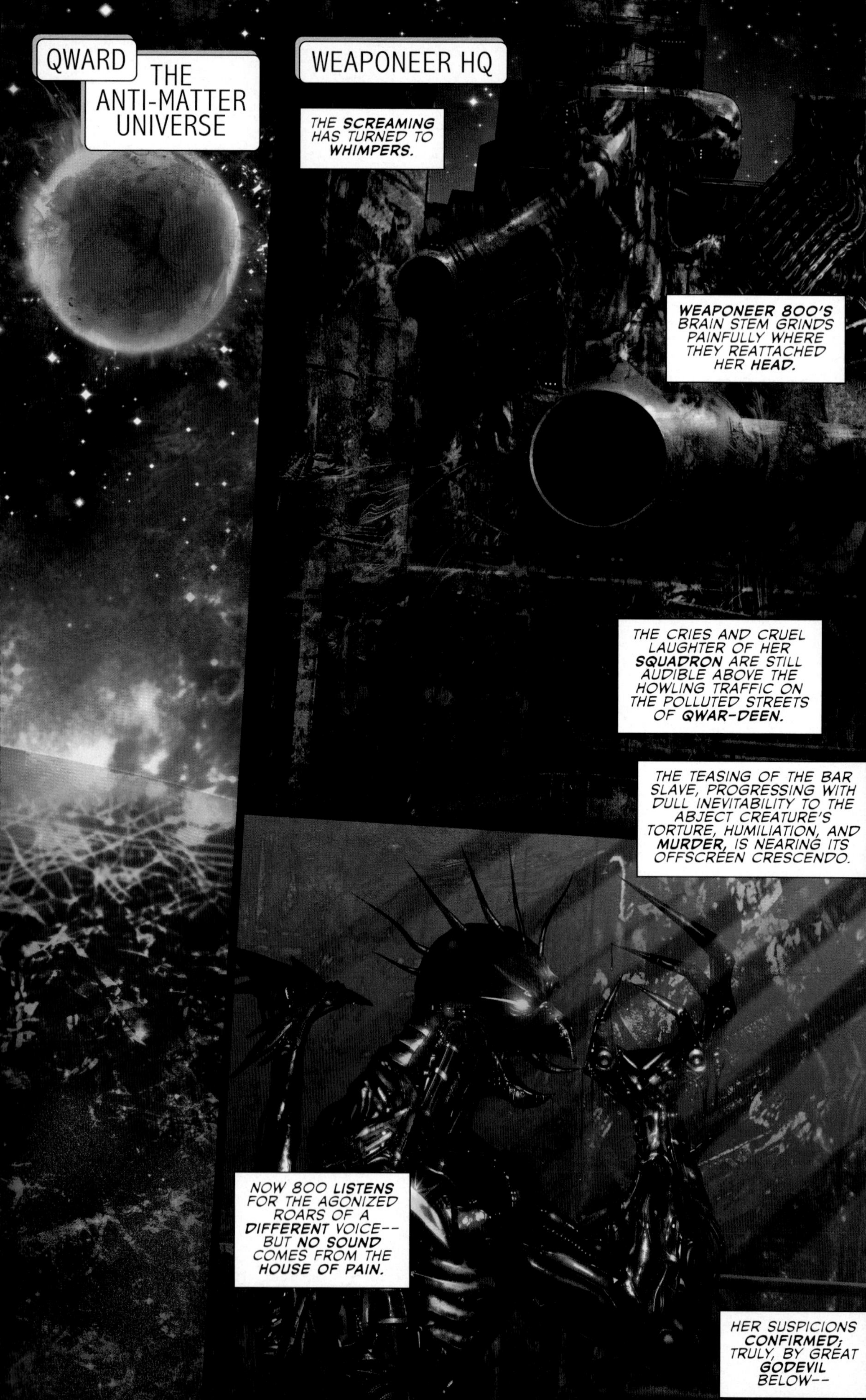
QWARD
THE ANTI-MATTER UNIVERSE
WEAPONEER HQ
THE SCREAMING HAS TURNED TO WHIMPERS.
WEAPONEER 800'S BRAIN STEM GRINDS PAINFULLY WHERE THEY REATTACHED HER HEAD.
THE CRIES AND CRUEL LAUGHTER OF HER SQUADRON ARE STILL AUDIBLE ABOVE THE HOWLING TRAFFIC ON THE POLLUTED STREETS OF QWAR-DEEN.
THE TEASING OF THE BAR SLAVE, PROGRESSING WITH DULL INEVITABILITY TO THE ABJECT CREATURE'S TORTURE, HUMILIATION, AND MURDER, IS NEARING ITS OFFSCREEN CRESCENDO.
NOW 800 LISTENS FOR THE AGONIZED ROARS OF A DIFFERENT VOICE-- BUT NO SOUND COMES FROM THE HOUSE OF PAIN.
HER SUSPICIONS CONFIRMED; TRULY, BY GREAT GODEVIL BELOW--

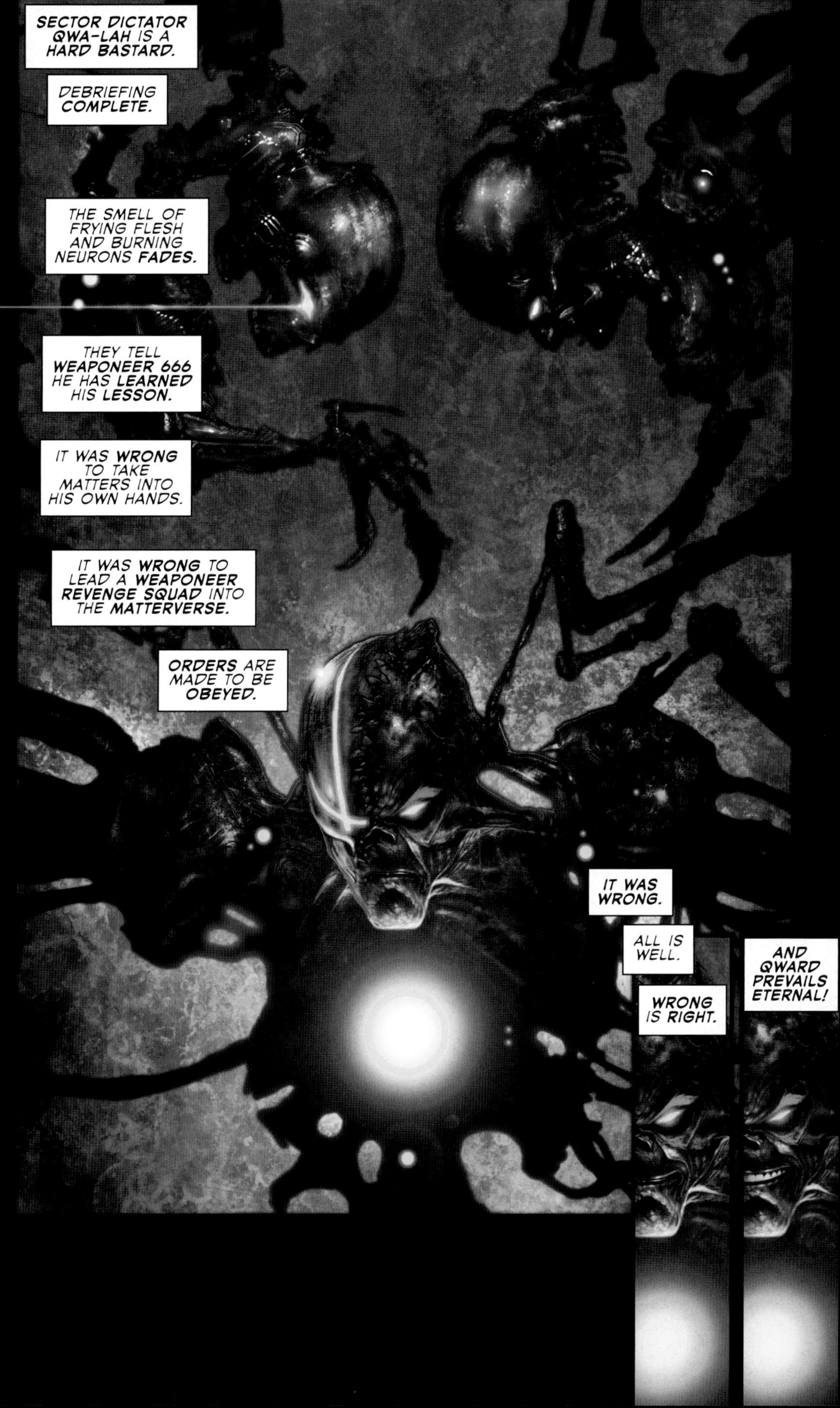
SECTOR DICTATOR QWA-LAH IS A HARD BASTARD.
DEBRIEFING COMPLETE.
THE SMELL OF FRYING FLESH AND BURNING NEURONS FADES.
THEY TELL WEAPONEER 666 HE HAS LEARNED HIS LESSON.
IT WAS WRONG TO TAKE MATTERS INTO HIS OWN HANDS.
IT WAS WRONG TO LEAD A WEAPONEER REVENGE SQUAD INTO THE MATTERVERSE.
ORDERS ARE MADE TO BE OBEYED.
IT WAS WRONG.
ALL IS WELL.
WRONG IS RIGHT.
AND QWARD PREVAILS ETERNAL!

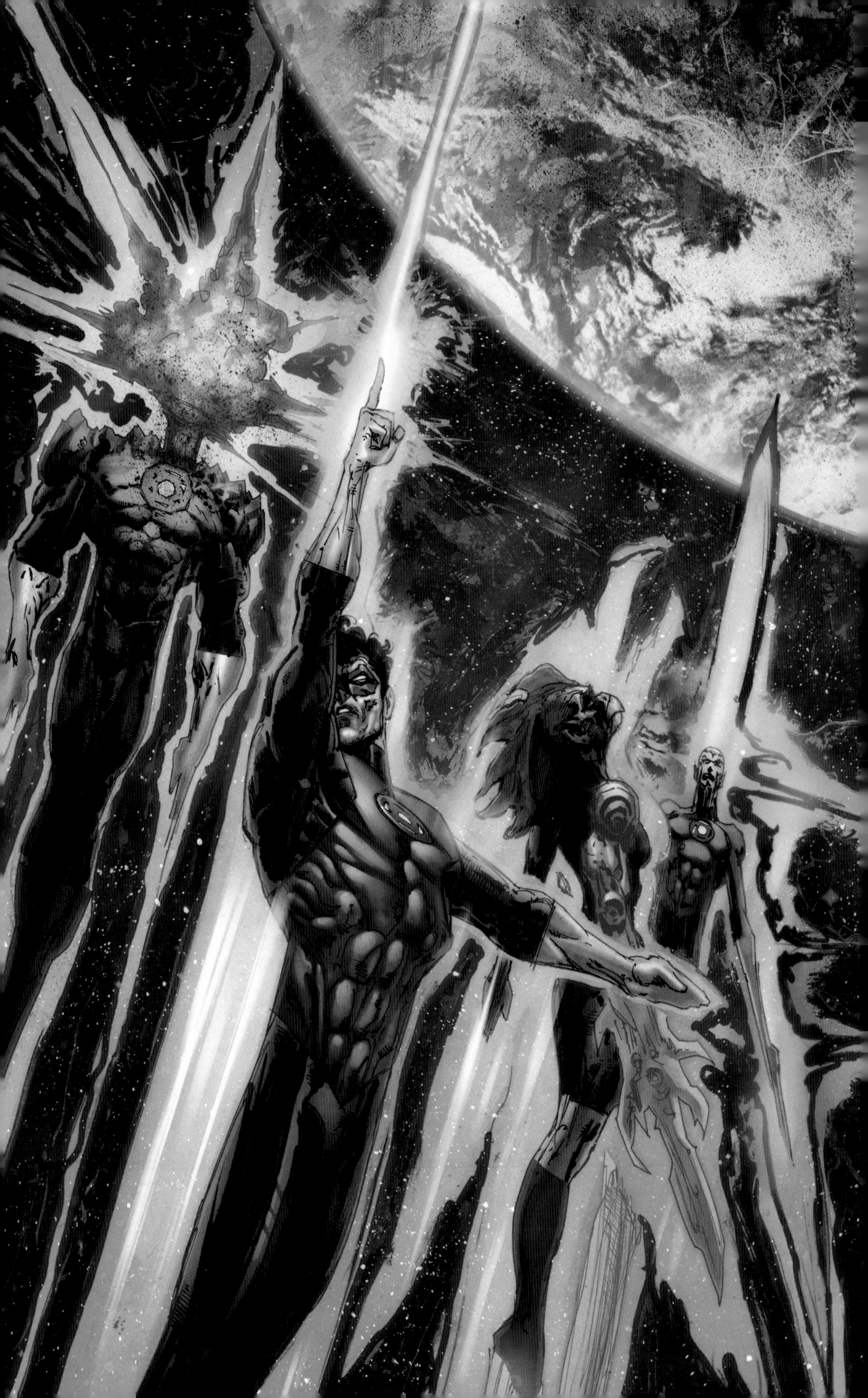

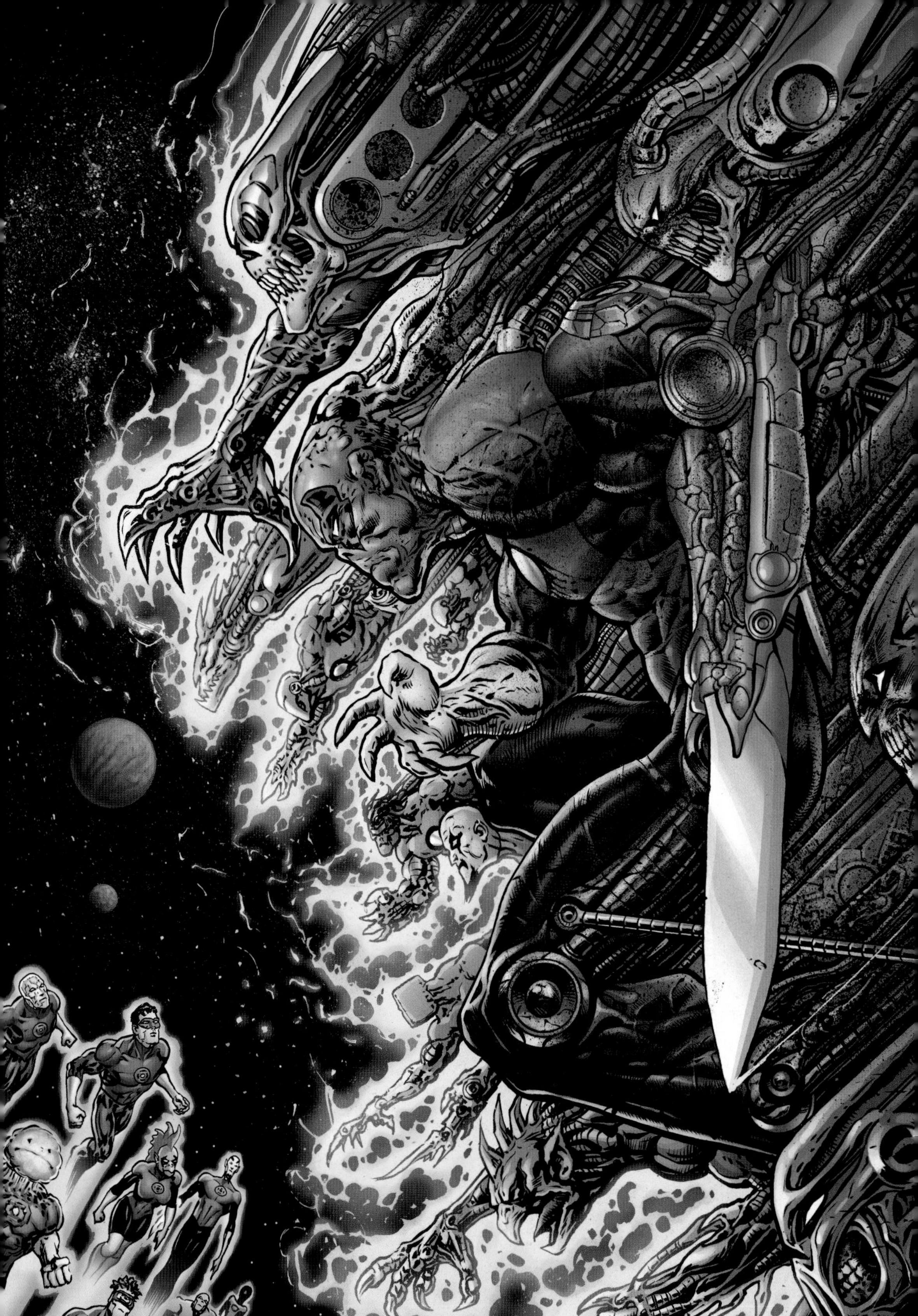

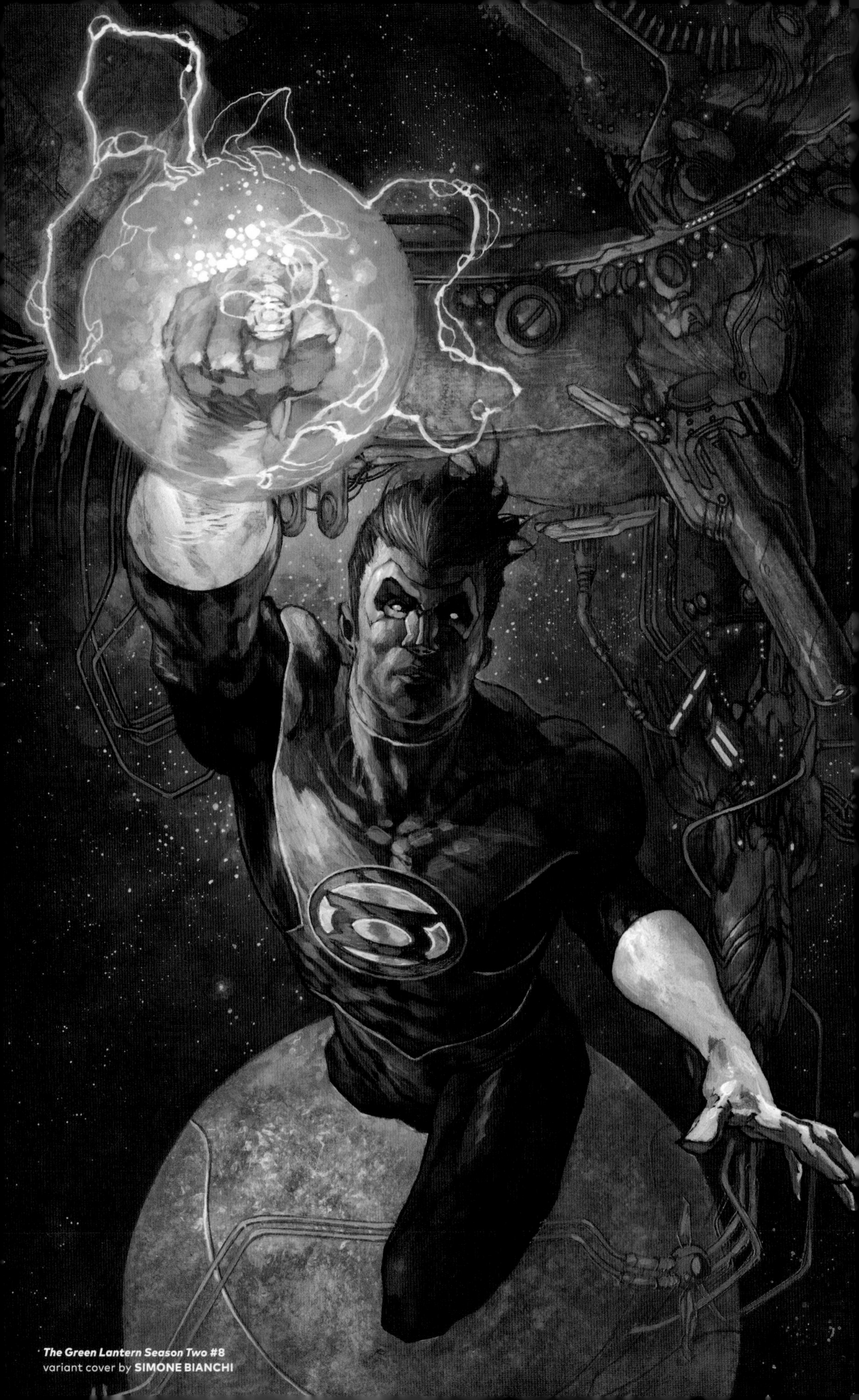

The Green Lantern Season Two #8
variant cover by **SIMONE BIANCHI**

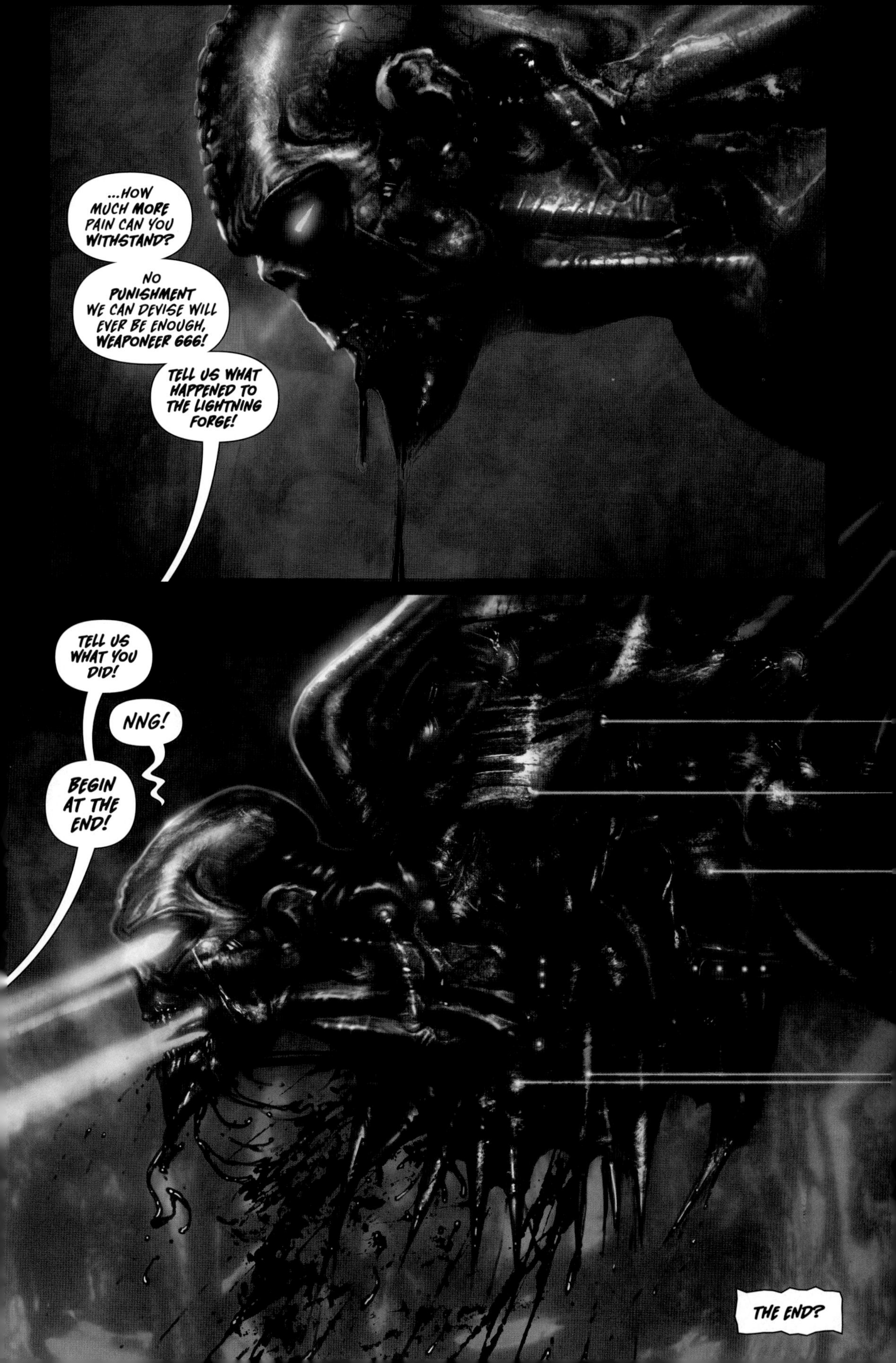
...HOW MUCH MORE PAIN CAN YOU WITHSTAND?
NO PUNISHMENT WE CAN DEVISE WILL EVER BE ENOUGH, WEAPONEER 666!
TELL US WHAT HAPPENED TO THE LIGHTNING FORGE!
TELL US WHAT YOU DID!
NNG!
BEGIN AT THE END!
THE END?

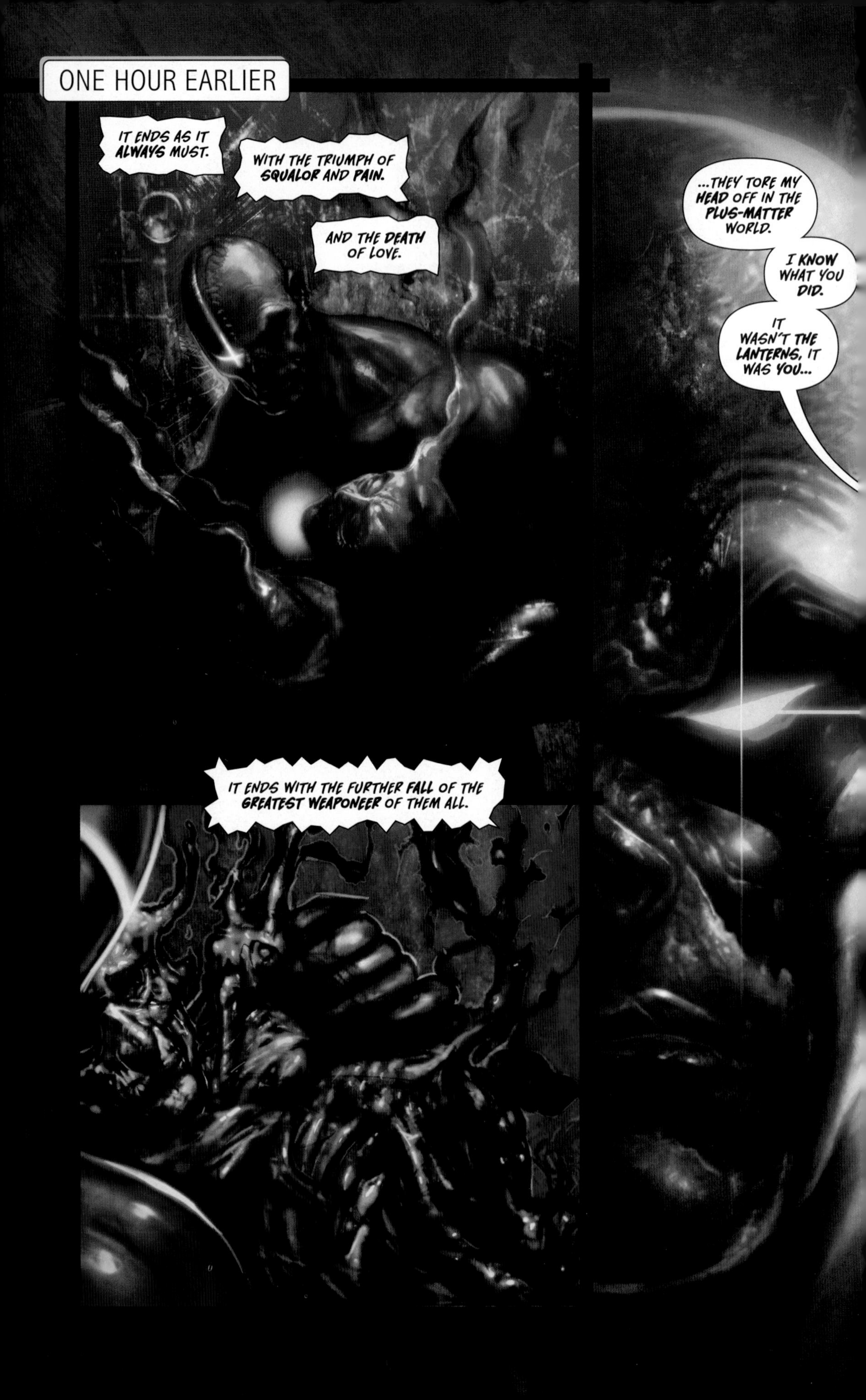
ONE HOUR EARLIER
IT ENDS AS IT ALWAYS MUST.
WITH THE TRIUMPH OF SQUALOR AND PAIN.
AND THE DEATH OF LOVE.
...THEY TORE MY HEAD OFF IN THE PLUS-MATTER WORLD.
I KNOW WHAT YOU DID.
IT WASN'T THE LANTERNS, IT WAS YOU...
IT ENDS WITH THE FURTHER FALL OF THE GREATEST WEAPONEER OF THEM ALL.

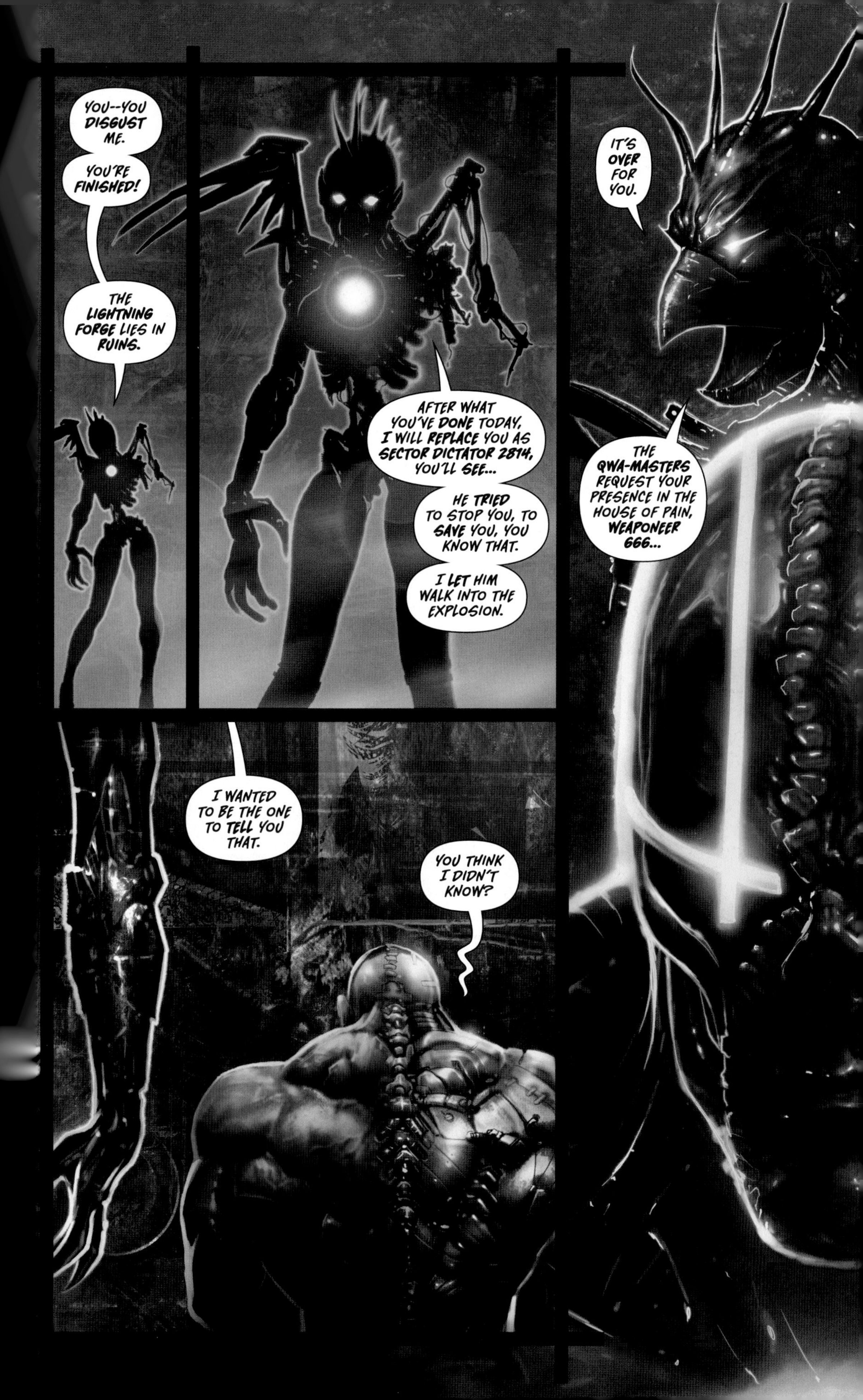
YOU--YOU DISGUST ME.
YOU'RE FINISHED!
THE LIGHTNING FORGE LIES IN RUINS.
AFTER WHAT YOU'VE DONE TODAY, I WILL REPLACE YOU AS SECTOR DICTATOR 2814, YOU'LL SEE...
HE TRIED TO STOP YOU, TO SAVE YOU, YOU KNOW THAT.
I LET HIM WALK INTO THE EXPLOSION.
IT'S OVER FOR YOU.
THE QWA-MASTERS REQUEST YOUR PRESENCE IN THE HOUSE OF PAIN, WEAPONEER 666...
I WANTED TO BE THE ONE TO TELL YOU THAT.
YOU THINK I DIDN'T KNOW?

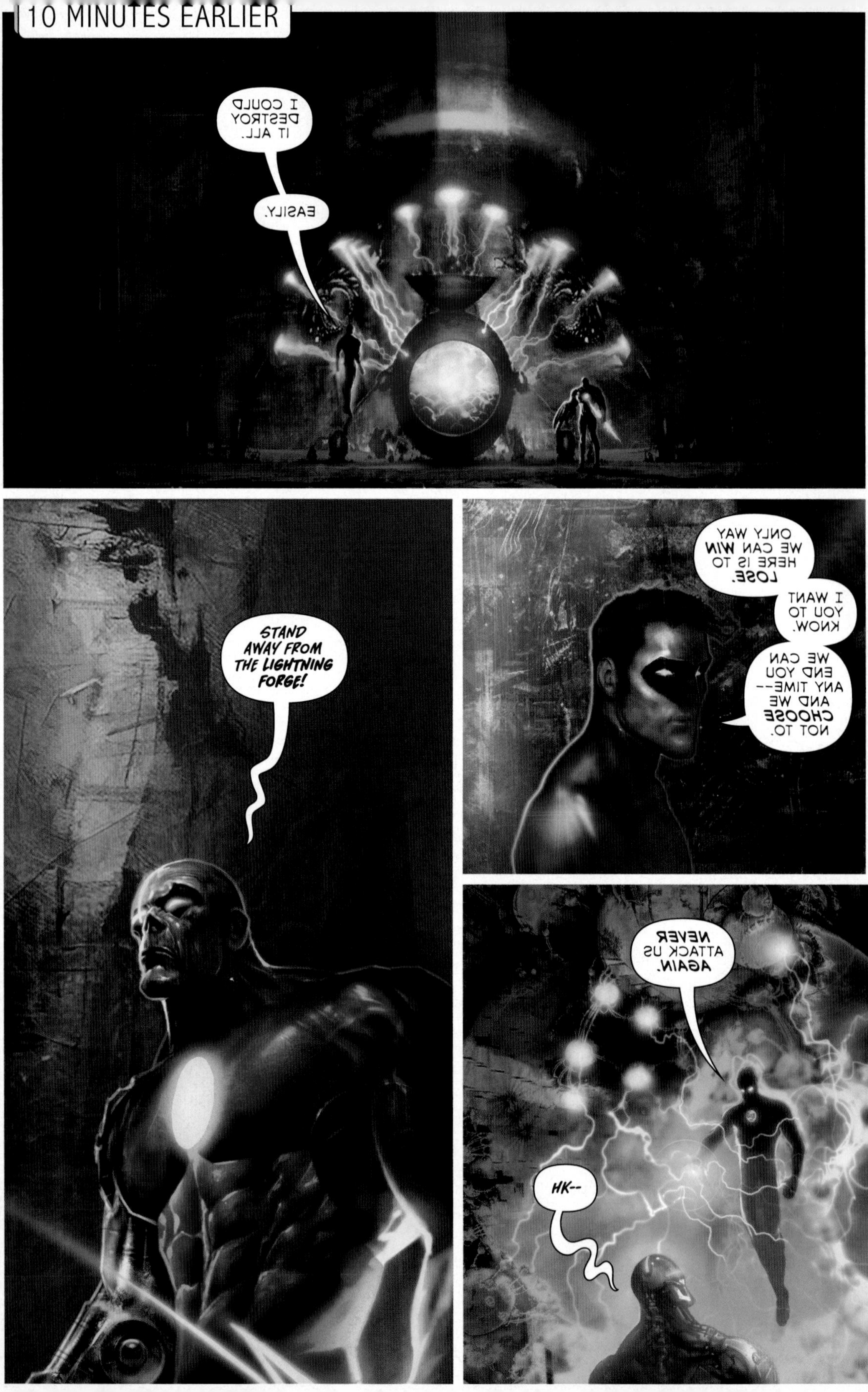

10 MINUTES EARLIER
I COULD DESTROY IT ALL.
EASILY.
STAND AWAY FROM THE LIGHTNING FORGE!
ONLY WAY WE CAN WIN HERE IS TO LOSE.
I WANT YOU TO KNOW.
WE CAN END YOU ANY TIME-- AND WE CHOOSE NOT TO.
NEVER ATTACK US AGAIN.
HK--

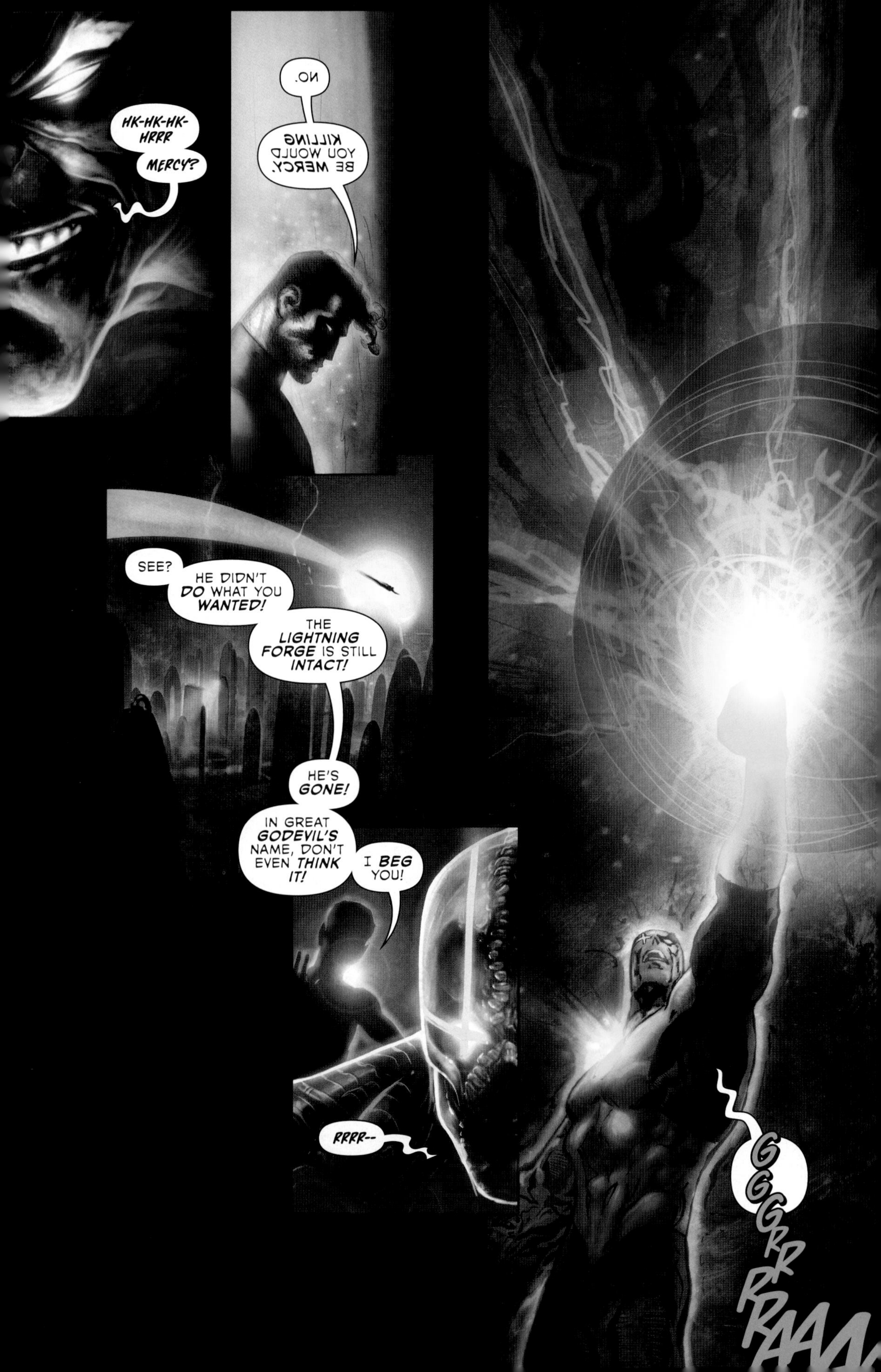
HK-HK-HK-HRRR
MERCY?
NO.
KILLING YOU WOULD BE MERCY.
SEE?
HE DIDN'T DO WHAT YOU WANTED!
THE LIGHTNING FORGE IS STILL INTACT!
HE'S GONE!
IN GREAT GODEVIL'S NAME, DON'T EVEN THINK IT!
I BEG YOU!
RRRR--
GGGRRRAAA

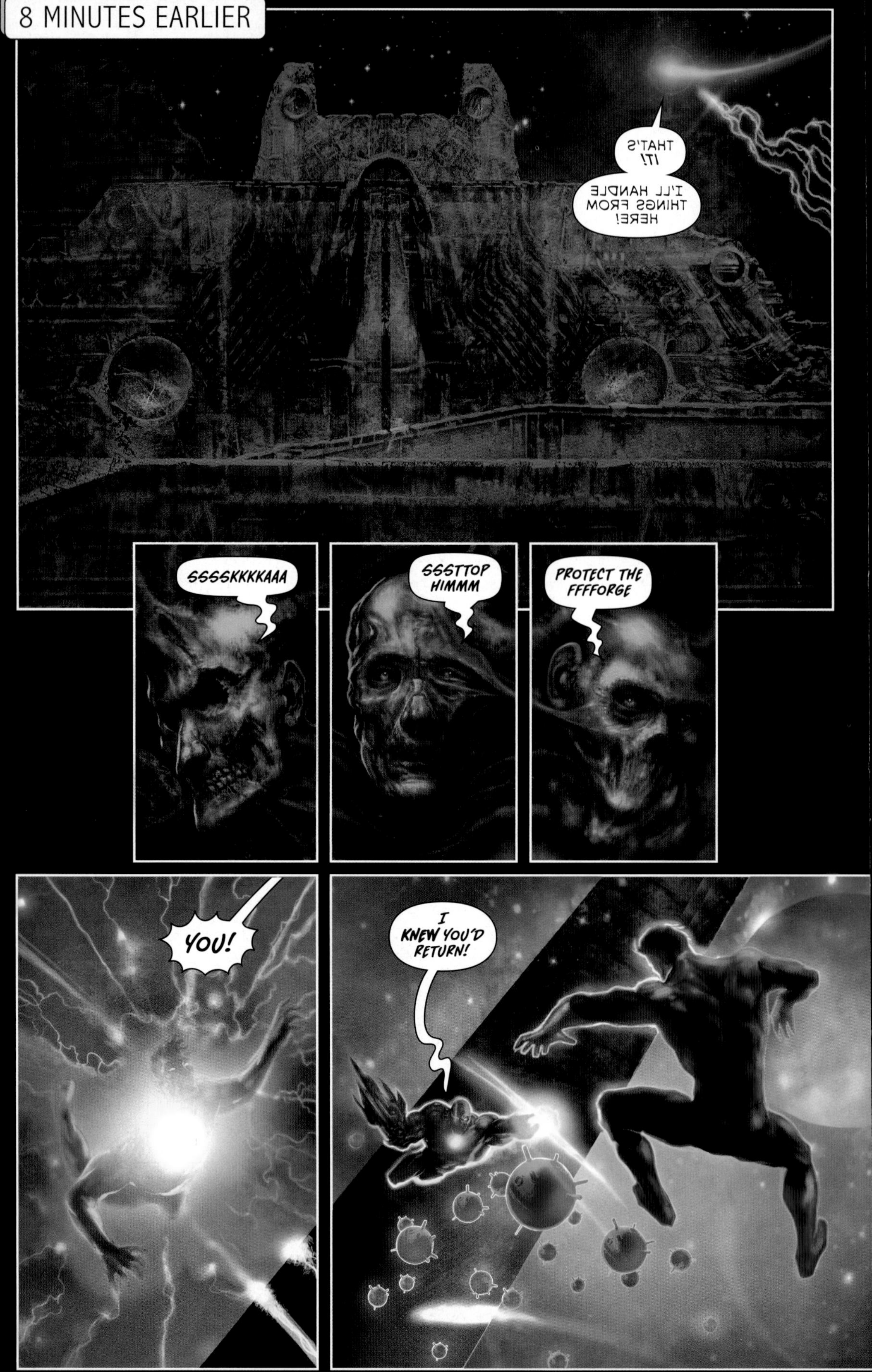
8 MINUTES EARLIER
THAT'S IT!
I'LL HANDLE THINGS FROM HERE!
SSSSKKKKAAA
SSSTTOP HIMMM
PROTECT THE FFFFORGE
YOU!
I KNEW YOU'D RETURN!

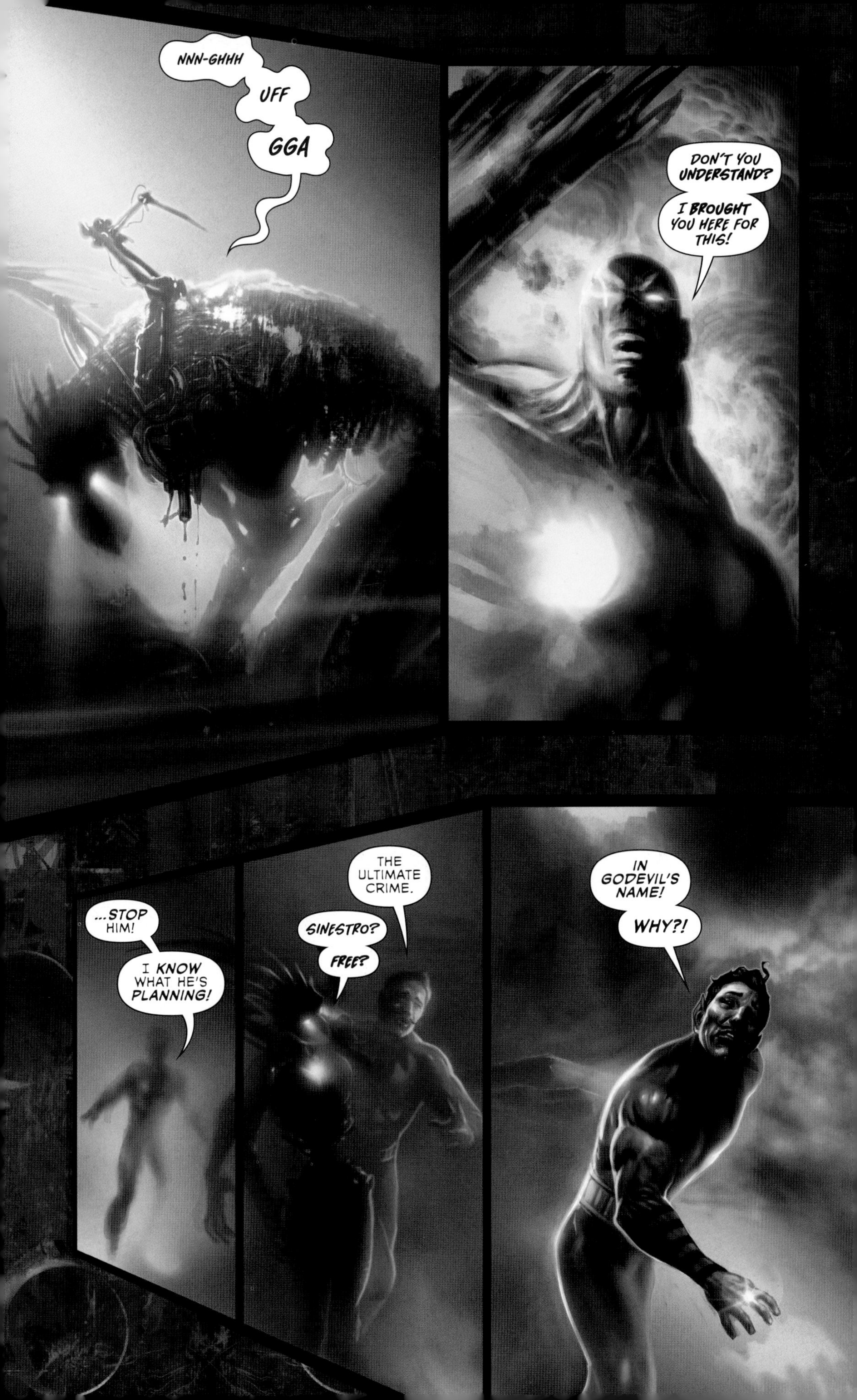
NNN-GHHH
UFF
GGA
DON'T YOU UNDERSTAND?
I BROUGHT YOU HERE FOR THIS!
...STOP HIM!
I KNOW WHAT HE'S PLANNING!
THE ULTIMATE CRIME.
SINESTRO?
FREE?
IN GODEVIL'S NAME!
WHY?!

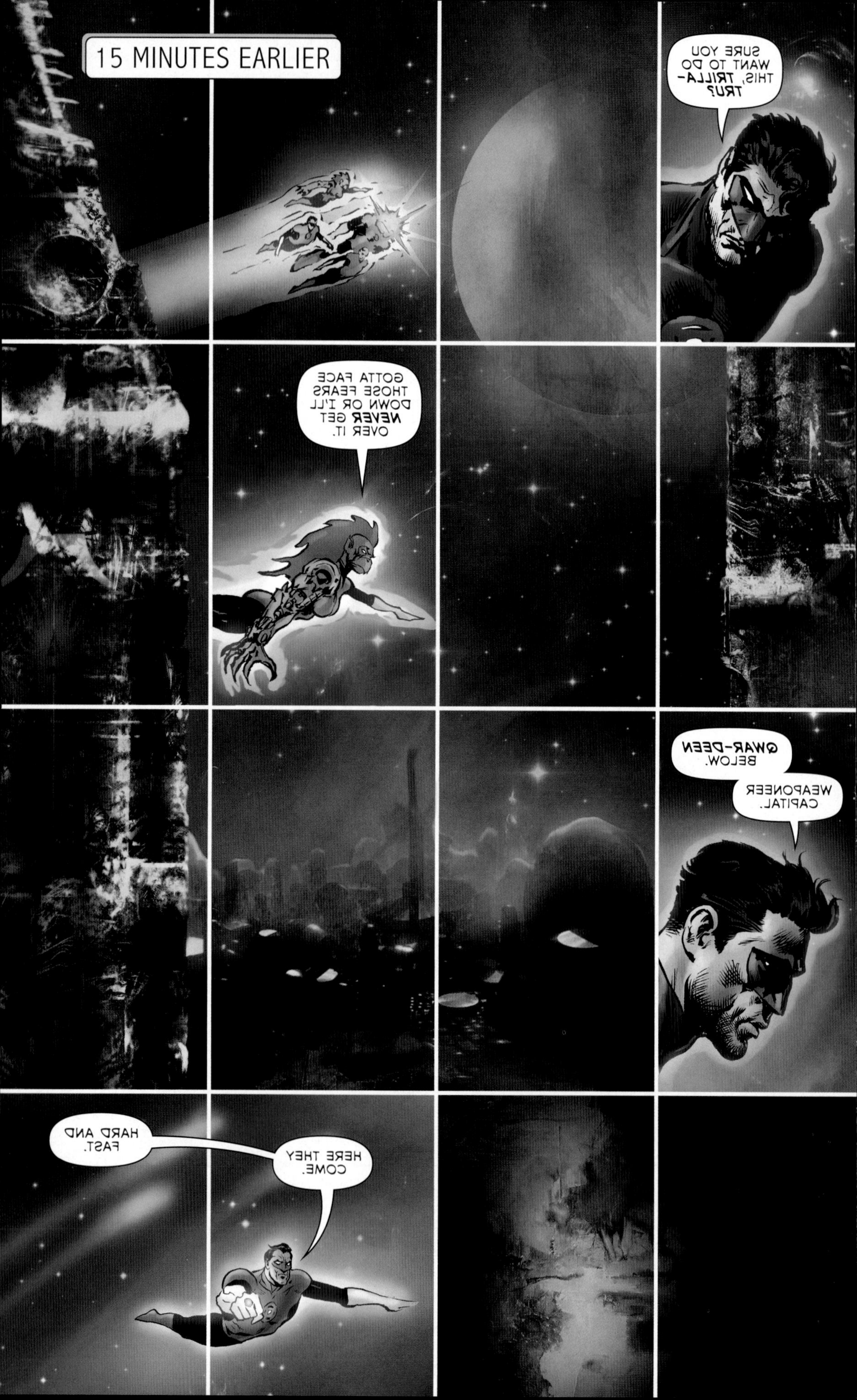
15 MINUTES EARLIER
SURE YOU WANT TO DO THIS, TRILLA-TRU?
GOTTA FACE THOSE FEARS DOWN OR I'LL NEVER GET OVER IT.
QWAR-DEEN BELOW.
WEAPONEER CAPITAL.
HERE THEY COME.
HARD AND FAST.

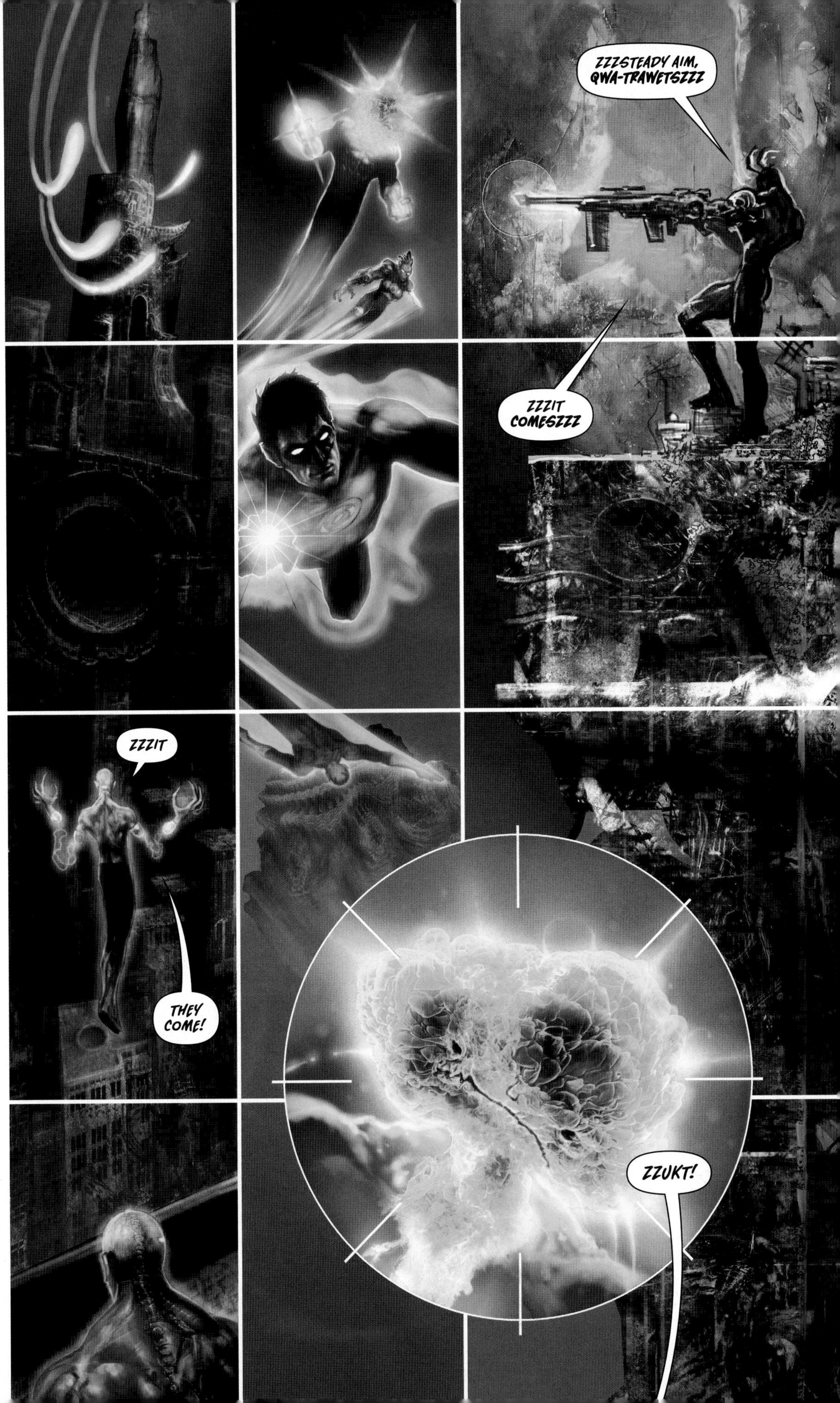
ZZZSTEADY AIM, QWA-TRAWETSZZZ
ZZZIT COMESZZZ
ZZZIT
THEY COME!
ZZUKT!

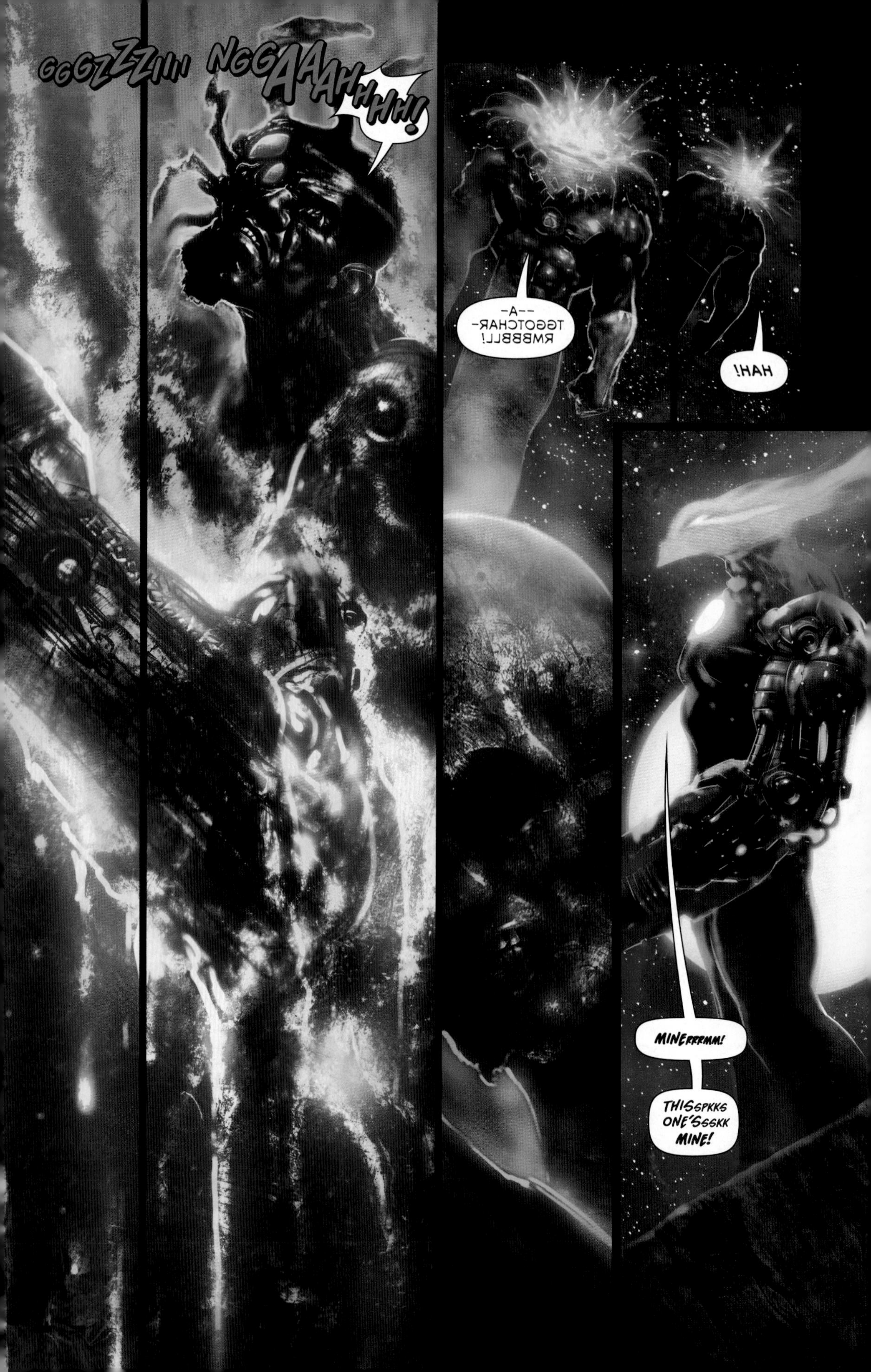

GGGZZZIIII NGGAAAAHHHH!
—A— TGGOTCHAR— RMBBLL!
!HAH
MINErrrmm!
THISspkks ONE'Ssskk MINE!

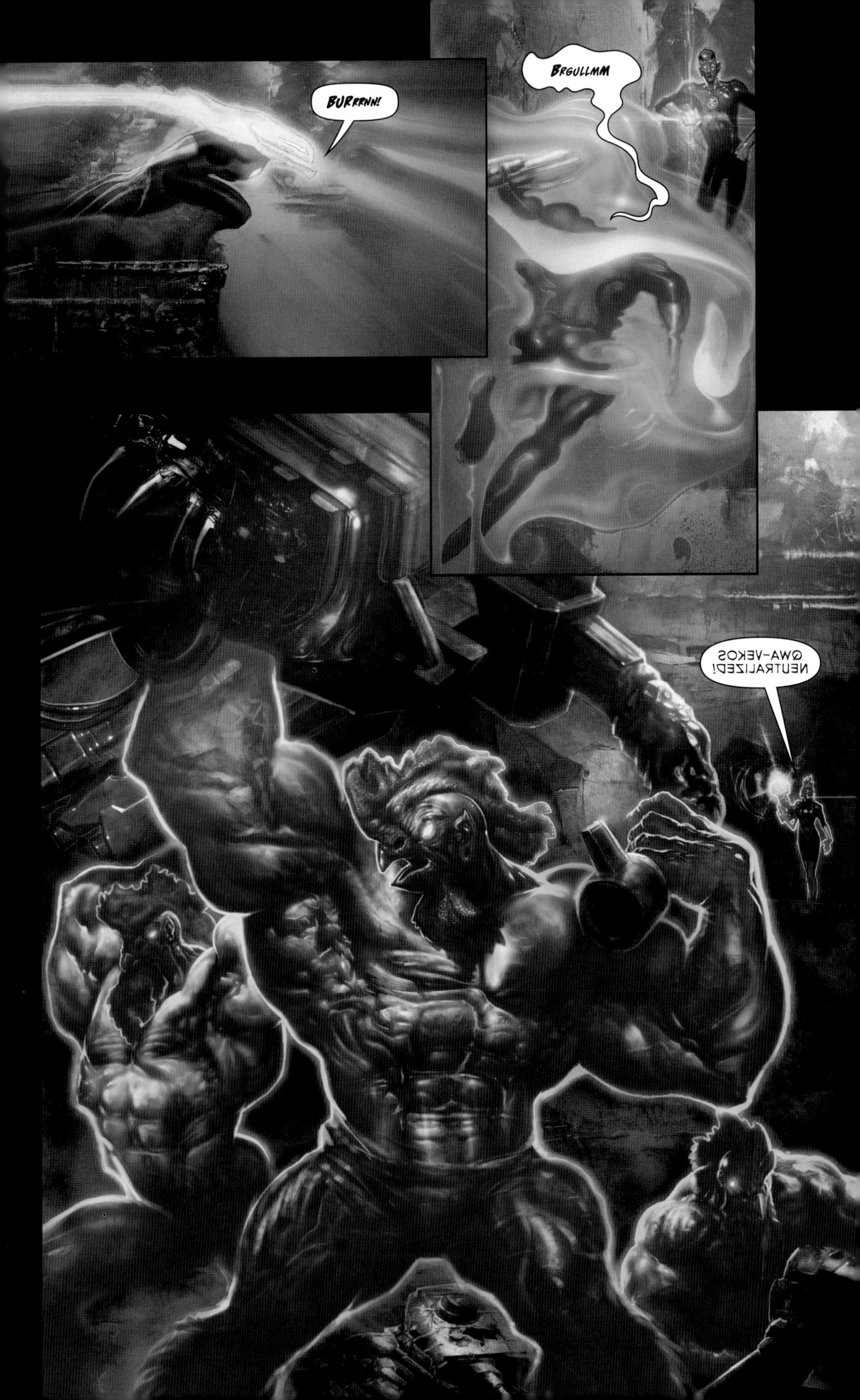
BURrrnn!
BRGULLMM
QWA-VEKOS NEUTRALIZED!

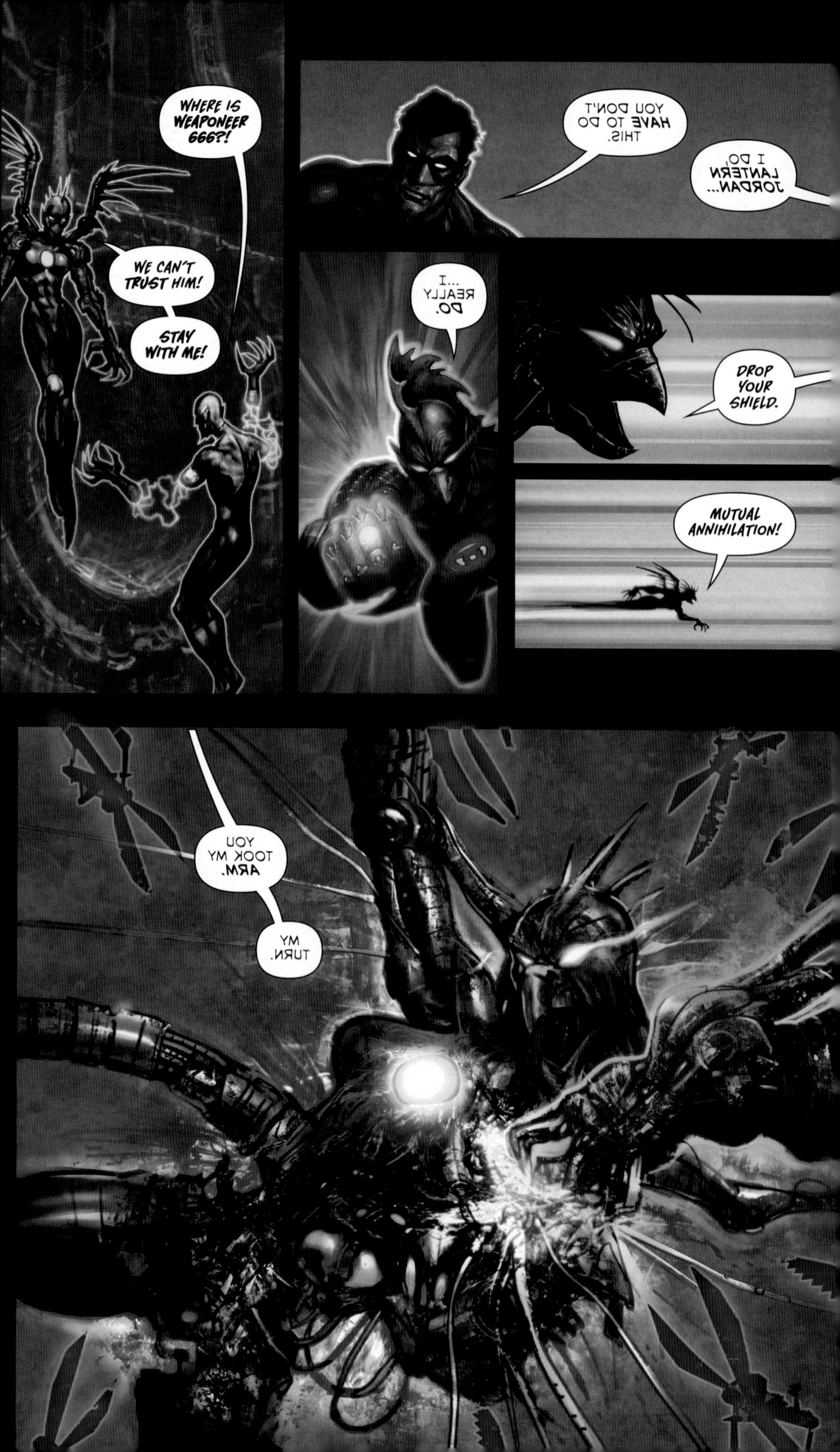
WHERE IS WEAPONEER 666?!
WE CAN'T TRUST HIM!
STAY WITH ME!
YOU DON'T HAVE TO DO THIS.
I DO, LANTERN JORDAN...
I... REALLY DO.
DROP YOUR SHIELD.
MUTUAL ANNIHILATION!
YOU TOOK MY ARM.
MY TURN.

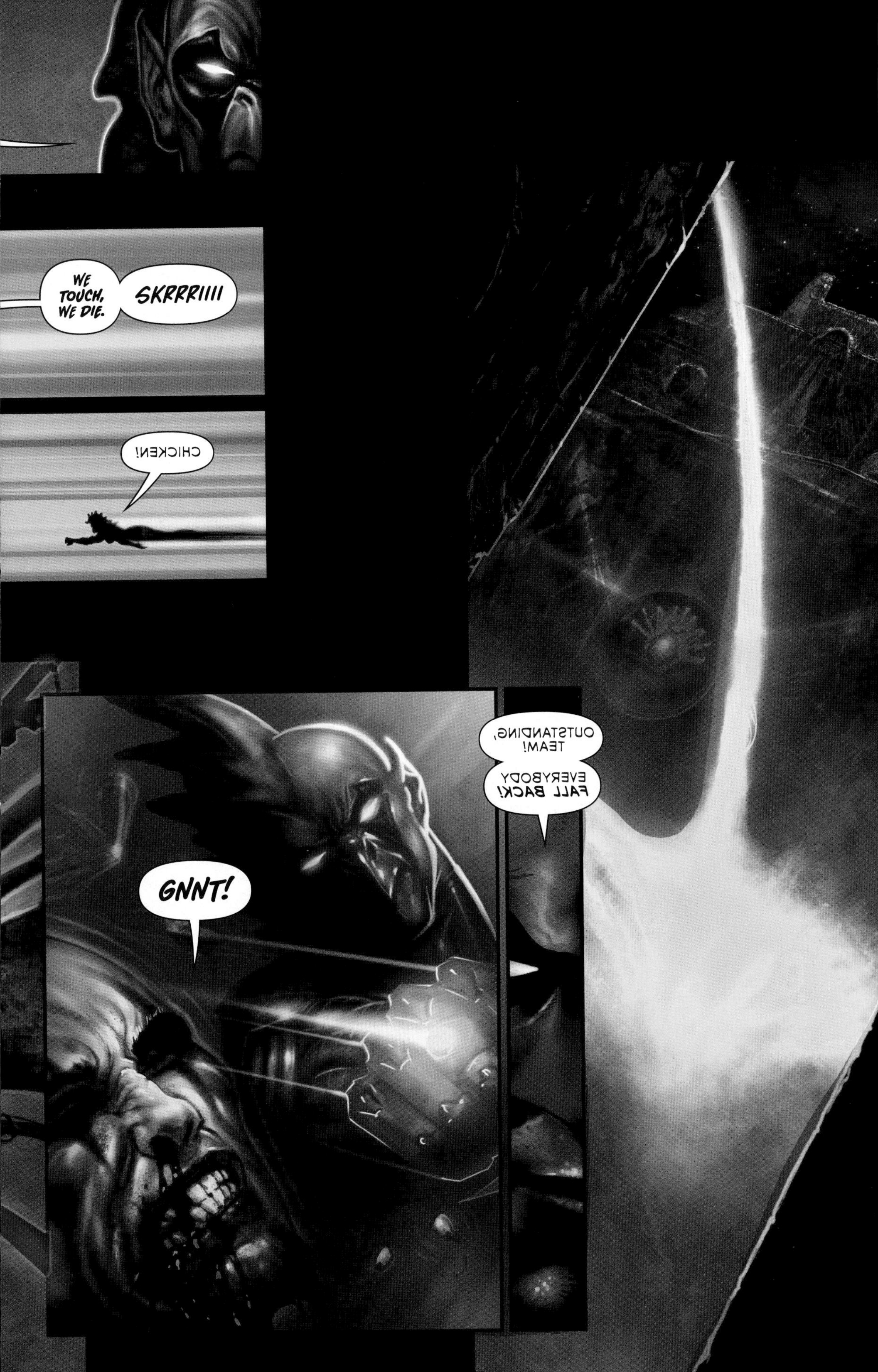
WE TOUCH, WE DIE.
SKRRRIIII
CHICKEN!
OUTSTANDING, TEAM!
EVERYBODY FALL BACK!
GNNT!

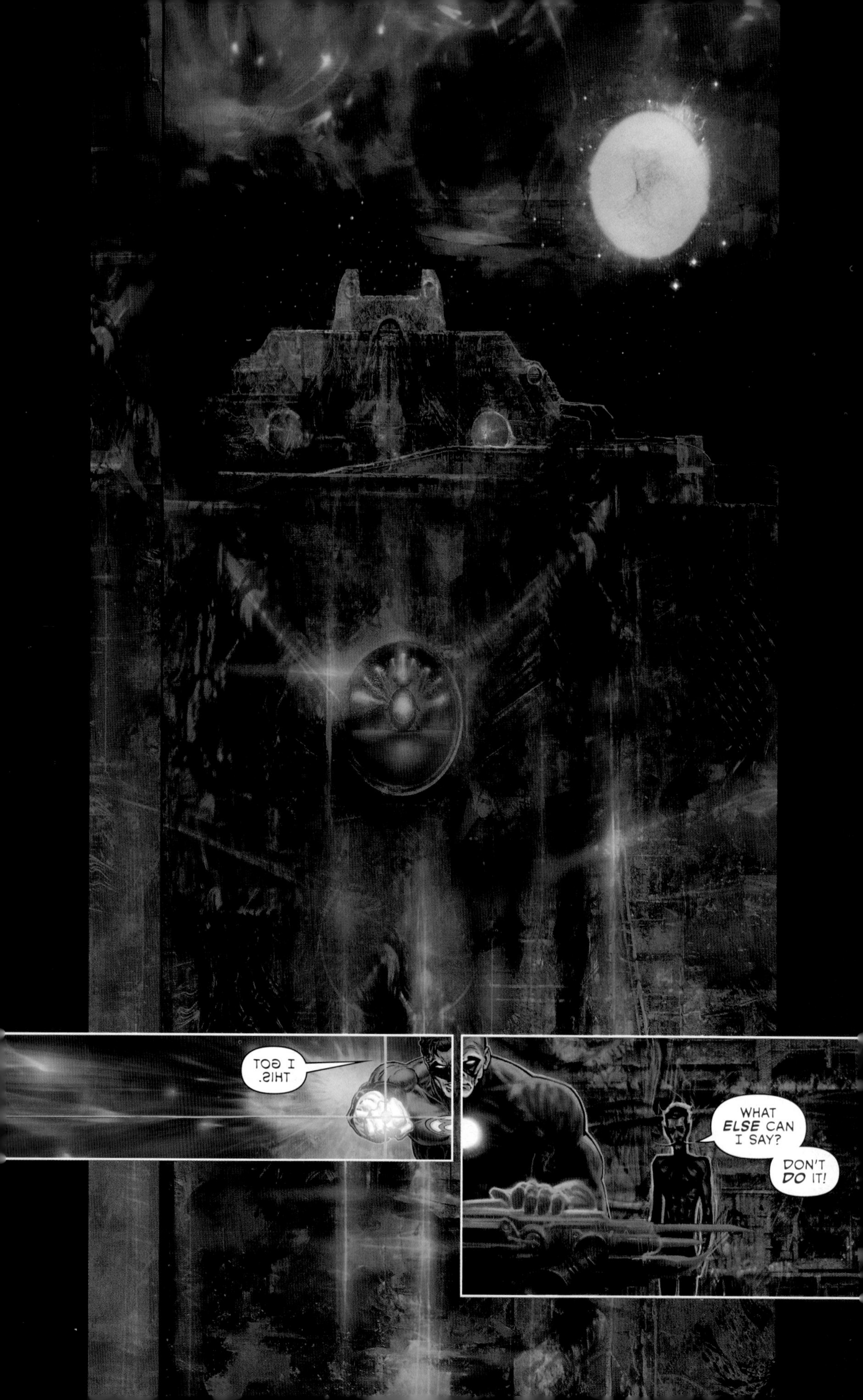
I GOT THIS.
WHAT ELSE CAN I SAY?
DON'T DO IT!

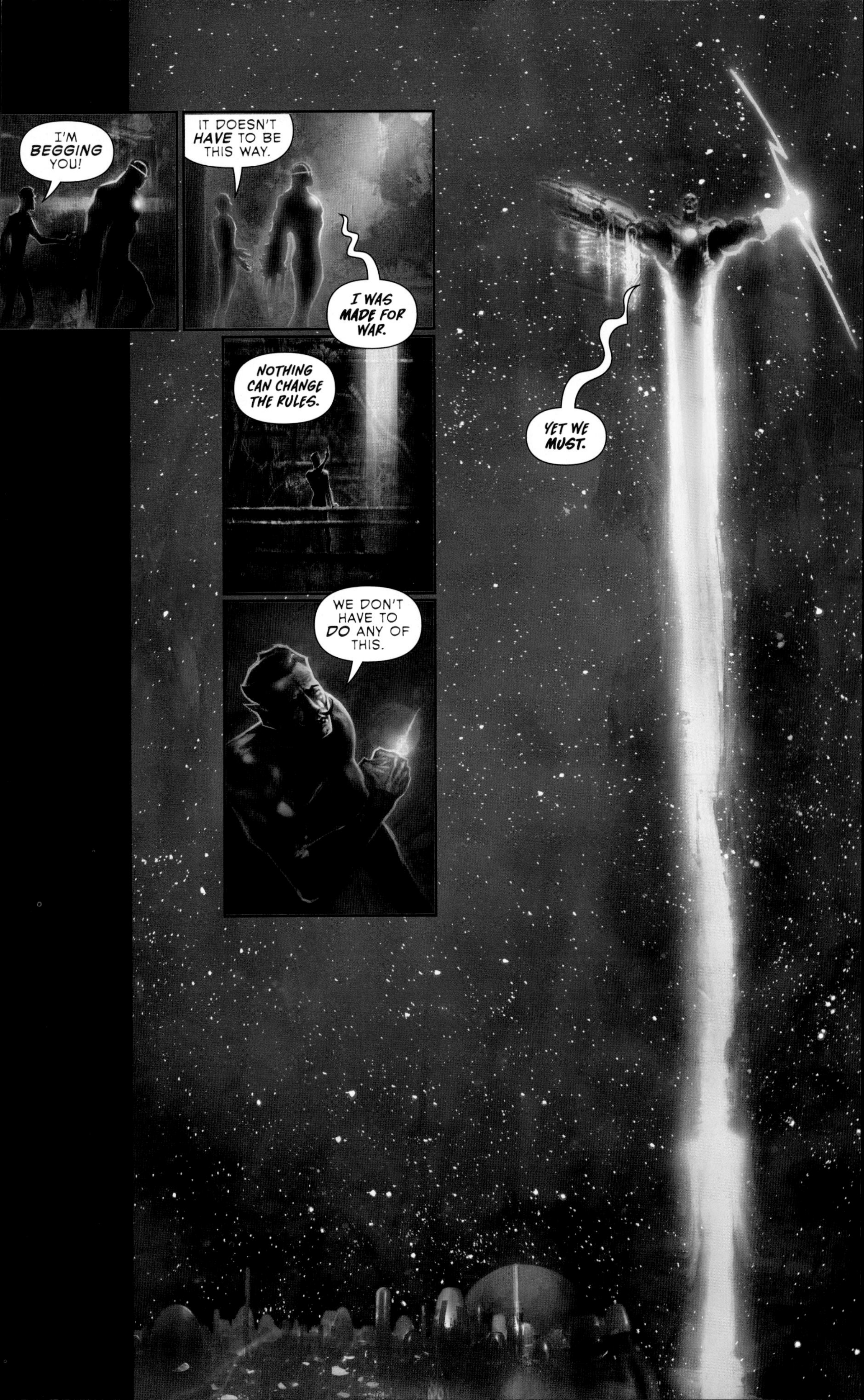

I'M BEGGING YOU!
IT DOESN'T HAVE TO BE THIS WAY.
I WAS MADE FOR WAR.
NOTHING CAN CHANGE THE RULES.
WE DON'T HAVE TO DO ANY OF THIS.
YET WE MUST.

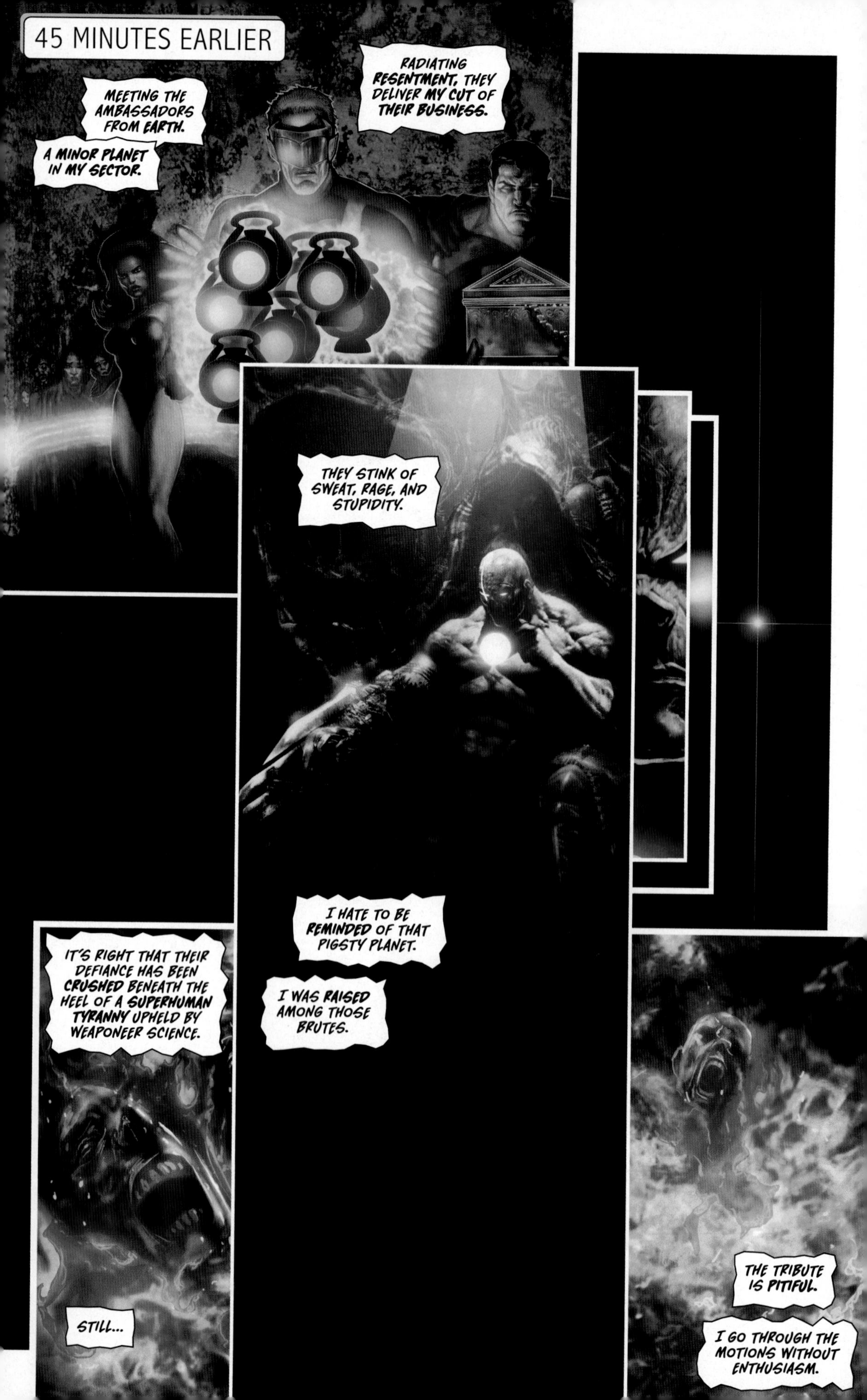
45 MINUTES EARLIER
MEETING THE AMBASSADORS FROM EARTH.
A MINOR PLANET IN MY SECTOR.
RADIATING RESENTMENT, THEY DELIVER MY CUT OF THEIR BUSINESS.
THEY STINK OF SWEAT, RAGE, AND STUPIDITY.
I HATE TO BE REMINDED OF THAT PIGSTY PLANET.
I WAS RAISED AMONG THOSE BRUTES.
IT'S RIGHT THAT THEIR DEFIANCE HAS BEEN CRUSHED BENEATH THE HEEL OF A SUPERHUMAN TYRANNY UPHELD BY WEAPONEER SCIENCE.
STILL...
THE TRIBUTE IS PITIFUL.
I GO THROUGH THE MOTIONS WITHOUT ENTHUSIASM.

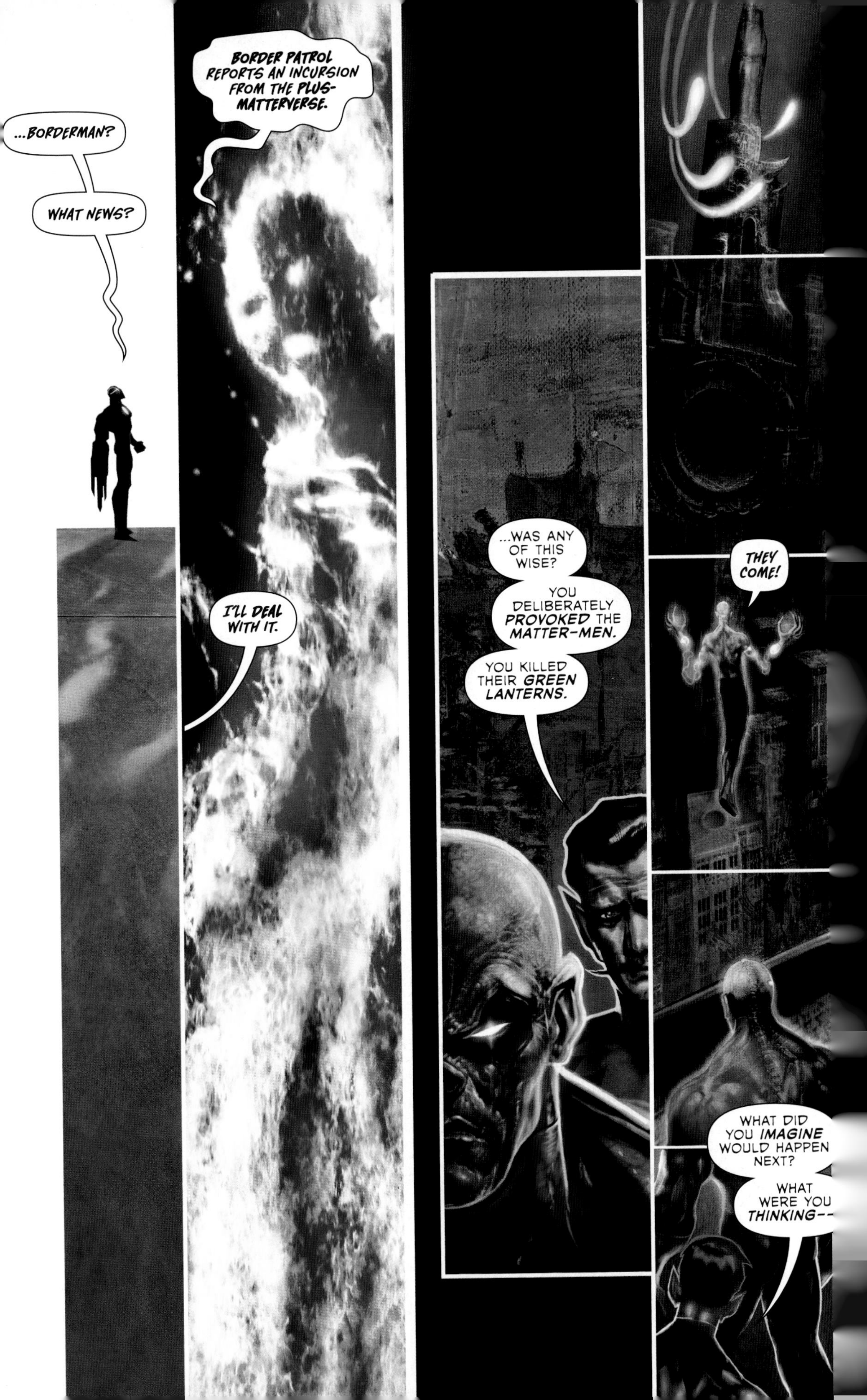
...BORDERMAN?
WHAT NEWS?
BORDER PATROL REPORTS AN INCURSION FROM THE PLUS-MATTERVERSE.
I'LL DEAL WITH IT.
...WAS ANY OF THIS WISE?
YOU DELIBERATELY PROVOKED THE MATTER-MEN.
YOU KILLED THEIR GREEN LANTERNS.
THEY COME!
WHAT DID YOU IMAGINE WOULD HAPPEN NEXT?
WHAT WERE YOU THINKING--

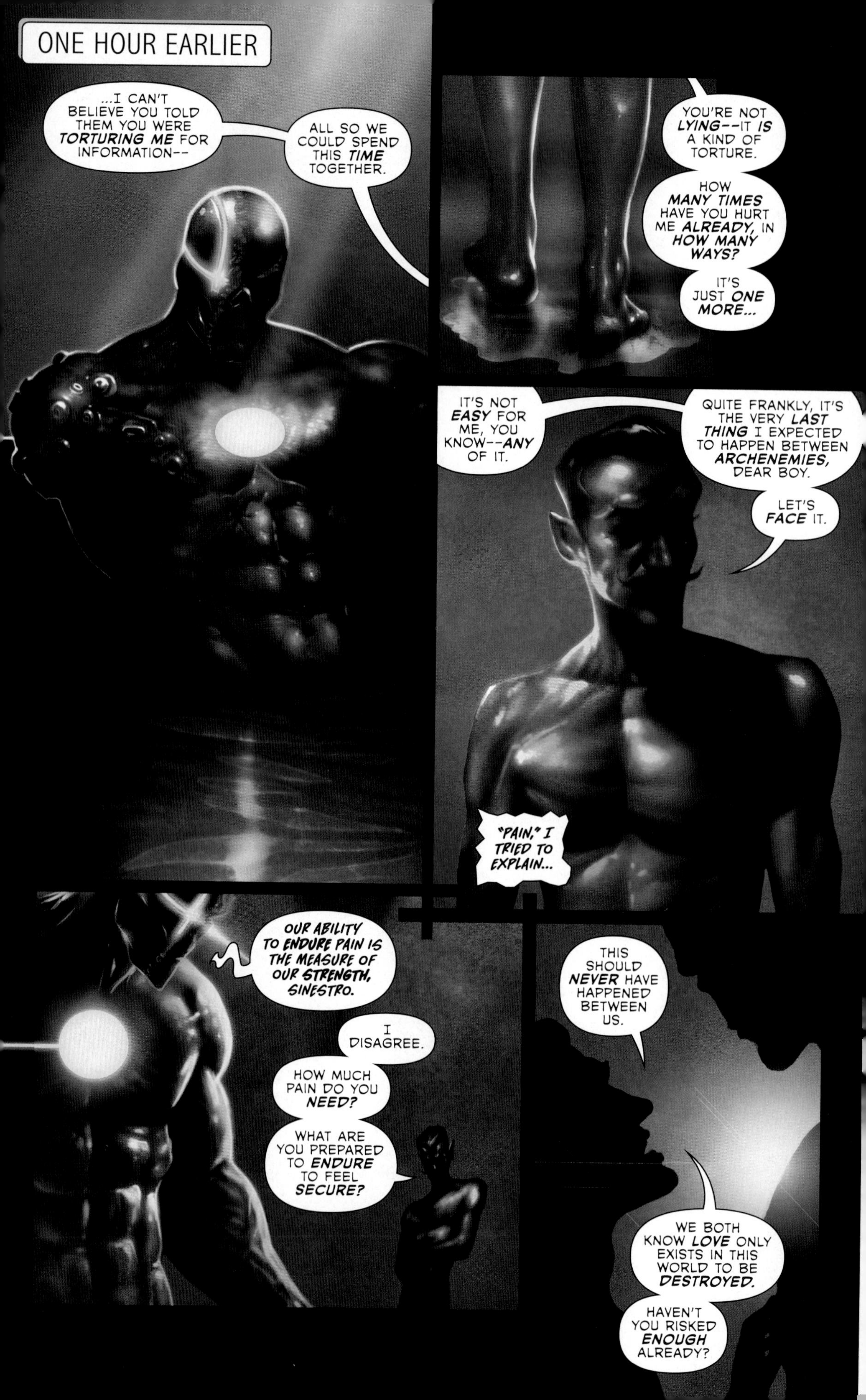
ONE HOUR EARLIER
...I CAN'T BELIEVE YOU TOLD THEM YOU WERE TORTURING ME FOR INFORMATION--
ALL SO WE COULD SPEND THIS TIME TOGETHER.
YOU'RE NOT LYING--IT IS A KIND OF TORTURE.
HOW MANY TIMES HAVE YOU HURT ME ALREADY, IN HOW MANY WAYS?
IT'S JUST ONE MORE...
IT'S NOT EASY FOR ME, YOU KNOW--ANY OF IT.
QUITE FRANKLY, IT'S THE VERY LAST THING I EXPECTED TO HAPPEN BETWEEN ARCHENEMIES, DEAR BOY.
LET'S FACE IT.
"PAIN," I TRIED TO EXPLAIN...
OUR ABILITY TO ENDURE PAIN IS THE MEASURE OF OUR STRENGTH, SINESTRO.
I DISAGREE.
HOW MUCH PAIN DO YOU NEED?
WHAT ARE YOU PREPARED TO ENDURE TO FEEL SECURE?
THIS SHOULD NEVER HAVE HAPPENED BETWEEN US.
WE BOTH KNOW LOVE ONLY EXISTS IN THIS WORLD TO BE DESTROYED.
HAVEN'T YOU RISKED ENOUGH ALREADY?

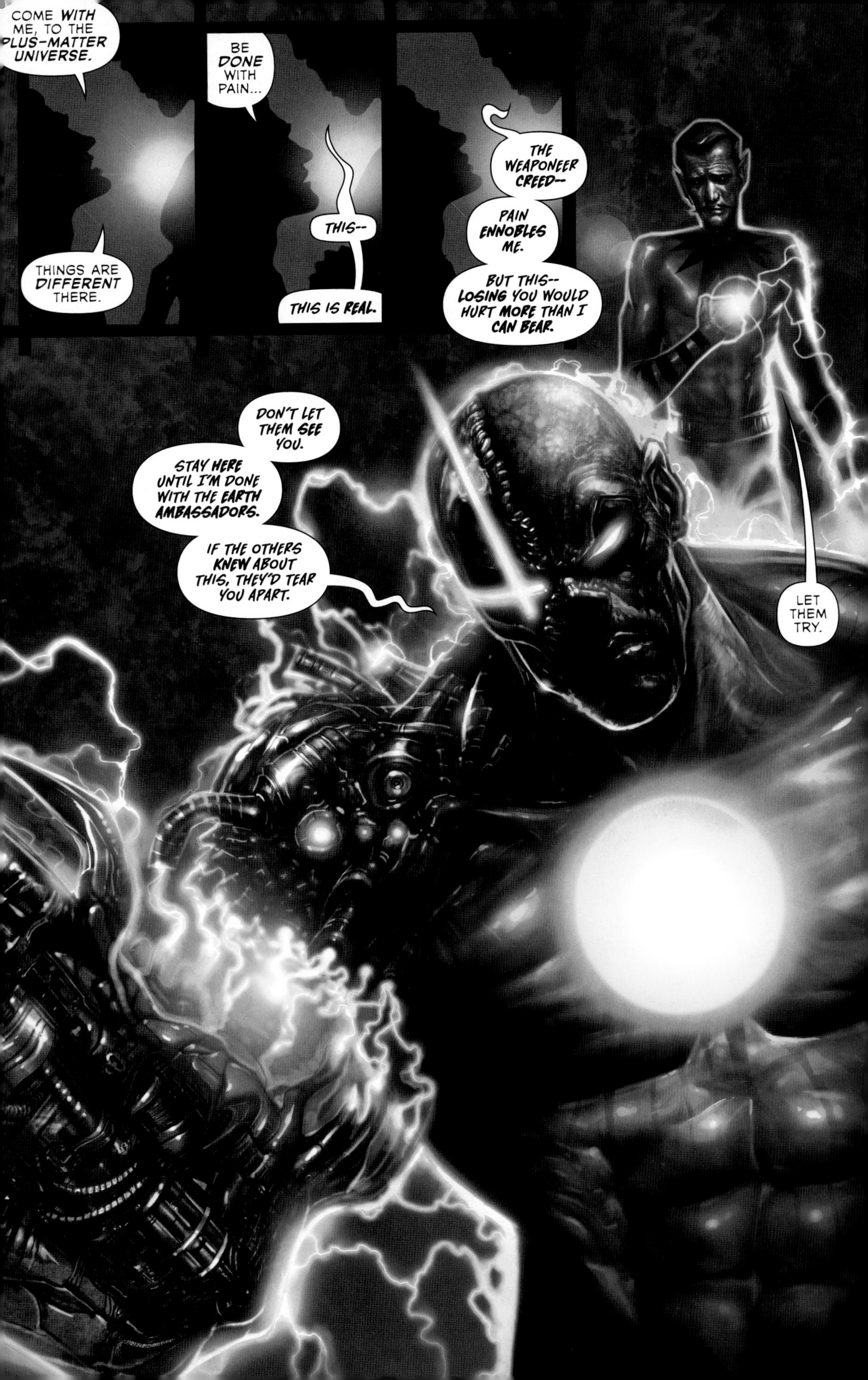

COME WITH ME, TO THE PLUS-MATTER UNIVERSE.
THINGS ARE DIFFERENT THERE.
BE DONE WITH PAIN...
THIS--
THIS IS REAL.
THE WEAPONEER CREED--
PAIN ENNOBLES ME.
BUT THIS-- LOSING YOU WOULD HURT MORE THAN I CAN BEAR.
DON'T LET THEM SEE YOU.
STAY HERE UNTIL I'M DONE WITH THE EARTH AMBASSADORS.
IF THE OTHERS KNEW ABOUT THIS, THEY'D TEAR YOU APART.
LET THEM TRY.

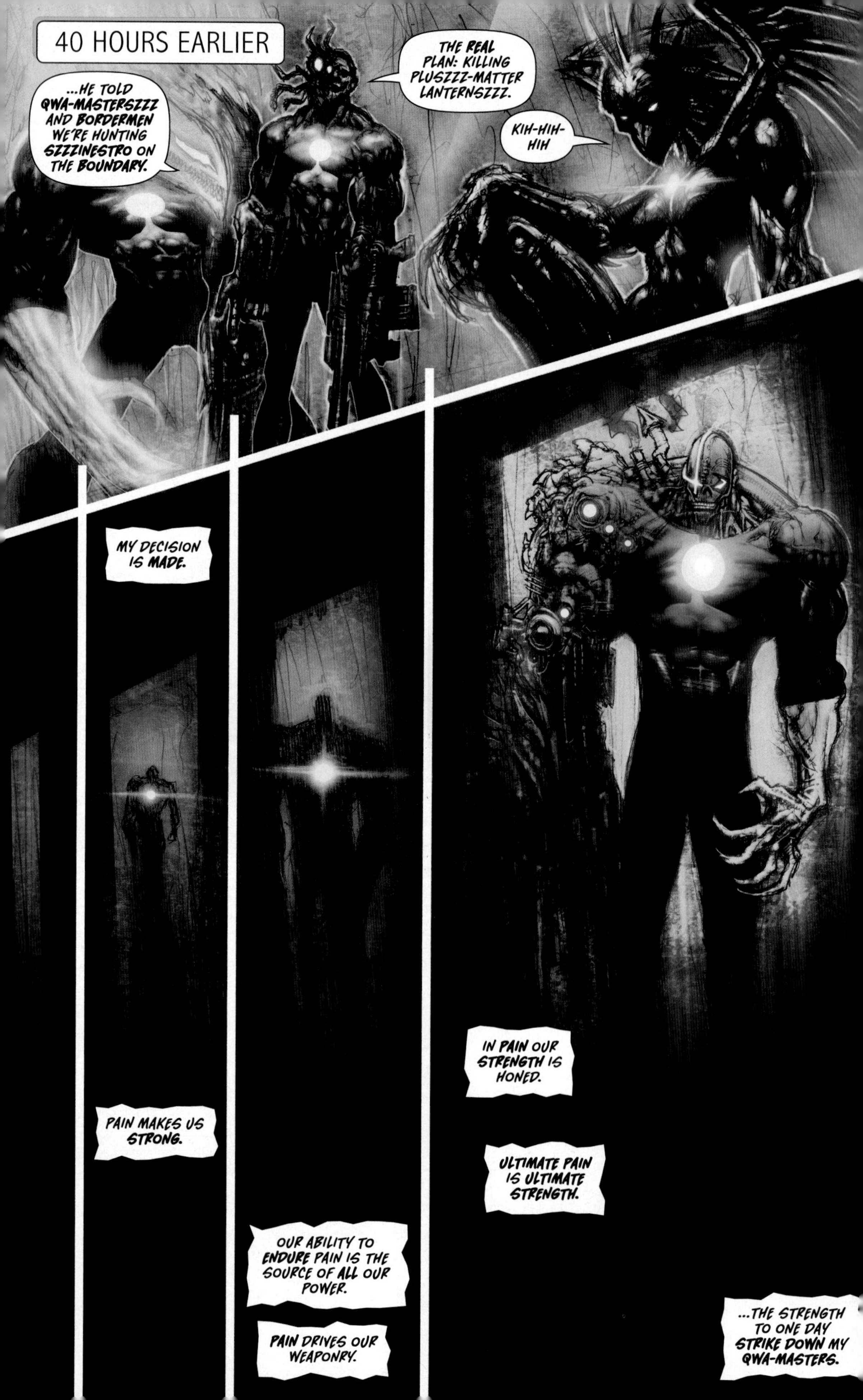
40 HOURS EARLIER
...HE TOLD QWA-MASTERSZZZ AND BORDERMEN WE'RE HUNTING SZZZINESTRO ON THE BOUNDARY.
THE REAL PLAN: KILLING PLUSZZZ-MATTER LANTERNSZZZ.
KIH-HIH-HIH
MY DECISION IS MADE.
PAIN MAKES US STRONG.
OUR ABILITY TO ENDURE PAIN IS THE SOURCE OF ALL OUR POWER.
PAIN DRIVES OUR WEAPONRY.
IN PAIN OUR STRENGTH IS HONED.
ULTIMATE PAIN IS ULTIMATE STRENGTH.
...THE STRENGTH TO ONE DAY STRIKE DOWN MY QWA-MASTERS.

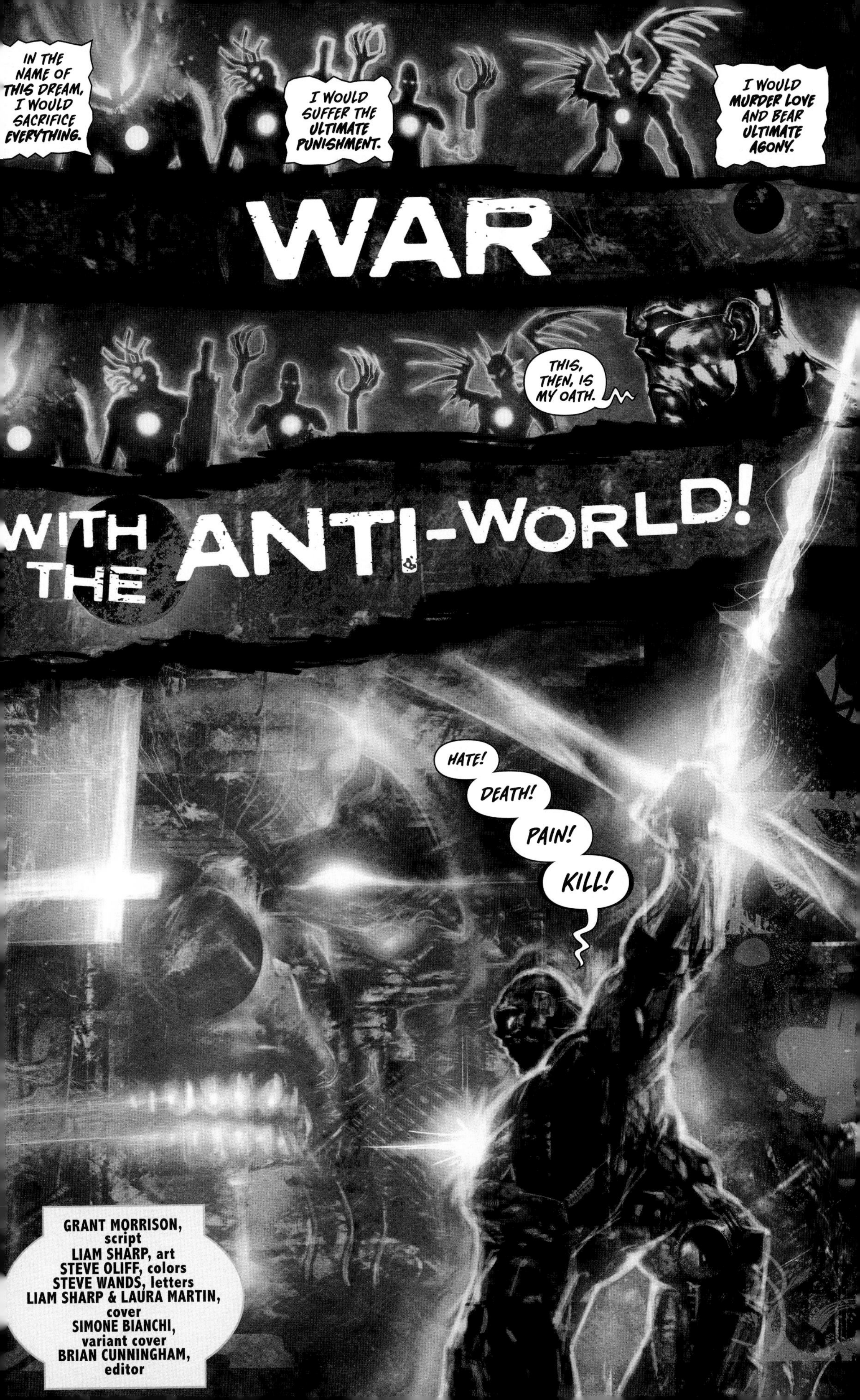
IN THE NAME OF THIS DREAM, I WOULD SACRIFICE EVERYTHING.
I WOULD SUFFER THE ULTIMATE PUNISHMENT.
I WOULD MURDER LOVE AND BEAR ULTIMATE AGONY.
WAR
THIS, THEN, IS MY OATH.
WITH THE ANTI-WORLD!
HATE!
DEATH!
PAIN!
KILL!
GRANT MORRISON, script
LIAM SHARP, art
STEVE OLIFF, colors
STEVE WANDS, letters
LIAM SHARP & LAURA MARTIN, cover
SIMONE BIANCHI, variant cover
BRIAN CUNNINGHAM, editor

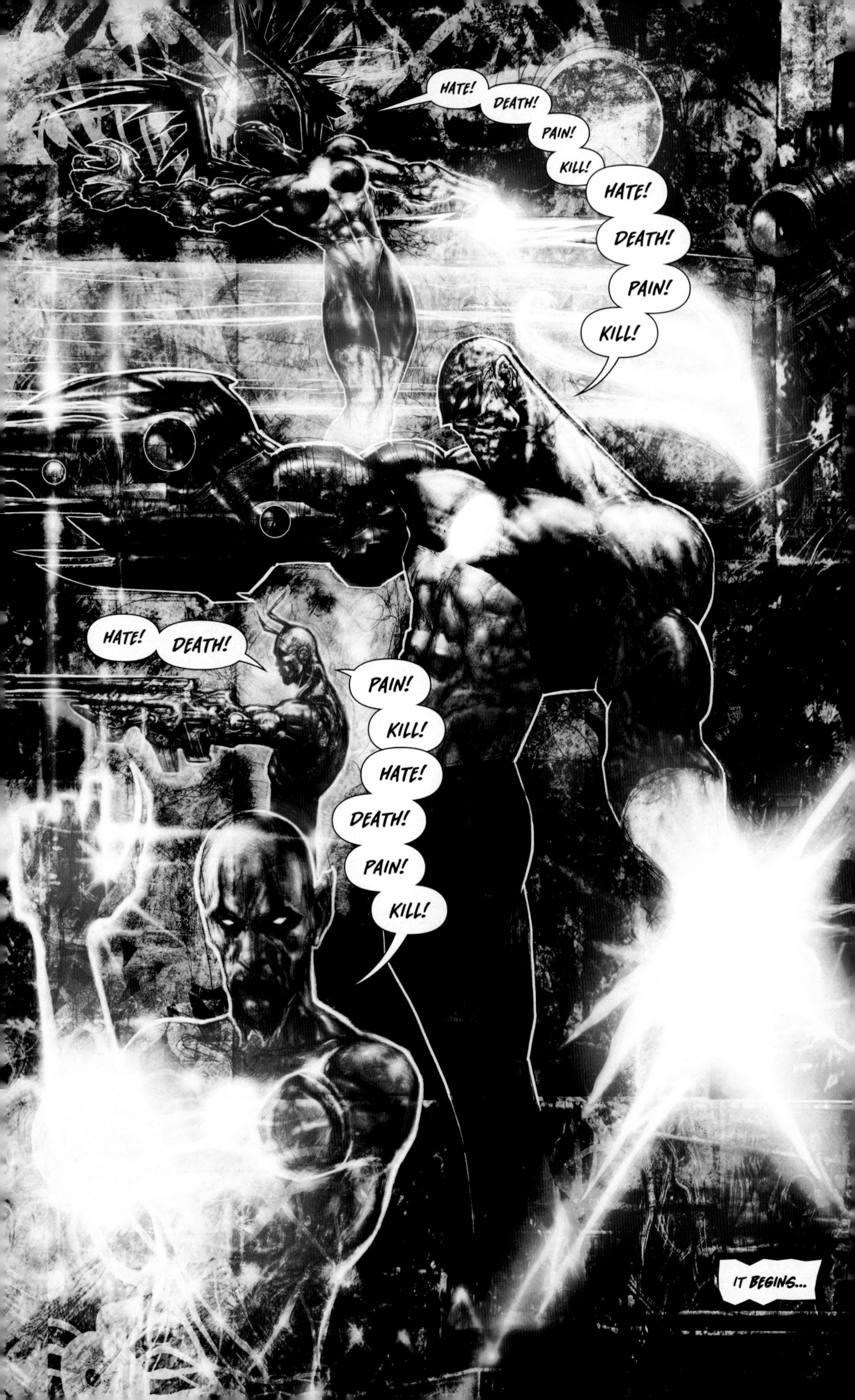
HATE!
DEATH!
PAIN!
KILL!
HATE!
DEATH!
PAIN!
KILL!
HATE!
DEATH!
PAIN!
KILL!
HATE!
DEATH!
PAIN!
KILL!
IT BEGINS...

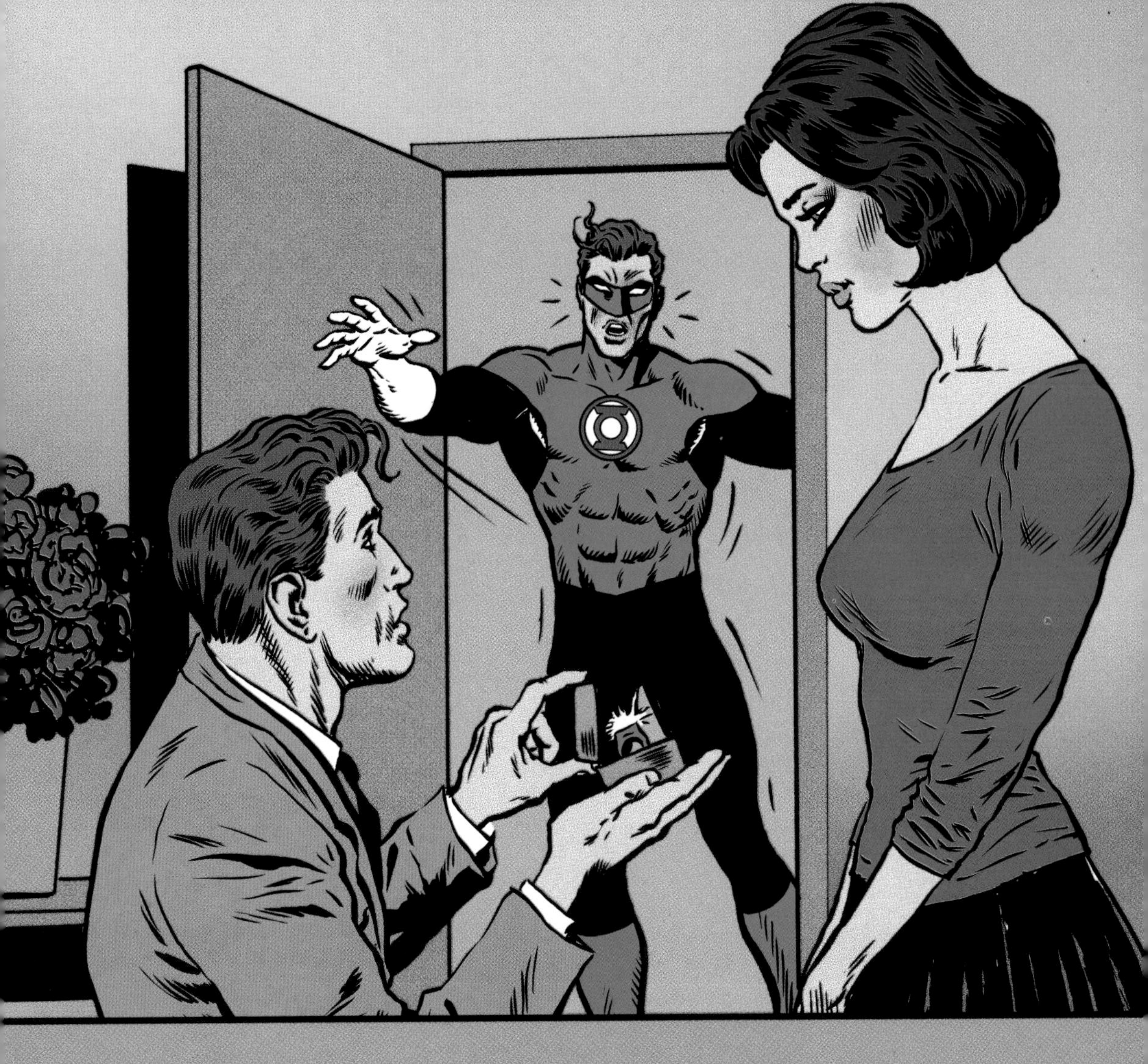

The Green Lantern Season Two #9
variant cover by **CHRIS BURNHAM** & **RICO RENZI**

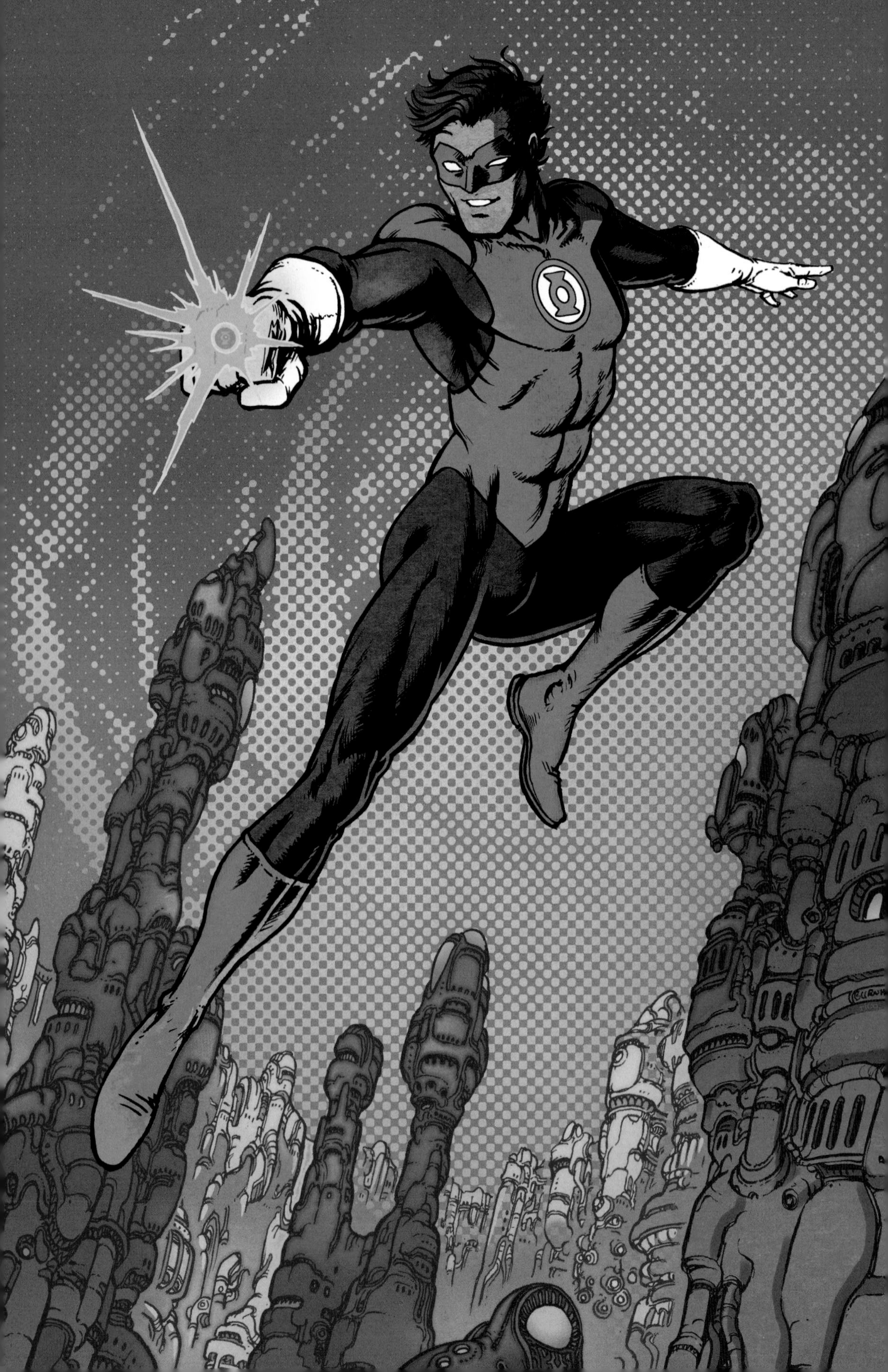

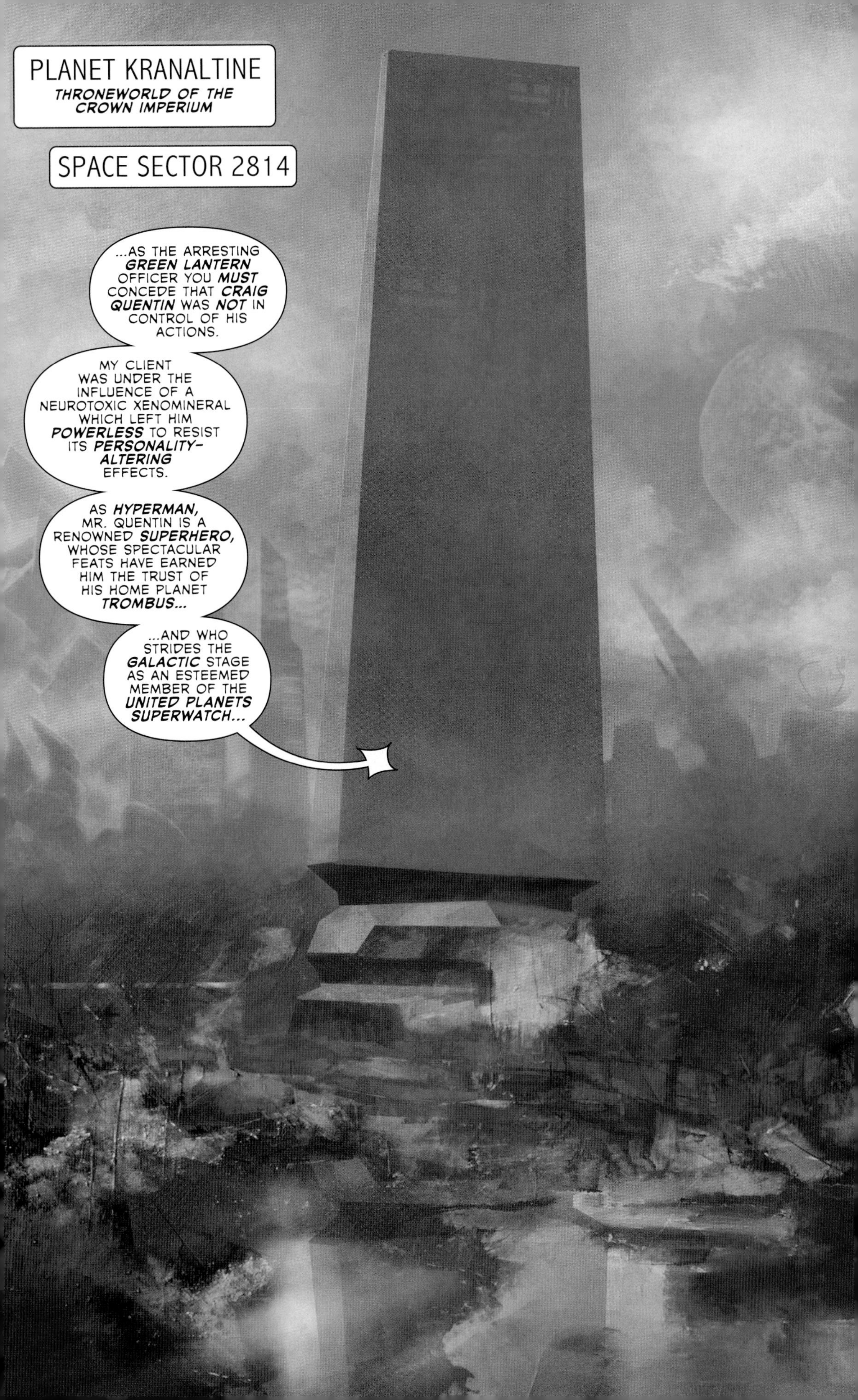
PLANET KRANALTINE
THRONEWORLD OF THE CROWN IMPERIUM
SPACE SECTOR 2814
...AS THE ARRESTING GREEN LANTERN OFFICER YOU MUST CONCEDE THAT CRAIG QUENTIN WAS NOT IN CONTROL OF HIS ACTIONS.
MY CLIENT WAS UNDER THE INFLUENCE OF A NEUROTOXIC XENOMINERAL WHICH LEFT HIM POWERLESS TO RESIST ITS PERSONALITY-ALTERING EFFECTS.
AS HYPERMAN, MR. QUENTIN IS A RENOWNED SUPERHERO, WHOSE SPECTACULAR FEATS HAVE EARNED HIM THE TRUST OF HIS HOME PLANET TROMBUS...
...AND WHO STRIDES THE GALACTIC STAGE AS AN ESTEEMED MEMBER OF THE UNITED PLANETS SUPERWATCH...

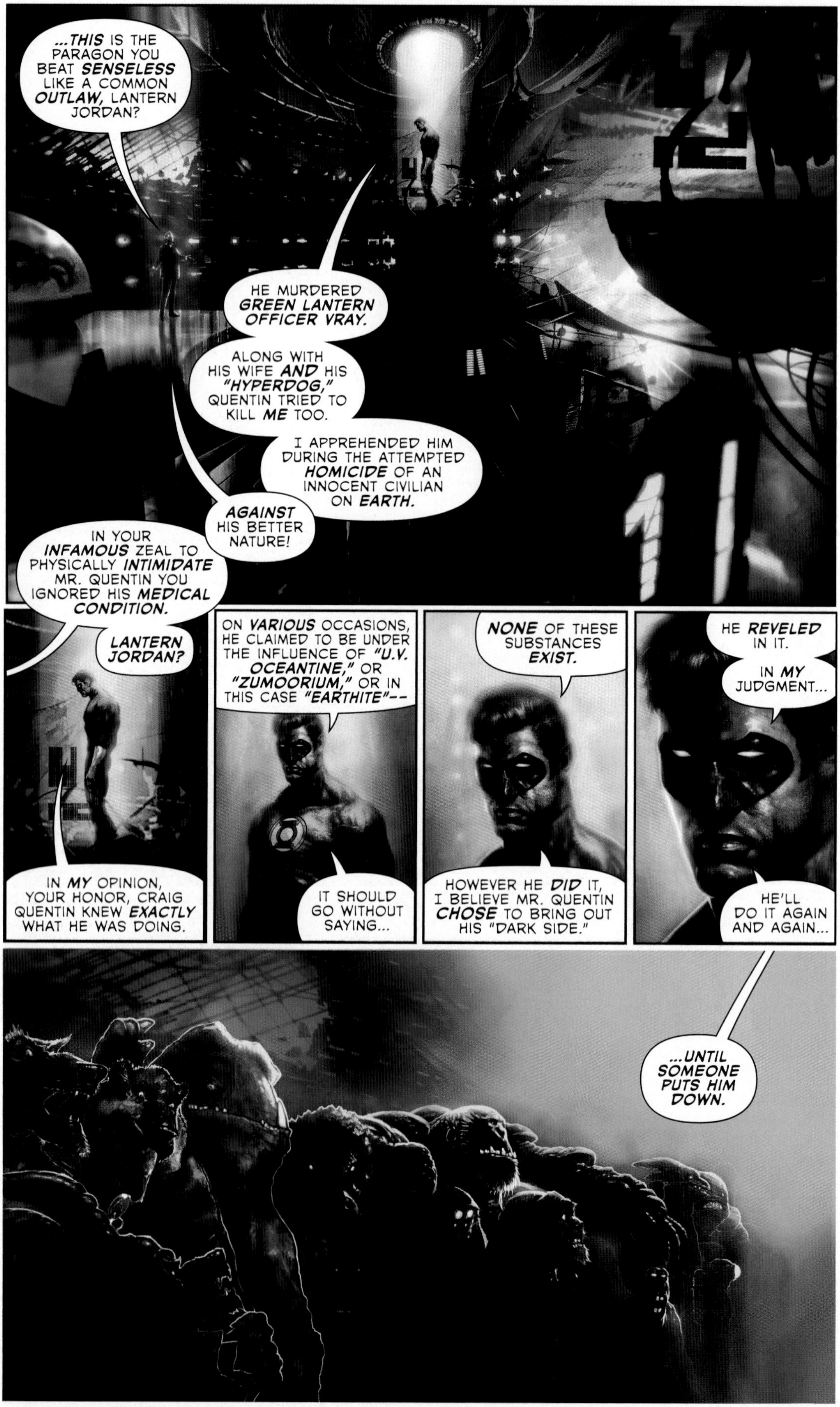
...THIS IS THE PARAGON YOU BEAT SENSELESS LIKE A COMMON OUTLAW, LANTERN JORDAN?
HE MURDERED GREEN LANTERN OFFICER VRAY.
ALONG WITH HIS WIFE AND HIS "HYPERDOG," QUENTIN TRIED TO KILL ME TOO.
I APPREHENDED HIM DURING THE ATTEMPTED HOMICIDE OF AN INNOCENT CIVILIAN ON EARTH.
AGAINST HIS BETTER NATURE!
IN YOUR INFAMOUS ZEAL TO PHYSICALLY INTIMIDATE MR. QUENTIN YOU IGNORED HIS MEDICAL CONDITION.
LANTERN JORDAN?
IN MY OPINION, YOUR HONOR, CRAIG QUENTIN KNEW EXACTLY WHAT HE WAS DOING.
ON VARIOUS OCCASIONS, HE CLAIMED TO BE UNDER THE INFLUENCE OF "U.V. OCEANTINE," OR "ZUMOORIUM," OR IN THIS CASE "EARTHITE"--
IT SHOULD GO WITHOUT SAYING...
NONE OF THESE SUBSTANCES EXIST.
HOWEVER HE DID IT, I BELIEVE MR. QUENTIN CHOSE TO BRING OUT HIS "DARK SIDE."
HE REVELED IN IT.
IN MY JUDGMENT...
HE'LL DO IT AGAIN AND AGAIN...
...UNTIL SOMEONE PUTS HIM DOWN.

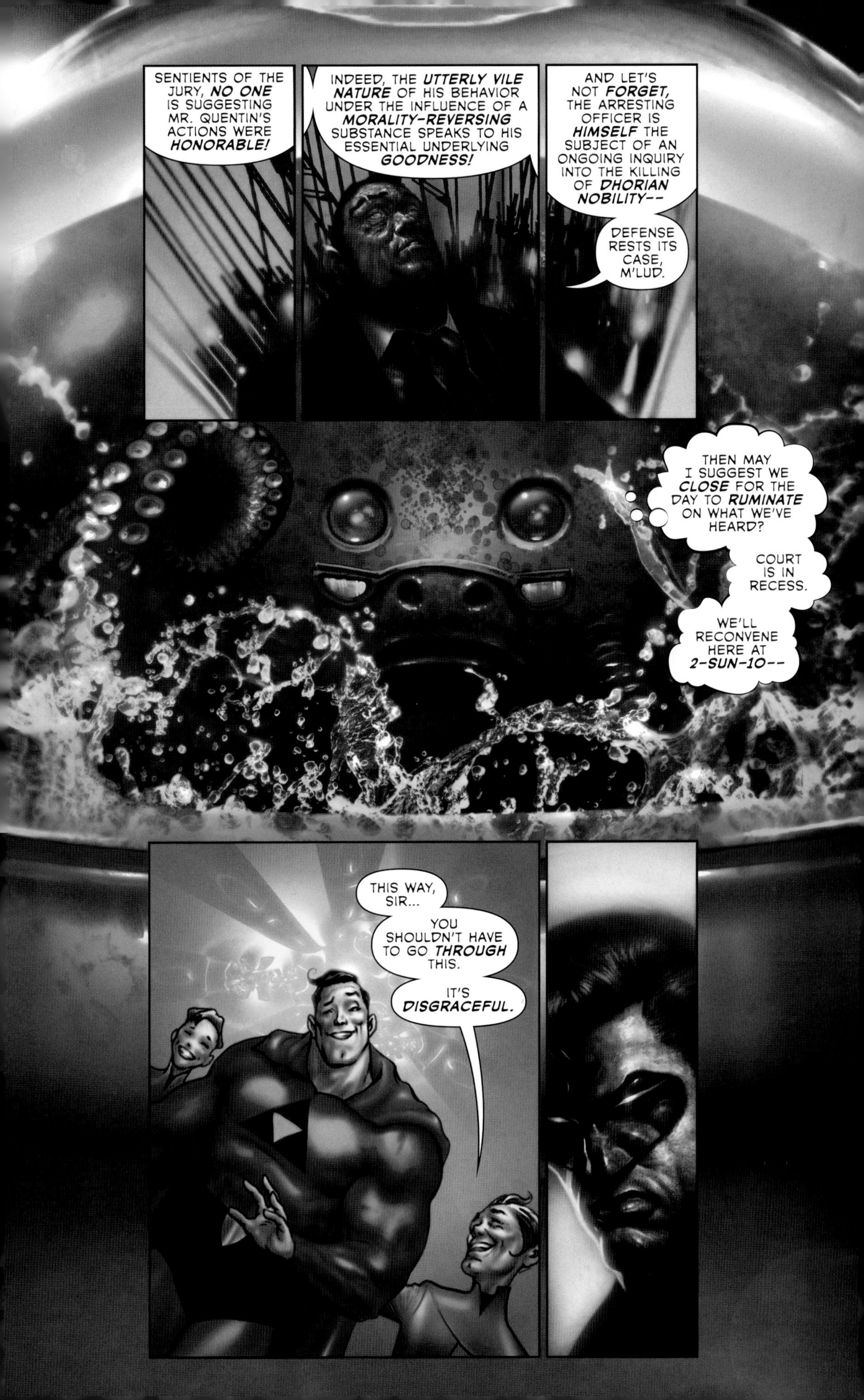
SENTIENTS OF THE JURY, NO ONE IS SUGGESTING MR. QUENTIN'S ACTIONS WERE HONORABLE!
INDEED, THE UTTERLY VILE NATURE OF HIS BEHAVIOR UNDER THE INFLUENCE OF A MORALITY-REVERSING SUBSTANCE SPEAKS TO HIS ESSENTIAL UNDERLYING GOODNESS!
AND LET'S NOT FORGET, THE ARRESTING OFFICER IS HIMSELF THE SUBJECT OF AN ONGOING INQUIRY INTO THE KILLING OF DHORIAN NOBILITY--
DEFENSE RESTS ITS CASE, M'LUD.
THEN MAY I SUGGEST WE CLOSE FOR THE DAY TO RUMINATE ON WHAT WE'VE HEARD?
COURT IS IN RECESS.
WE'LL RECONVENE HERE AT 2-SUN-10--
THIS WAY, SIR...
YOU SHOULDN'T HAVE TO GO THROUGH THIS.
IT'S DISGRACEFUL.

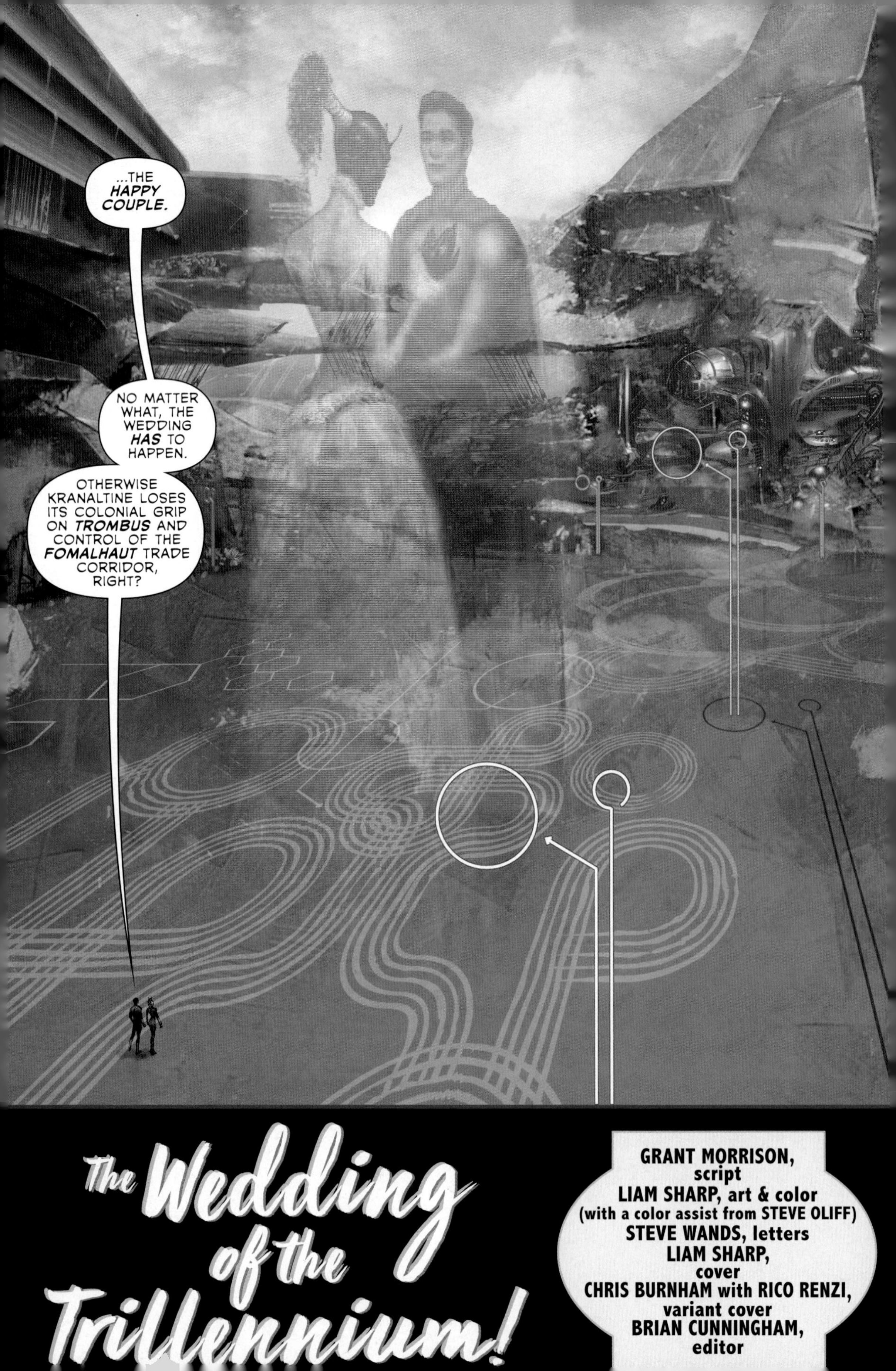
...THE *HAPPY COUPLE.*
NO MATTER WHAT, THE WEDDING *HAS* TO HAPPEN.
OTHERWISE KRANALTINE LOSES ITS COLONIAL GRIP ON *TROMBUS* AND CONTROL OF THE *FOMALHAUT* TRADE CORRIDOR, RIGHT?

The Wedding of the Trillennium!

GRANT MORRISON, script
LIAM SHARP, art & color
(with a color assist from STEVE OLIFF)
STEVE WANDS, letters
LIAM SHARP, cover
CHRIS BURNHAM with RICO RENZI, variant cover
BRIAN CUNNINGHAM, editor

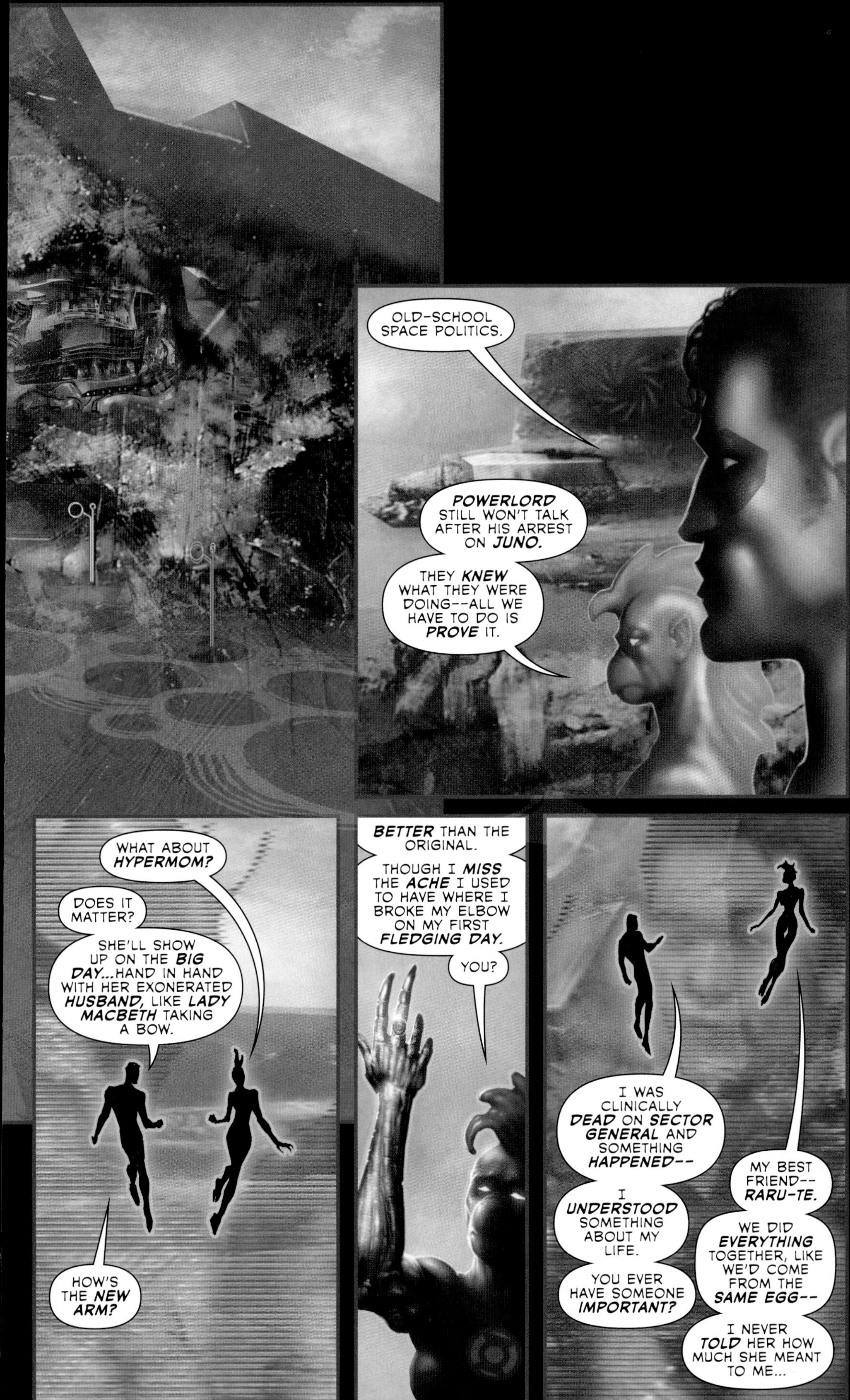
OLD-SCHOOL SPACE POLITICS.
POWERLORD STILL WON'T TALK AFTER HIS ARREST ON JUNO.
THEY KNEW WHAT THEY WERE DOING--ALL WE HAVE TO DO IS PROVE IT.
WHAT ABOUT HYPERMOM?
DOES IT MATTER?
SHE'LL SHOW UP ON THE BIG DAY...HAND IN HAND WITH HER EXONERATED HUSBAND, LIKE LADY MACBETH TAKING A BOW.
HOW'S THE NEW ARM?
BETTER THAN THE ORIGINAL.
THOUGH I MISS THE ACHE I USED TO HAVE WHERE I BROKE MY ELBOW ON MY FIRST FLEDGING DAY.
YOU?
I WAS CLINICALLY DEAD ON SECTOR GENERAL AND SOMETHING HAPPENED--
I UNDERSTOOD SOMETHING ABOUT MY LIFE.
YOU EVER HAVE SOMEONE IMPORTANT?
MY BEST FRIEND-- RARU-TE.
WE DID EVERYTHING TOGETHER, LIKE WE'D COME FROM THE SAME EGG--
I NEVER TOLD HER HOW MUCH SHE MEANT TO ME...

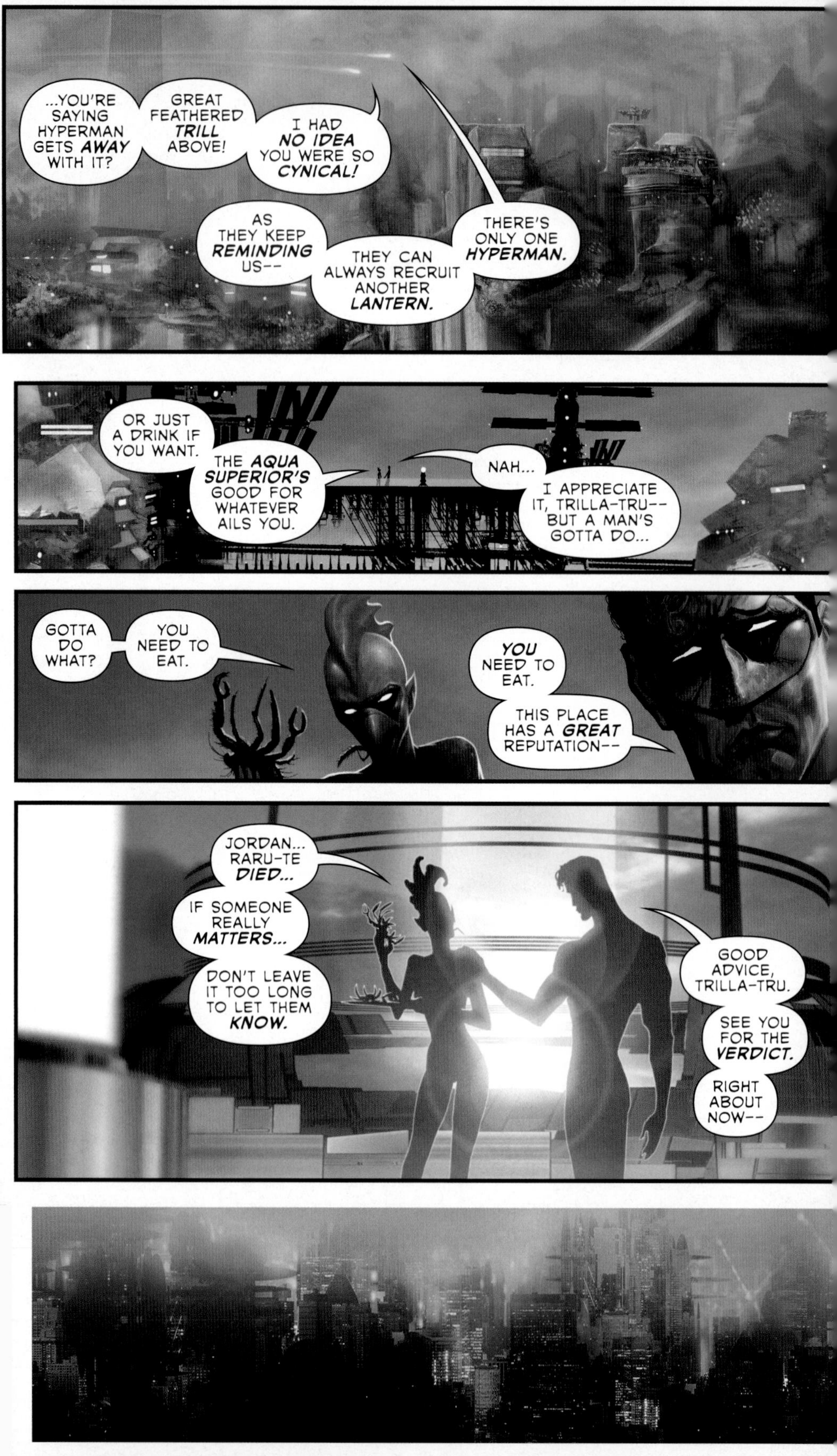
...YOU'RE SAYING HYPERMAN GETS AWAY WITH IT?
GREAT FEATHERED TRILL ABOVE!
I HAD NO IDEA YOU WERE SO CYNICAL!
THERE'S ONLY ONE HYPERMAN.
AS THEY KEEP REMINDING US--
THEY CAN ALWAYS RECRUIT ANOTHER LANTERN.
OR JUST A DRINK IF YOU WANT.
THE AQUA SUPERIOR'S GOOD FOR WHATEVER AILS YOU.
NAH...
I APPRECIATE IT, TRILLA-TRU-- BUT A MAN'S GOTTA DO...
GOTTA DO WHAT?
YOU NEED TO EAT.
YOU NEED TO EAT.
THIS PLACE HAS A GREAT REPUTATION--
JORDAN... RARU-TE DIED...
IF SOMEONE REALLY MATTERS...
DON'T LEAVE IT TOO LONG TO LET THEM KNOW.
GOOD ADVICE, TRILLA-TRU.
SEE YOU FOR THE VERDICT.
RIGHT ABOUT NOW--

KAW! SO, WHAT'S YOUR TAKE ON THE *YOUNG GUARDIANS?*

I DIDN'T GET TO KNOW THE *OLD* ONES BUT...

THEY MOVE IN *MYSTERIOUS WAYS.*

THEY TALKED ABOUT AN *ULTRAWAR*-- SOME ALL-OUT *CONCEPTUAL BATTLE*--

SUPPOSEDLY ABOUT TO SPILL OUT *EVERY-WHERE.*

THING IS-- I WAS MANEUVERED INTO ENCOUNTERS WITH A BUNCH OF MY *EXES* AND I'M NOT SURE *HOW* IT ALL RELATES.

IT MADE ME *THINK...*

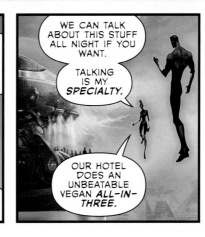

WE CAN TALK ABOUT THIS STUFF ALL NIGHT IF YOU WANT.

TALKING IS MY *SPECIALTY.*

OUR HOTEL DOES AN UNBEATABLE VEGAN *ALL-IN-THREE.*

YOU HAVE TO TRY THE *DECON-STRUCTED MILLINUT ROAST.*

GOT SOMETHING I HAVE TO DO.

2814 SECTOR H.Q.

COMMENCING INTERSPACE ACCELERATION.

DESTINATION: PLANET *EARTH.*

SPACEFOLD.

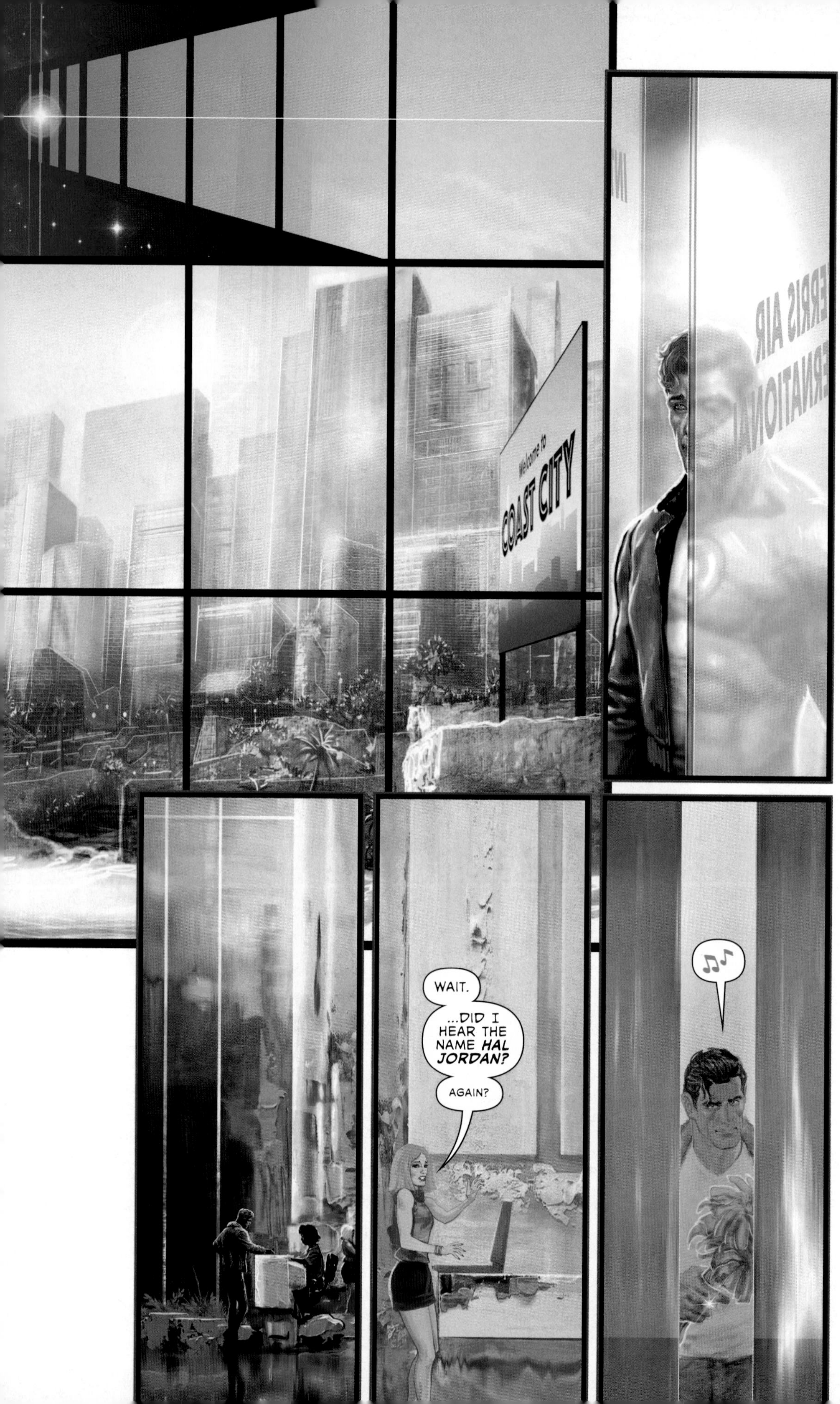
Welcome to
COAST CITY
WAIT.
...DID I HEAR THE NAME HAL JORDAN?
AGAIN?
♫

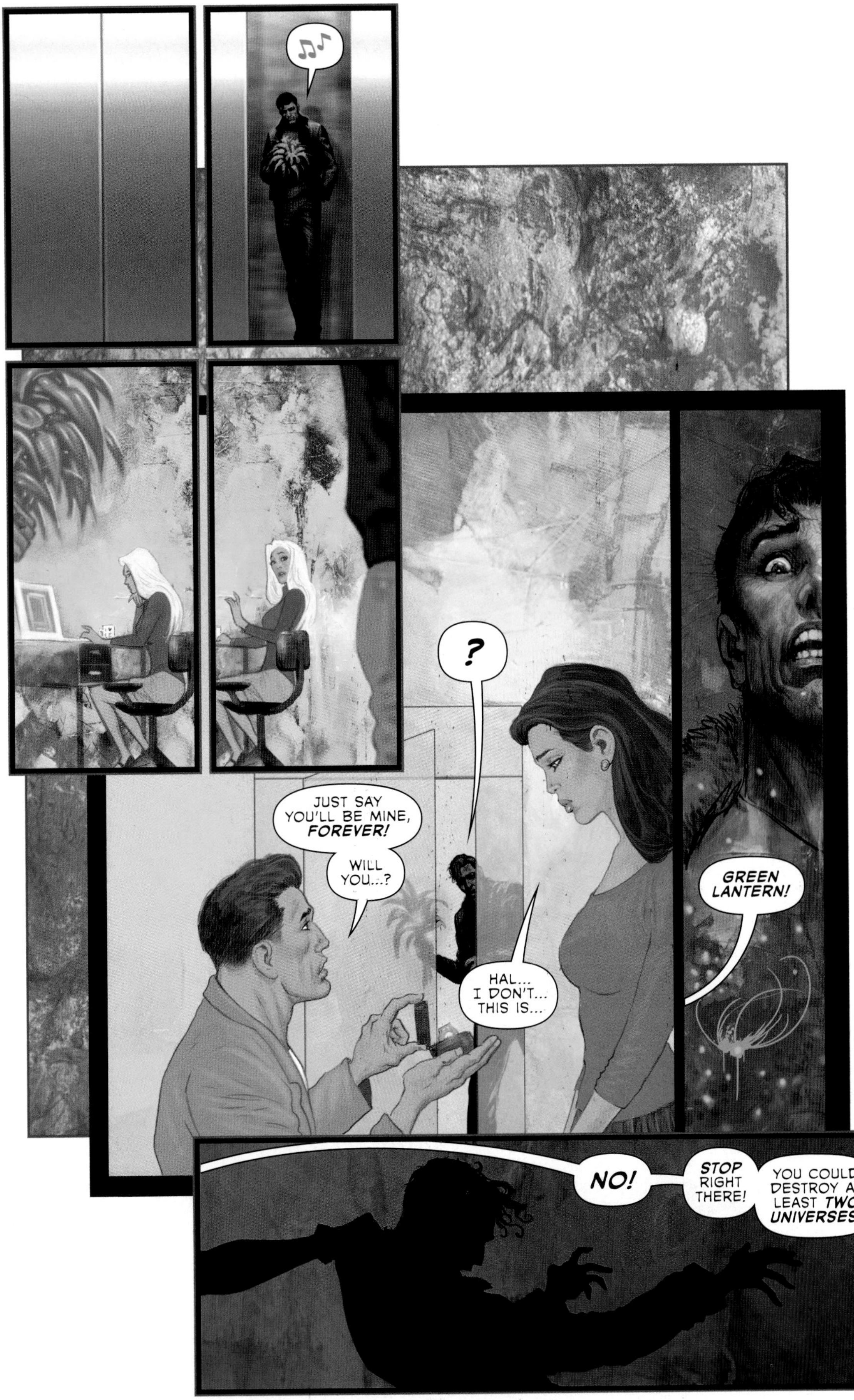
♫♪
?
JUST SAY YOU'LL BE MINE, FOREVER!
WILL YOU...?
HAL... I DON'T... THIS IS...
GREEN LANTERN!
NO!
STOP RIGHT THERE!
YOU COULD DESTROY AT LEAST TWO UNIVERSES!

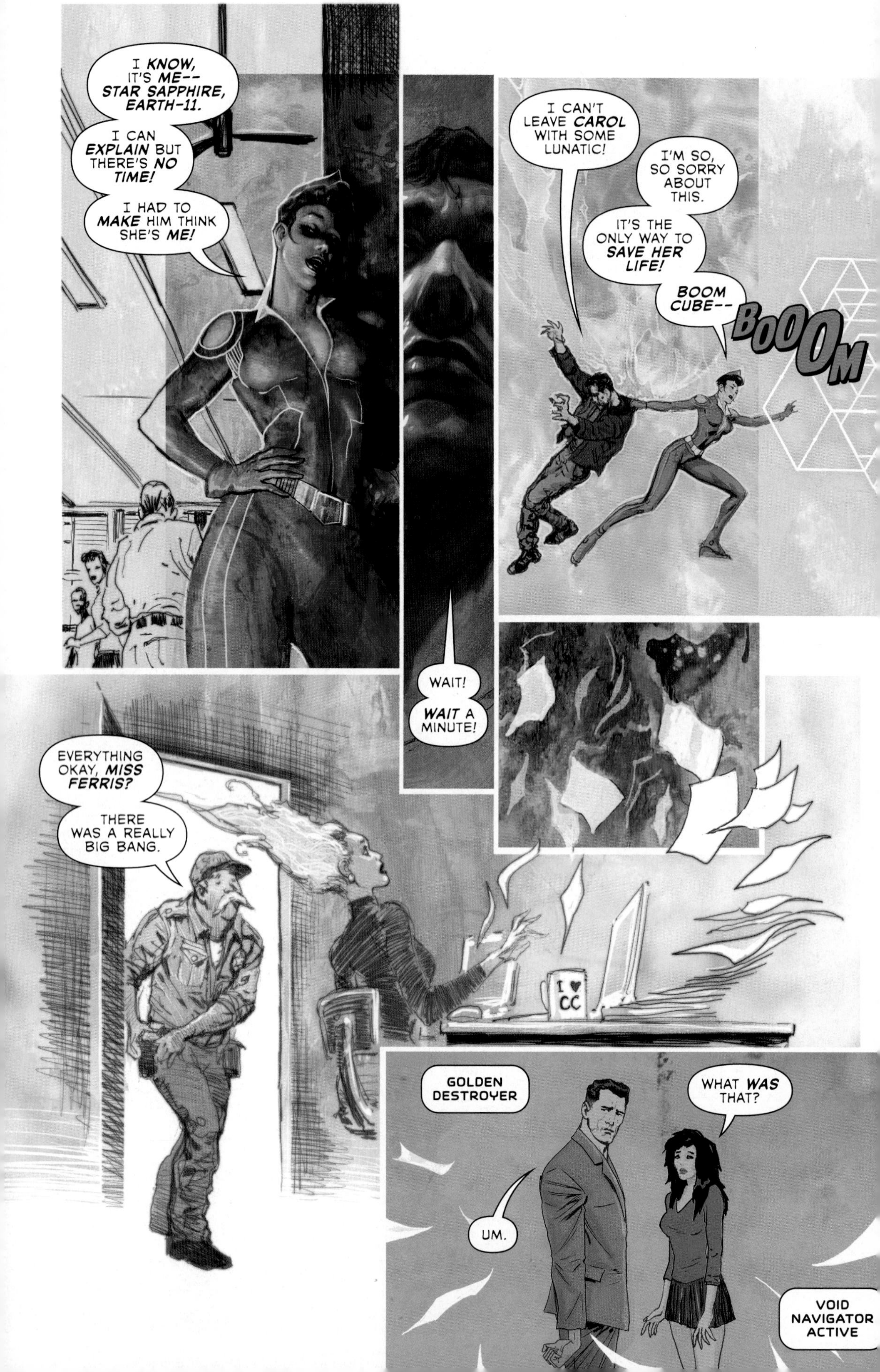
I KNOW, IT'S ME-- STAR SAPPHIRE, EARTH-11.
I CAN EXPLAIN BUT THERE'S NO TIME!
I HAD TO MAKE HIM THINK SHE'S ME!
WAIT! WAIT A MINUTE!
I CAN'T LEAVE CAROL WITH SOME LUNATIC!
I'M SO, SO SORRY ABOUT THIS.
IT'S THE ONLY WAY TO SAVE HER LIFE!
BOOM CUBE--
BOOOM
EVERYTHING OKAY, MISS FERRIS?
THERE WAS A REALLY BIG BANG.
I ♥ CC
GOLDEN DESTROYER
WHAT WAS THAT?
UM.
VOID NAVIGATOR ACTIVE

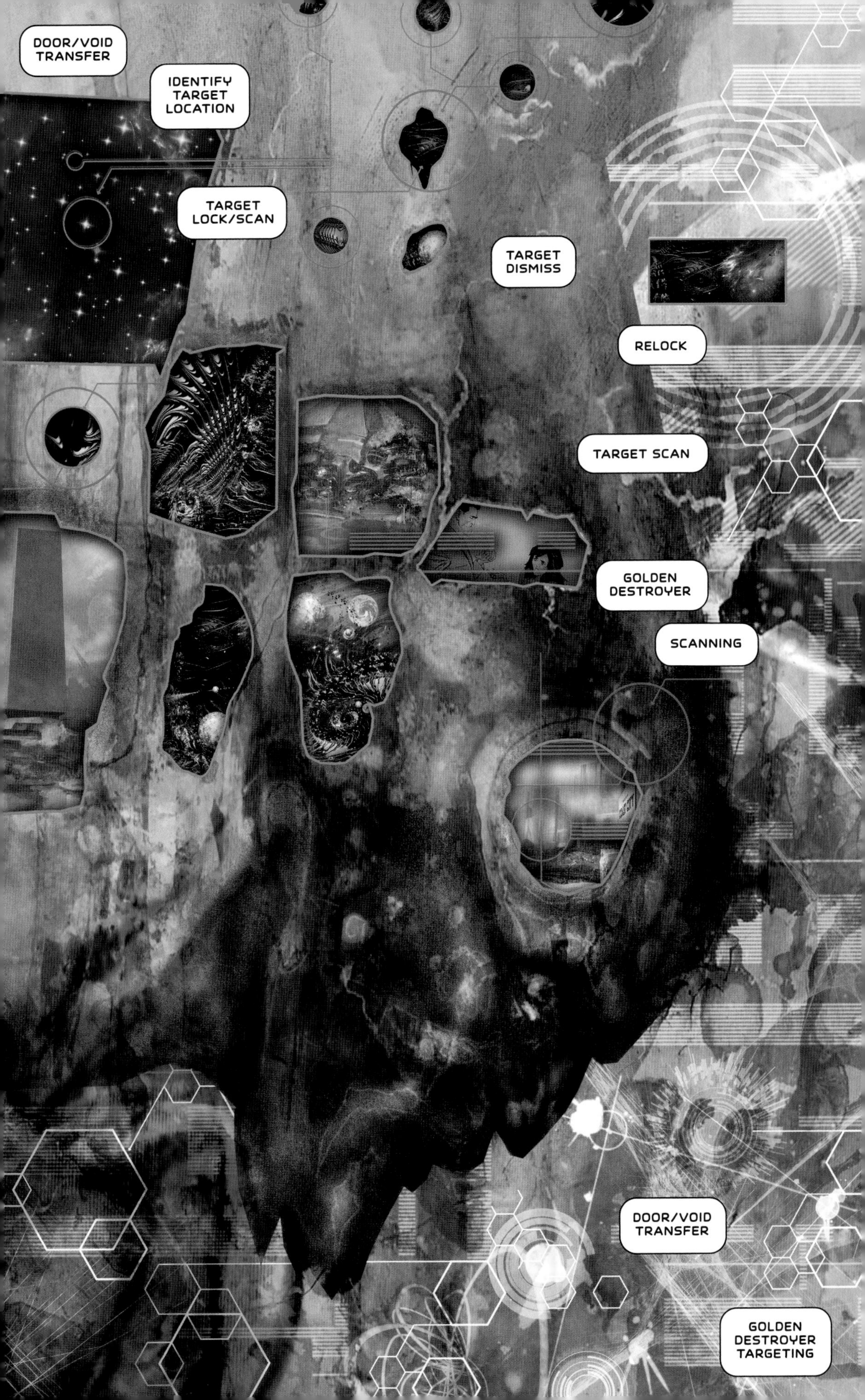
DOOR/VOID TRANSFER
IDENTIFY TARGET LOCATION
TARGET LOCK/SCAN
TARGET DISMISS
RELOCK
TARGET SCAN
GOLDEN DESTROYER
SCANNING
DOOR/VOID TRANSFER
GOLDEN DESTROYER TARGETING

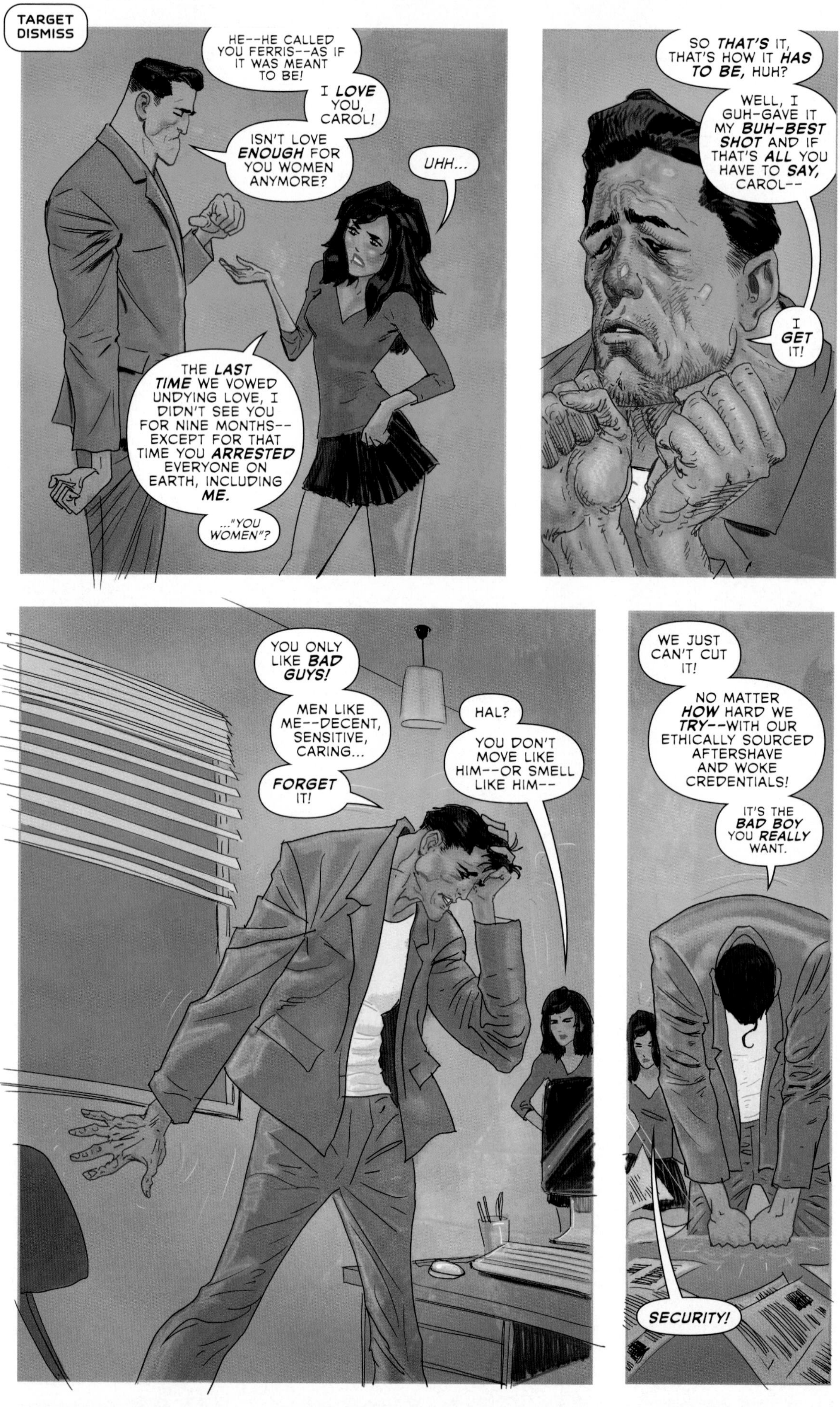
TARGET DISMISS
HE--HE CALLED YOU FERRIS--AS IF IT WAS MEANT TO BE!
I LOVE YOU, CAROL!
ISN'T LOVE ENOUGH FOR YOU WOMEN ANYMORE?
UHH...
THE LAST TIME WE VOWED UNDYING LOVE, I DIDN'T SEE YOU FOR NINE MONTHS--EXCEPT FOR THAT TIME YOU ARRESTED EVERYONE ON EARTH, INCLUDING ME.
..."YOU WOMEN"?
SO THAT'S IT, THAT'S HOW IT HAS TO BE, HUH?
WELL, I GUH-GAVE IT MY BUH-BEST SHOT AND IF THAT'S ALL YOU HAVE TO SAY, CAROL--
I GET IT!
YOU ONLY LIKE BAD GUYS!
MEN LIKE ME--DECENT, SENSITIVE, CARING...
FORGET IT!
HAL?
YOU DON'T MOVE LIKE HIM--OR SMELL LIKE HIM--
WE JUST CAN'T CUT IT!
NO MATTER HOW HARD WE TRY--WITH OUR ETHICALLY SOURCED AFTERSHAVE AND WOKE CREDENTIALS!
IT'S THE BAD BOY YOU REALLY WANT.
SECURITY!

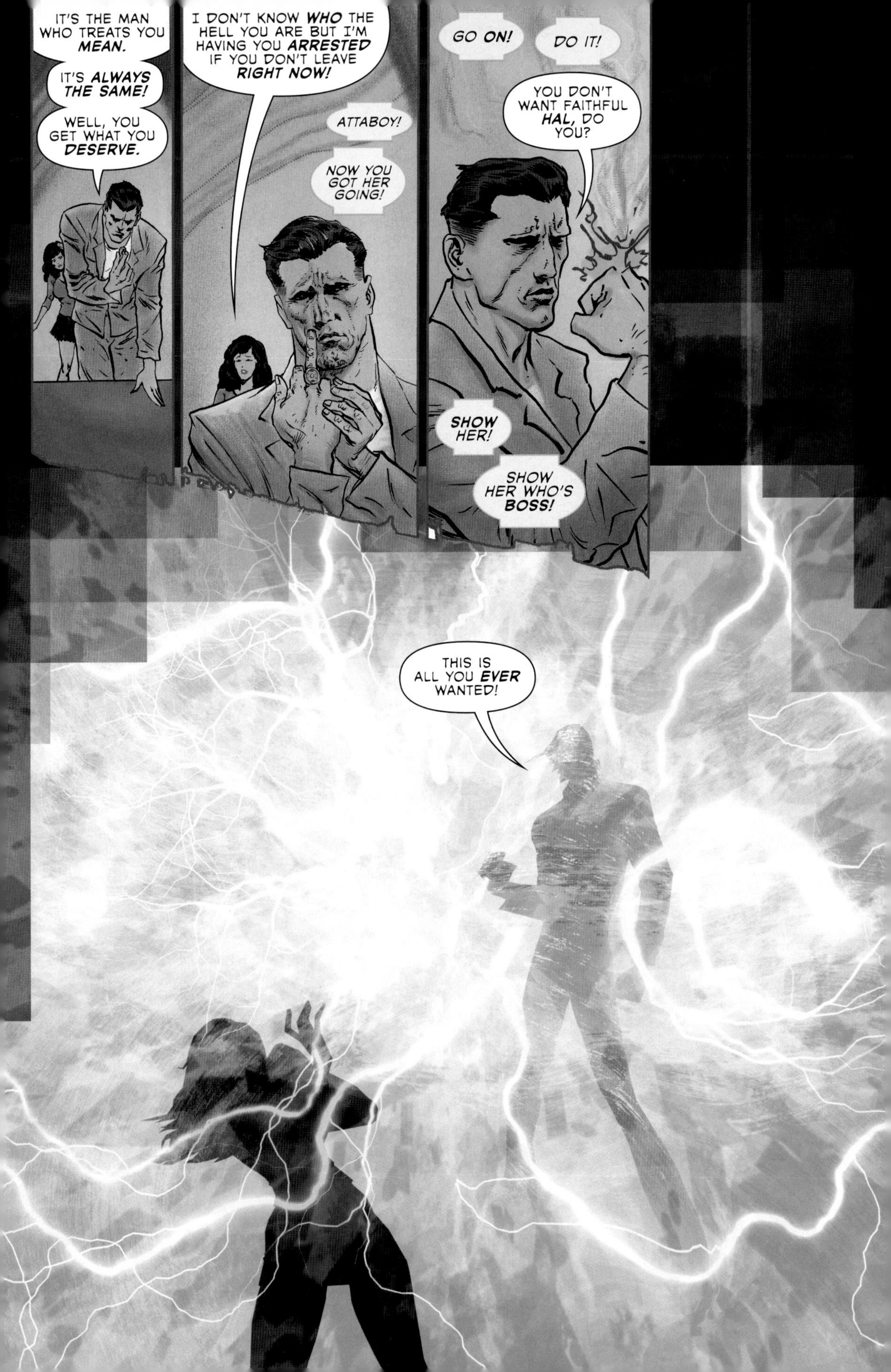
IT'S THE MAN WHO TREATS YOU **MEAN.**
IT'S **ALWAYS THE SAME!**
WELL, YOU GET WHAT YOU **DESERVE.**
I DON'T KNOW **WHO** THE HELL YOU ARE BUT I'M HAVING YOU **ARRESTED** IF YOU DON'T LEAVE **RIGHT NOW!**
ATTABOY!
NOW YOU GOT HER GOING!
GO **ON!**
DO IT!
YOU DON'T WANT FAITHFUL **HAL,** DO YOU?
SHOW HER!
SHOW HER WHO'S **BOSS!**
THIS IS ALL YOU **EVER** WANTED!

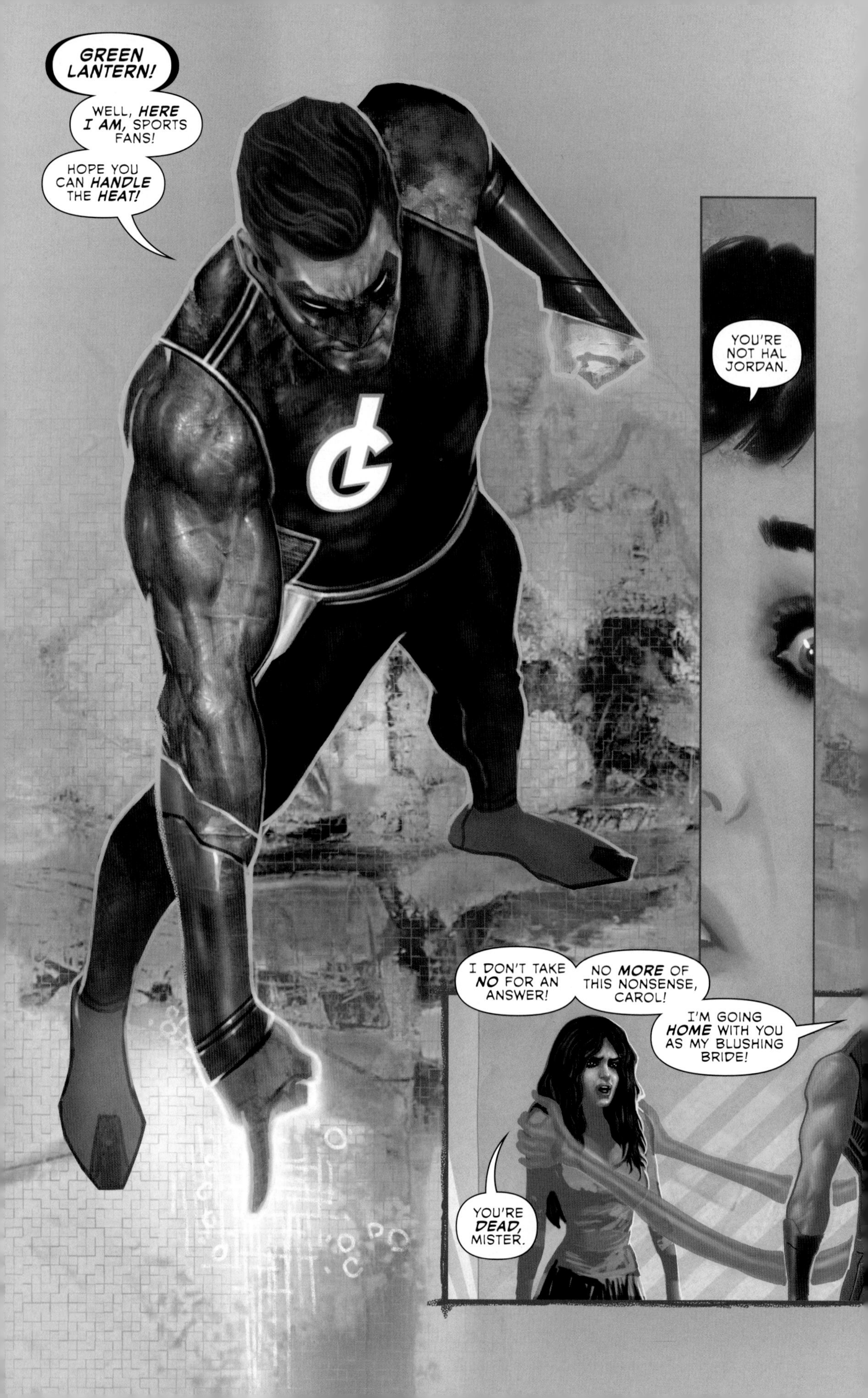
GREEN LANTERN!
WELL, HERE I AM, SPORTS FANS!
HOPE YOU CAN HANDLE THE HEAT!
YOU'RE NOT HAL JORDAN.
I DON'T TAKE NO FOR AN ANSWER!
NO MORE OF THIS NONSENSE, CAROL!
I'M GOING HOME WITH YOU AS MY BLUSHING BRIDE!
YOU'RE DEAD, MISTER.

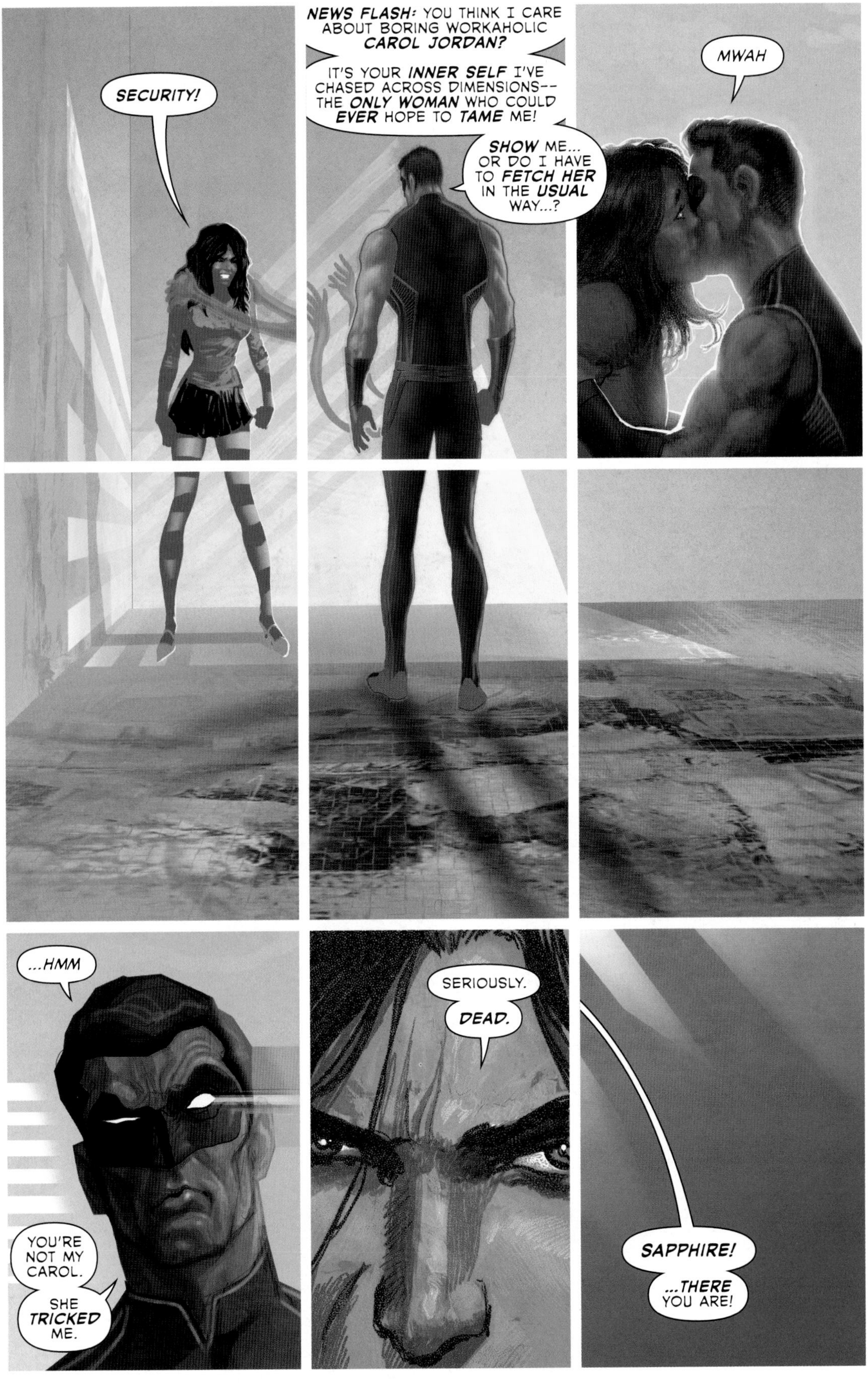
SECURITY!
NEWS FLASH: YOU THINK I CARE ABOUT BORING WORKAHOLIC CAROL JORDAN?
IT'S YOUR INNER SELF I'VE CHASED ACROSS DIMENSIONS-- THE ONLY WOMAN WHO COULD EVER HOPE TO TAME ME!
SHOW ME... OR DO I HAVE TO FETCH HER IN THE USUAL WAY...?
MWAH
...HMM
YOU'RE NOT MY CAROL.
SHE TRICKED ME.
SERIOUSLY.
DEAD.
SAPPHIRE!
...THERE YOU ARE!

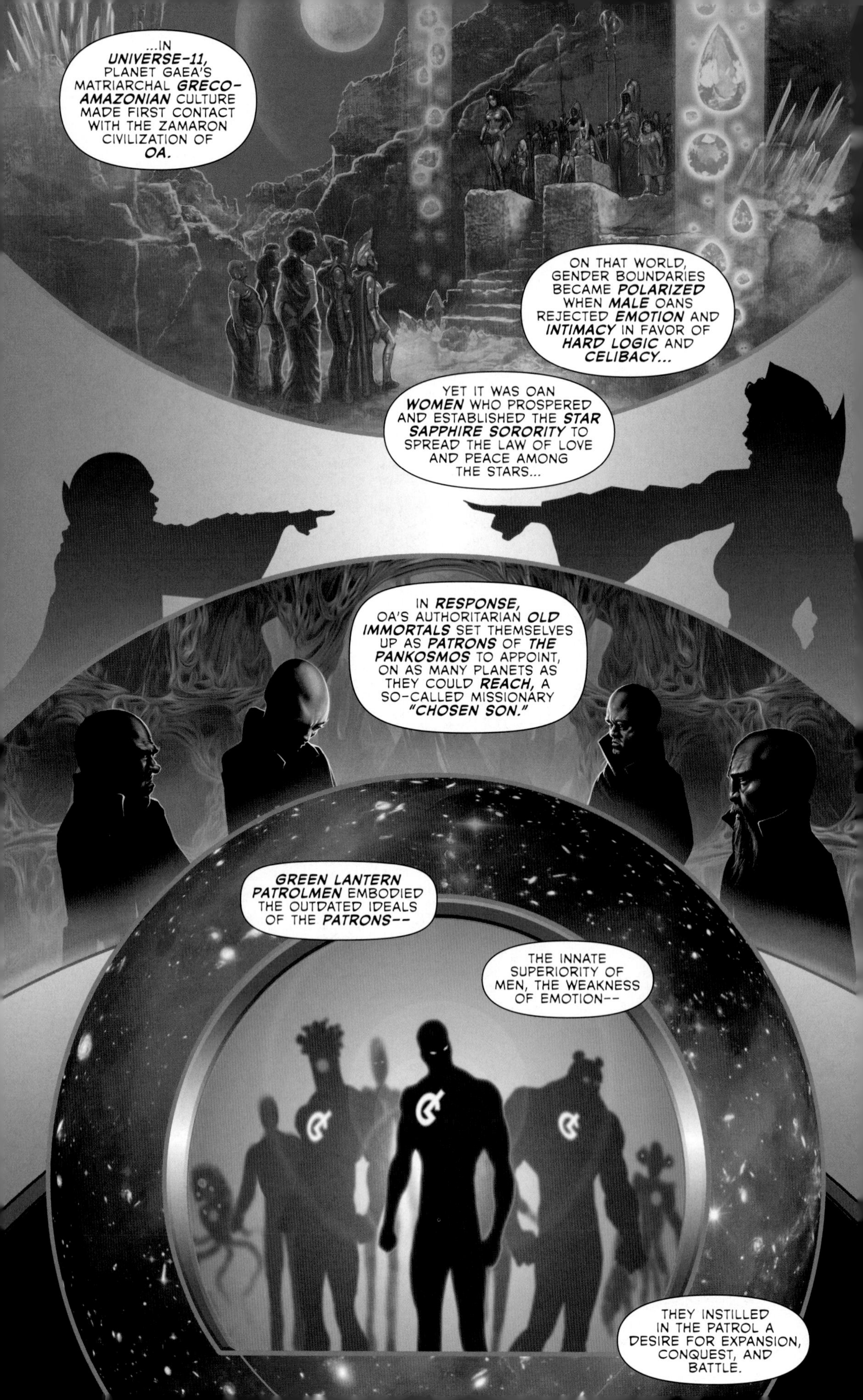
...IN UNIVERSE-11, PLANET GAEA'S MATRIARCHAL GRECO-AMAZONIAN CULTURE MADE FIRST CONTACT WITH THE ZAMARON CIVILIZATION OF OA.
ON THAT WORLD, GENDER BOUNDARIES BECAME POLARIZED WHEN MALE OANS REJECTED EMOTION AND INTIMACY IN FAVOR OF HARD LOGIC AND CELIBACY...
YET IT WAS OAN WOMEN WHO PROSPERED AND ESTABLISHED THE STAR SAPPHIRE SORORITY TO SPREAD THE LAW OF LOVE AND PEACE AMONG THE STARS...
IN RESPONSE, OA'S AUTHORITARIAN OLD IMMORTALS SET THEMSELVES UP AS PATRONS OF THE PANKOSMOS TO APPOINT, ON AS MANY PLANETS AS THEY COULD REACH, A SO-CALLED MISSIONARY "CHOSEN SON."
GREEN LANTERN PATROLMEN EMBODIED THE OUTDATED IDEALS OF THE PATRONS--
THE INNATE SUPERIORITY OF MEN, THE WEAKNESS OF EMOTION--
THEY INSTILLED IN THE PATROL A DESIRE FOR EXPANSION, CONQUEST, AND BATTLE.

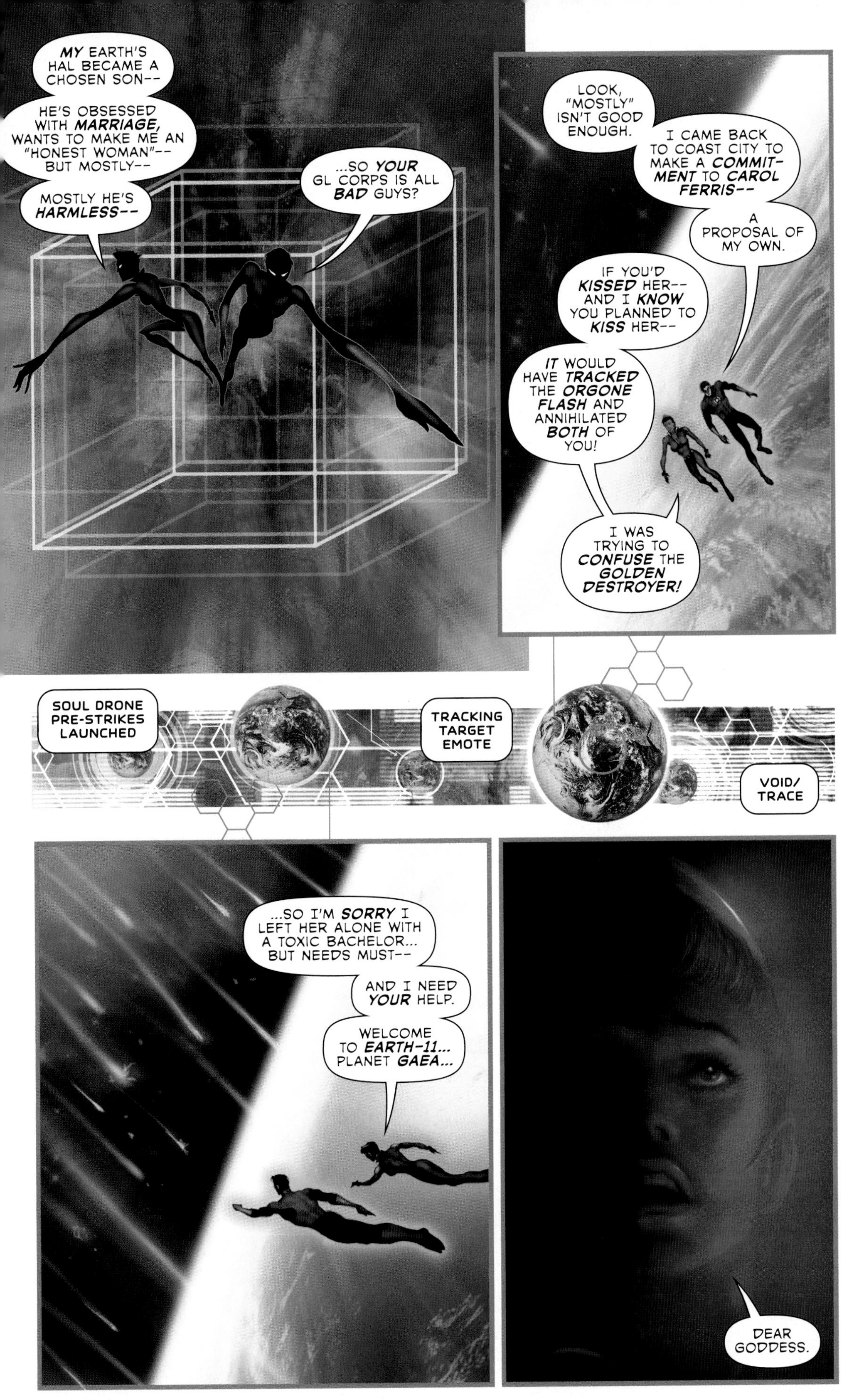
MY EARTH'S HAL BECAME A CHOSEN SON--
HE'S OBSESSED WITH MARRIAGE, WANTS TO MAKE ME AN "HONEST WOMAN"-- BUT MOSTLY--
MOSTLY HE'S HARMLESS--
...SO YOUR GL CORPS IS ALL BAD GUYS?
LOOK, "MOSTLY" ISN'T GOOD ENOUGH.
I CAME BACK TO COAST CITY TO MAKE A COMMIT-MENT TO CAROL FERRIS--
A PROPOSAL OF MY OWN.
IF YOU'D KISSED HER-- AND I KNOW YOU PLANNED TO KISS HER--
IT WOULD HAVE TRACKED THE ORGONE FLASH AND ANNIHILATED BOTH OF YOU!
I WAS TRYING TO CONFUSE THE GOLDEN DESTROYER!
SOUL DRONE PRE-STRIKES LAUNCHED
TRACKING TARGET EMOTE
VOID/ TRACE
...SO I'M SORRY I LEFT HER ALONE WITH A TOXIC BACHELOR... BUT NEEDS MUST--
AND I NEED YOUR HELP.
WELCOME TO EARTH-11... PLANET GAEA...
DEAR GODDESS.

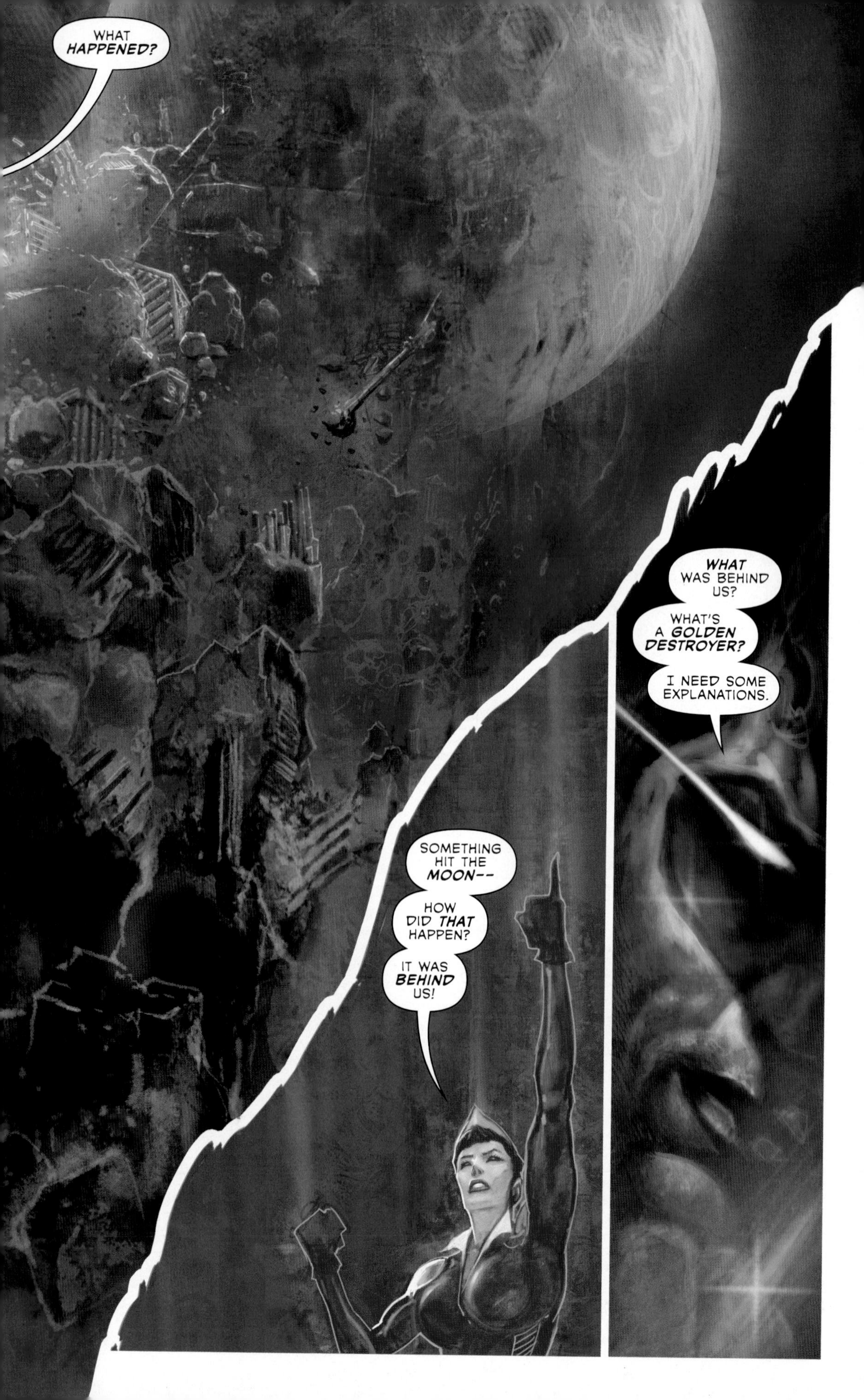
WHAT *HAPPENED?*
SOMETHING HIT THE *MOON--*
HOW DID *THAT* HAPPEN?
IT WAS *BEHIND* US!
WHAT WAS BEHIND US?
WHAT'S A *GOLDEN DESTROYER?*
I NEED SOME EXPLANATIONS.

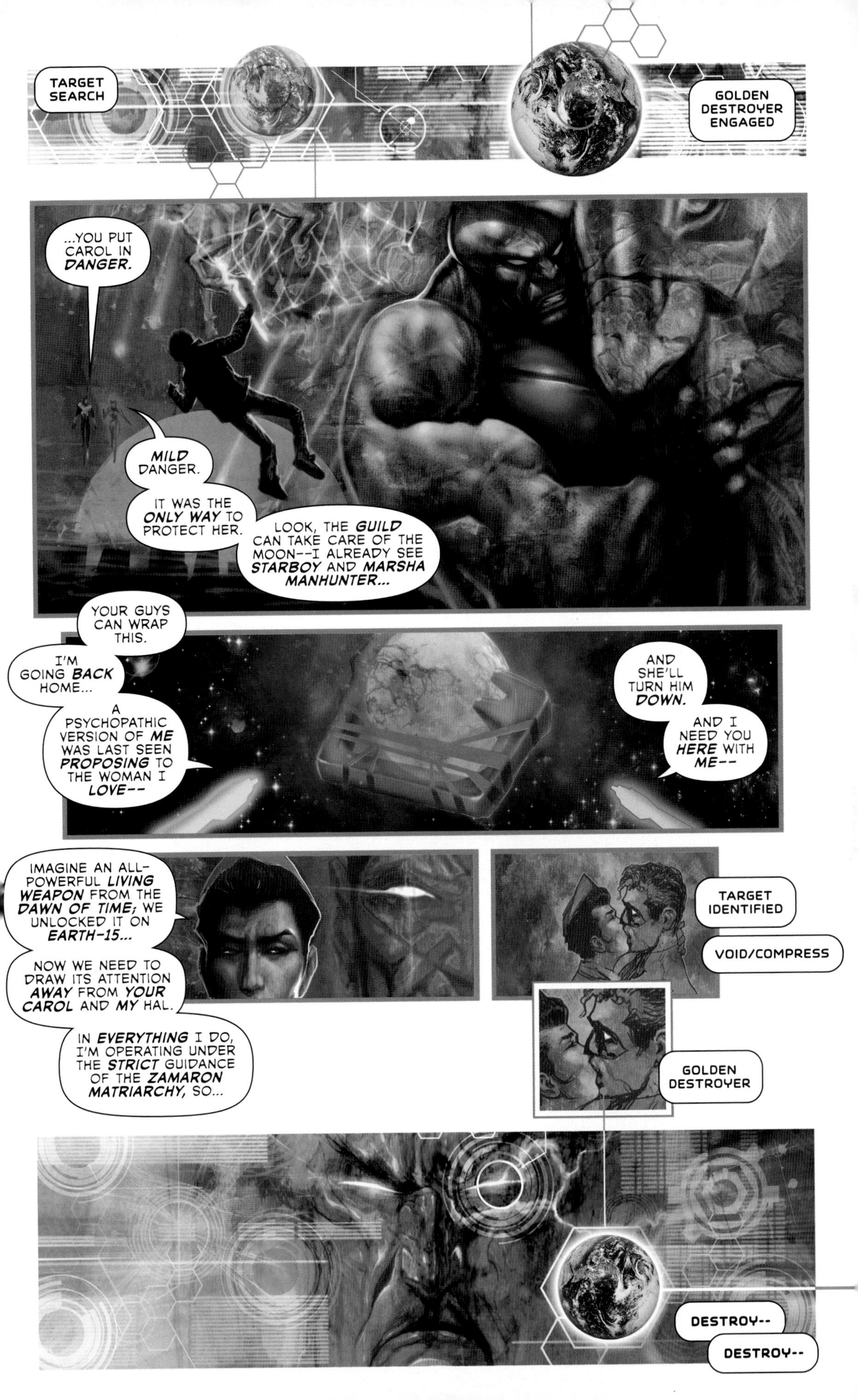
TARGET SEARCH
GOLDEN DESTROYER ENGAGED
...YOU PUT CAROL IN DANGER.
MILD DANGER.
IT WAS THE ONLY WAY TO PROTECT HER.
LOOK, THE GUILD CAN TAKE CARE OF THE MOON--I ALREADY SEE STARBOY AND MARSHA MANHUNTER...
YOUR GUYS CAN WRAP THIS.
I'M GOING BACK HOME...
A PSYCHOPATHIC VERSION OF ME WAS LAST SEEN PROPOSING TO THE WOMAN I LOVE--
AND SHE'LL TURN HIM DOWN.
AND I NEED YOU HERE WITH ME--
IMAGINE AN ALL-POWERFUL LIVING WEAPON FROM THE DAWN OF TIME; WE UNLOCKED IT ON EARTH-15...
NOW WE NEED TO DRAW ITS ATTENTION AWAY FROM YOUR CAROL AND MY HAL.
IN EVERYTHING I DO, I'M OPERATING UNDER THE STRICT GUIDANCE OF THE ZAMARON MATRIARCHY, SO...
TARGET IDENTIFIED
VOID/COMPRESS
GOLDEN DESTROYER
DESTROY--
DESTROY--

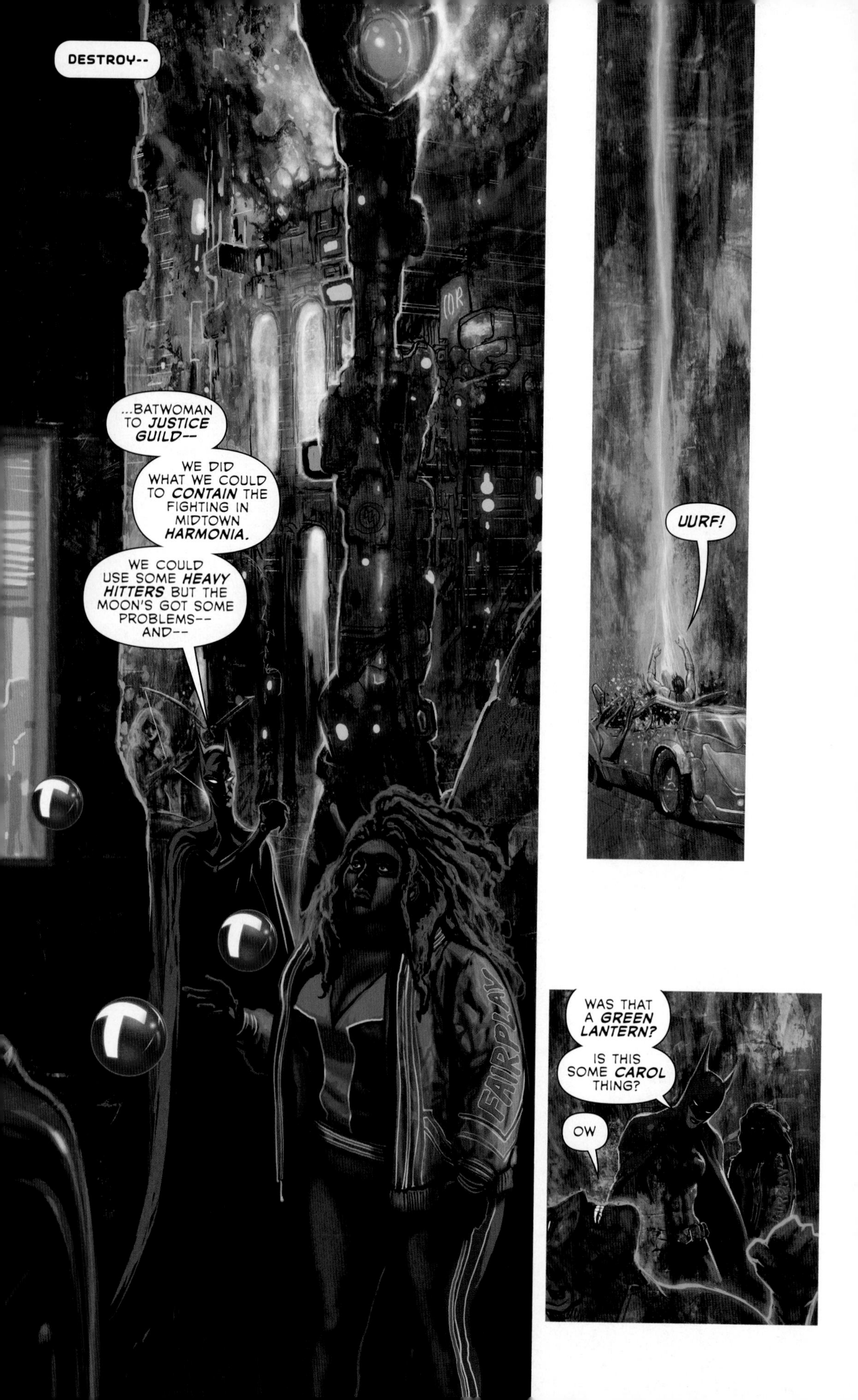
DESTROY--
...BATWOMAN TO *JUSTICE GUILD*--
WE DID WHAT WE COULD TO *CONTAIN* THE FIGHTING IN MIDTOWN *HARMONIA.*
WE COULD USE SOME *HEAVY HITTERS* BUT THE MOON'S GOT SOME PROBLEMS-- AND--
FAIRPLAY
UURF!
WAS THAT A *GREEN LANTERN?*
IS THIS SOME *CAROL* THING?
OW

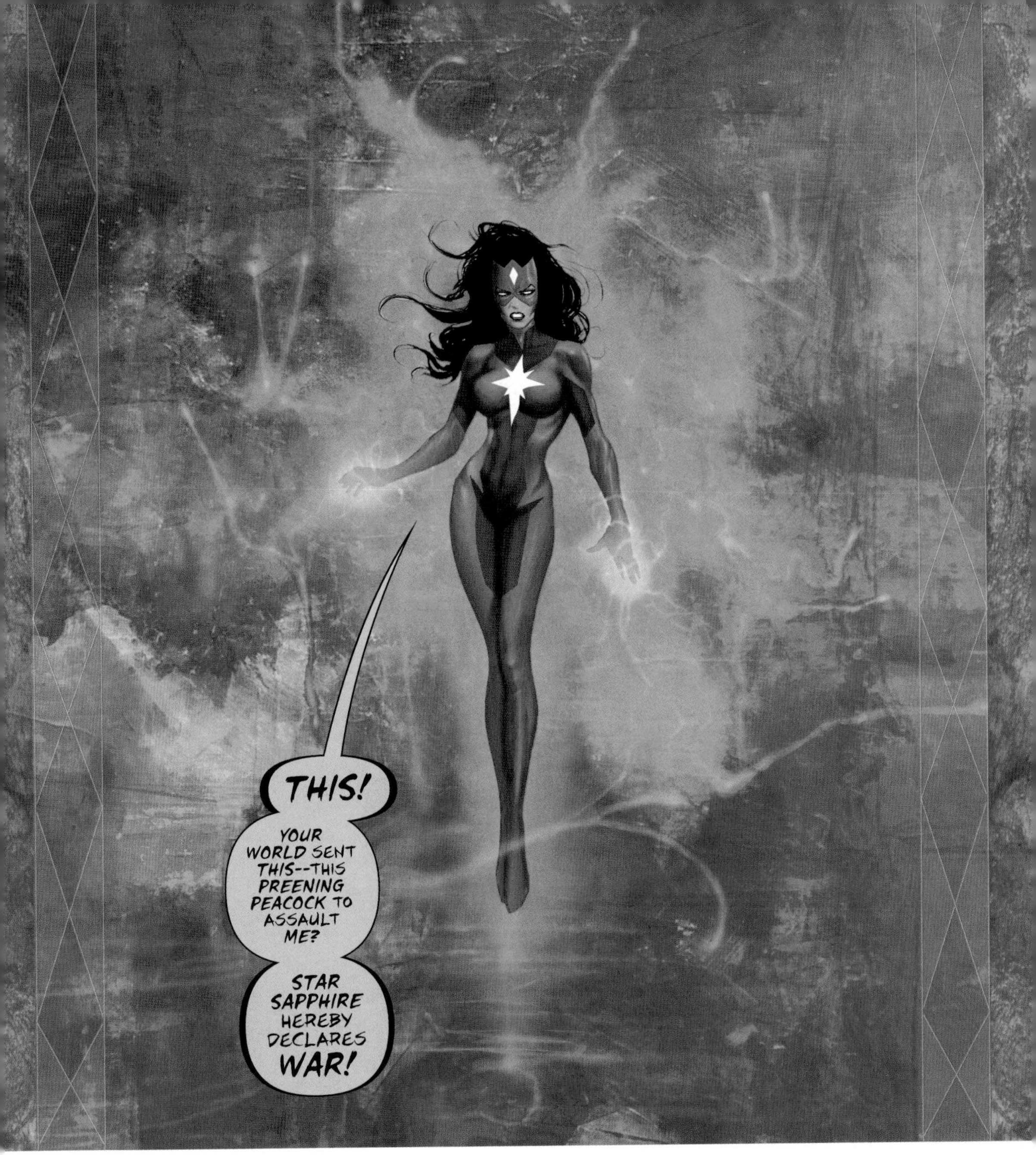
THIS!
YOUR WORLD SENT THIS--THIS PREENING PEACOCK TO ASSAULT ME?
STAR SAPPHIRE HEREBY DECLARES WAR!

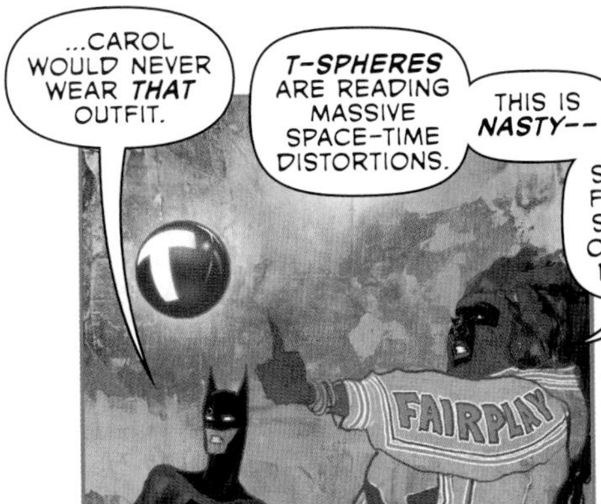
...CAROL WOULD NEVER WEAR THAT OUTFIT.
T-SPHERES ARE READING MASSIVE SPACE-TIME DISTORTIONS.
THIS IS NASTY--
SCALAR FORCES SPIKING OFF THE DIAL--
FAIRPLAY

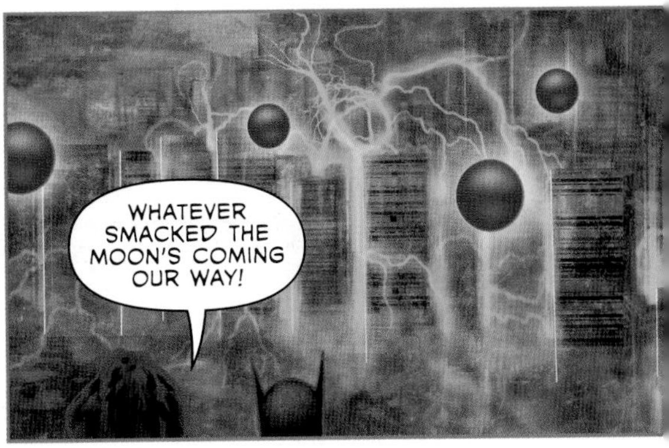
WHATEVER SMACKED THE MOON'S COMING OUR WAY!

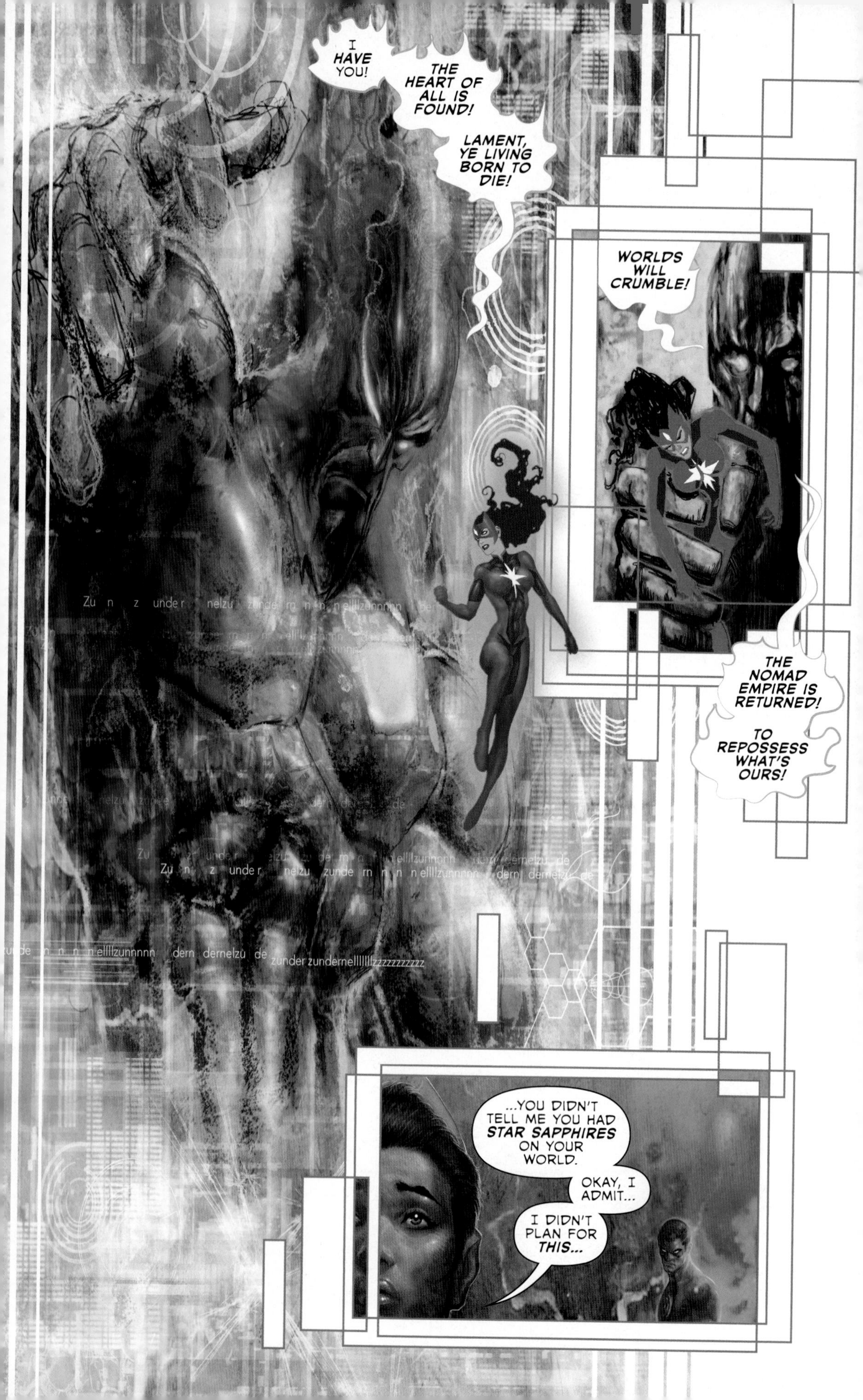
I HAVE YOU!
THE HEART OF ALL IS FOUND!
LAMENT, YE LIVING BORN TO DIE!
WORLDS WILL CRUMBLE!
THE NOMAD EMPIRE IS RETURNED!
TO REPOSSESS WHAT'S OURS!
...YOU DIDN'T TELL ME YOU HAD STAR SAPPHIRES ON YOUR WORLD.
OKAY, I ADMIT...
I DIDN'T PLAN FOR THIS...

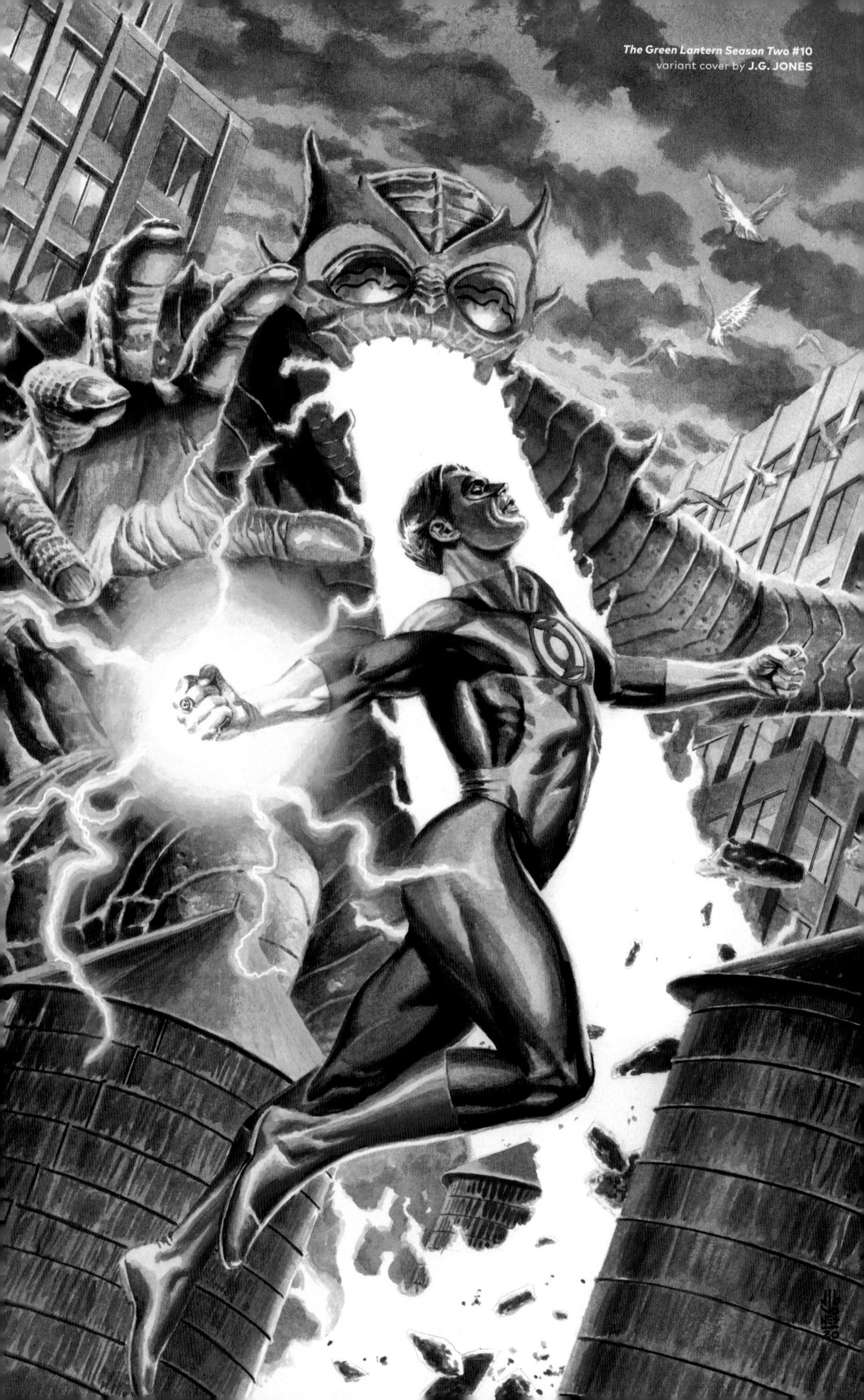

The Green Lantern Season Two #10
variant cover by **J.G. JONES**

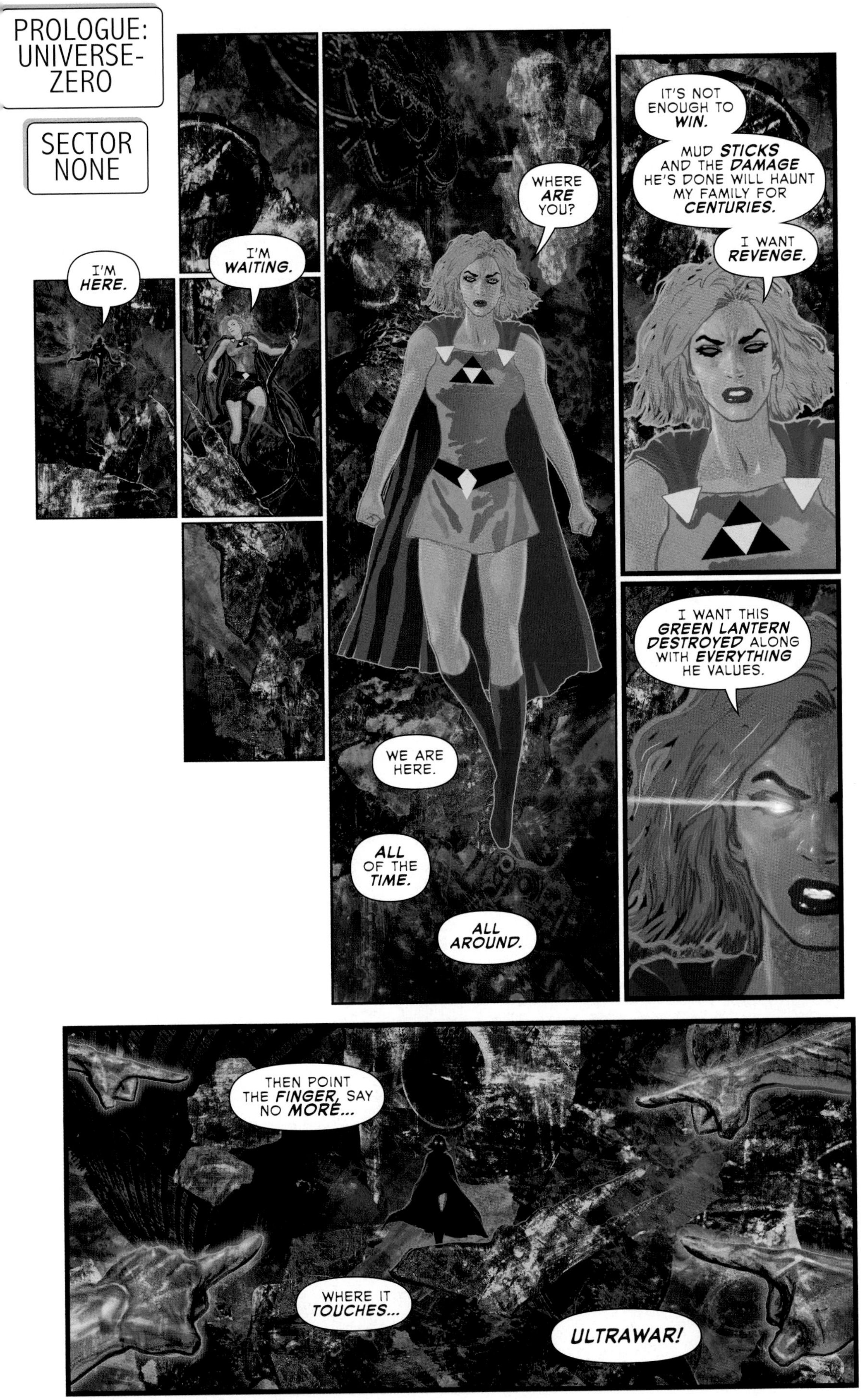
PROLOGUE: UNIVERSE-ZERO
SECTOR NONE
I'M HERE.
I'M WAITING.
WHERE ARE YOU?
WE ARE HERE.
ALL OF THE TIME.
ALL AROUND.
IT'S NOT ENOUGH TO WIN.
MUD STICKS AND THE DAMAGE HE'S DONE WILL HAUNT MY FAMILY FOR CENTURIES.
I WANT REVENGE.
I WANT THIS GREEN LANTERN DESTROYED ALONG WITH EVERYTHING HE VALUES.
THEN POINT THE FINGER, SAY NO MORE...
WHERE IT TOUCHES...
ULTRAWAR!

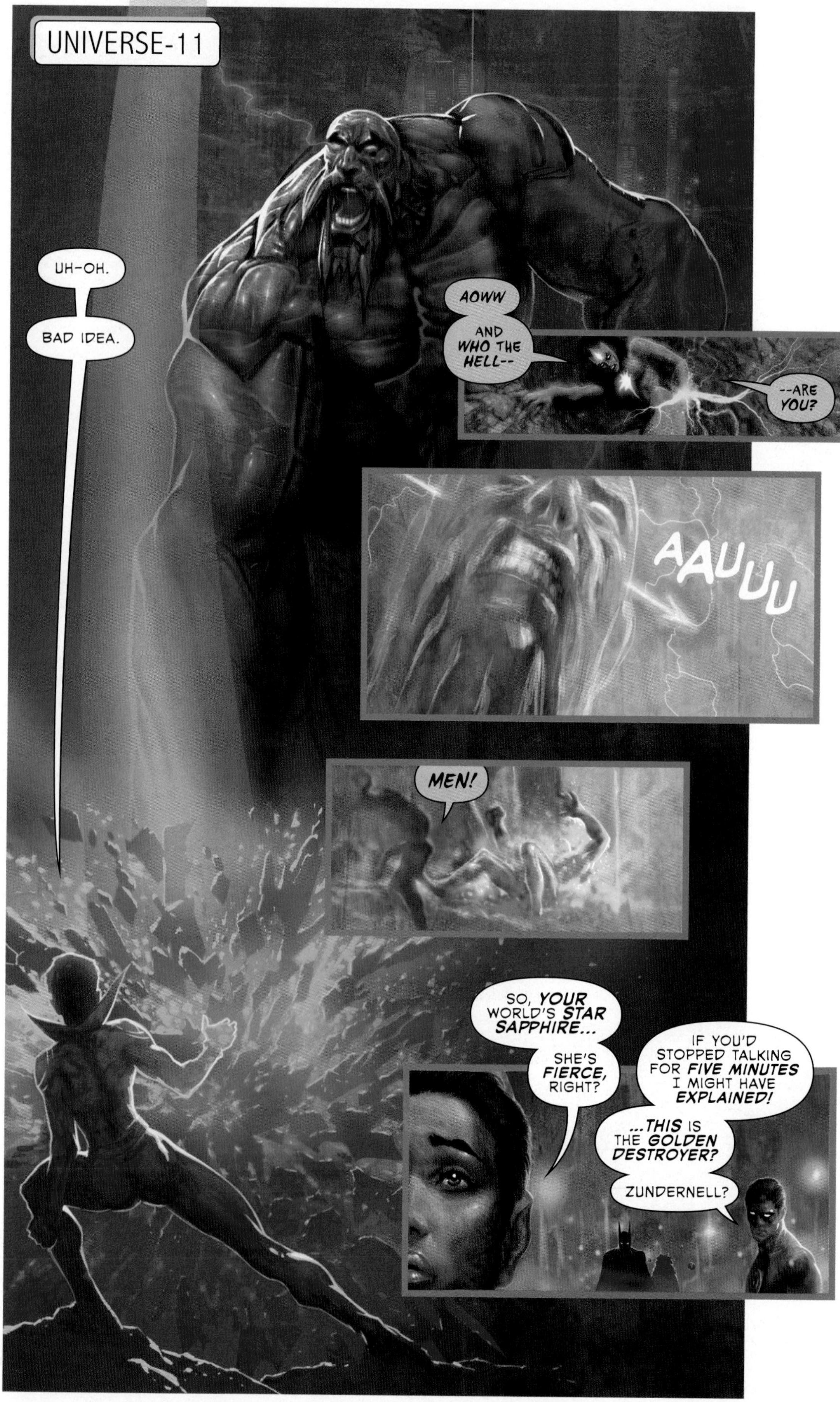
UNIVERSE-11
UH-OH.
BAD IDEA.
AOWW
AND WHO THE HELL--
--ARE YOU?
AAUUUU
MEN!
SO, YOUR WORLD'S STAR SAPPHIRE...
SHE'S FIERCE, RIGHT?
IF YOU'D STOPPED TALKING FOR FIVE MINUTES I MIGHT HAVE EXPLAINED!
...THIS IS THE GOLDEN DESTROYER?
ZUNDERNELL?

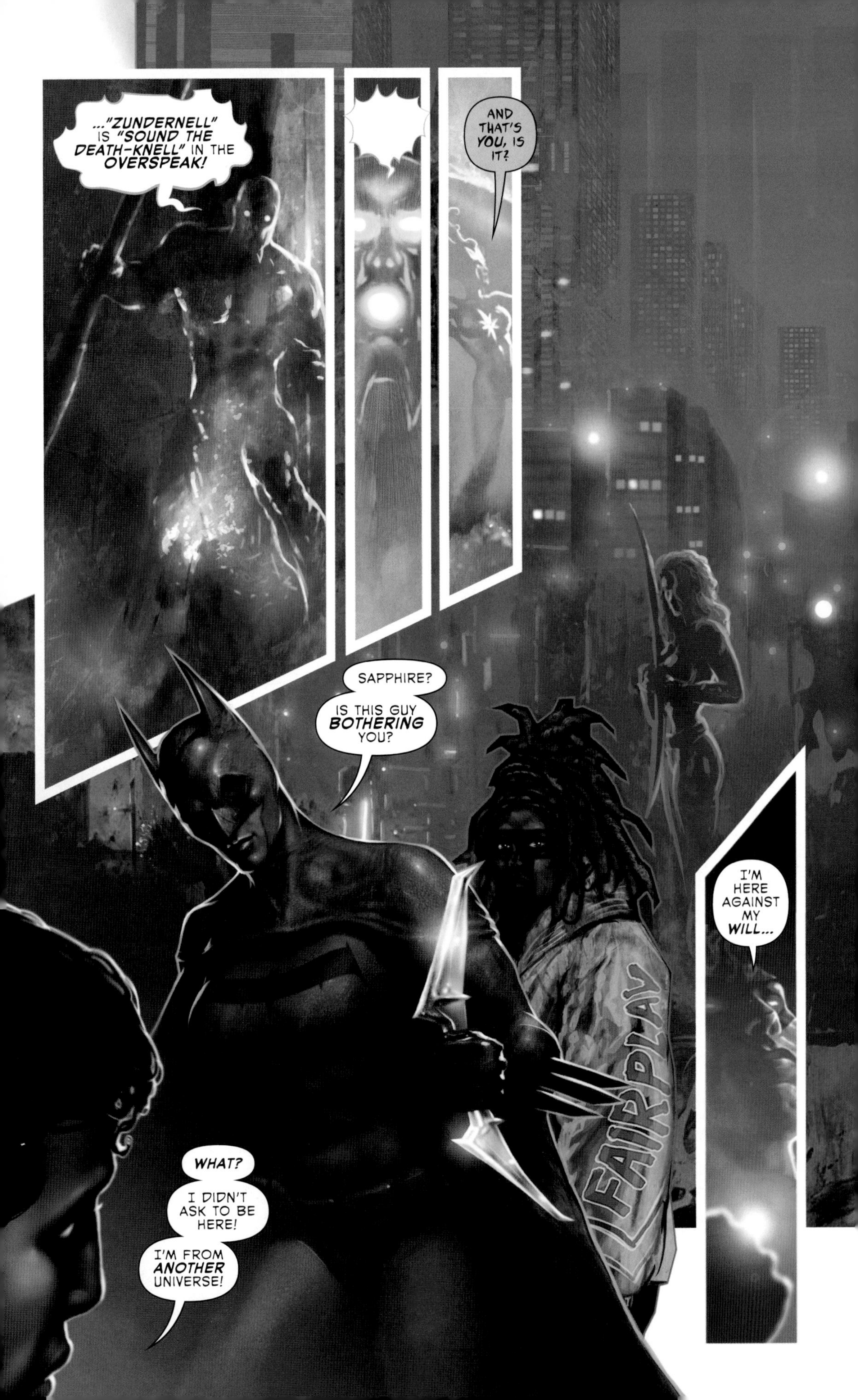
..."ZUNDERNELL" IS "SOUND THE DEATH-KNELL" IN THE OVERSPEAK!
AND THAT'S YOU, IS IT?
SAPPHIRE?
IS THIS GUY BOTHERING YOU?
I'M HERE AGAINST MY WILL...
WHAT?
I DIDN'T ASK TO BE HERE!
I'M FROM ANOTHER UNIVERSE!
FAIR PLAY

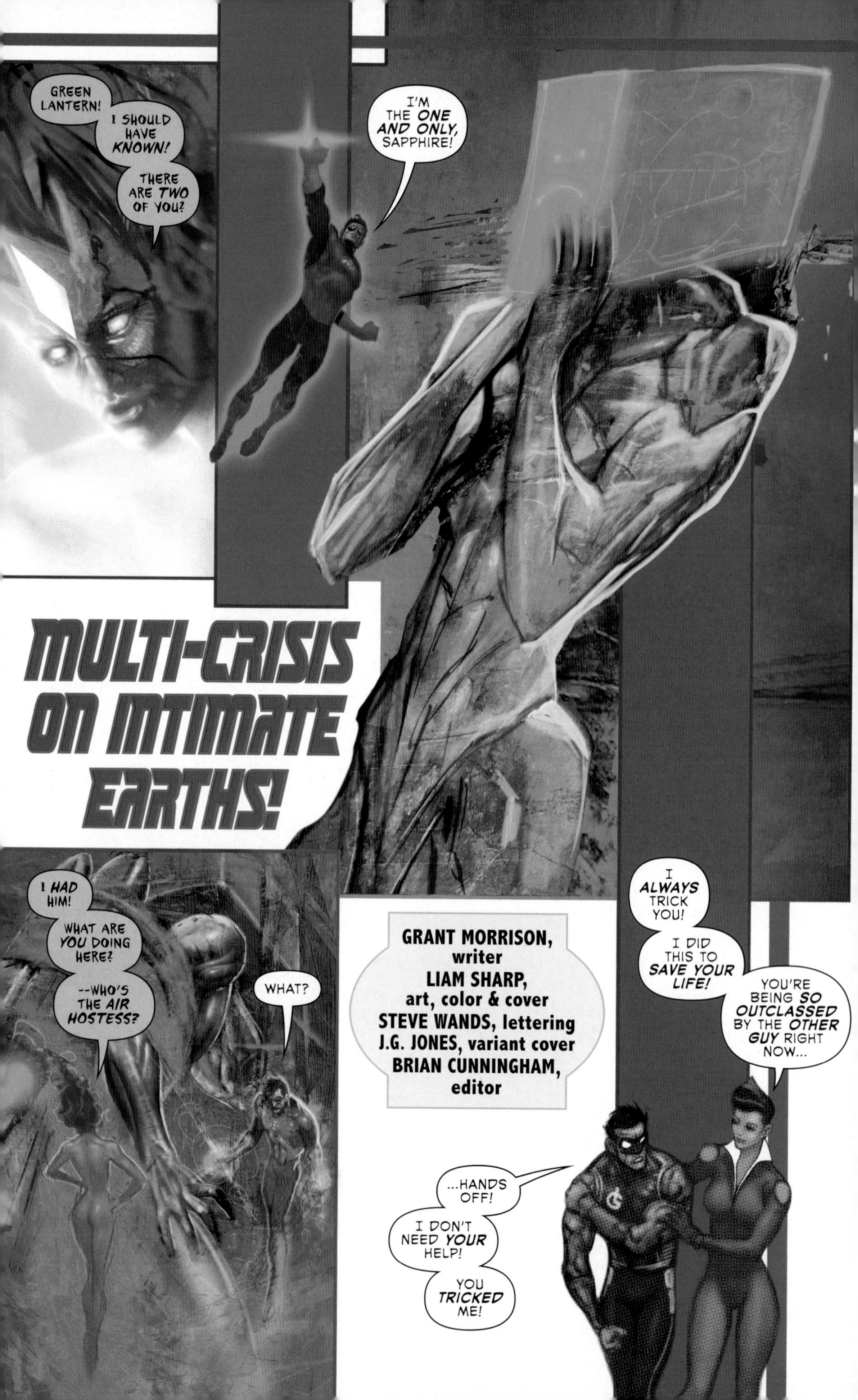
GREEN LANTERN!
I SHOULD HAVE KNOWN!
THERE ARE TWO OF YOU?
I'M THE ONE AND ONLY, SAPPHIRE!
MULTI-CRISIS ON INTIMATE EARTHS!
I HAD HIM!
WHAT ARE YOU DOING HERE?
--WHO'S THE AIR HOSTESS?
WHAT?
GRANT MORRISON, writer
LIAM SHARP, art, color & cover
STEVE WANDS, lettering
J.G. JONES, variant cover
BRIAN CUNNINGHAM, editor
I ALWAYS TRICK YOU!
I DID THIS TO SAVE YOUR LIFE!
YOU'RE BEING SO OUTCLASSED BY THE OTHER GUY RIGHT NOW...
...HANDS OFF!
I DON'T NEED YOUR HELP!
YOU TRICKED ME!

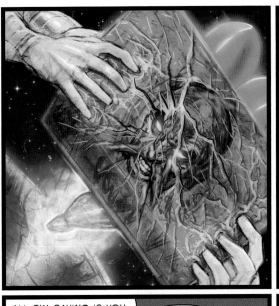

LOOK, WE DON'T **NEED** TO FIGHT.

CAROL, THIS IS AS MUCH A SHOCK TO **ME** AS IT IS TO **YOU**...

I DON'T KNOW **WHO** TO START WITH!

THESE PEOPLE ARE **MAD**!

WE DON'T ACT LIKE THAT--DO WE...?

ALL I'M SAYING IS YOU DO **NOT** WANT TO GO TO WAR OVER A **MIS**-UNDERSTANDING.

YOU JUST CHASED A **VERSION OF ME** TO A **PARALLEL EARTH**.

WOMEN ARE **IN CHARGE** HERE--

AS THEY **SHOULD** BE!

AND I NEARLY STARTED A **WAR**?

SEE, **THIS** IS THE SORT OF THING THAT HAPPENS AROUND YOU **ALL THE TIME**!

GUYS!

END OF THE WORLD ALERT!

YOU DO THIS **ALL THE TIME**!

DON'T LET HER GET AWAY WITH IT!

TRICKING PEOPLE INTO DOING WHAT **YOU** WANT!

YEAH, YEAH, YEAH.

DON'T THINK YOU CAN JUST PEACE AND LOVE **THIS** AWAY!

I SAW HOW YOU LOOKED AT HIM!

YOU!

AS FOR **YOU**!

YOU **KISSED** ME!

YOU TRIGGERED THE **STAR SAPPHIRE**!

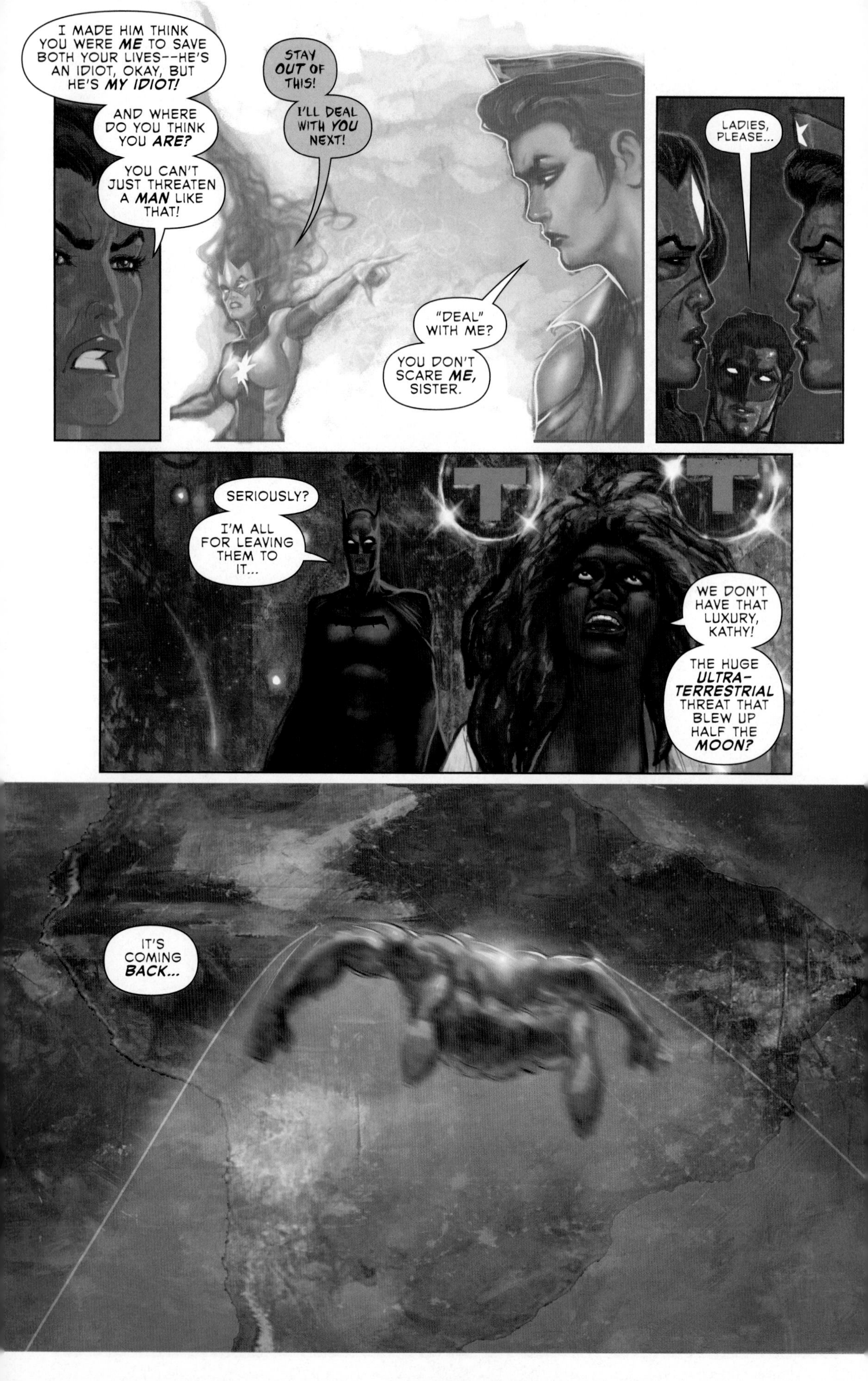
I MADE HIM THINK YOU WERE *ME* TO SAVE BOTH YOUR LIVES--HE'S AN IDIOT, OKAY, BUT HE'S *MY IDIOT!*
AND WHERE DO YOU THINK YOU *ARE?*
YOU CAN'T JUST THREATEN A *MAN* LIKE THAT!
STAY *OUT* OF THIS!
I'LL DEAL WITH *YOU* NEXT!
"DEAL" WITH ME?
YOU DON'T SCARE *ME,* SISTER.
LADIES, PLEASE...
SERIOUSLY?
I'M ALL FOR LEAVING THEM TO IT...
WE DON'T HAVE THAT LUXURY, KATHY!
THE HUGE *ULTRA-TERRESTRIAL* THREAT THAT BLEW UP HALF THE *MOON?*
IT'S COMING *BACK...*

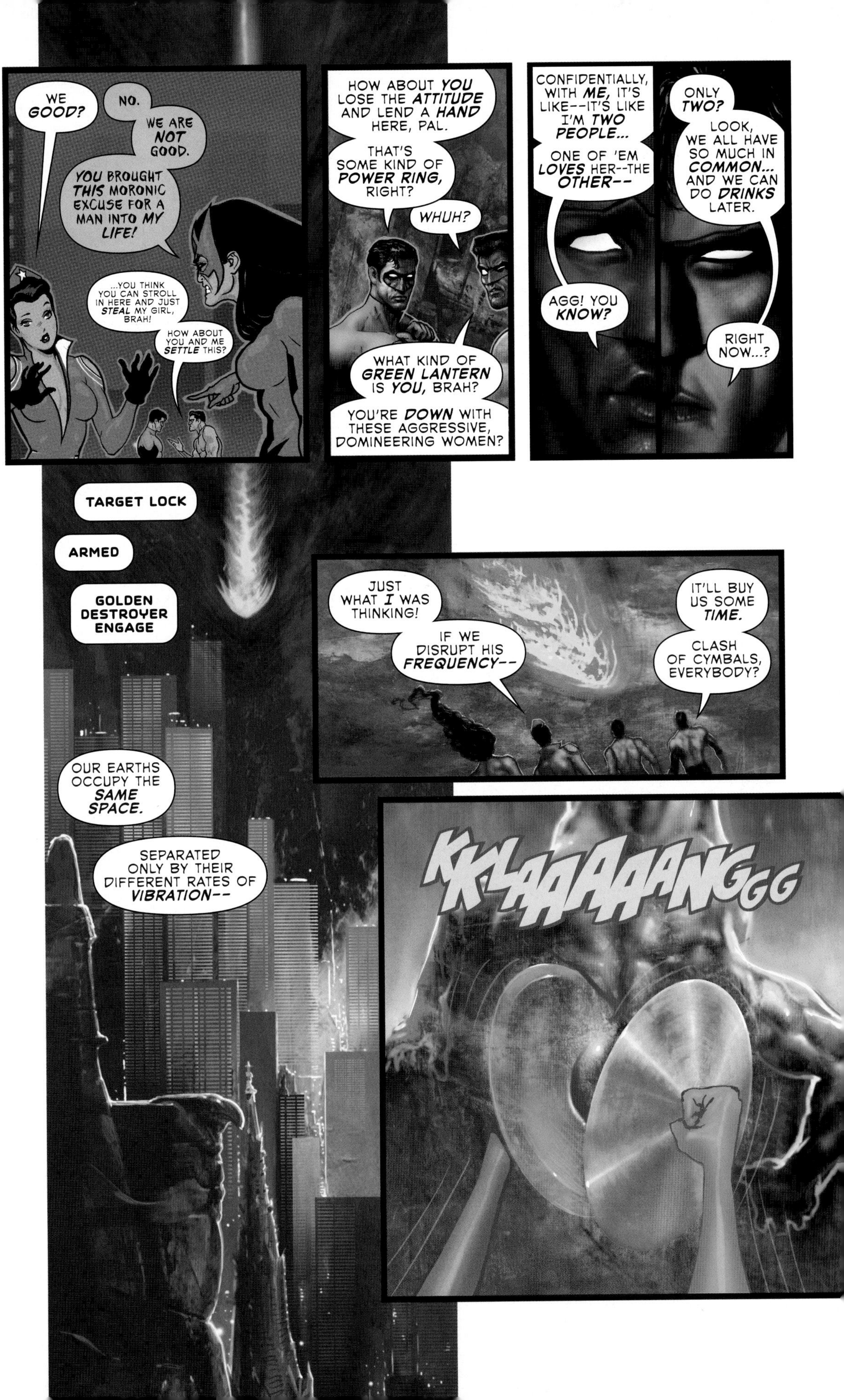
WE GOOD?
NO.
WE ARE NOT GOOD.
YOU BROUGHT THIS MORONIC EXCUSE FOR A MAN INTO MY LIFE!
...YOU THINK YOU CAN STROLL IN HERE AND JUST STEAL MY GIRL, BRAH!
HOW ABOUT YOU AND ME SETTLE THIS?
HOW ABOUT YOU LOSE THE ATTITUDE AND LEND A HAND HERE, PAL.
THAT'S SOME KIND OF POWER RING, RIGHT?
WHUH?
WHAT KIND OF GREEN LANTERN IS YOU, BRAH?
YOU'RE DOWN WITH THESE AGGRESSIVE, DOMINEERING WOMEN?
CONFIDENTIALLY, WITH ME, IT'S LIKE--IT'S LIKE I'M TWO PEOPLE...
ONE OF 'EM LOVES HER--THE OTHER--
ONLY TWO?
LOOK, WE ALL HAVE SO MUCH IN COMMON... AND WE CAN DO DRINKS LATER.
AGG! YOU KNOW?
RIGHT NOW...?
TARGET LOCK
ARMED
GOLDEN DESTROYER ENGAGE
JUST WHAT I WAS THINKING!
IF WE DISRUPT HIS FREQUENCY--
IT'LL BUY US SOME TIME.
CLASH OF CYMBALS, EVERYBODY?
OUR EARTHS OCCUPY THE SAME SPACE.
SEPARATED ONLY BY THEIR DIFFERENT RATES OF VIBRATION--
KKLAAAAAANGGG

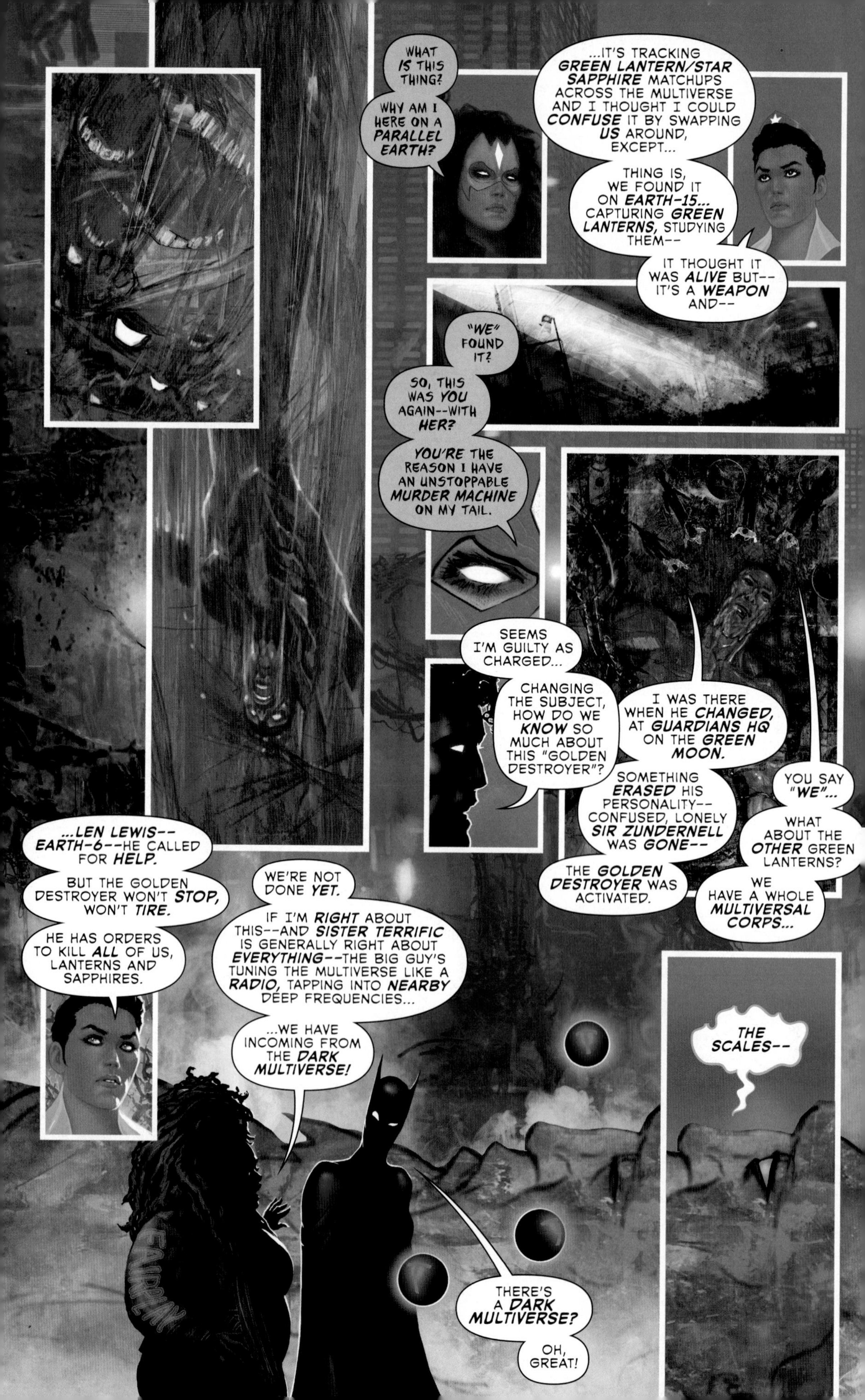

WHAT IS THIS THING?
WHY AM I HERE ON A PARALLEL EARTH?
...IT'S TRACKING GREEN LANTERN/STAR SAPPHIRE MATCHUPS ACROSS THE MULTIVERSE AND I THOUGHT I COULD CONFUSE IT BY SWAPPING US AROUND, EXCEPT...
THING IS, WE FOUND IT ON EARTH-15... CAPTURING GREEN LANTERNS, STUDYING THEM--
IT THOUGHT IT WAS ALIVE BUT-- IT'S A WEAPON AND--
"WE" FOUND IT?
SO, THIS WAS YOU AGAIN--WITH HER?
YOU'RE THE REASON I HAVE AN UNSTOPPABLE MURDER MACHINE ON MY TAIL.
SEEMS I'M GUILTY AS CHARGED...
CHANGING THE SUBJECT, HOW DO WE KNOW SO MUCH ABOUT THIS "GOLDEN DESTROYER"?
I WAS THERE WHEN HE CHANGED, AT GUARDIANS HQ ON THE GREEN MOON.
SOMETHING ERASED HIS PERSONALITY-- CONFUSED, LONELY SIR ZUNDERNELL WAS GONE--
THE GOLDEN DESTROYER WAS ACTIVATED.
YOU SAY "WE"...
WHAT ABOUT THE OTHER GREEN LANTERNS?
WE HAVE A WHOLE MULTIVERSAL CORPS...
...LEN LEWIS-- EARTH-6--HE CALLED FOR HELP.
BUT THE GOLDEN DESTROYER WON'T STOP, WON'T TIRE.
HE HAS ORDERS TO KILL ALL OF US, LANTERNS AND SAPPHIRES.
WE'RE NOT DONE YET.
IF I'M RIGHT ABOUT THIS--AND SISTER TERRIFIC IS GENERALLY RIGHT ABOUT EVERYTHING--THE BIG GUY'S TUNING THE MULTIVERSE LIKE A RADIO, TAPPING INTO NEARBY DEEP FREQUENCIES...
...WE HAVE INCOMING FROM THE DARK MULTIVERSE!
THERE'S A DARK MULTIVERSE?
OH, GREAT!
THE SCALES--

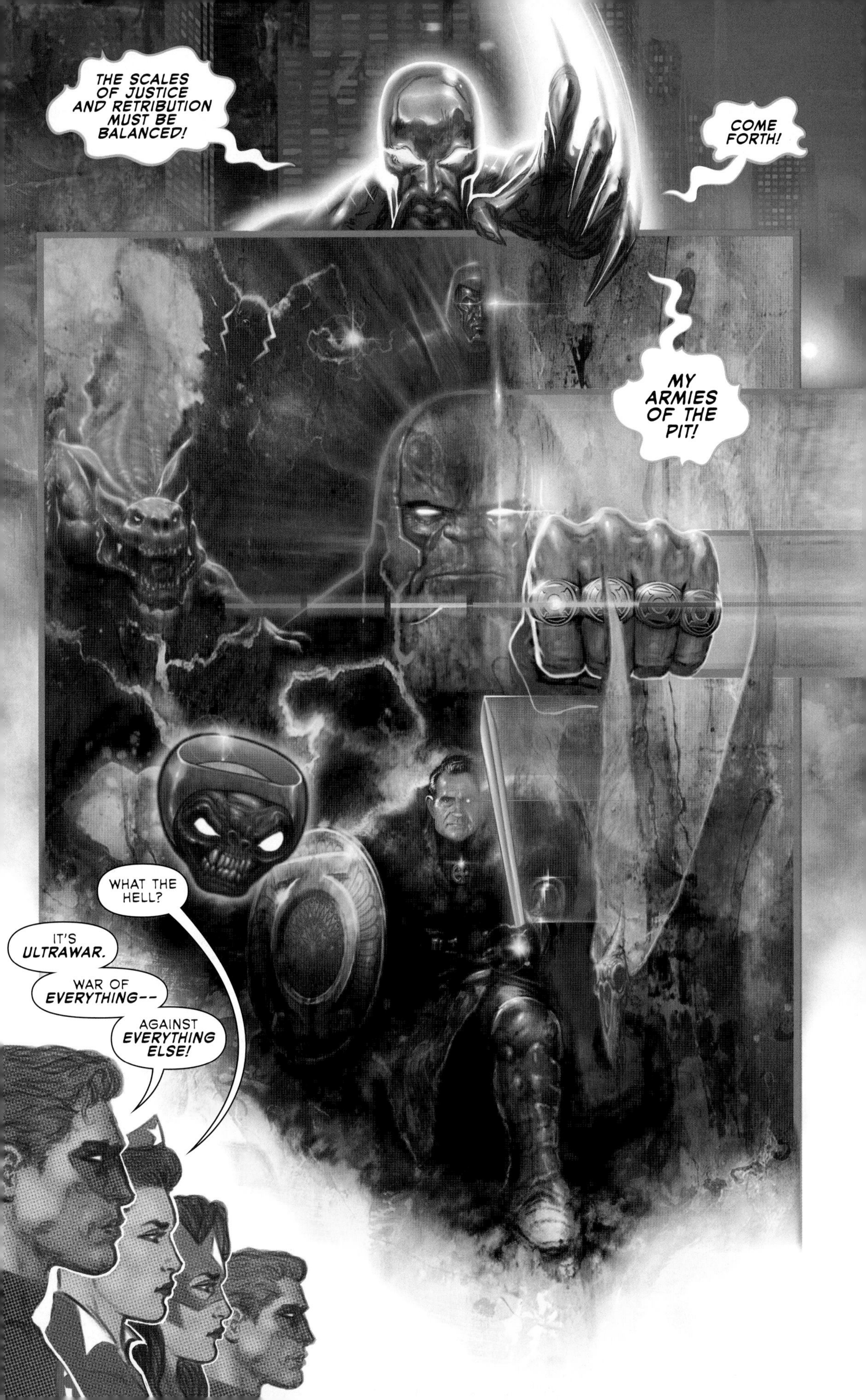
THE SCALES OF JUSTICE AND RETRIBUTION MUST BE BALANCED!
COME FORTH!
MY ARMIES OF THE PIT!
WHAT THE HELL?
IT'S ULTRAWAR.
WAR OF EVERYTHING--
AGAINST EVERYTHING ELSE!

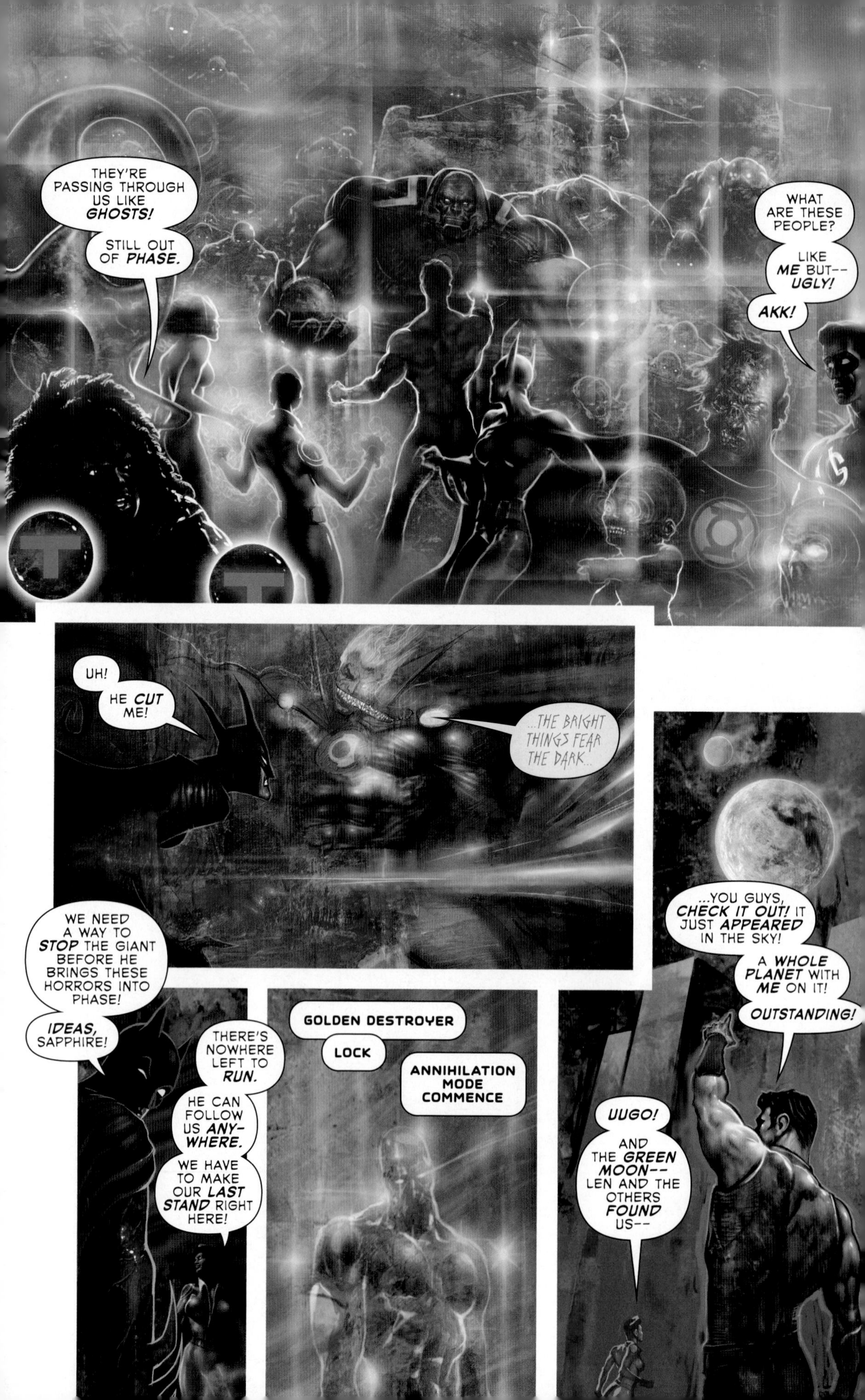
THEY'RE PASSING THROUGH US LIKE GHOSTS!
STILL OUT OF PHASE.
WHAT ARE THESE PEOPLE?
LIKE ME BUT-- UGLY!
AKK!
UH!
HE CUT ME!
...THE BRIGHT THINGS FEAR THE DARK...
...YOU GUYS, CHECK IT OUT! IT JUST APPEARED IN THE SKY!
A WHOLE PLANET WITH ME ON IT!
OUTSTANDING!
WE NEED A WAY TO STOP THE GIANT BEFORE HE BRINGS THESE HORRORS INTO PHASE!
IDEAS, SAPPHIRE!
THERE'S NOWHERE LEFT TO RUN.
HE CAN FOLLOW US ANY-WHERE.
WE HAVE TO MAKE OUR LAST STAND RIGHT HERE!
GOLDEN DESTROYER
LOCK
ANNIHILATION MODE COMMENCE
UUGO!
AND THE GREEN MOON-- LEN AND THE OTHERS FOUND US--

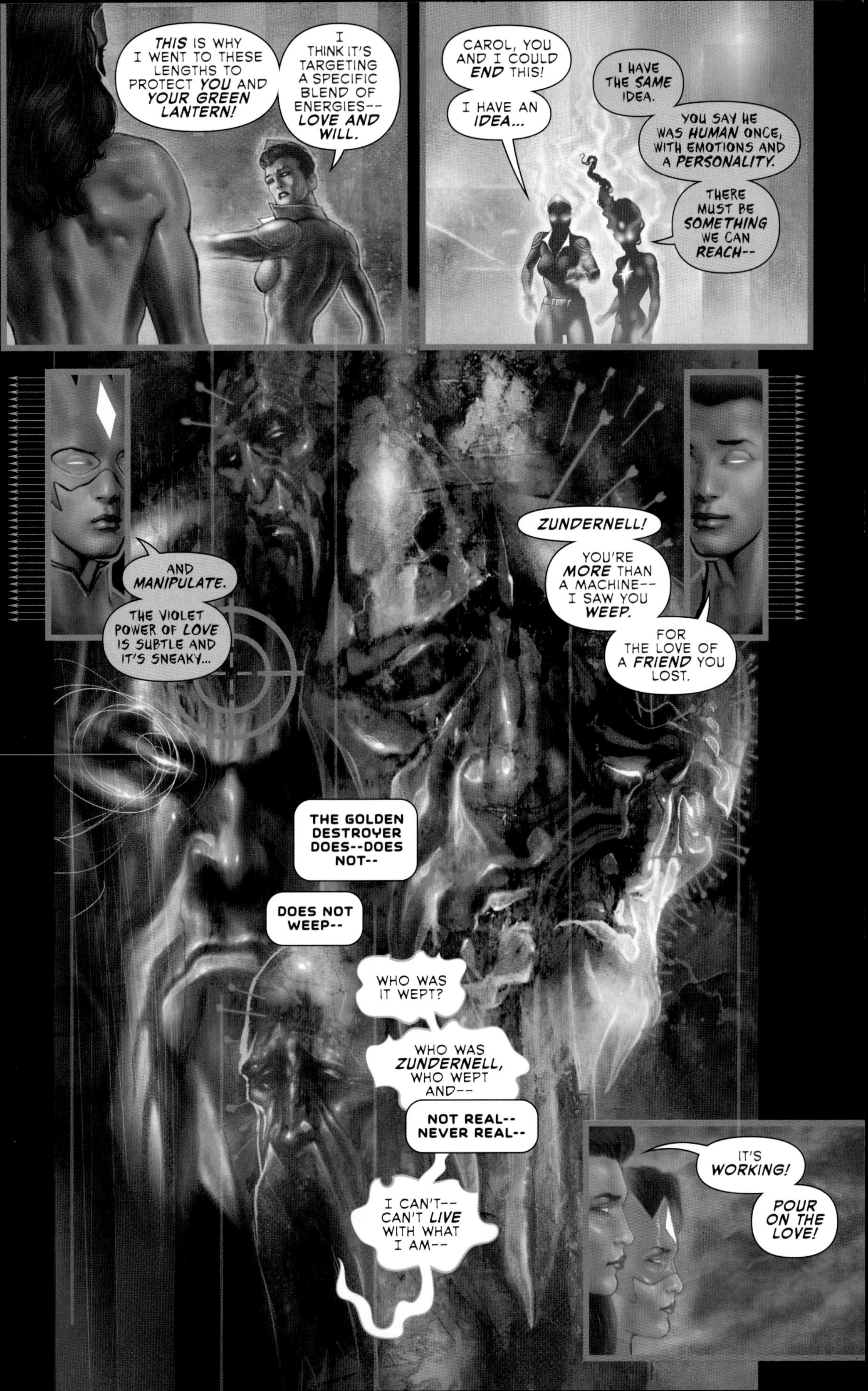
THIS IS WHY I WENT TO THESE LENGTHS TO PROTECT YOU AND YOUR GREEN LANTERN!
I THINK IT'S TARGETING A SPECIFIC BLEND OF ENERGIES-- LOVE AND WILL.
CAROL, YOU AND I COULD END THIS!
I HAVE AN IDEA...
I HAVE THE SAME IDEA.
YOU SAY HE WAS HUMAN ONCE, WITH EMOTIONS AND A PERSONALITY.
THERE MUST BE SOMETHING WE CAN REACH--
AND MANIPULATE.
THE VIOLET POWER OF LOVE IS SUBTLE AND IT'S SNEAKY...
ZUNDERNELL!
YOU'RE MORE THAN A MACHINE-- I SAW YOU WEEP.
FOR THE LOVE OF A FRIEND YOU LOST.
THE GOLDEN DESTROYER DOES--DOES NOT--
DOES NOT WEEP--
WHO WAS IT WEPT?
WHO WAS ZUNDERNELL, WHO WEPT AND--
NOT REAL-- NEVER REAL--
I CAN'T-- CAN'T LIVE WITH WHAT I AM--
IT'S WORKING!
POUR ON THE LOVE!

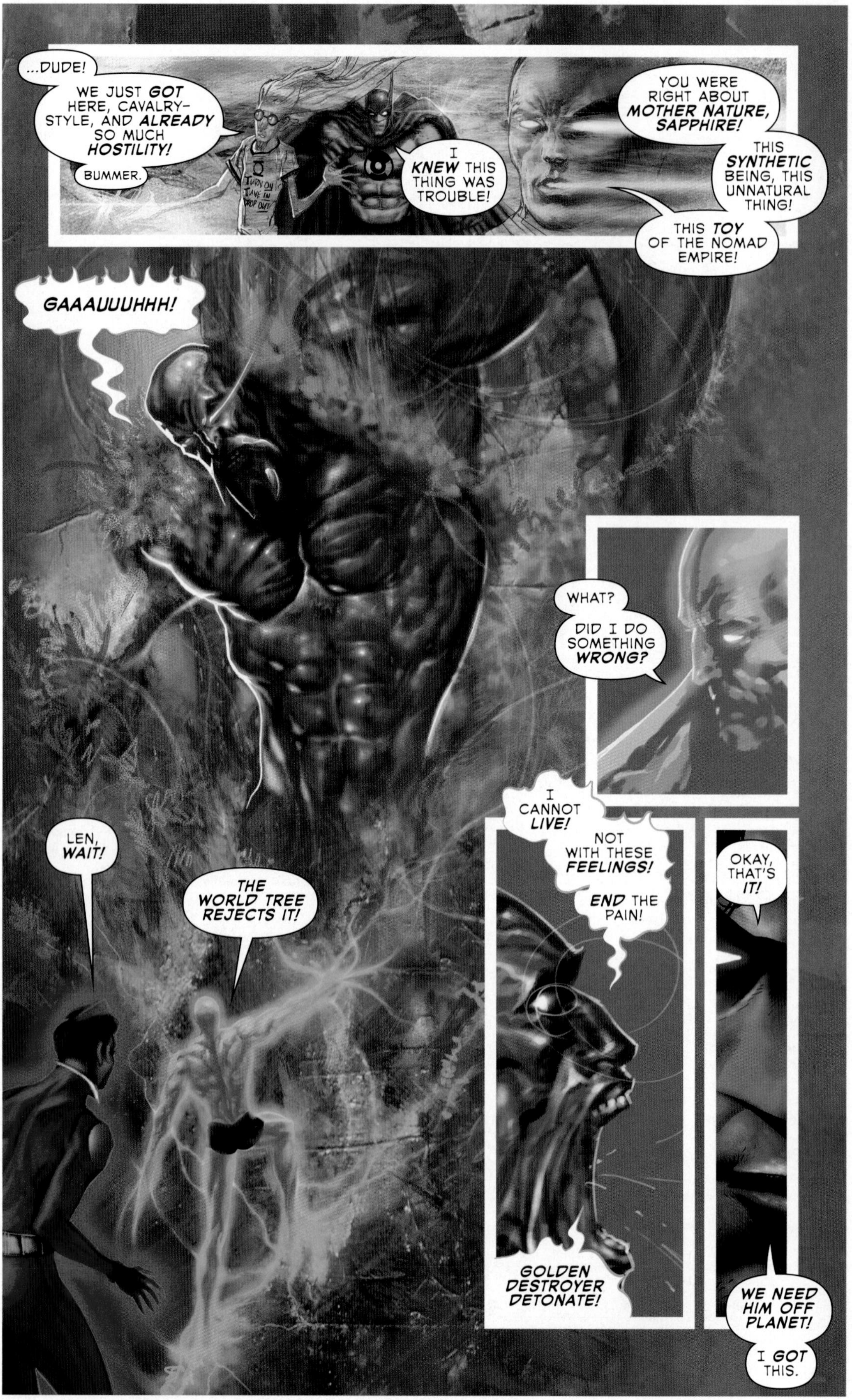
...DUDE!
WE JUST GOT HERE, CAVALRY-STYLE, AND ALREADY SO MUCH HOSTILITY!
BUMMER.
I KNEW THIS THING WAS TROUBLE!
YOU WERE RIGHT ABOUT MOTHER NATURE, SAPPHIRE!
THIS SYNTHETIC BEING, THIS UNNATURAL THING!
THIS TOY OF THE NOMAD EMPIRE!
GAAAUUUHHH!
WHAT?
DID I DO SOMETHING WRONG?
LEN, WAIT!
THE WORLD TREE REJECTS IT!
I CANNOT LIVE!
NOT WITH THESE FEELINGS!
END THE PAIN!
GOLDEN DESTROYER DETONATE!
OKAY, THAT'S IT!
WE NEED HIM OFF PLANET!
I GOT THIS.

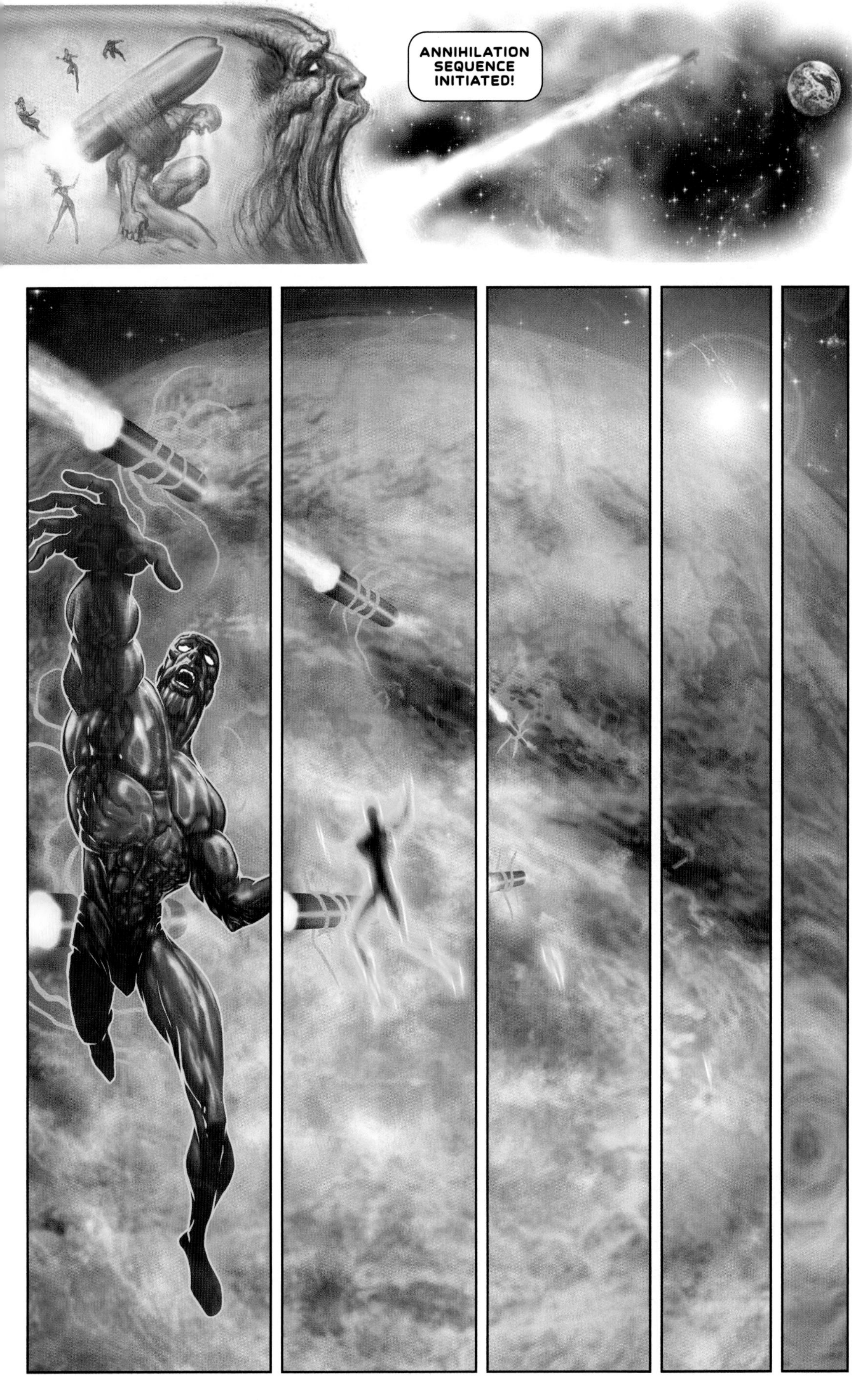
ANNIHILATION SEQUENCE INITIATED!

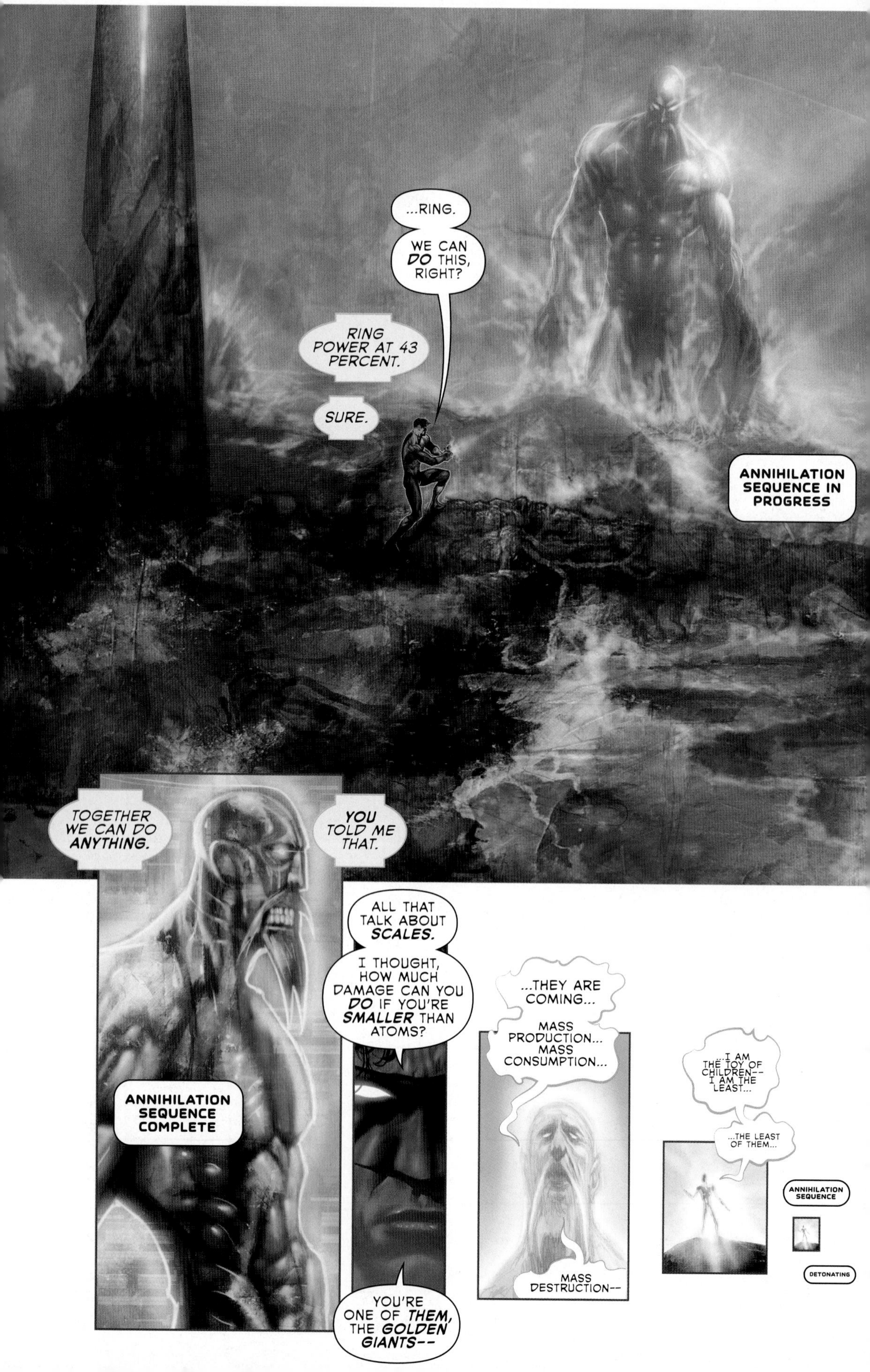

...RING.
WE CAN DO THIS, RIGHT?
RING POWER AT 43 PERCENT.
SURE.
ANNIHILATION SEQUENCE IN PROGRESS
TOGETHER WE CAN DO ANYTHING.
YOU TOLD ME THAT.
ANNIHILATION SEQUENCE COMPLETE
ALL THAT TALK ABOUT SCALES.
I THOUGHT, HOW MUCH DAMAGE CAN YOU DO IF YOU'RE SMALLER THAN ATOMS?
YOU'RE ONE OF THEM, THE GOLDEN GIANTS--
...THEY ARE COMING...
MASS PRODUCTION... MASS CONSUMPTION...
MASS DESTRUCTION--
...I AM THE TOY OF CHILDREN-- I AM THE LEAST...
...THE LEAST OF THEM...
ANNIHILATION SEQUENCE
DETONATING

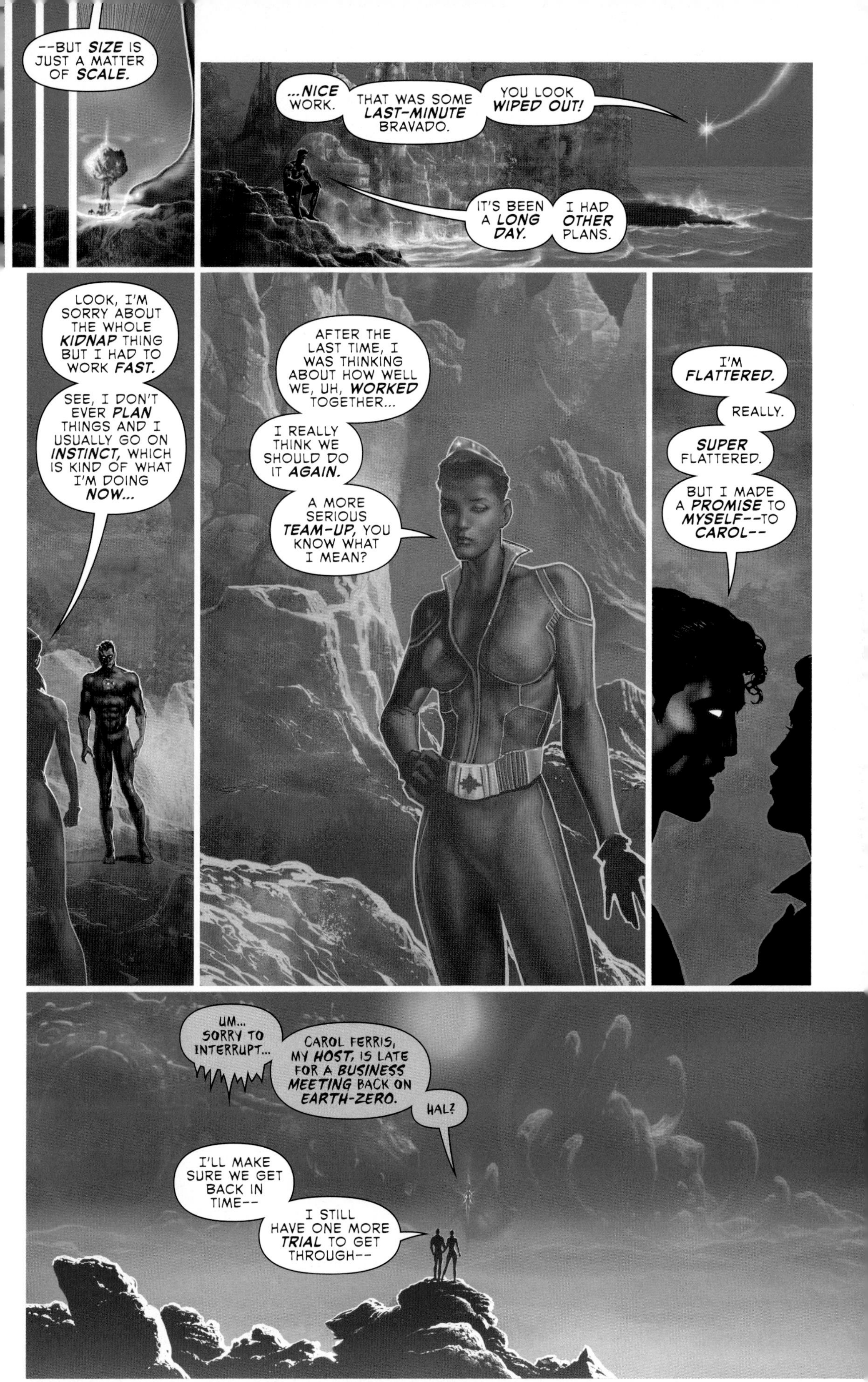
--BUT SIZE IS JUST A MATTER OF SCALE.
...NICE WORK.
THAT WAS SOME LAST-MINUTE BRAVADO.
YOU LOOK WIPED OUT!
IT'S BEEN A LONG DAY.
I HAD OTHER PLANS.
LOOK, I'M SORRY ABOUT THE WHOLE KIDNAP THING BUT I HAD TO WORK FAST.
SEE, I DON'T EVER PLAN THINGS AND I USUALLY GO ON INSTINCT, WHICH IS KIND OF WHAT I'M DOING NOW...
AFTER THE LAST TIME, I WAS THINKING ABOUT HOW WELL WE, UH, WORKED TOGETHER...
I REALLY THINK WE SHOULD DO IT AGAIN.
A MORE SERIOUS TEAM-UP, YOU KNOW WHAT I MEAN?
I'M FLATTERED.
REALLY.
SUPER FLATTERED.
BUT I MADE A PROMISE TO MYSELF--TO CAROL--
UM... SORRY TO INTERRUPT...
CAROL FERRIS, MY HOST, IS LATE FOR A BUSINESS MEETING BACK ON EARTH-ZERO.
HAL?
I'LL MAKE SURE WE GET BACK IN TIME--
I STILL HAVE ONE MORE TRIAL TO GET THROUGH--

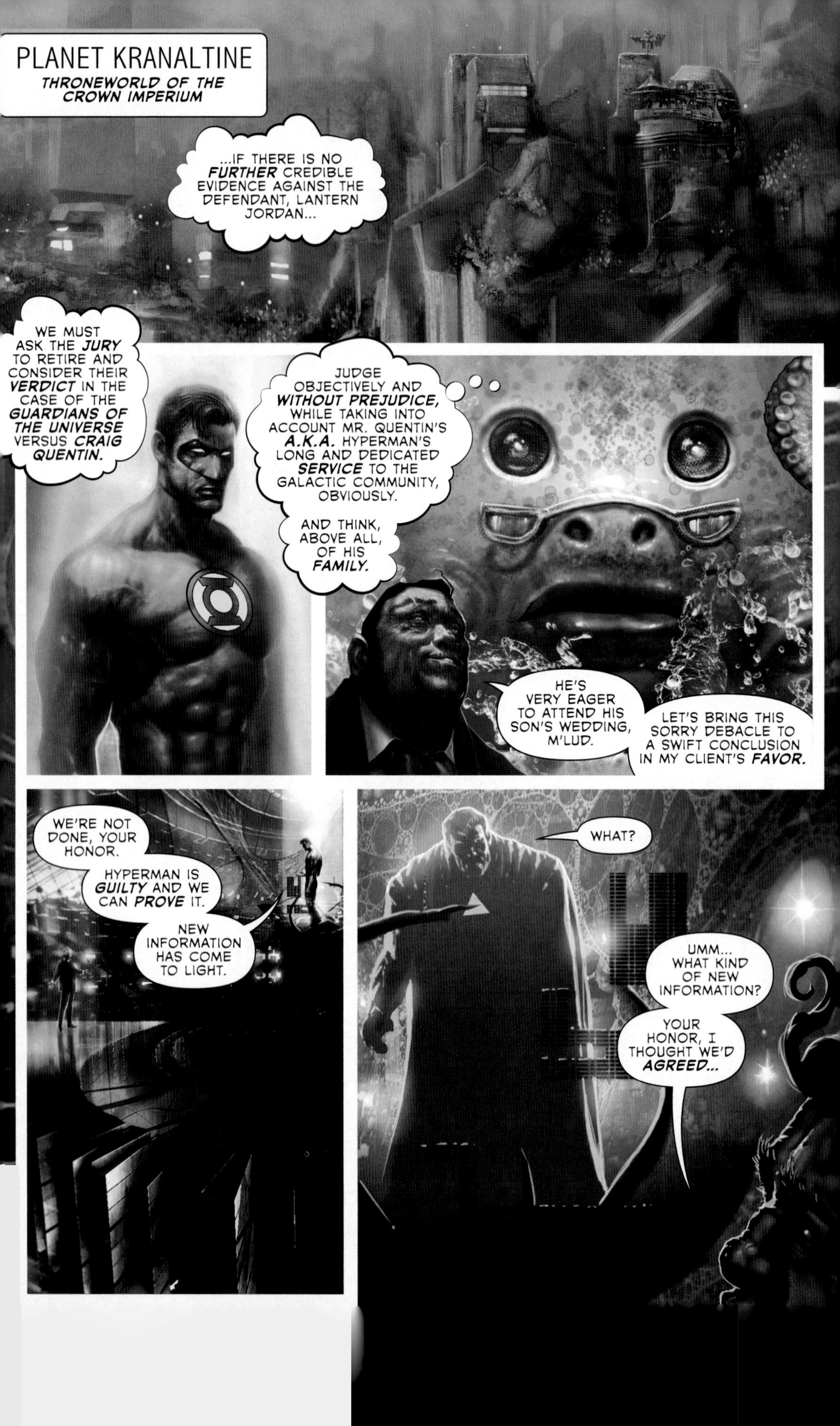
PLANET KRANALTINE
THRONEWORLD OF THE CROWN IMPERIUM
...IF THERE IS NO FURTHER CREDIBLE EVIDENCE AGAINST THE DEFENDANT, LANTERN JORDAN...
WE MUST ASK THE JURY TO RETIRE AND CONSIDER THEIR VERDICT IN THE CASE OF THE GUARDIANS OF THE UNIVERSE VERSUS CRAIG QUENTIN.
JUDGE OBJECTIVELY AND WITHOUT PREJUDICE, WHILE TAKING INTO ACCOUNT MR. QUENTIN'S A.K.A. HYPERMAN'S LONG AND DEDICATED SERVICE TO THE GALACTIC COMMUNITY, OBVIOUSLY.
AND THINK, ABOVE ALL, OF HIS FAMILY.
HE'S VERY EAGER TO ATTEND HIS SON'S WEDDING, M'LUD.
LET'S BRING THIS SORRY DEBACLE TO A SWIFT CONCLUSION IN MY CLIENT'S FAVOR.
WE'RE NOT DONE, YOUR HONOR.
HYPERMAN IS GUILTY AND WE CAN PROVE IT.
NEW INFORMATION HAS COME TO LIGHT.
WHAT?
UMM... WHAT KIND OF NEW INFORMATION?
YOUR HONOR, I THOUGHT WE'D AGREED...

...MY COLLEAGUE LANTERN JORDAN IS *CORRECT.*

THERE WAS *ONE WITNESS* WE FAILED TO CONSULT.

POWERLORD'S SO-CALLED "RO-BUTLER," *MECHANDRO...*

ZVVRZZ!

WHAT'S *THIS!*

POWERLORD SAID *NOTHING!*

...THAT THING *KNOWS* NOTHING.

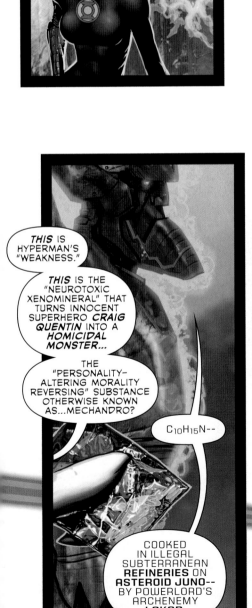

THIS IS HYPERMAN'S "WEAKNESS."

THIS IS THE "NEUROTOXIC XENOMINERAL" THAT TURNS INNOCENT SUPERHERO *CRAIG QUENTIN* INTO A *HOMICIDAL MONSTER...*

THE "PERSONALITY-ALTERING MORALITY REVERSING" SUBSTANCE OTHERWISE KNOWN AS...MECHANDRO?

$C_{10}H_{15}N$--

COOKED IN ILLEGAL SUBTERRANEAN *REFINERIES* ON *ASTEROID JUNO*-- BY POWERLORD'S ARCHENEMY *LOKAR.*

TRANSFERRED BY *BOOM CUBE* TO CRAIG QUENTIN'S IMPREGNABLE *AERO-CITADEL* ON *TROMBUS.*

AS MECHANDRO'S MEMORY STORE WILL REVEAL, *BOOM CUBE KEYS* HAVE *UNIQUE* ENERGY SIGNATURES.

IN *THIS* CASE, THE RECEIVING TERMINAL BELONGED TO THE *HYPER-FAMILY.*

MRS. QUENTIN'S ATTEMPTS TO PROTECT HER HUSBAND'S REPUTATION MADE HER A WILLING ACCESSORY TO *MURDER.*

SHE *ENABLED* HER HUSBAND'S HABIT AND COVERED HIS TRACKS.

WHICH IS WHY I'M CURRENTLY BEING *TARGETED* BY HYPERWOMAN'S *OPTIC POWERS.*

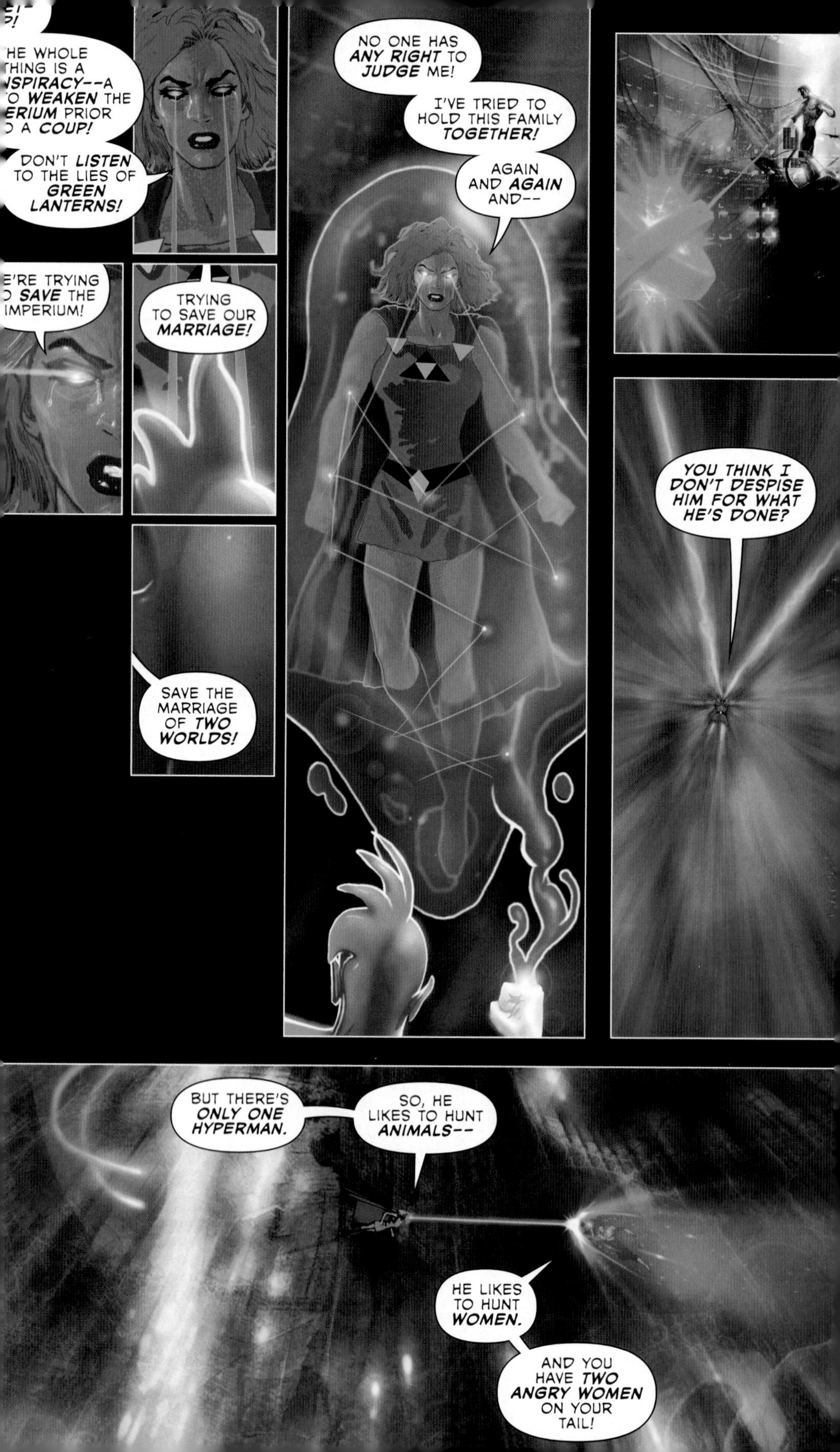

HE WHOLE THING IS A NSPIRACY--A O WEAKEN THE ERIUM PRIOR O A COUP!
DON'T LISTEN TO THE LIES OF GREEN LANTERNS!
E'RE TRYING O SAVE THE IMPERIUM!
TRYING TO SAVE OUR MARRIAGE!
SAVE THE MARRIAGE OF TWO WORLDS!
NO ONE HAS ANY RIGHT TO JUDGE ME!
I'VE TRIED TO HOLD THIS FAMILY TOGETHER!
AGAIN AND AGAIN AND--
YOU THINK I DON'T DESPISE HIM FOR WHAT HE'S DONE?
BUT THERE'S ONLY ONE HYPERMAN.
SO, HE LIKES TO HUNT ANIMALS--
HE LIKES TO HUNT WOMEN.
AND YOU HAVE TWO ANGRY WOMEN ON YOUR TAIL!

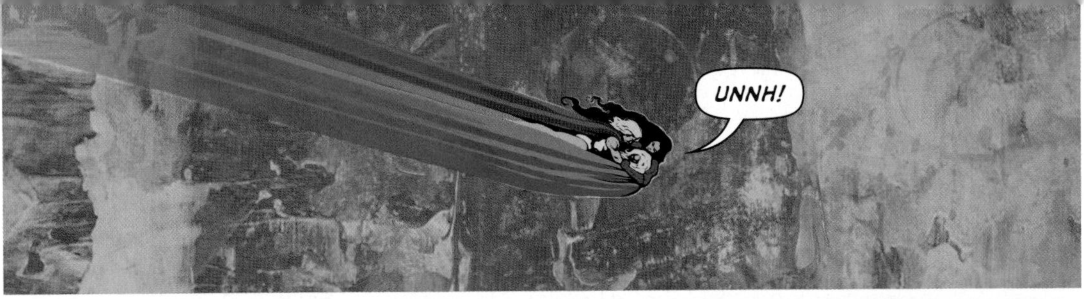
UNNH!

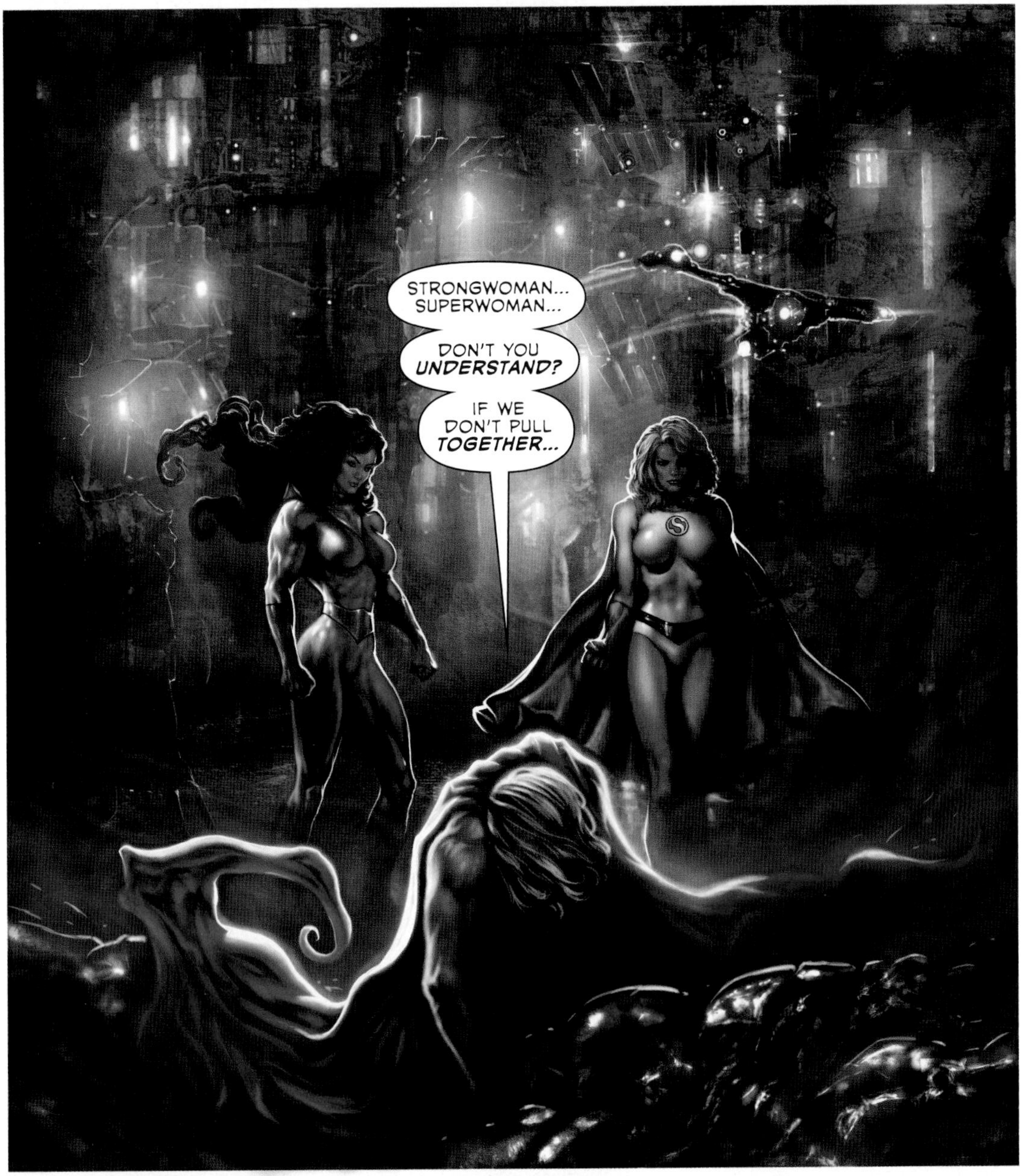
STRONGWOMAN... SUPERWOMAN...
DON'T YOU UNDERSTAND?
IF WE DON'T PULL TOGETHER...

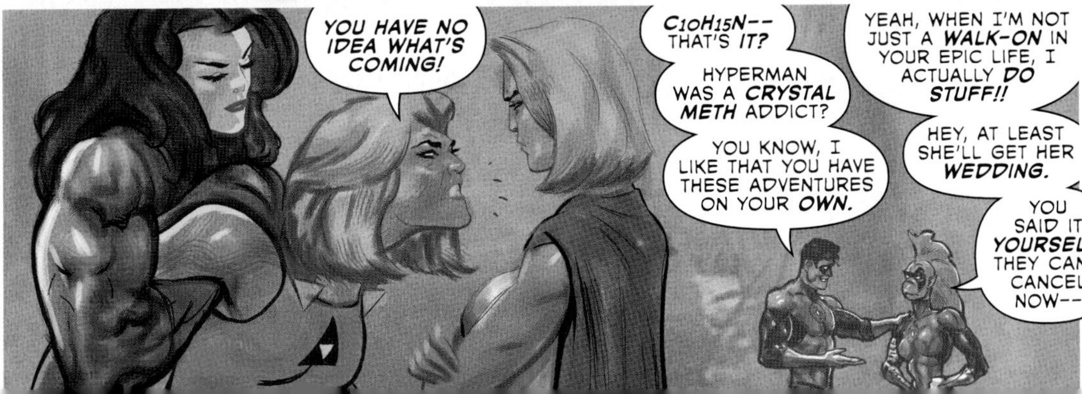
YOU HAVE NO IDEA WHAT'S COMING!
$C_{10}H_{15}N$-- THAT'S IT?
HYPERMAN WAS A CRYSTAL METH ADDICT?
YOU KNOW, I LIKE THAT YOU HAVE THESE ADVENTURES ON YOUR OWN.
YEAH, WHEN I'M NOT JUST A WALK-ON IN YOUR EPIC LIFE, I ACTUALLY DO STUFF!!
HEY, AT LEAST SHE'LL GET HER WEDDING.
YOU SAID IT YOURSELF; THEY CAN'T CANCEL NOW--

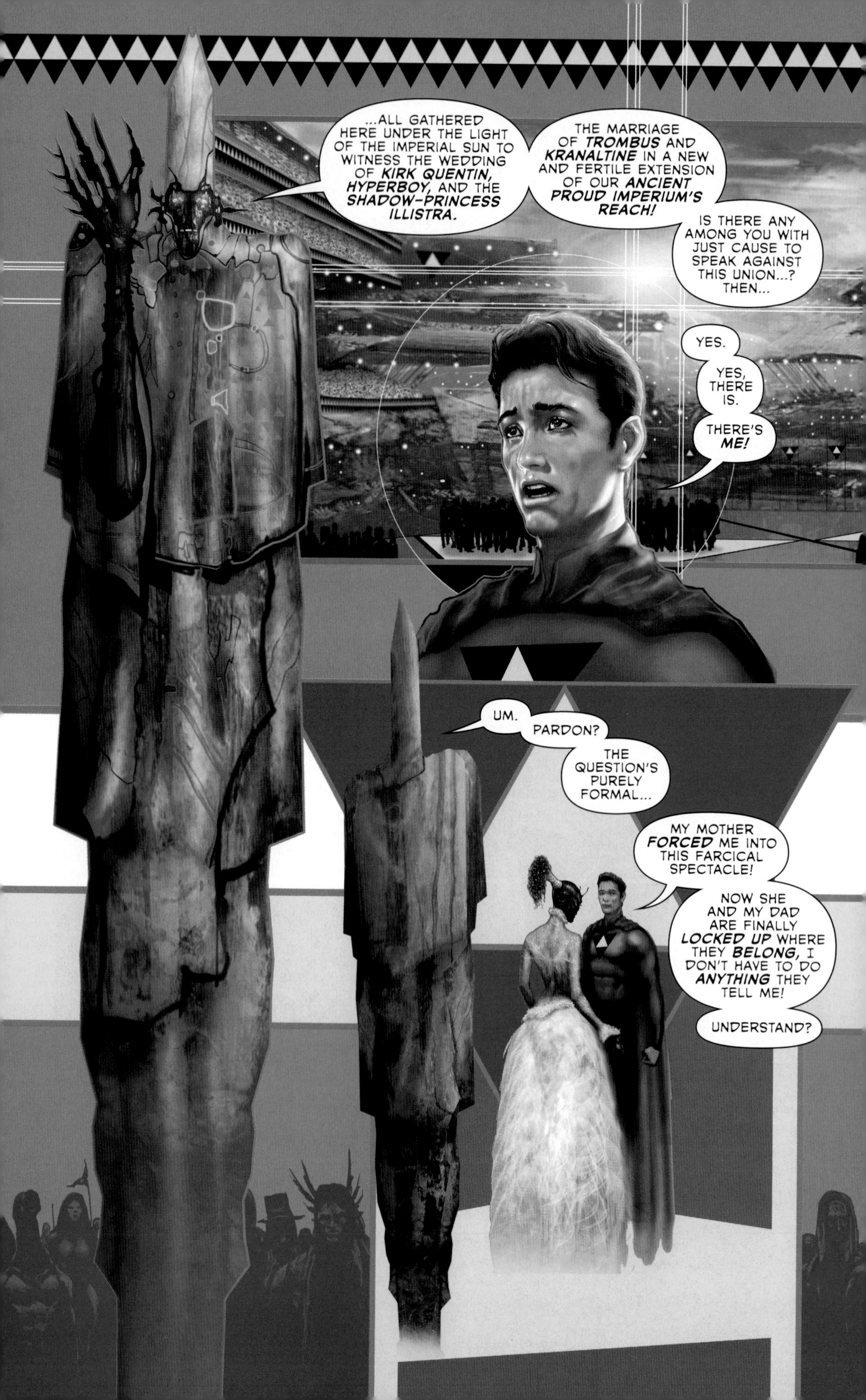
...ALL GATHERED HERE UNDER THE LIGHT OF THE IMPERIAL SUN TO WITNESS THE WEDDING OF KIRK QUENTIN, HYPERBOY, AND THE SHADOW-PRINCESS ILLISTRA.
THE MARRIAGE OF TROMBUS AND KRANALTINE IN A NEW AND FERTILE EXTENSION OF OUR ANCIENT PROUD IMPERIUM'S REACH!
IS THERE ANY AMONG YOU WITH JUST CAUSE TO SPEAK AGAINST THIS UNION...? THEN...
YES.
YES, THERE IS.
THERE'S ME!
UM.
PARDON?
THE QUESTION'S PURELY FORMAL...
MY MOTHER FORCED ME INTO THIS FARCICAL SPECTACLE!
NOW SHE AND MY DAD ARE FINALLY LOCKED UP WHERE THEY BELONG, I DON'T HAVE TO DO ANYTHING THEY TELL ME!
UNDERSTAND?

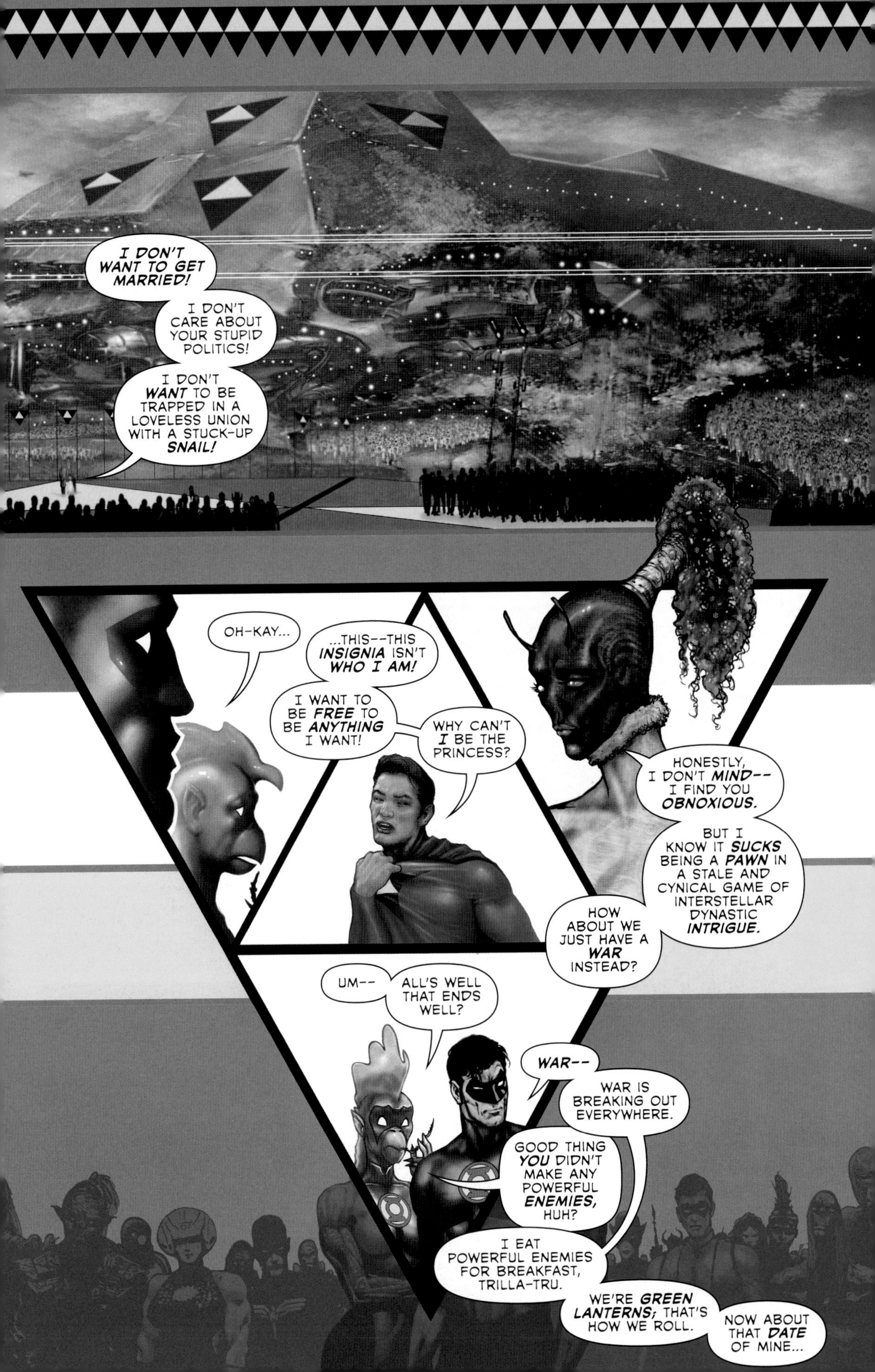
I DON'T WANT TO GET MARRIED!
I DON'T CARE ABOUT YOUR STUPID POLITICS!
I DON'T WANT TO BE TRAPPED IN A LOVELESS UNION WITH A STUCK-UP SNAIL!
OH-KAY...
...THIS--THIS INSIGNIA ISN'T WHO I AM!
I WANT TO BE FREE TO BE ANYTHING I WANT!
WHY CAN'T I BE THE PRINCESS?
HONESTLY, I DON'T MIND-- I FIND YOU OBNOXIOUS.
BUT I KNOW IT SUCKS BEING A PAWN IN A STALE AND CYNICAL GAME OF INTERSTELLAR DYNASTIC INTRIGUE.
HOW ABOUT WE JUST HAVE A WAR INSTEAD?
UM--
ALL'S WELL THAT ENDS WELL?
WAR--
WAR IS BREAKING OUT EVERYWHERE.
GOOD THING YOU DIDN'T MAKE ANY POWERFUL ENEMIES, HUH?
I EAT POWERFUL ENEMIES FOR BREAKFAST, TRILLA-TRU.
WE'RE GREEN LANTERNS; THAT'S HOW WE ROLL.
NOW ABOUT THAT DATE OF MINE...

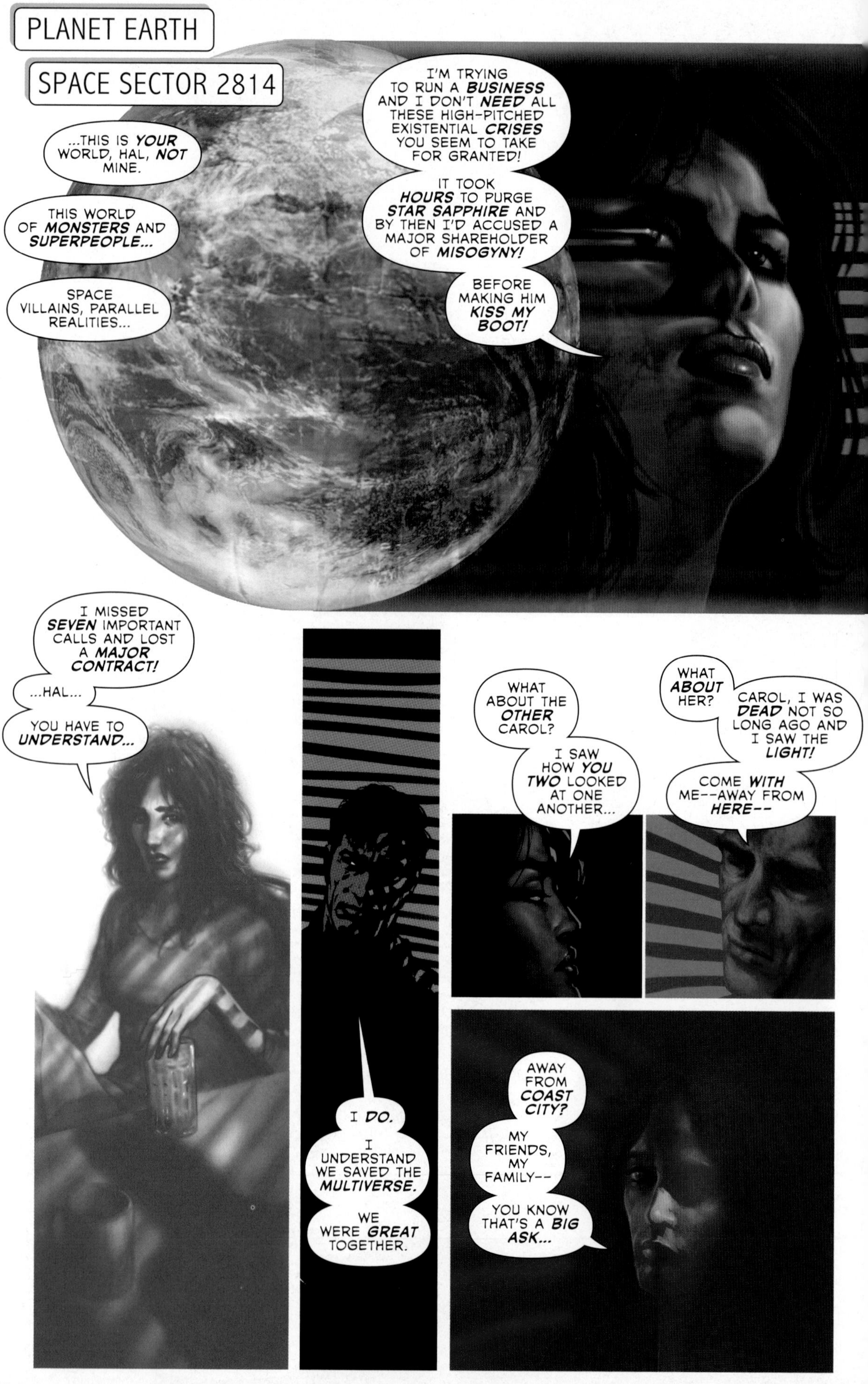
PLANET EARTH
SPACE SECTOR 2814
...THIS IS YOUR WORLD, HAL, NOT MINE.
THIS WORLD OF MONSTERS AND SUPERPEOPLE...
SPACE VILLAINS, PARALLEL REALITIES...
I'M TRYING TO RUN A BUSINESS AND I DON'T NEED ALL THESE HIGH-PITCHED EXISTENTIAL CRISES YOU SEEM TO TAKE FOR GRANTED!
IT TOOK HOURS TO PURGE STAR SAPPHIRE AND BY THEN I'D ACCUSED A MAJOR SHAREHOLDER OF MISOGYNY!
BEFORE MAKING HIM KISS MY BOOT!
I MISSED SEVEN IMPORTANT CALLS AND LOST A MAJOR CONTRACT!
...HAL...
YOU HAVE TO UNDERSTAND...
I DO.
I UNDERSTAND WE SAVED THE MULTIVERSE.
WE WERE GREAT TOGETHER.
WHAT ABOUT THE OTHER CAROL?
I SAW HOW YOU TWO LOOKED AT ONE ANOTHER...
WHAT ABOUT HER?
CAROL, I WAS DEAD NOT SO LONG AGO AND I SAW THE LIGHT!
COME WITH ME--AWAY FROM HERE--
AWAY FROM COAST CITY?
MY FRIENDS, MY FAMILY--
YOU KNOW THAT'S A BIG ASK...

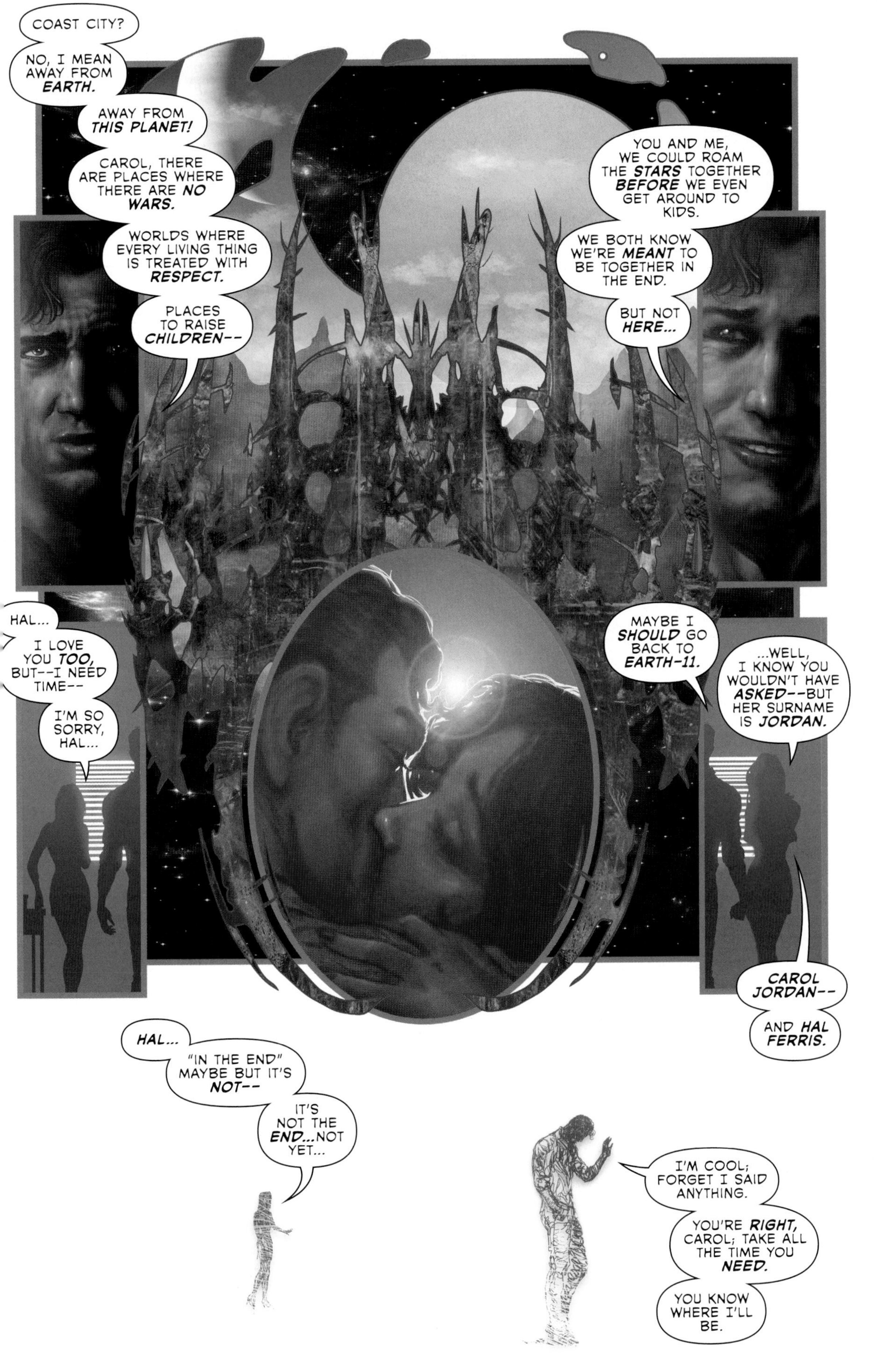
COAST CITY?
NO, I MEAN AWAY FROM EARTH.
AWAY FROM THIS PLANET!
CAROL, THERE ARE PLACES WHERE THERE ARE NO WARS.
WORLDS WHERE EVERY LIVING THING IS TREATED WITH RESPECT.
PLACES TO RAISE CHILDREN--
YOU AND ME, WE COULD ROAM THE STARS TOGETHER BEFORE WE EVEN GET AROUND TO KIDS.
WE BOTH KNOW WE'RE MEANT TO BE TOGETHER IN THE END.
BUT NOT HERE...
HAL...
I LOVE YOU TOO, BUT--I NEED TIME--
I'M SO SORRY, HAL...
MAYBE I SHOULD GO BACK TO EARTH-11.
...WELL, I KNOW YOU WOULDN'T HAVE ASKED--BUT HER SURNAME IS JORDAN.
CAROL JORDAN--
AND HAL FERRIS.
HAL...
"IN THE END" MAYBE BUT IT'S NOT--
IT'S NOT THE END...NOT YET...
I'M COOL; FORGET I SAID ANYTHING.
YOU'RE RIGHT, CAROL; TAKE ALL THE TIME YOU NEED.
YOU KNOW WHERE I'LL BE.

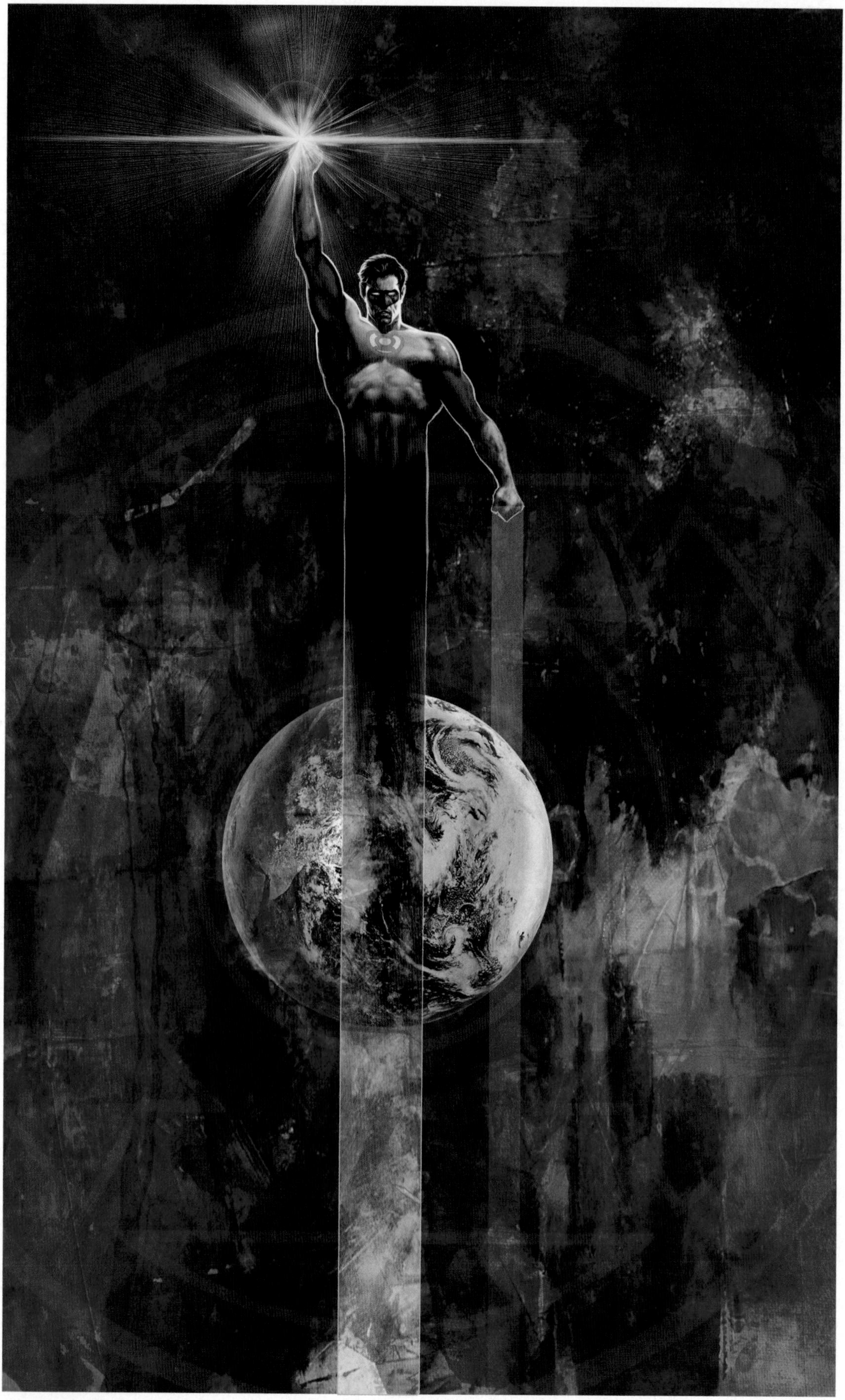

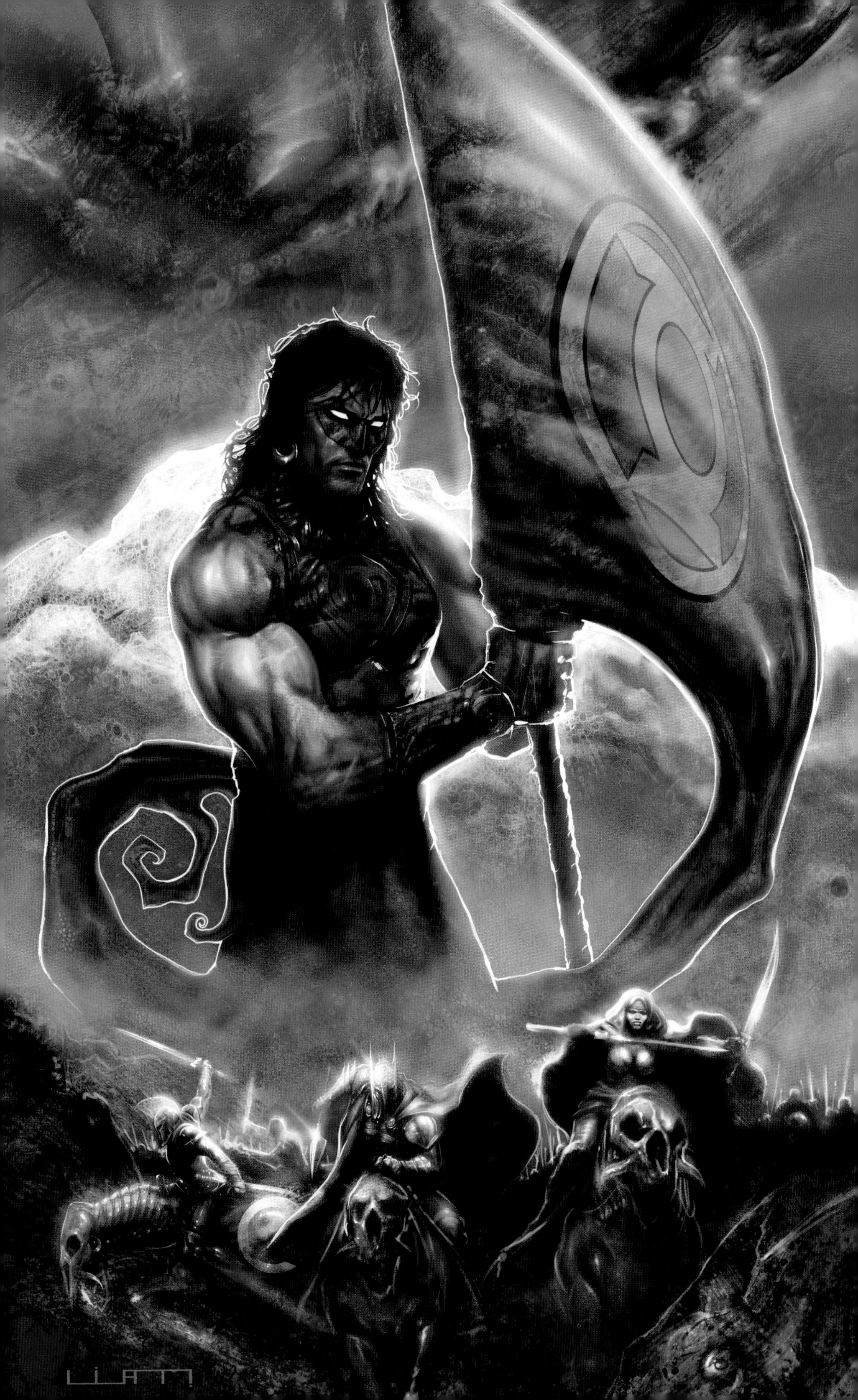

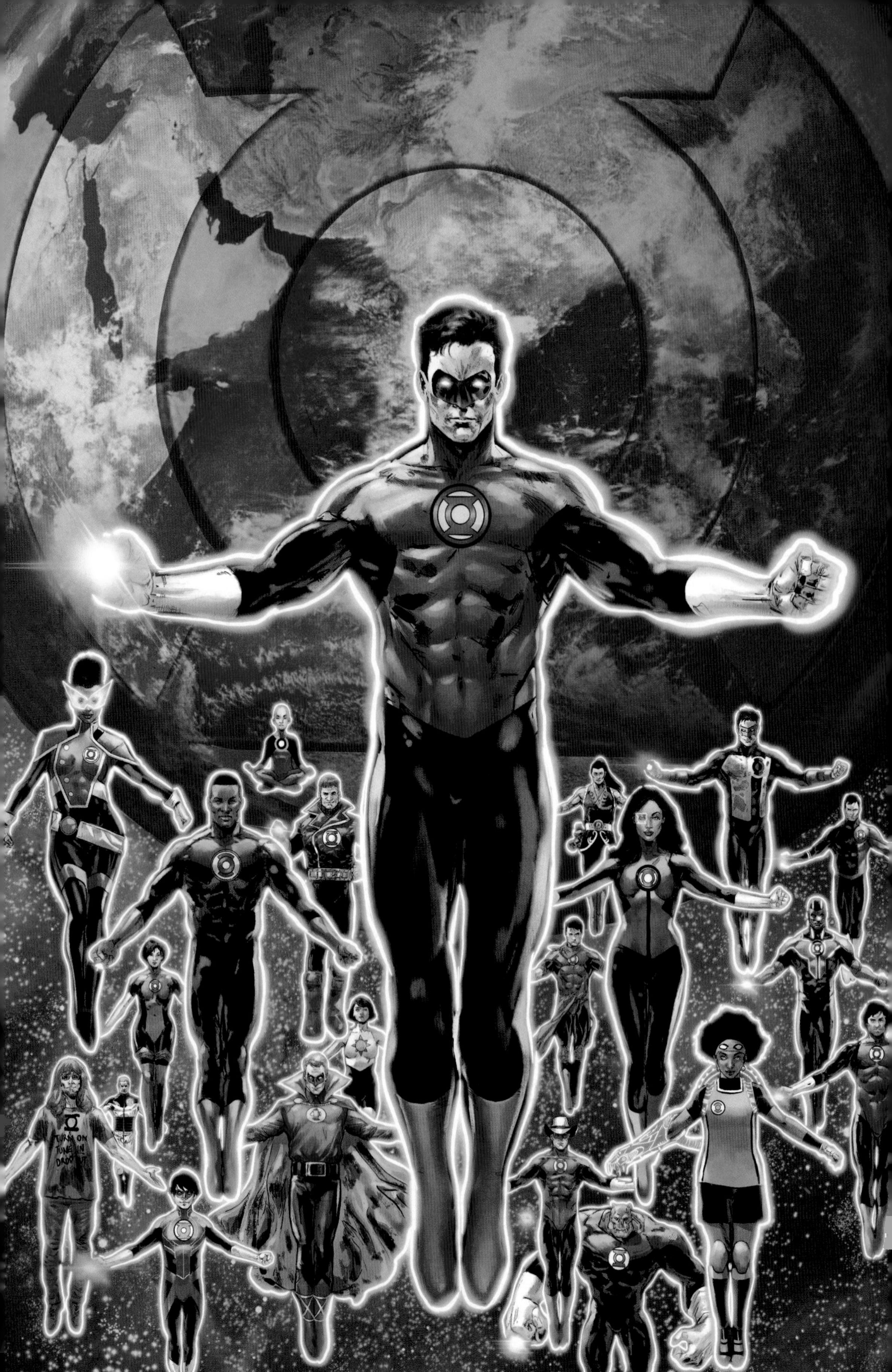
TURN ON
TUNE IN

The Green Lantern Season Two #11 variant cover by **PHIL JIMENEZ** & **ARIF PRIANTO**

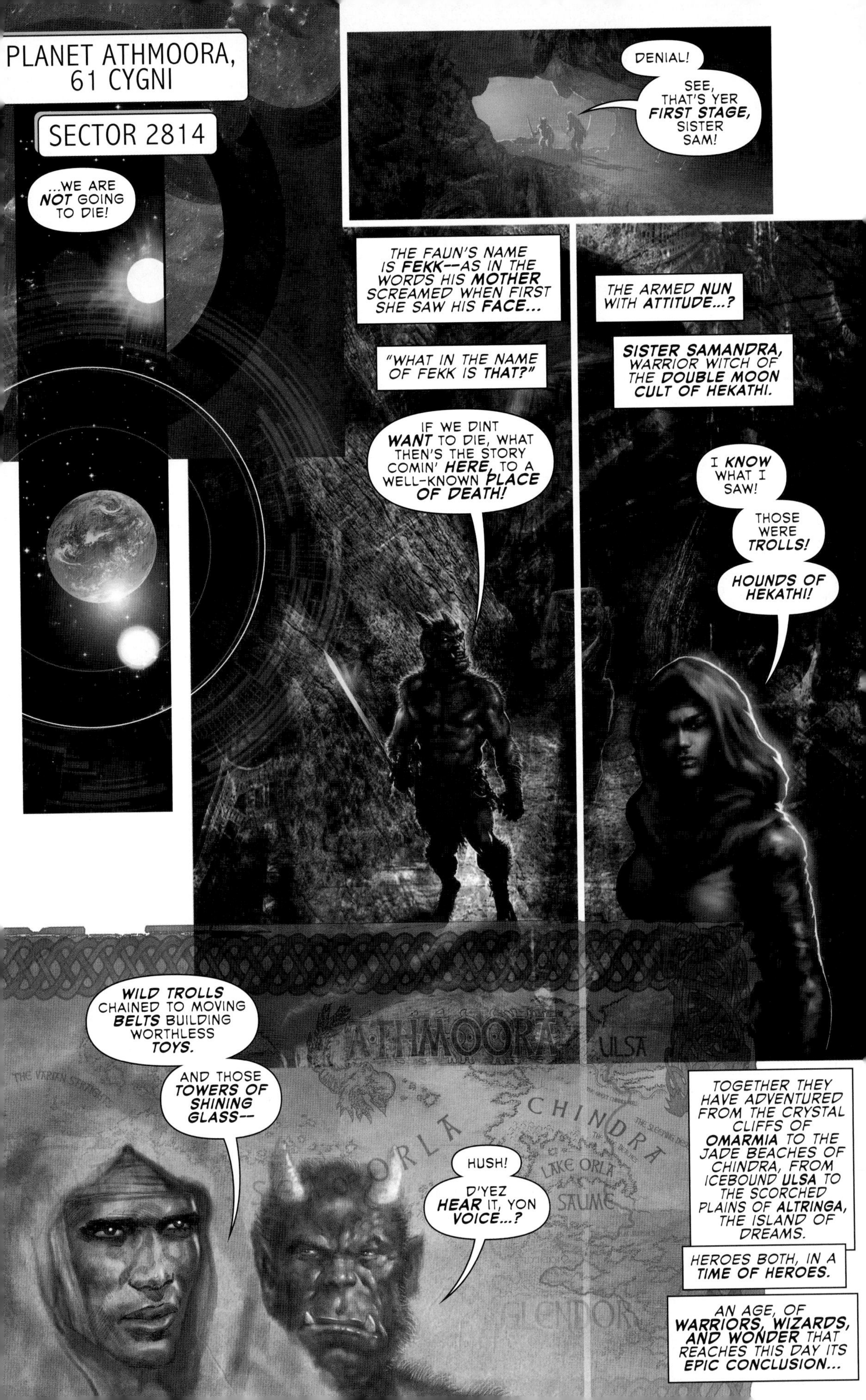
PLANET ATHMOORA, 61 CYGNI
SECTOR 2814
...WE ARE NOT GOING TO DIE!
DENIAL!
SEE, THAT'S YER FIRST STAGE, SISTER SAM!
THE FAUN'S NAME IS FEKK--AS IN THE WORDS HIS MOTHER SCREAMED WHEN FIRST SHE SAW HIS FACE...
"WHAT IN THE NAME OF FEKK IS THAT?"
IF WE DINT WANT TO DIE, WHAT THEN'S THE STORY COMIN' HERE, TO A WELL-KNOWN PLACE OF DEATH!
THE ARMED NUN WITH ATTITUDE...?
SISTER SAMANDRA, WARRIOR WITCH OF THE DOUBLE MOON CULT OF HEKATHI.
I KNOW WHAT I SAW!
THOSE WERE TROLLS!
HOUNDS OF HEKATHI!
WILD TROLLS CHAINED TO MOVING BELTS BUILDING WORTHLESS TOYS.
AND THOSE TOWERS OF SHINING GLASS--
ATHMOORA
ULSA
CHINDRA
ORLA
LAKE ORLA
SAUME
HUSH!
D'YEZ HEAR IT, YON VOICE...?
TOGETHER THEY HAVE ADVENTURED FROM THE CRYSTAL CLIFFS OF OMARMIA TO THE JADE BEACHES OF CHINDRA, FROM ICEBOUND ULSA TO THE SCORCHED PLAINS OF ALTRINGA, THE ISLAND OF DREAMS.
HEROES BOTH, IN A TIME OF HEROES.
AN AGE, OF WARRIORS, WIZARDS, AND WONDER THAT REACHES THIS DAY ITS EPIC CONCLUSION...

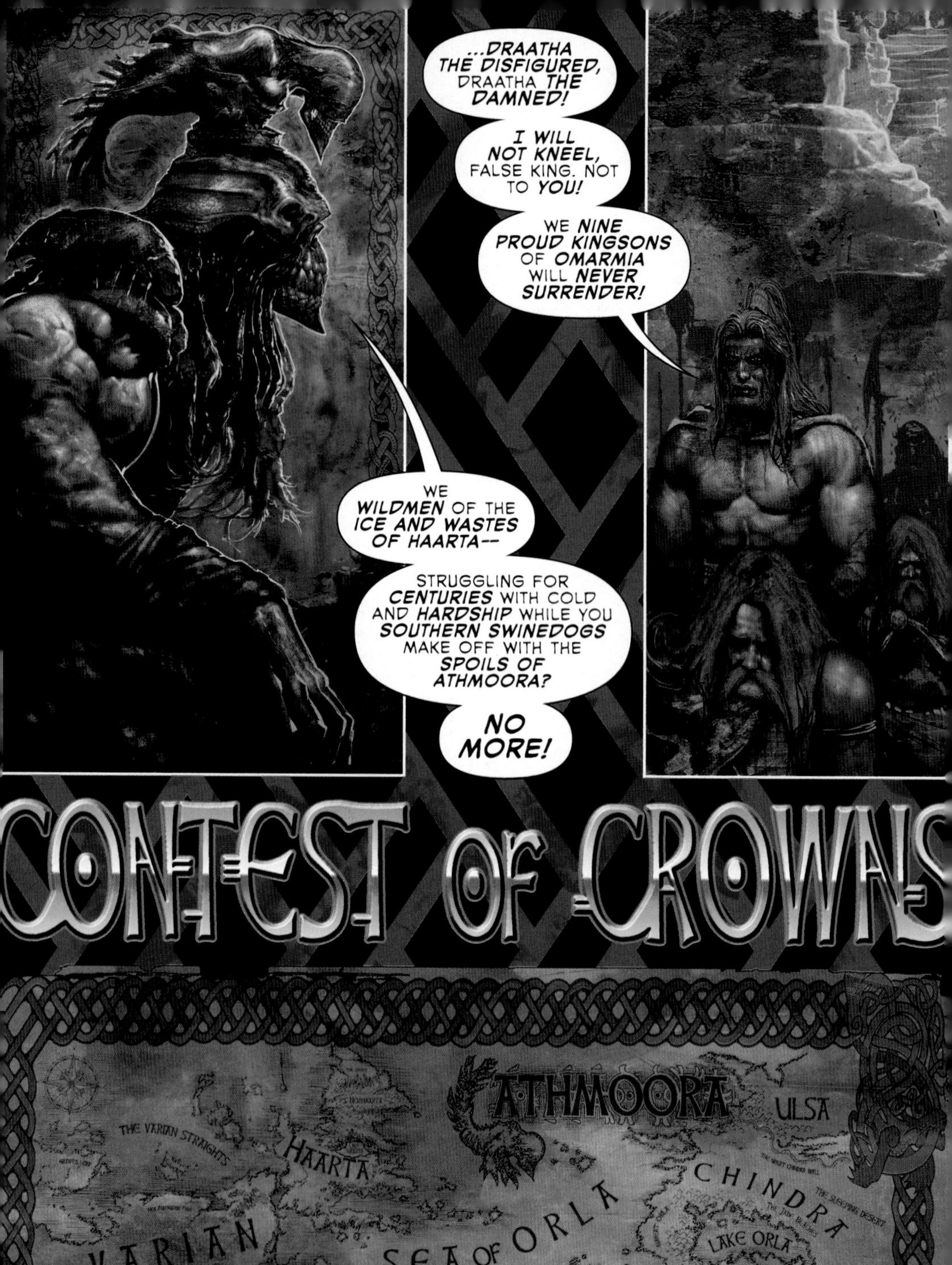
...DRAATHA THE DISFIGURED, DRAATHA THE DAMNED!
I WILL NOT KNEEL, FALSE KING. NOT TO YOU!
WE NINE PROUD KINGSONS OF OMARMIA WILL NEVER SURRENDER!
WE WILDMEN OF THE ICE AND WASTES OF HAARTA--
STRUGGLING FOR CENTURIES WITH COLD AND HARDSHIP WHILE YOU SOUTHERN SWINEDOGS MAKE OFF WITH THE SPOILS OF ATHMOORA?
NO MORE!
CONTEST OF CROWNS
ATHMOORA
ULSA
THE VARIAN STRAIGHTS
HAARTA
CHINDRA
THE SLEEPING DESERT
VARIAN
SEA OF ORLA
LAKE ORLA
SAUME
THE VITRIFIED DESERT
DORDRUM
OMARMIA
GLENDOR
SEA OF RATHMOOR
ALTRINGA

Writer: Grant Morrison Art and Color: Liam Sharp
Letters: Steve Wands Cover: Liam Sharp
Variant Cover: Phil Jimenez and Arif Prianto
Assistant Editor: Marquis Draper Editor: Andrew Marino

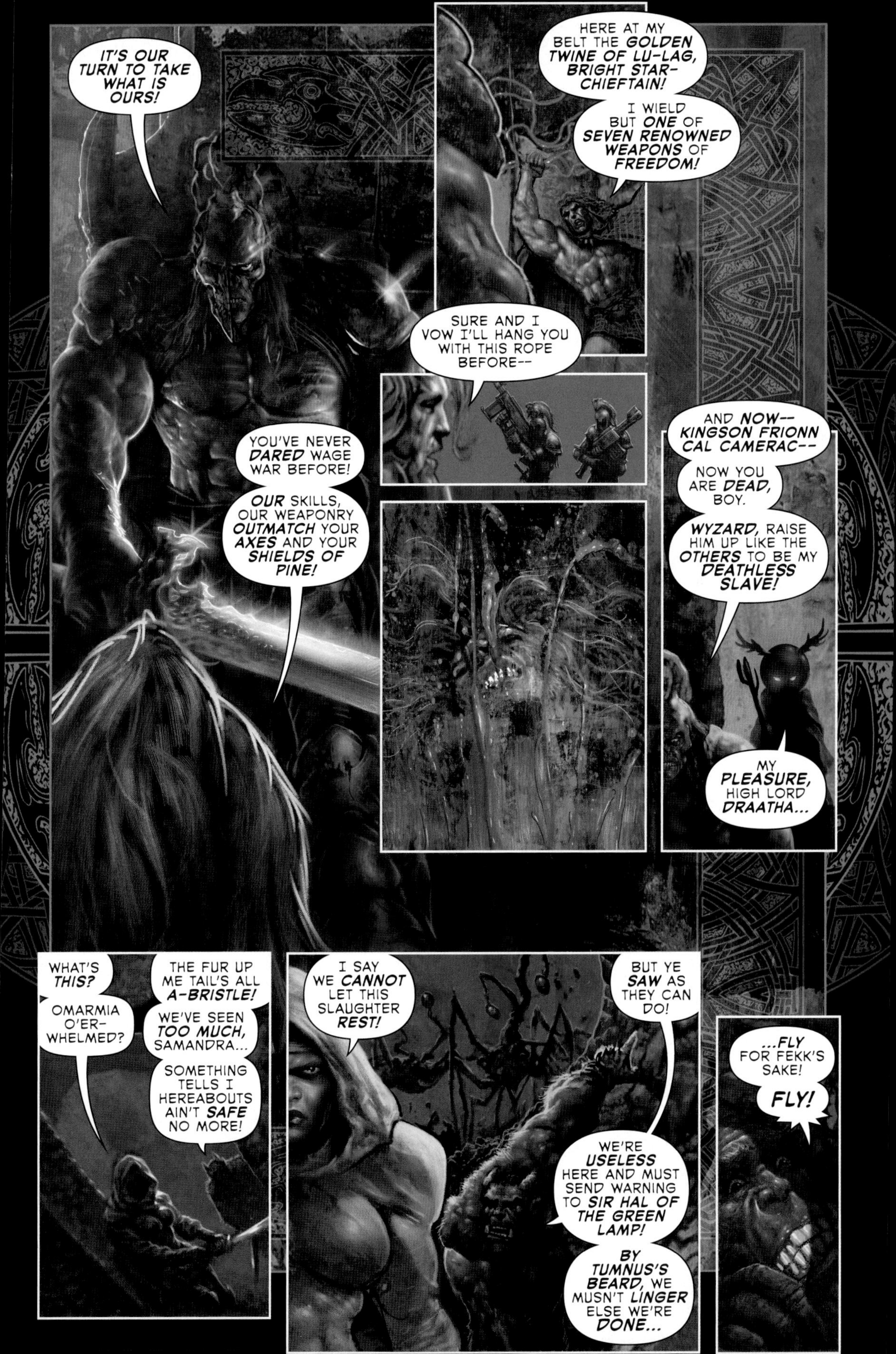
IT'S OUR TURN TO TAKE WHAT IS OURS!
HERE AT MY BELT THE GOLDEN TWINE OF LU-LAG, BRIGHT STAR-CHIEFTAIN!
I WIELD BUT ONE OF SEVEN RENOWNED WEAPONS OF FREEDOM!
SURE AND I VOW I'LL HANG YOU WITH THIS ROPE BEFORE--
YOU'VE NEVER DARED WAGE WAR BEFORE!
OUR SKILLS, OUR WEAPONRY OUTMATCH YOUR AXES AND YOUR SHIELDS OF PINE!
AND NOW--KINGSON FRIONN CAL CAMERAC--
NOW YOU ARE DEAD, BOY.
WYZARD, RAISE HIM UP LIKE THE OTHERS TO BE MY DEATHLESS SLAVE!
MY PLEASURE, HIGH LORD DRAATHA...
WHAT'S THIS?
OMARMIA O'ER-WHELMED?
THE FUR UP ME TAIL'S ALL A-BRISTLE!
WE'VE SEEN TOO MUCH, SAMANDRA...
SOMETHING TELLS I HEREABOUTS AIN'T SAFE NO MORE!
I SAY WE CANNOT LET THIS SLAUGHTER REST!
BUT YE SAW AS THEY CAN DO!
WE'RE USELESS HERE AND MUST SEND WARNING TO SIR HAL OF THE GREEN LAMP!
BY TUMNUS'S BEARD, WE MUSN'T LINGER ELSE WE'RE DONE...
...FLY FOR FEKK'S SAKE!
FLY!

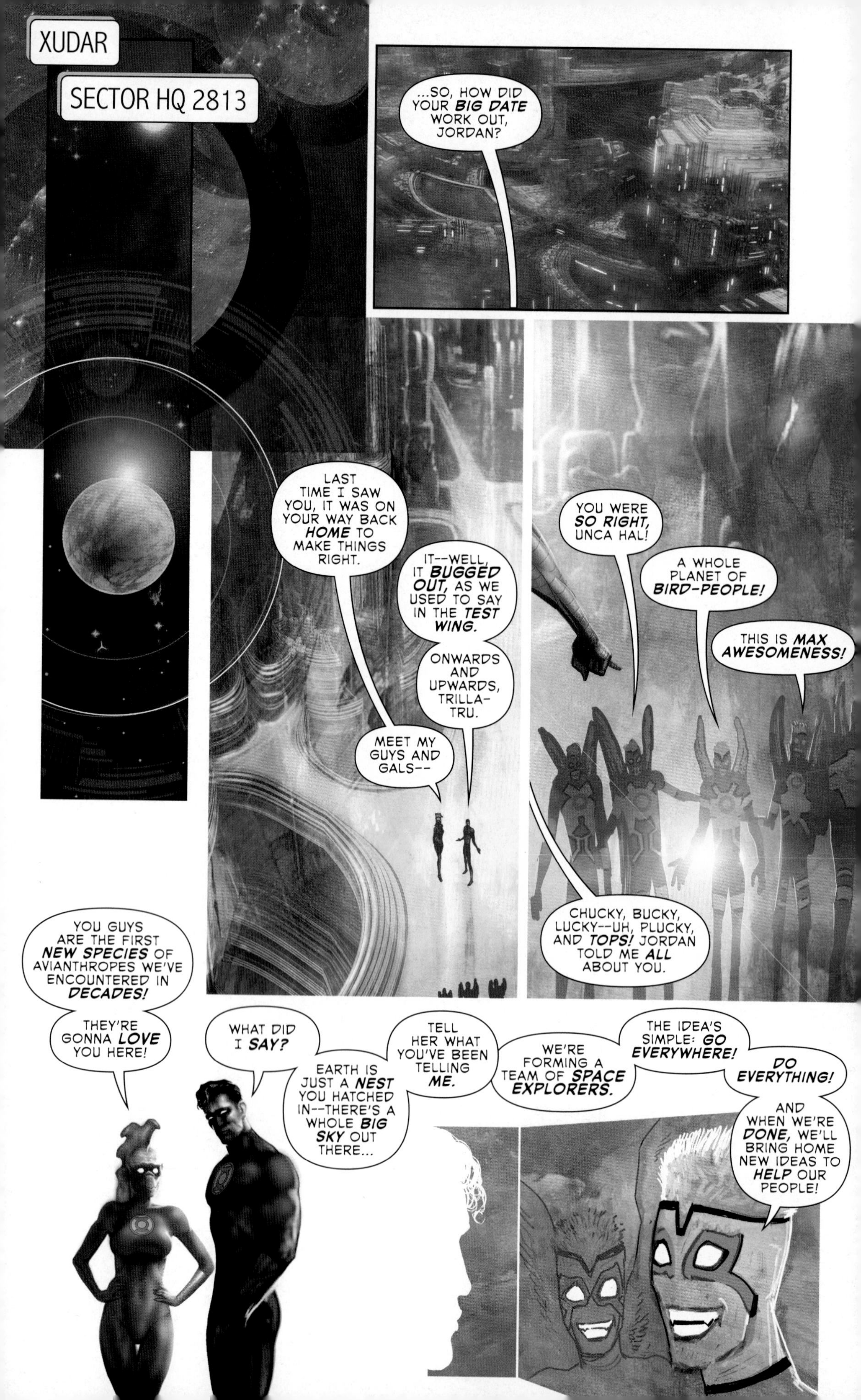
XUDAR
SECTOR HQ 2813
...SO, HOW DID YOUR BIG DATE WORK OUT, JORDAN?
LAST TIME I SAW YOU, IT WAS ON YOUR WAY BACK HOME TO MAKE THINGS RIGHT.
IT--WELL, IT BUGGED OUT, AS WE USED TO SAY IN THE TEST WING.
ONWARDS AND UPWARDS, TRILLA-TRU.
MEET MY GUYS AND GALS--
YOU WERE SO RIGHT, UNCA HAL!
A WHOLE PLANET OF BIRD-PEOPLE!
THIS IS MAX AWESOMENESS!
CHUCKY, BUCKY, LUCKY--UH, PLUCKY, AND TOPS! JORDAN TOLD ME ALL ABOUT YOU.
YOU GUYS ARE THE FIRST NEW SPECIES OF AVIANTHROPES WE'VE ENCOUNTERED IN DECADES!
THEY'RE GONNA LOVE YOU HERE!
WHAT DID I SAY?
EARTH IS JUST A NEST YOU HATCHED IN--THERE'S A WHOLE BIG SKY OUT THERE...
TELL HER WHAT YOU'VE BEEN TELLING ME.
WE'RE FORMING A TEAM OF SPACE EXPLORERS.
THE IDEA'S SIMPLE: GO EVERYWHERE!
DO EVERYTHING!
AND WHEN WE'RE DONE, WE'LL BRING HOME NEW IDEAS TO HELP OUR PEOPLE!

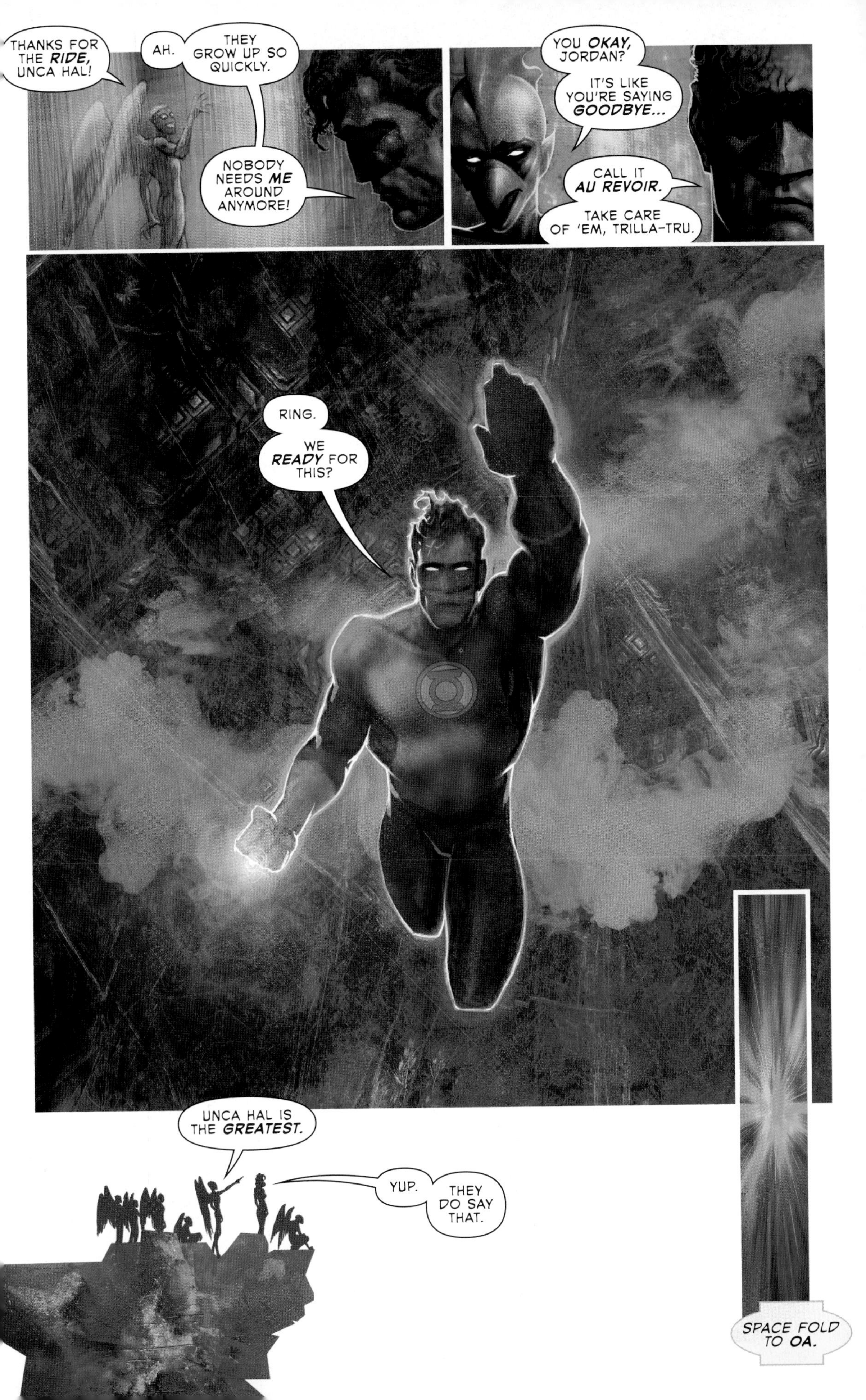
THANKS FOR THE RIDE, UNCA HAL!
AH.
THEY GROW UP SO QUICKLY.
NOBODY NEEDS ME AROUND ANYMORE!
YOU OKAY, JORDAN?
IT'S LIKE YOU'RE SAYING GOODBYE...
CALL IT AU REVOIR.
TAKE CARE OF 'EM, TRILLA-TRU.
RING.
WE READY FOR THIS?
UNCA HAL IS THE GREATEST.
YUP.
THEY DO SAY THAT.
SPACE FOLD TO OA.

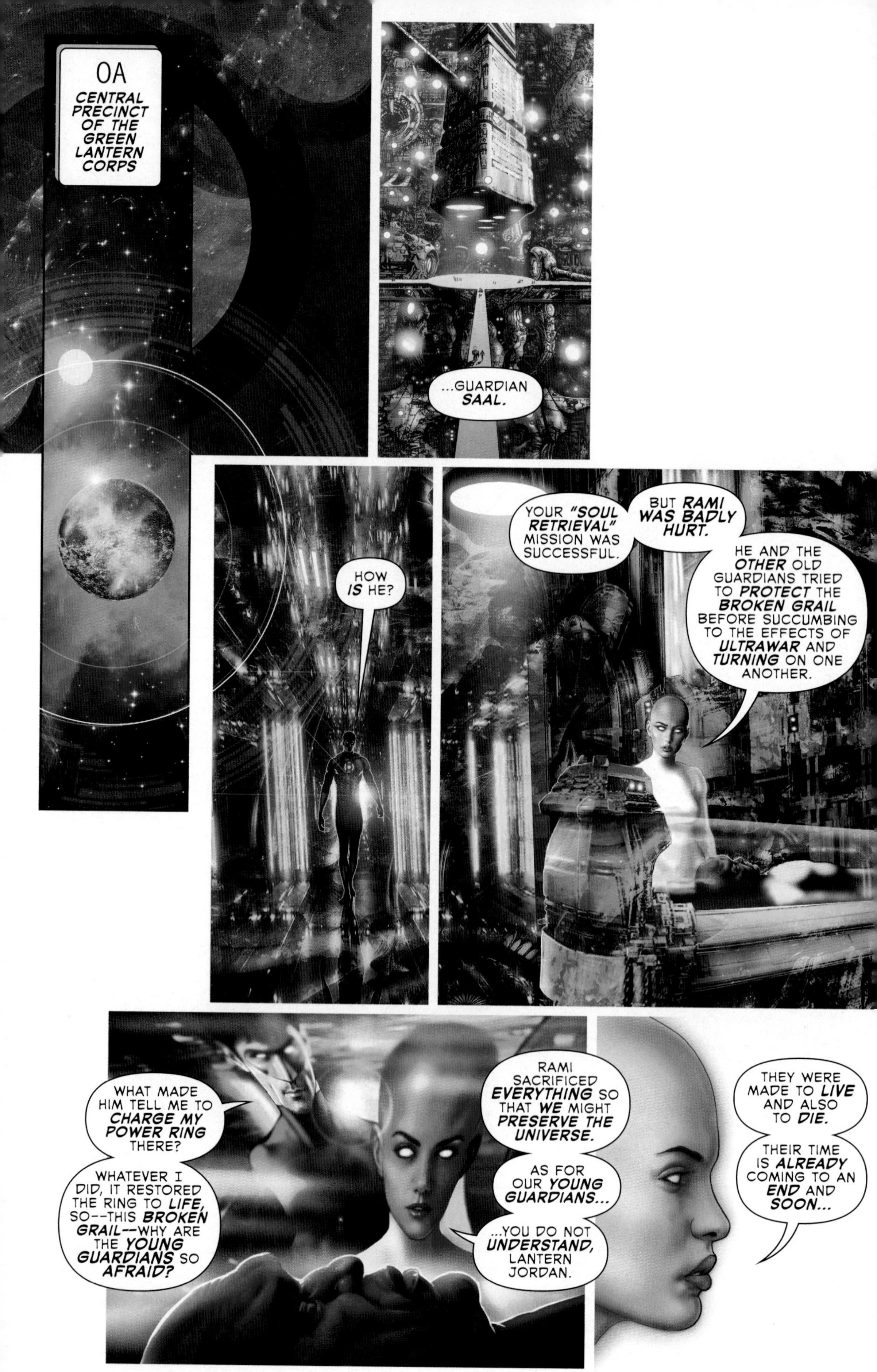
OA
CENTRAL PRECINCT OF THE GREEN LANTERN CORPS
...GUARDIAN SAAL.
HOW IS HE?
YOUR "SOUL RETRIEVAL" MISSION WAS SUCCESSFUL.
BUT RAMI WAS BADLY HURT.
HE AND THE OTHER OLD GUARDIANS TRIED TO PROTECT THE BROKEN GRAIL BEFORE SUCCUMBING TO THE EFFECTS OF ULTRAWAR AND TURNING ON ONE ANOTHER.
WHAT MADE HIM TELL ME TO CHARGE MY POWER RING THERE?
WHATEVER I DID, IT RESTORED THE RING TO LIFE, SO--THIS BROKEN GRAIL--WHY ARE THE YOUNG GUARDIANS SO AFRAID?
RAMI SACRIFICED EVERYTHING SO THAT WE MIGHT PRESERVE THE UNIVERSE.
AS FOR OUR YOUNG GUARDIANS...
...YOU DO NOT UNDERSTAND, LANTERN JORDAN.
THEY WERE MADE TO LIVE AND ALSO TO DIE.
THEIR TIME IS ALREADY COMING TO AN END AND SOON...

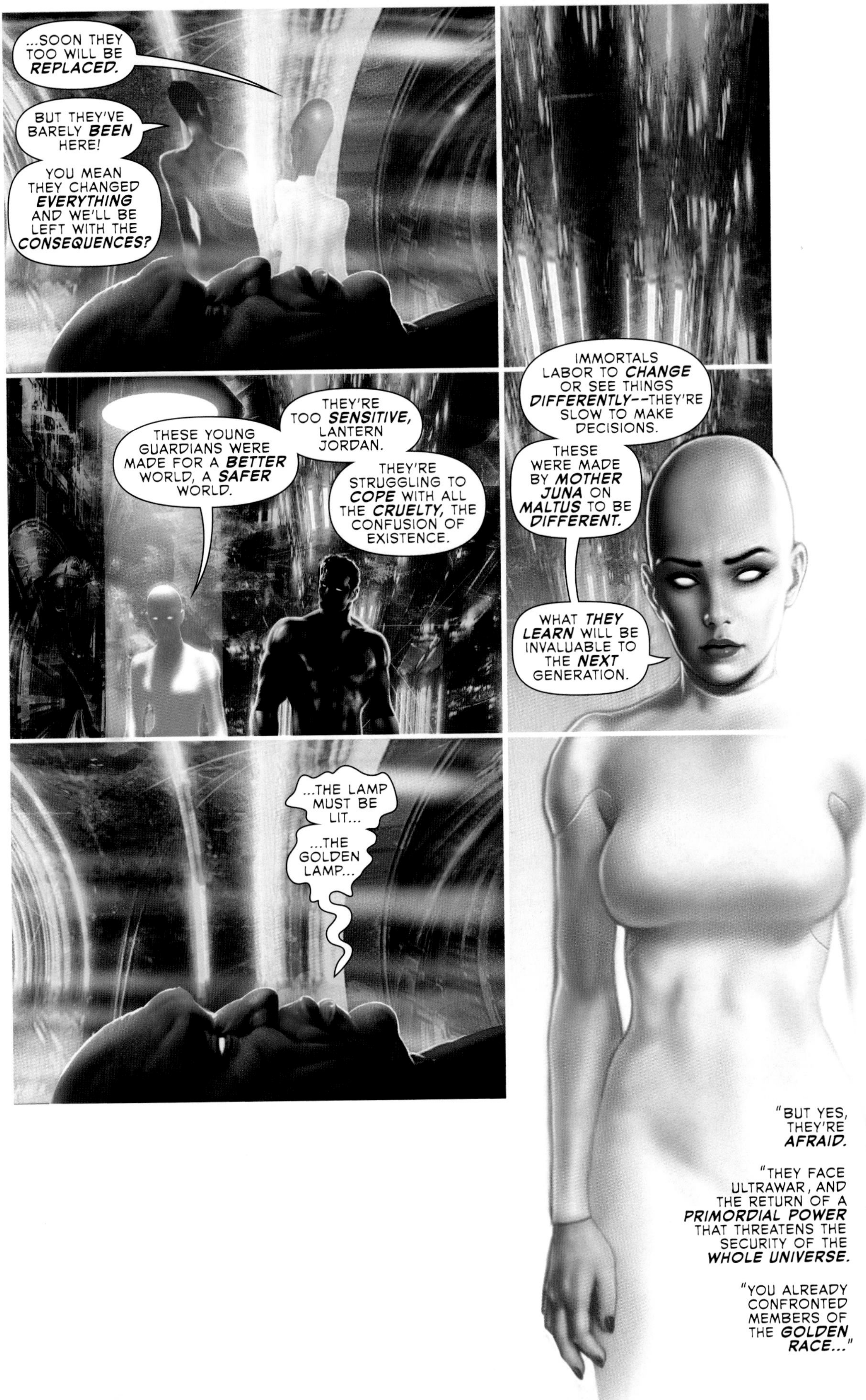
...SOON THEY TOO WILL BE REPLACED.
BUT THEY'VE BARELY BEEN HERE!
YOU MEAN THEY CHANGED EVERYTHING AND WE'LL BE LEFT WITH THE CONSEQUENCES?
IMMORTALS LABOR TO CHANGE OR SEE THINGS DIFFERENTLY--THEY'RE SLOW TO MAKE DECISIONS.
THESE WERE MADE BY MOTHER JUNA ON MALTUS TO BE DIFFERENT.
THESE YOUNG GUARDIANS WERE MADE FOR A BETTER WORLD, A SAFER WORLD.
THEY'RE TOO SENSITIVE, LANTERN JORDAN.
THEY'RE STRUGGLING TO COPE WITH ALL THE CRUELTY, THE CONFUSION OF EXISTENCE.
WHAT THEY LEARN WILL BE INVALUABLE TO THE NEXT GENERATION.
...THE LAMP MUST BE LIT...
...THE GOLDEN LAMP...
"BUT YES, THEY'RE AFRAID.
"THEY FACE ULTRAWAR, AND THE RETURN OF A PRIMORDIAL POWER THAT THREATENS THE SECURITY OF THE WHOLE UNIVERSE.
"YOU ALREADY CONFRONTED MEMBERS OF THE GOLDEN RACE..."

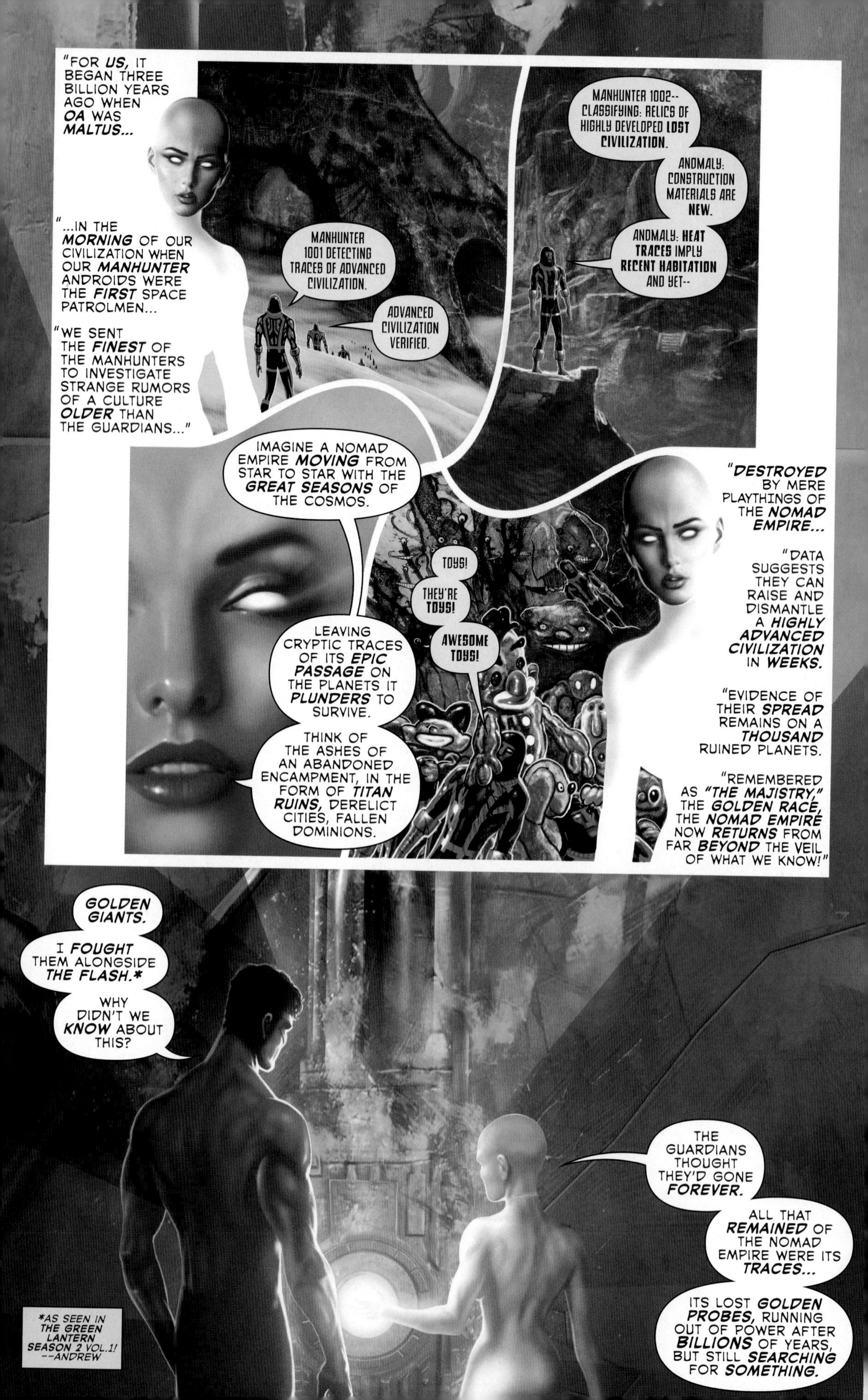
"FOR US, IT BEGAN THREE BILLION YEARS AGO WHEN OA WAS MALTUS...
"...IN THE MORNING OF OUR CIVILIZATION WHEN OUR MANHUNTER ANDROIDS WERE THE FIRST SPACE PATROLMEN...
"WE SENT THE FINEST OF THE MANHUNTERS TO INVESTIGATE STRANGE RUMORS OF A CULTURE OLDER THAN THE GUARDIANS..."
MANHUNTER 1001 DETECTING TRACES OF ADVANCED CIVILIZATION.
ADVANCED CIVILIZATION VERIFIED.
MANHUNTER 1002-- CLASSIFYING: RELICS OF HIGHLY DEVELOPED LOST CIVILIZATION.
ANOMALY: CONSTRUCTION MATERIALS ARE NEW.
ANOMALY: HEAT TRACES IMPLY RECENT HABITATION AND YET--
IMAGINE A NOMAD EMPIRE MOVING FROM STAR TO STAR WITH THE GREAT SEASONS OF THE COSMOS.
LEAVING CRYPTIC TRACES OF ITS EPIC PASSAGE ON THE PLANETS IT PLUNDERS TO SURVIVE.
THINK OF THE ASHES OF AN ABANDONED ENCAMPMENT, IN THE FORM OF TITAN RUINS, DERELICT CITIES, FALLEN DOMINIONS.
TOYS!
THEY'RE TOYS!
AWESOME TOYS!
"DESTROYED BY MERE PLAYTHINGS OF THE NOMAD EMPIRE...
"DATA SUGGESTS THEY CAN RAISE AND DISMANTLE A HIGHLY ADVANCED CIVILIZATION IN WEEKS.
"EVIDENCE OF THEIR SPREAD REMAINS ON A THOUSAND RUINED PLANETS.
"REMEMBERED AS "THE MAJISTRY," THE GOLDEN RACE, THE NOMAD EMPIRE NOW RETURNS FROM FAR BEYOND THE VEIL OF WHAT WE KNOW!"
GOLDEN GIANTS.
I FOUGHT THEM ALONGSIDE THE FLASH.*
WHY DIDN'T WE KNOW ABOUT THIS?
THE GUARDIANS THOUGHT THEY'D GONE FOREVER.
ALL THAT REMAINED OF THE NOMAD EMPIRE WERE ITS TRACES...
ITS LOST GOLDEN PROBES, RUNNING OUT OF POWER AFTER BILLIONS OF YEARS, BUT STILL SEARCHING FOR SOMETHING.
*AS SEEN IN THE GREEN LANTERN SEASON 2 VOL.1! --ANDREW

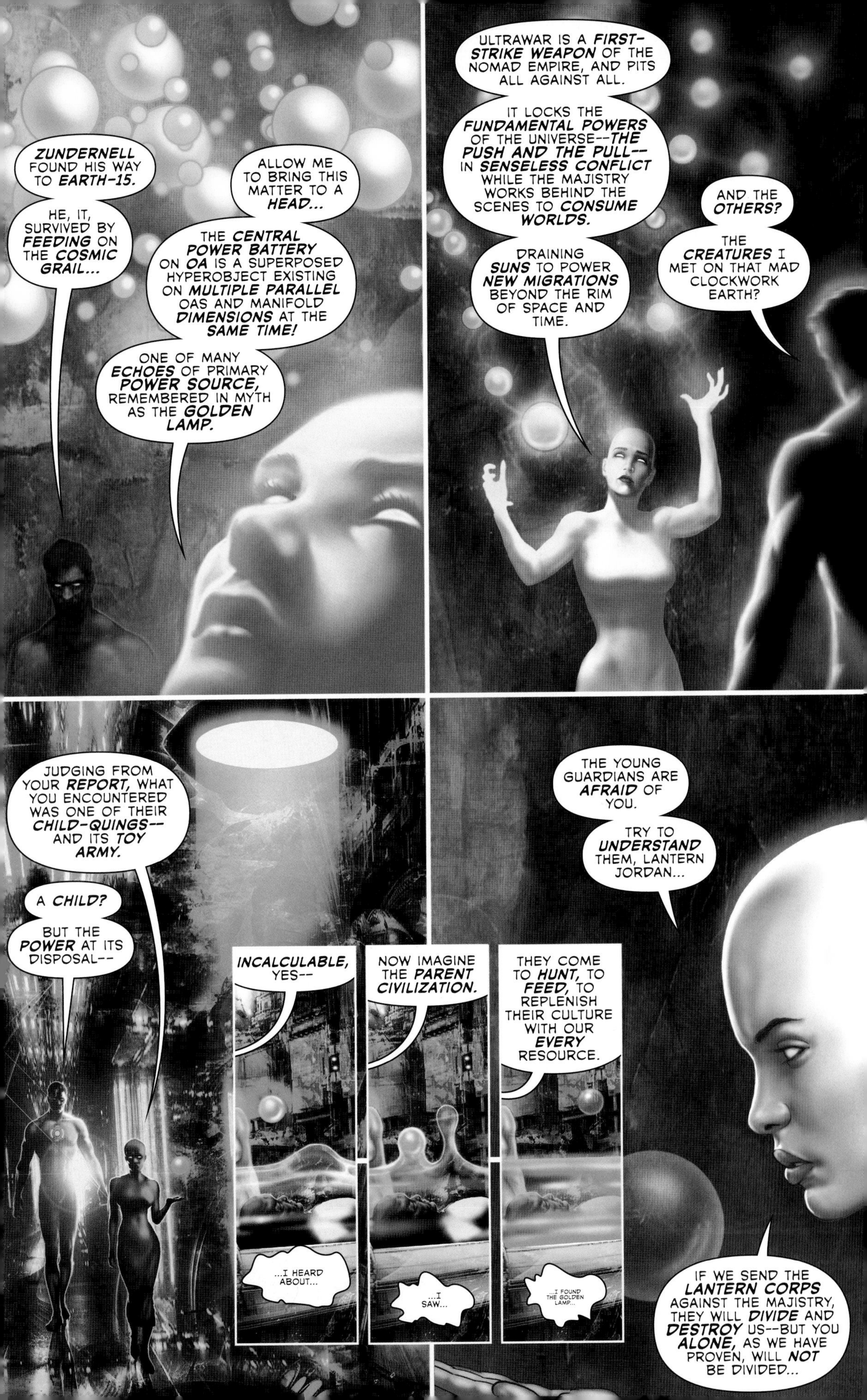

ZUNDERNELL FOUND HIS WAY TO EARTH-15.
HE, IT, SURVIVED BY FEEDING ON THE COSMIC GRAIL...
ALLOW ME TO BRING THIS MATTER TO A HEAD...
THE CENTRAL POWER BATTERY ON OA IS A SUPERPOSED HYPEROBJECT EXISTING ON MULTIPLE PARALLEL OAS AND MANIFOLD DIMENSIONS AT THE SAME TIME!
ONE OF MANY ECHOES OF PRIMARY POWER SOURCE, REMEMBERED IN MYTH AS THE GOLDEN LAMP.
ULTRAWAR IS A FIRST-STRIKE WEAPON OF THE NOMAD EMPIRE, AND PITS ALL AGAINST ALL.
IT LOCKS THE FUNDAMENTAL POWERS OF THE UNIVERSE--THE PUSH AND THE PULL--IN SENSELESS CONFLICT WHILE THE MAJISTRY WORKS BEHIND THE SCENES TO CONSUME WORLDS.
DRAINING SUNS TO POWER NEW MIGRATIONS BEYOND THE RIM OF SPACE AND TIME.
AND THE OTHERS?
THE CREATURES I MET ON THAT MAD CLOCKWORK EARTH?
JUDGING FROM YOUR REPORT, WHAT YOU ENCOUNTERED WAS ONE OF THEIR CHILD-QUINGS--AND ITS TOY ARMY.
A CHILD?
BUT THE POWER AT ITS DISPOSAL--
INCALCULABLE, YES--
...I HEARD ABOUT...
NOW IMAGINE THE PARENT CIVILIZATION.
...I SAW...
THEY COME TO HUNT, TO FEED, TO REPLENISH THEIR CULTURE WITH OUR EVERY RESOURCE.
...I FOUND THE GOLDEN LAMP...
THE YOUNG GUARDIANS ARE AFRAID OF YOU.
TRY TO UNDERSTAND THEM, LANTERN JORDAN...
IF WE SEND THE LANTERN CORPS AGAINST THE MAJISTRY, THEY WILL DIVIDE AND DESTROY US--BUT YOU ALONE, AS WE HAVE PROVEN, WILL NOT BE DIVIDED...

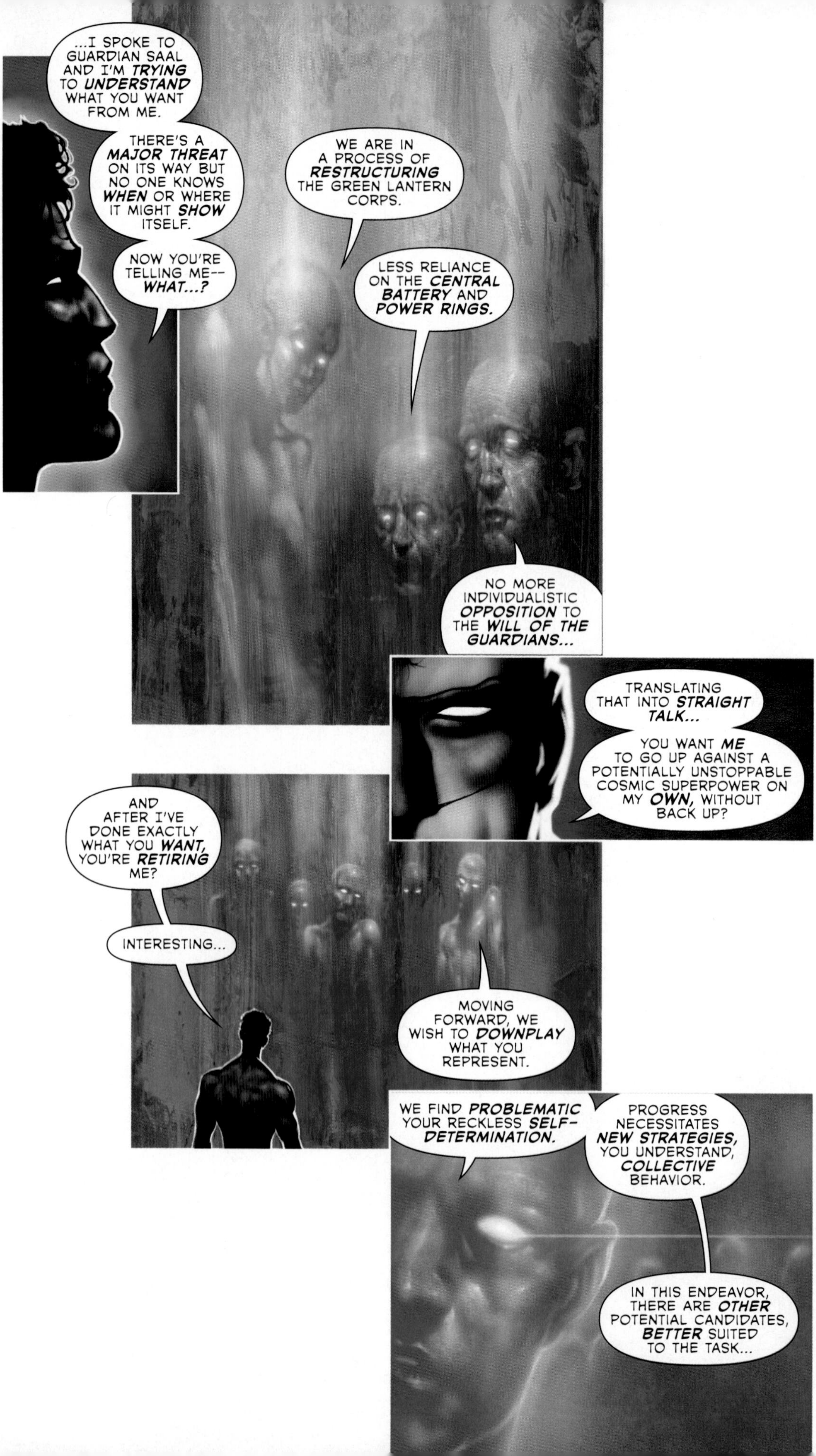

...I SPOKE TO GUARDIAN SAAL AND I'M TRYING TO UNDERSTAND WHAT YOU WANT FROM ME.
THERE'S A MAJOR THREAT ON ITS WAY BUT NO ONE KNOWS WHEN OR WHERE IT MIGHT SHOW ITSELF.
NOW YOU'RE TELLING ME-- WHAT...?
WE ARE IN A PROCESS OF RESTRUCTURING THE GREEN LANTERN CORPS.
LESS RELIANCE ON THE CENTRAL BATTERY AND POWER RINGS.
NO MORE INDIVIDUALISTIC OPPOSITION TO THE WILL OF THE GUARDIANS...
TRANSLATING THAT INTO STRAIGHT TALK...
YOU WANT ME TO GO UP AGAINST A POTENTIALLY UNSTOPPABLE COSMIC SUPERPOWER ON MY OWN, WITHOUT BACK UP?
AND AFTER I'VE DONE EXACTLY WHAT YOU WANT, YOU'RE RETIRING ME?
INTERESTING...
MOVING FORWARD, WE WISH TO DOWNPLAY WHAT YOU REPRESENT.
WE FIND PROBLEMATIC YOUR RECKLESS SELF-DETERMINATION.
PROGRESS NECESSITATES NEW STRATEGIES, YOU UNDERSTAND, COLLECTIVE BEHAVIOR.
IN THIS ENDEAVOR, THERE ARE OTHER POTENTIAL CANDIDATES, BETTER SUITED TO THE TASK...

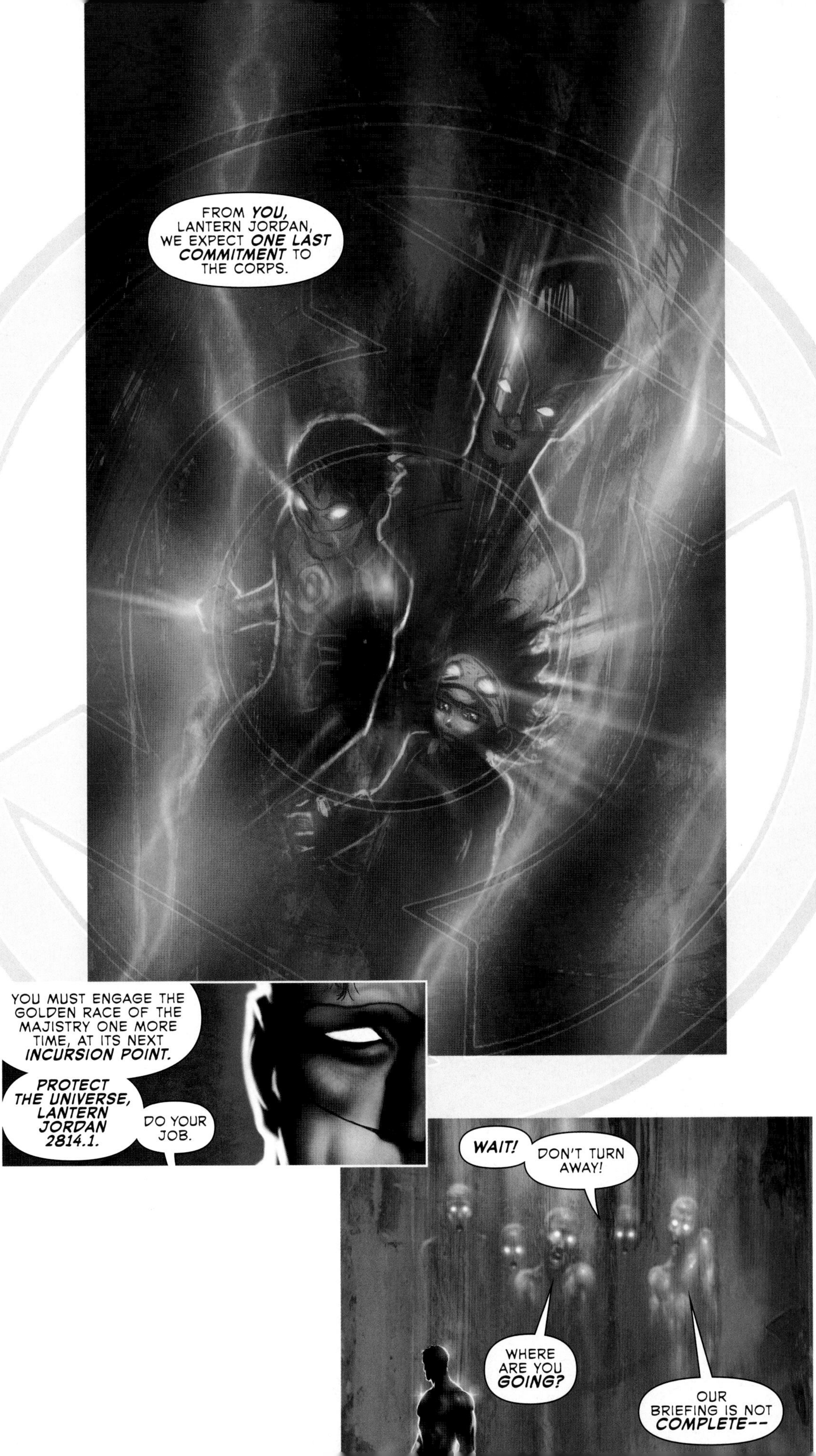

FROM YOU, LANTERN JORDAN, WE EXPECT ONE LAST COMMITMENT TO THE CORPS.
YOU MUST ENGAGE THE GOLDEN RACE OF THE MAJISTRY ONE MORE TIME, AT ITS NEXT INCURSION POINT.
PROTECT THE UNIVERSE, LANTERN JORDAN 2814.1.
DO YOUR JOB.
WAIT!
DON'T TURN AWAY!
WHERE ARE YOU GOING?
OUR BRIEFING IS NOT COMPLETE--

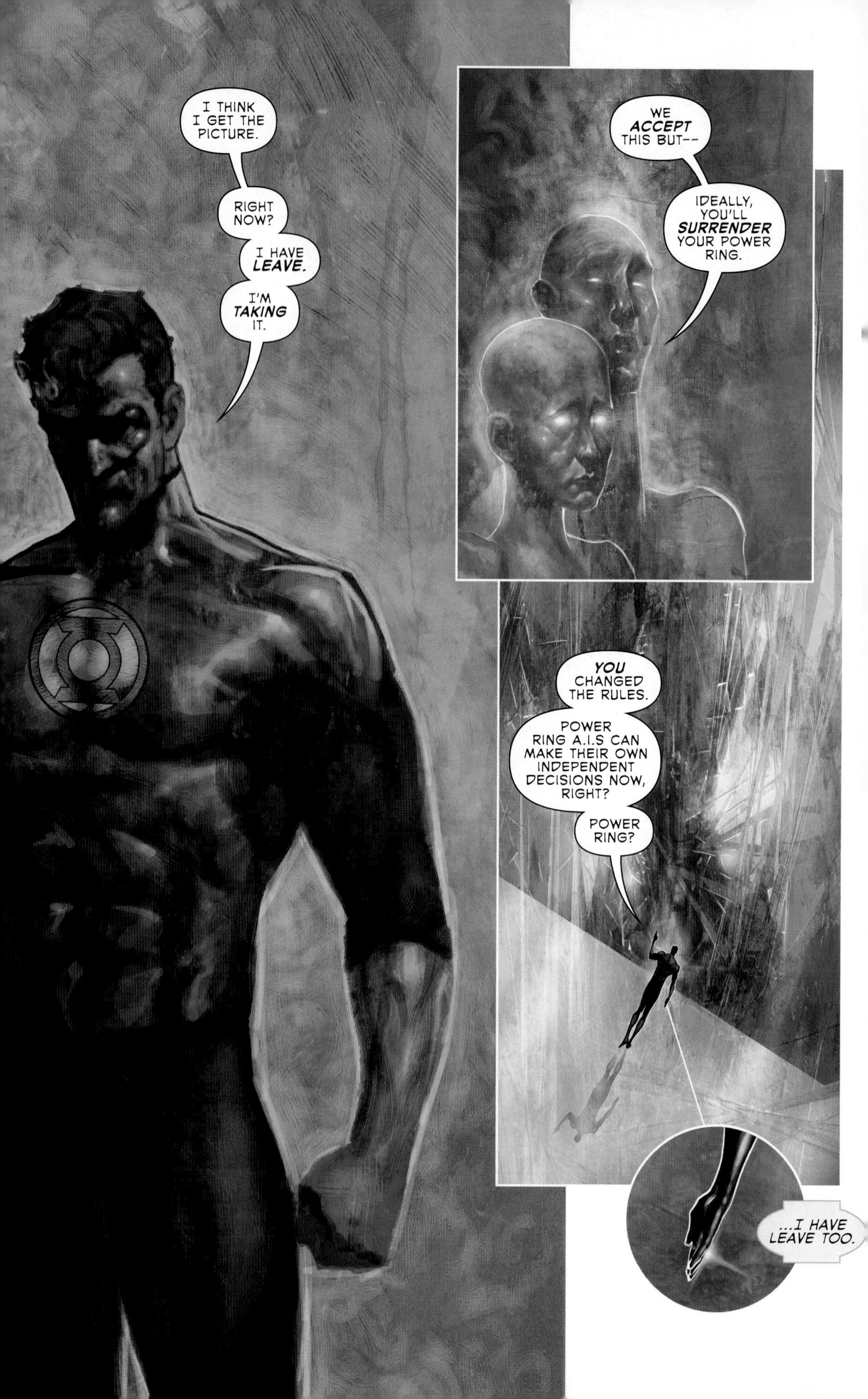
I THINK I GET THE PICTURE.
RIGHT NOW?
I HAVE LEAVE.
I'M TAKING IT.
WE ACCEPT THIS BUT--
IDEALLY, YOU'LL SURRENDER YOUR POWER RING.
YOU CHANGED THE RULES.
POWER RING A.I.S CAN MAKE THEIR OWN INDEPENDENT DECISIONS NOW, RIGHT?
POWER RING?
...I HAVE LEAVE TOO.

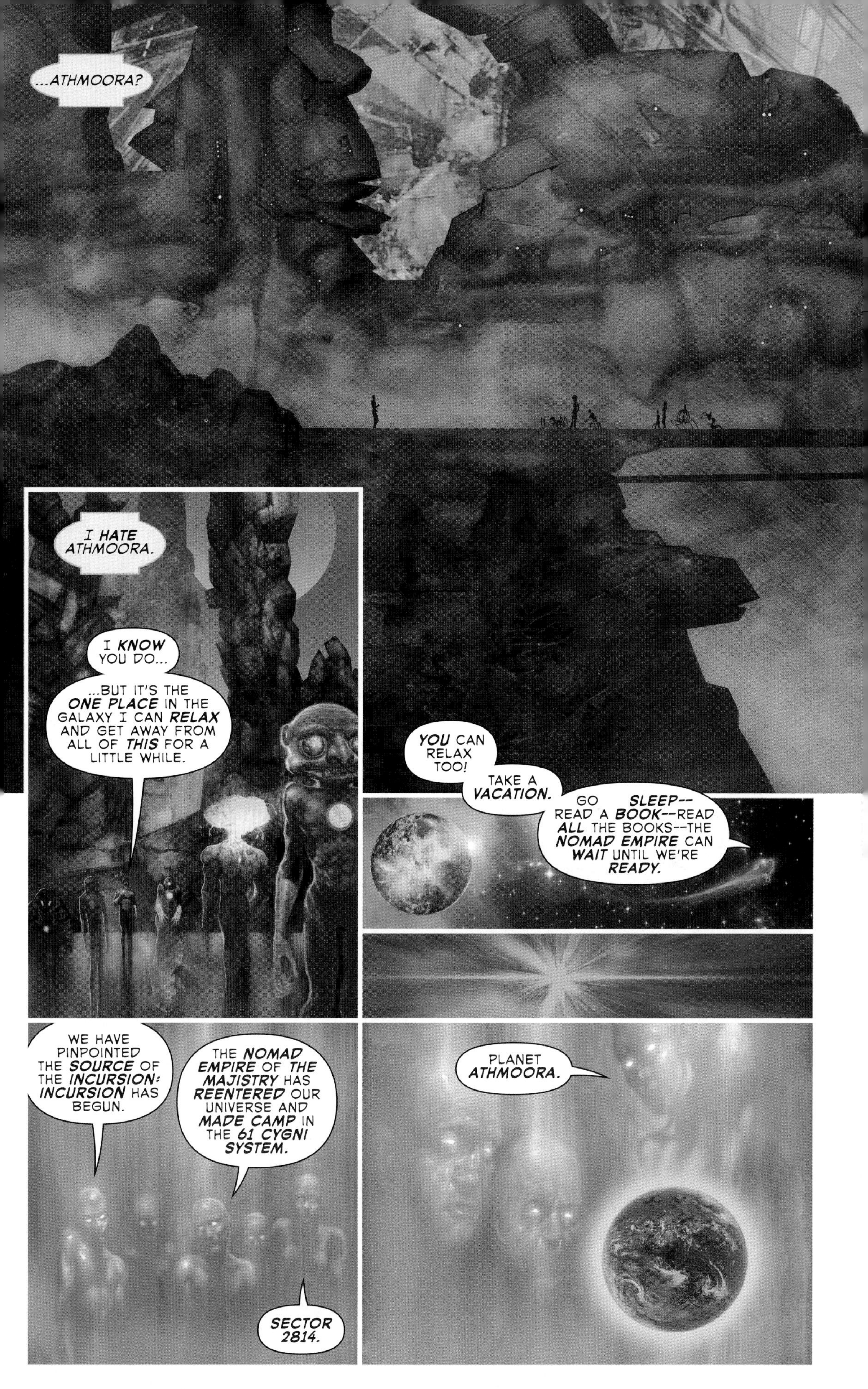
...ATHMOORA?
I HATE ATHMOORA.
I KNOW YOU DO...
...BUT IT'S THE ONE PLACE IN THE GALAXY I CAN RELAX AND GET AWAY FROM ALL OF THIS FOR A LITTLE WHILE.
YOU CAN RELAX TOO!
TAKE A VACATION.
GO SLEEP--READ A BOOK--READ ALL THE BOOKS--THE NOMAD EMPIRE CAN WAIT UNTIL WE'RE READY.
WE HAVE PINPOINTED THE SOURCE OF THE INCURSION: INCURSION HAS BEGUN.
THE NOMAD EMPIRE OF THE MAJISTRY HAS REENTERED OUR UNIVERSE AND MADE CAMP IN THE 61 CYGNI SYSTEM.
SECTOR 2814.
PLANET ATHMOORA.

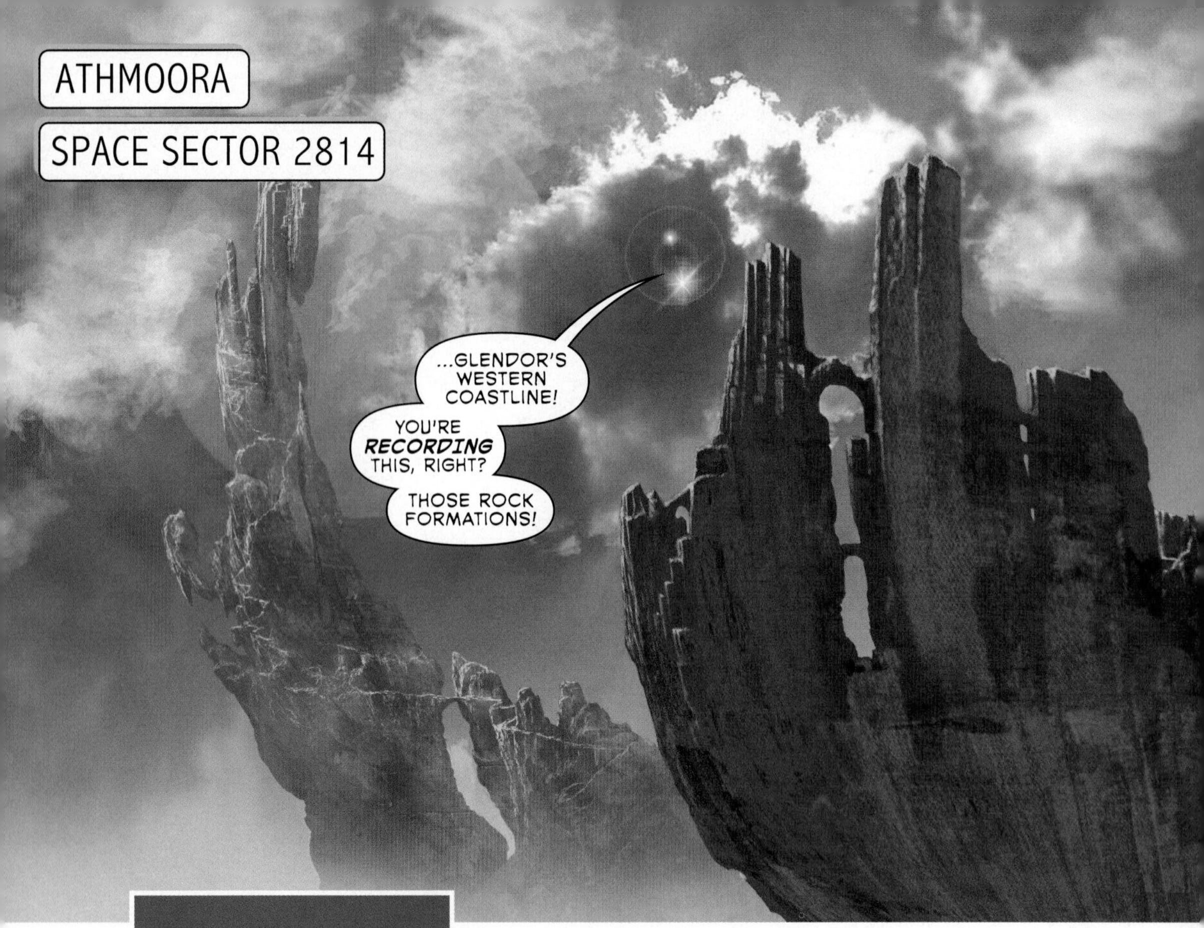
ATHMOORA
SPACE SECTOR 2814
...GLENDOR'S WESTERN COASTLINE!
YOU'RE RECORDING THIS, RIGHT?
THOSE ROCK FORMATIONS!

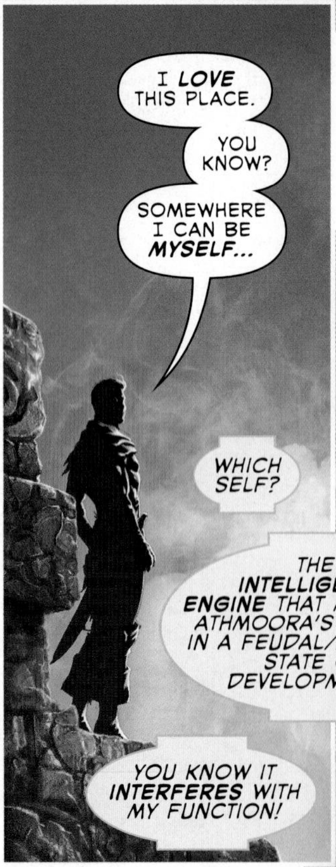
I LOVE THIS PLACE.
YOU KNOW?
SOMEWHERE I CAN BE MYSELF...
WHICH SELF?
THE INTELLIGENCE ENGINE THAT MAINTAINS ATHMOORA'S CULTURE IN A FEUDAL/MEDIEVAL STATE OF DEVELOPMENT...
YOU KNOW IT INTERFERES WITH MY FUNCTION!

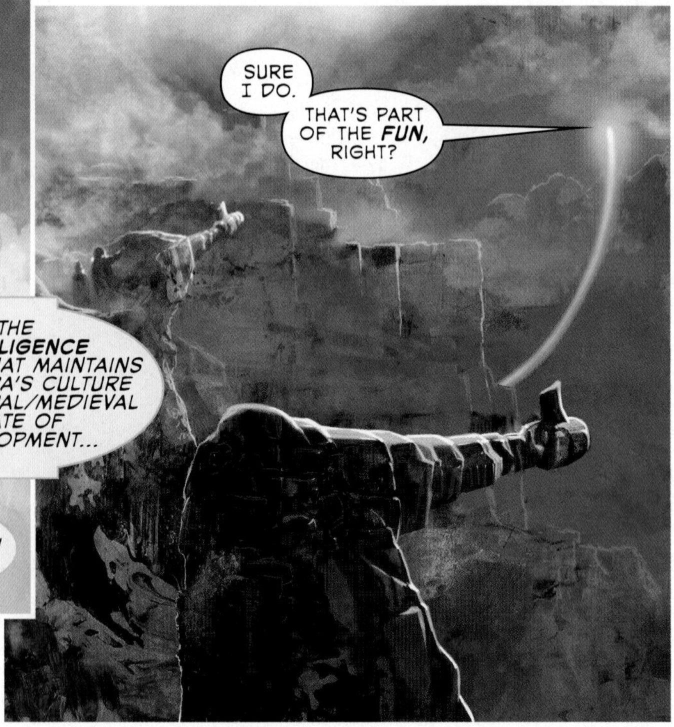
SURE I DO.
THAT'S PART OF THE FUN, RIGHT?

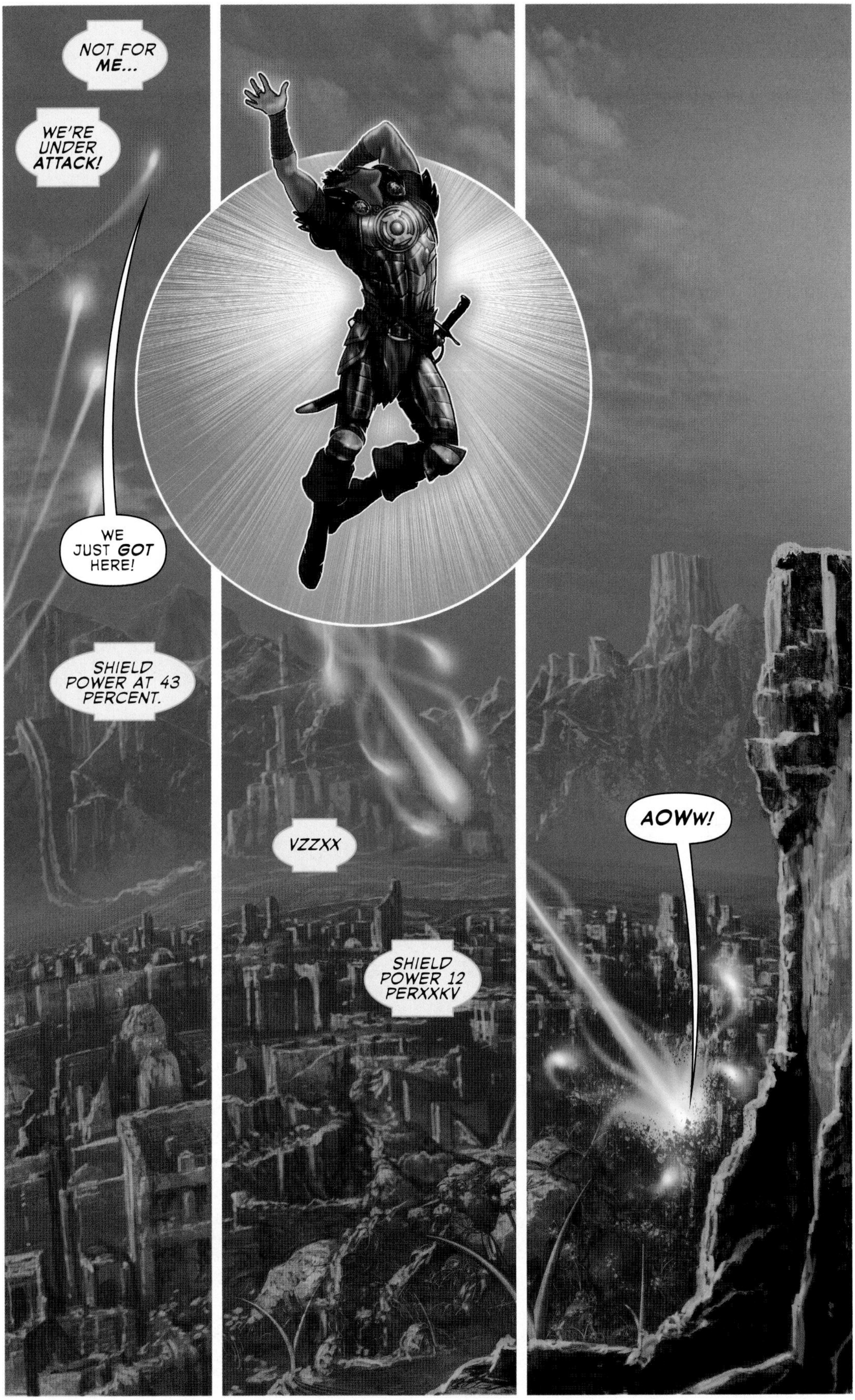

NOT FOR ME...
WE'RE UNDER ATTACK!
WE JUST GOT HERE!
SHIELD POWER AT 43 PERCENT.
VZZXX
SHIELD POWER 12 PERXXKV
AOWW!

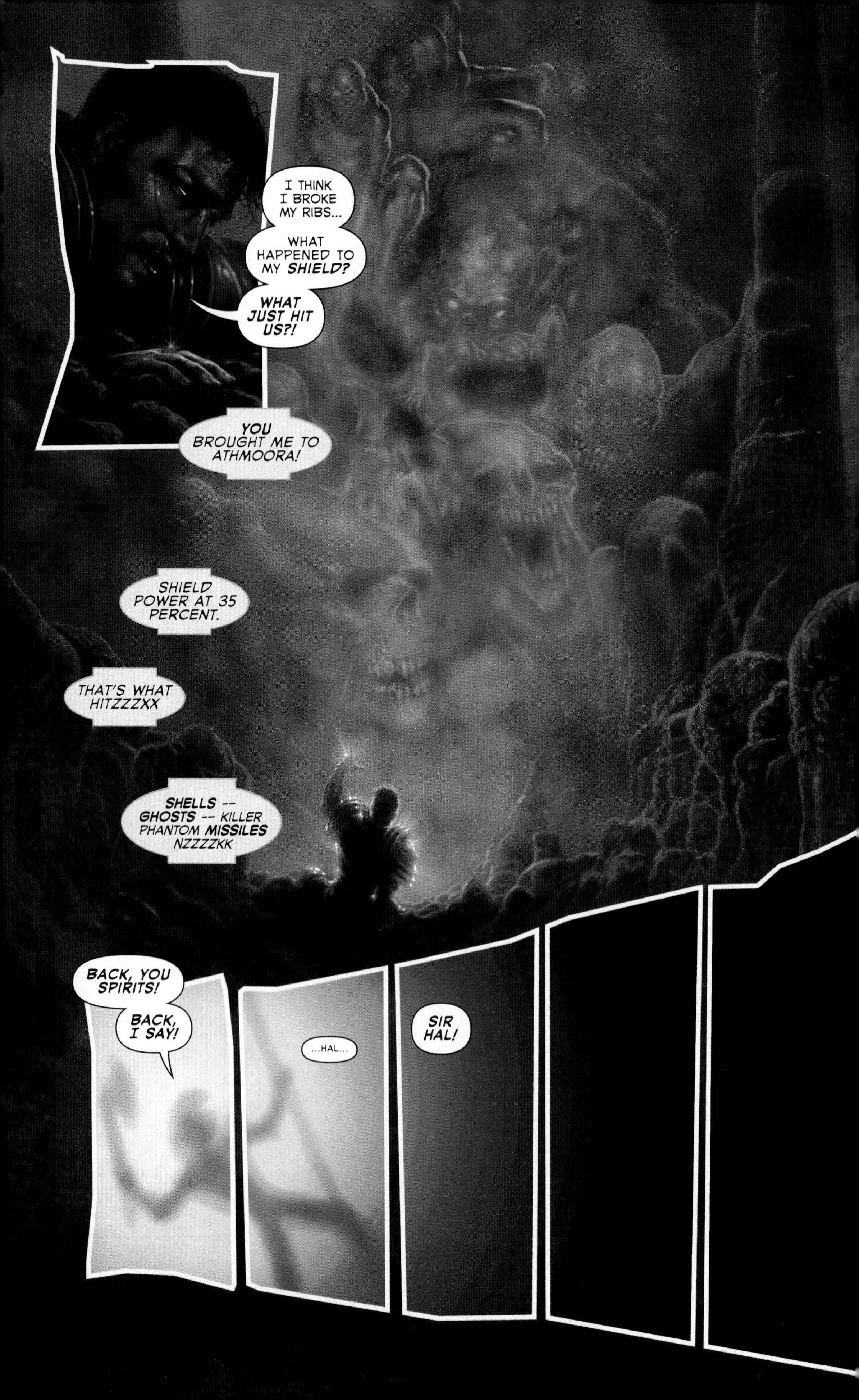

I THINK I BROKE MY RIBS...
WHAT HAPPENED TO MY SHIELD?
WHAT JUST HIT US?!
YOU BROUGHT ME TO ATHMOORA!
SHIELD POWER AT 35 PERCENT.
THAT'S WHAT HITZZZXX
SHELLS -- GHOSTS -- KILLER PHANTOM MISSILES NZZZZKK
BACK, YOU SPIRITS!
BACK, I SAY!
...HAL...
SIR HAL!

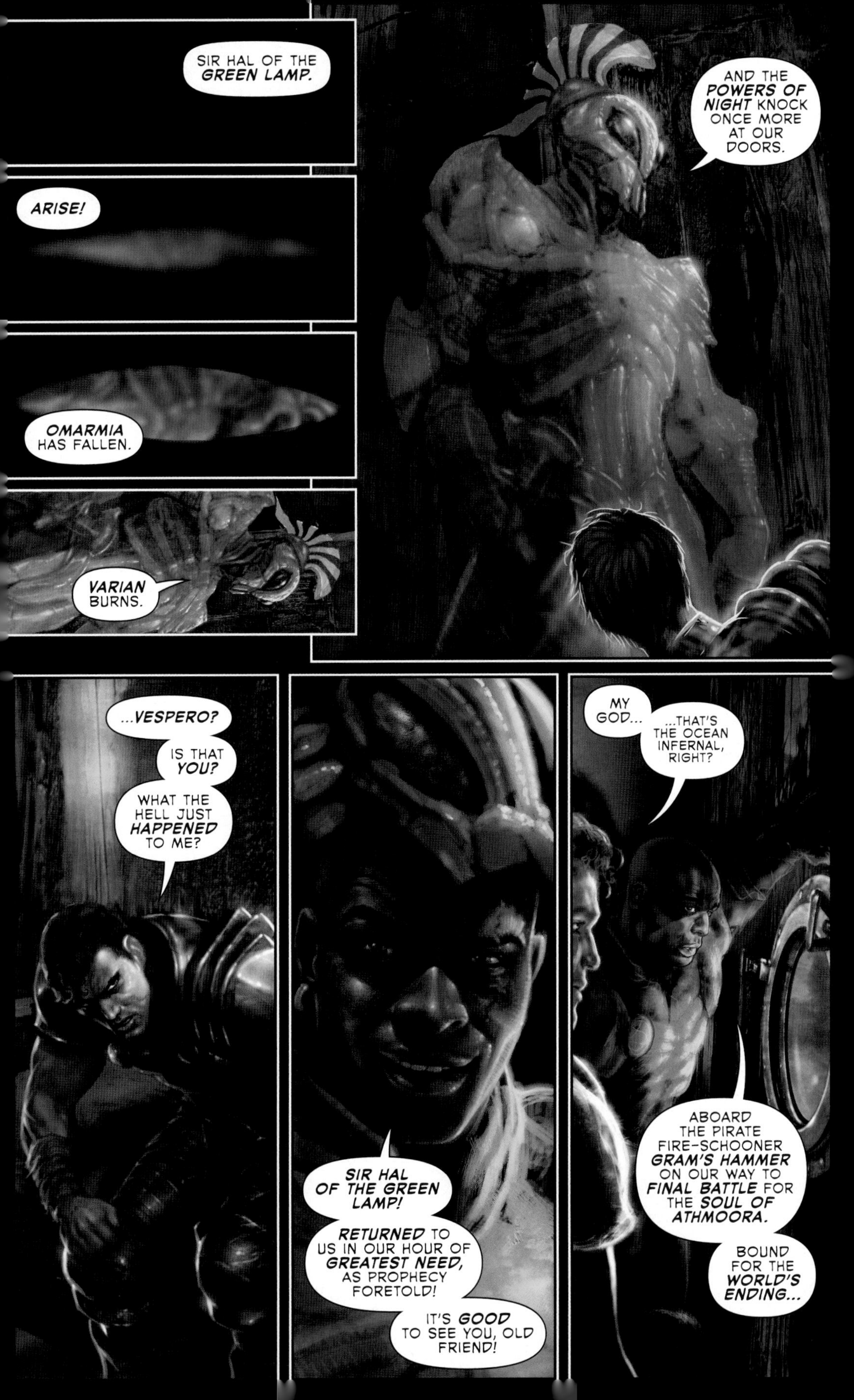
SIR HAL OF THE GREEN LAMP.
AND THE POWERS OF NIGHT KNOCK ONCE MORE AT OUR DOORS.
ARISE!
OMARMIA HAS FALLEN.
VARIAN BURNS.
...VESPERO?
IS THAT YOU?
WHAT THE HELL JUST HAPPENED TO ME?
SIR HAL OF THE GREEN LAMP!
RETURNED TO US IN OUR HOUR OF GREATEST NEED, AS PROPHECY FORETOLD!
IT'S GOOD TO SEE YOU, OLD FRIEND!
MY GOD...
...THAT'S THE OCEAN INFERNAL, RIGHT?
ABOARD THE PIRATE FIRE-SCHOONER GRAM'S HAMMER ON OUR WAY TO FINAL BATTLE FOR THE SOUL OF ATHMOORA.
BOUND FOR THE WORLD'S ENDING...

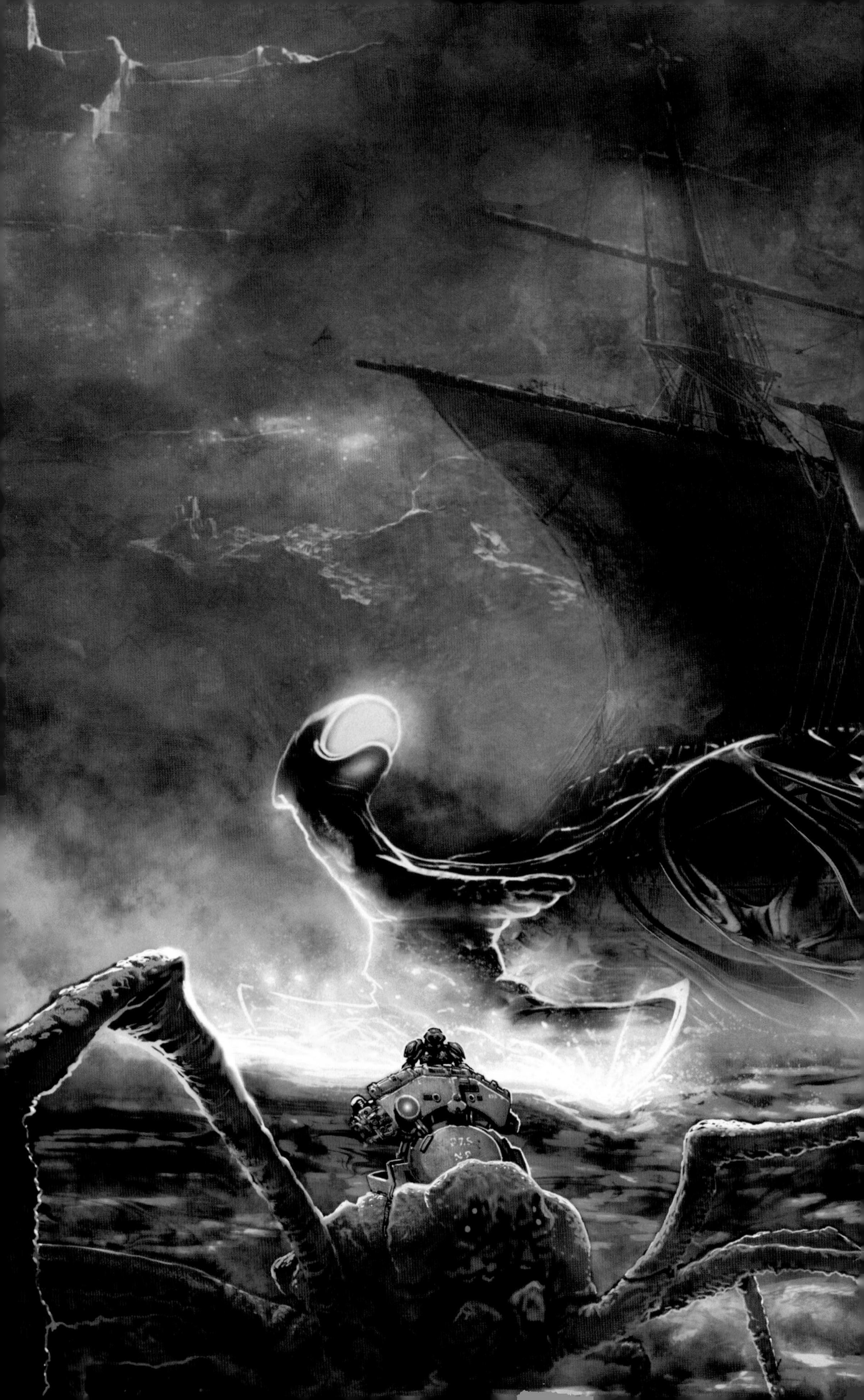

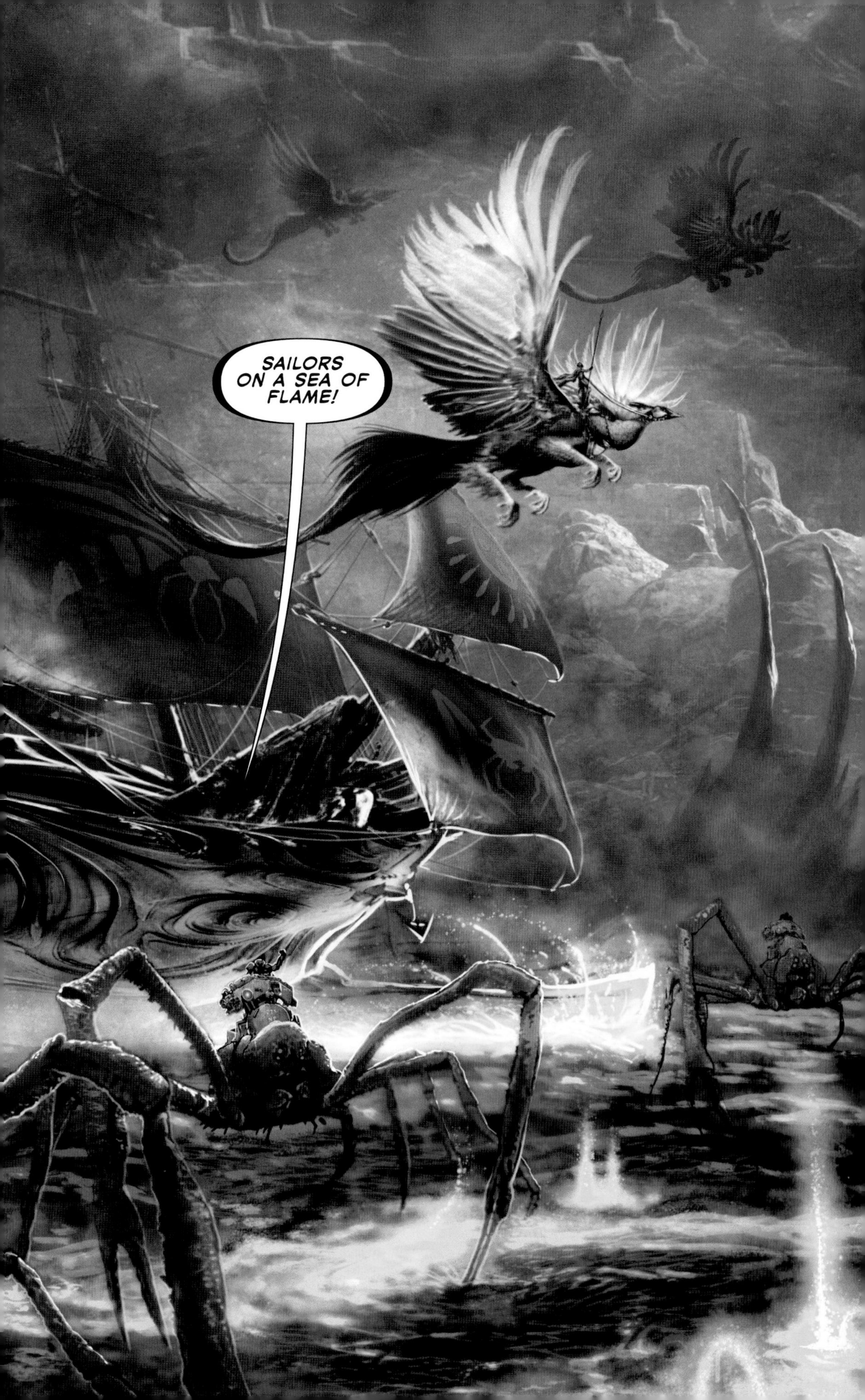
SAILORS ON A SEA OF FLAME!

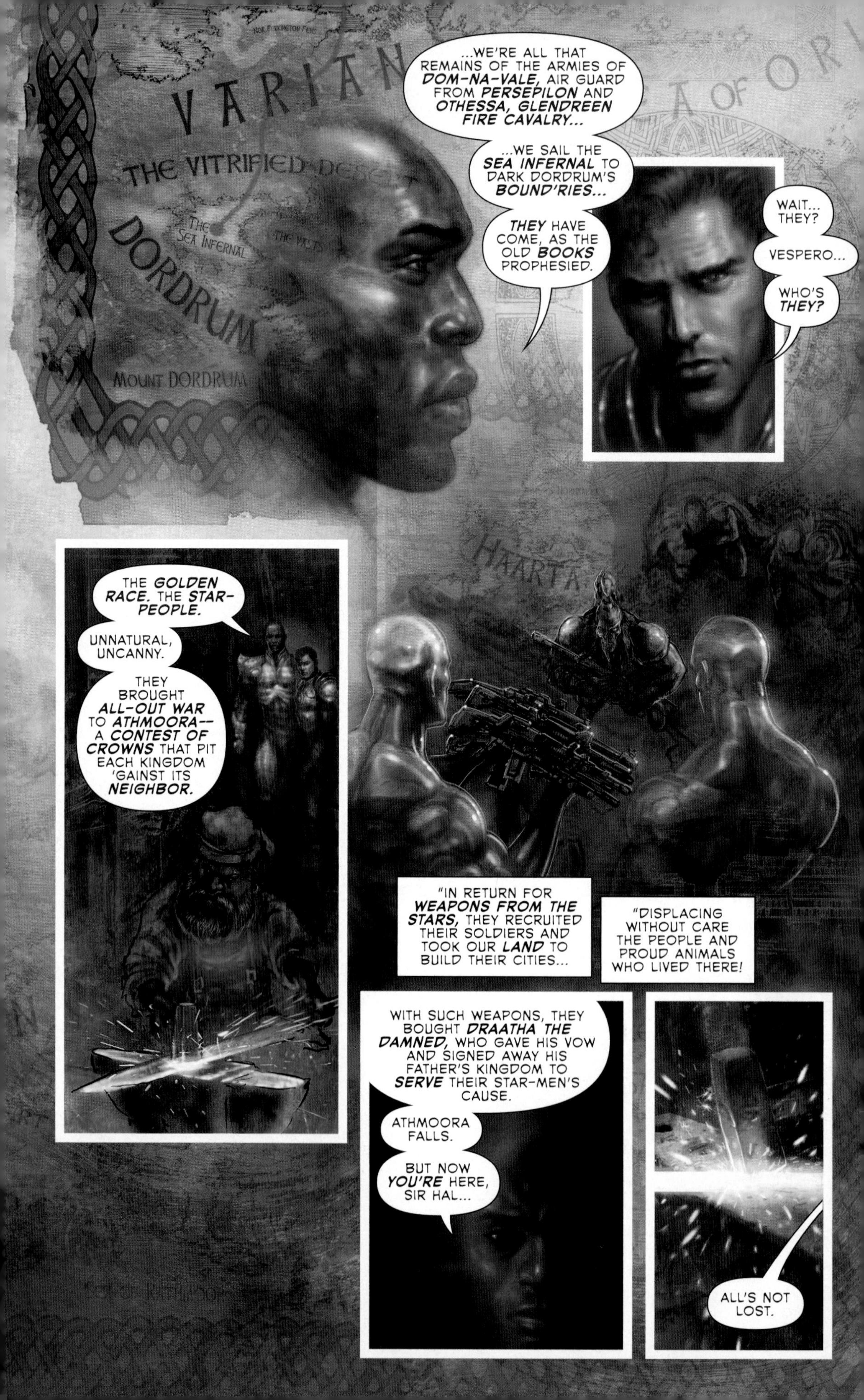
VARIAN
THE VITRIFIED
THE SEA INFERNAL
THE VASTS
DORDRUM
MOUNT DORDRUM
...WE'RE ALL THAT REMAINS OF THE ARMIES OF *DOM-NA-VALE*, AIR GUARD FROM *PERSEPILON* AND *OTHESSA, GLENDREEN FIRE CAVALRY...*
...WE SAIL THE *SEA INFERNAL* TO DARK DORDRUM'S *BOUND'RIES...*
THEY HAVE COME, AS THE OLD *BOOKS* PROPHESIED.
WAIT... THEY?
VESPERO...
WHO'S *THEY?*
HAARTA
THE *GOLDEN RACE.* THE *STAR-PEOPLE.*
UNNATURAL, UNCANNY.
THEY BROUGHT *ALL-OUT WAR* TO *ATHMOORA*-- A *CONTEST OF CROWNS* THAT PIT EACH KINGDOM 'GAINST ITS *NEIGHBOR.*
"IN RETURN FOR *WEAPONS FROM THE STARS,* THEY RECRUITED THEIR SOLDIERS AND TOOK OUR *LAND* TO BUILD THEIR CITIES...
"DISPLACING WITHOUT CARE THE PEOPLE AND PROUD ANIMALS WHO LIVED THERE!
WITH SUCH WEAPONS, THEY BOUGHT *DRAATHA THE DAMNED,* WHO GAVE HIS VOW AND SIGNED AWAY HIS FATHER'S KINGDOM TO *SERVE* THEIR STAR-MEN'S CAUSE.
ATHMOORA FALLS.
BUT NOW *YOU'RE* HERE, SIR HAL...
ALL'S NOT LOST.

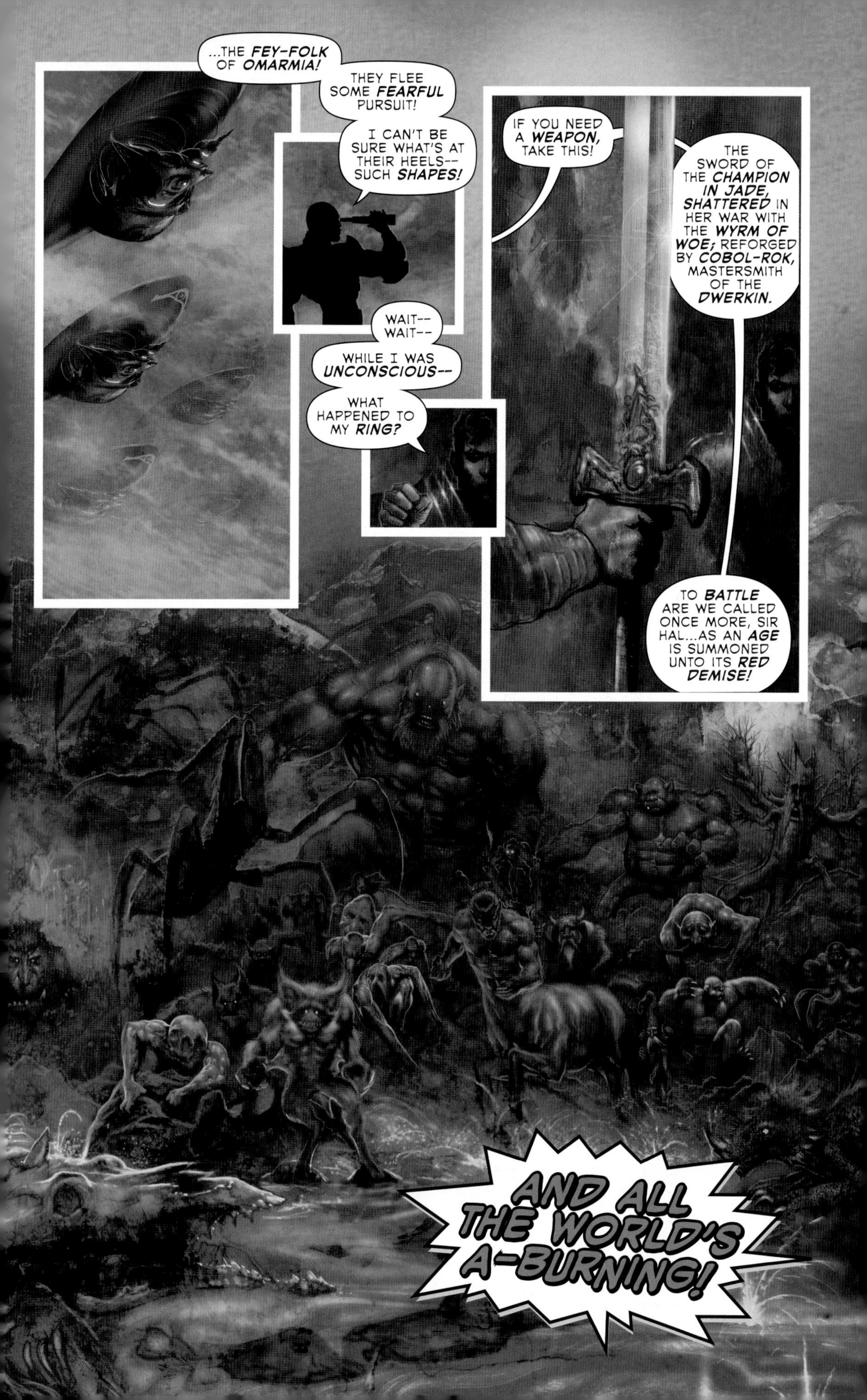
...THE FEY-FOLK OF OMARMIA!
THEY FLEE SOME FEARFUL PURSUIT!
I CAN'T BE SURE WHAT'S AT THEIR HEELS-- SUCH SHAPES!
WAIT-- WAIT--
WHILE I WAS UNCONSCIOUS--
WHAT HAPPENED TO MY RING?
IF YOU NEED A WEAPON, TAKE THIS!
THE SWORD OF THE CHAMPION IN JADE, SHATTERED IN HER WAR WITH THE WYRM OF WOE; REFORGED BY COBOL-ROK, MASTERSMITH OF THE DWERKIN.
TO BATTLE ARE WE CALLED ONCE MORE, SIR HAL...AS AN AGE IS SUMMONED UNTO ITS RED DEMISE!
AND ALL THE WORLD'S A-BURNING!

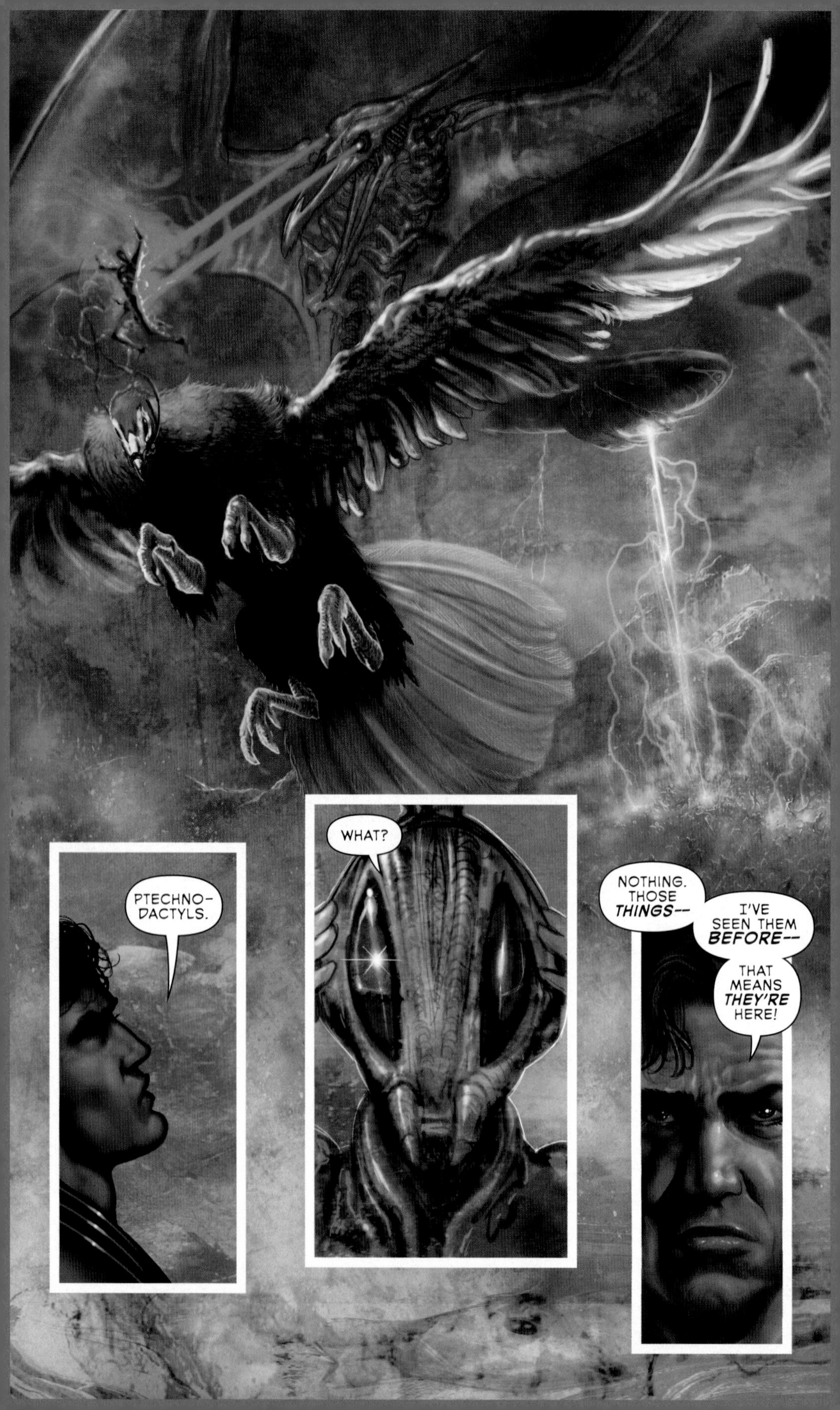
PTECHNO-DACTYLS.
WHAT?
NOTHING. THOSE *THINGS*--
I'VE SEEN THEM *BEFORE*--
THAT MEANS *THEY'RE* HERE!

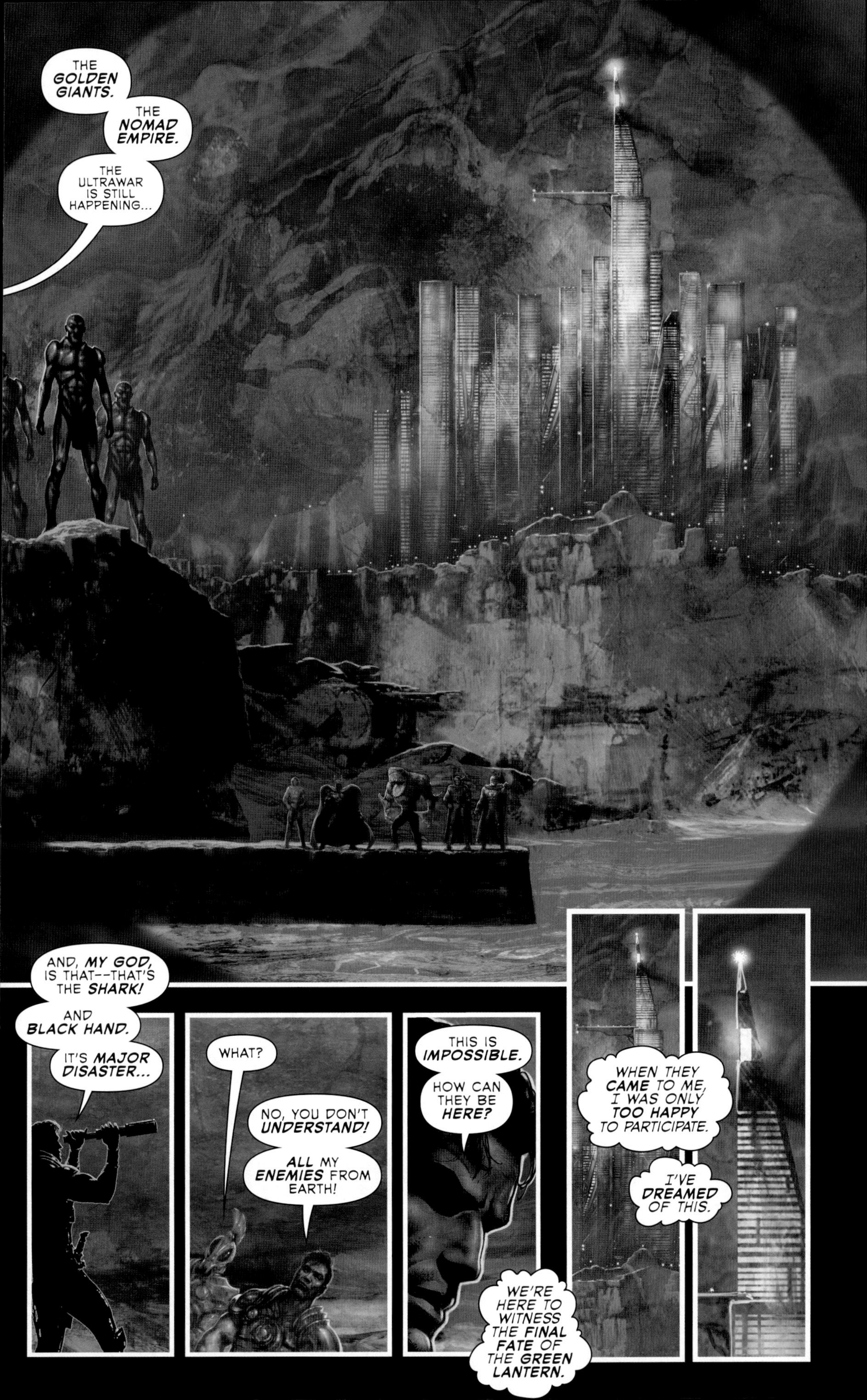
THE GOLDEN GIANTS.
THE NOMAD EMPIRE.
THE ULTRAWAR IS STILL HAPPENING...
AND, MY GOD, IS THAT--THAT'S THE SHARK!
AND BLACK HAND.
IT'S MAJOR DISASTER...
WHAT?
NO, YOU DON'T UNDERSTAND!
ALL MY ENEMIES FROM EARTH!
THIS IS IMPOSSIBLE.
HOW CAN THEY BE HERE?
WE'RE HERE TO WITNESS THE FINAL FATE OF THE GREEN LANTERN.
WHEN THEY CAME TO ME, I WAS ONLY TOO HAPPY TO PARTICIPATE.
I'VE DREAMED OF THIS.

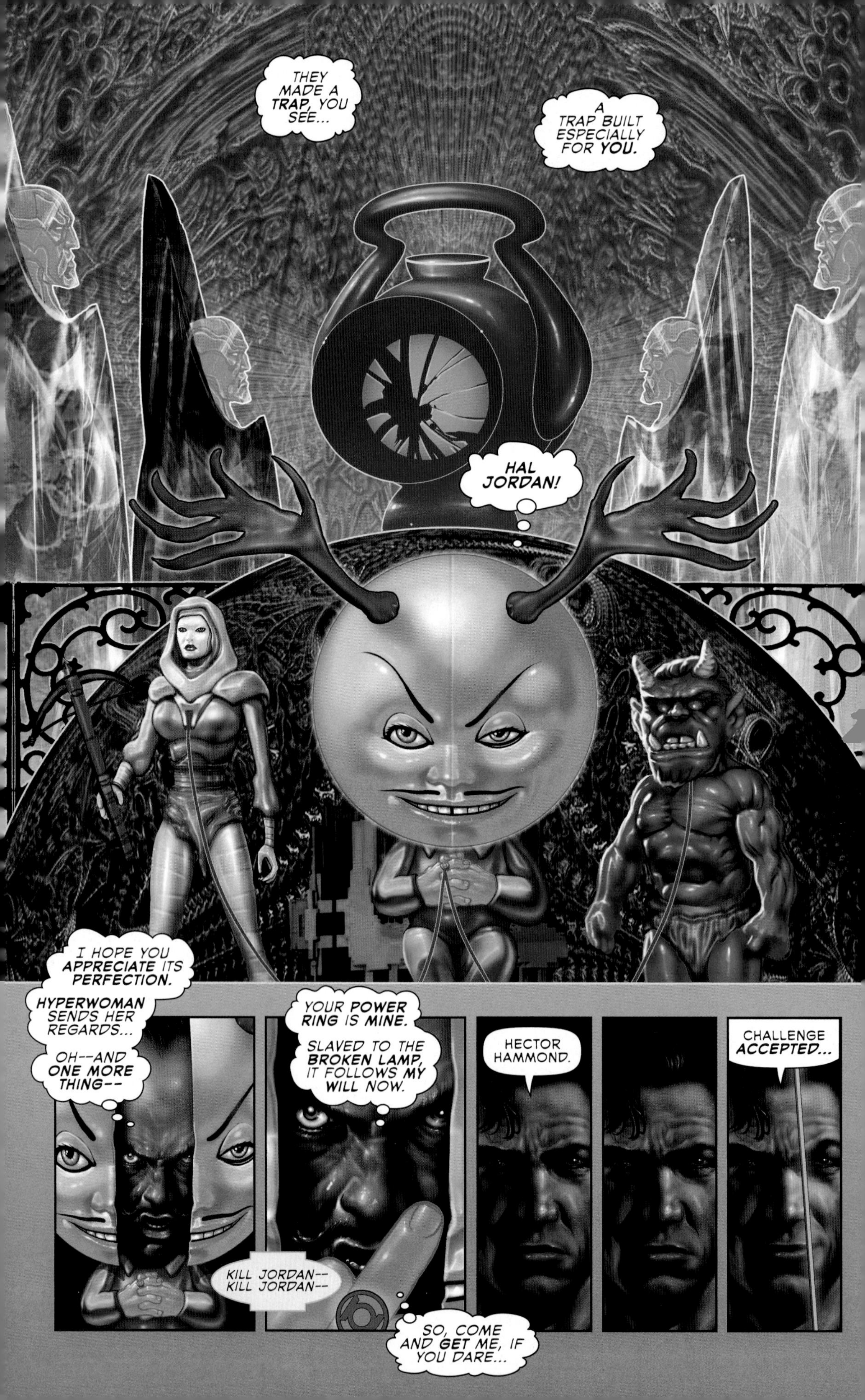
THEY MADE A TRAP, YOU SEE...
A TRAP BUILT ESPECIALLY FOR YOU.
HAL JORDAN!
I HOPE YOU APPRECIATE ITS PERFECTION.
HYPERWOMAN SENDS HER REGARDS...
OH--AND ONE MORE THING--
YOUR POWER RING IS MINE.
SLAVED TO THE BROKEN LAMP, IT FOLLOWS MY WILL NOW.
KILL JORDAN-- KILL JORDAN--
SO, COME AND GET ME, IF YOU DARE...
HECTOR HAMMOND.
CHALLENGE ACCEPTED...

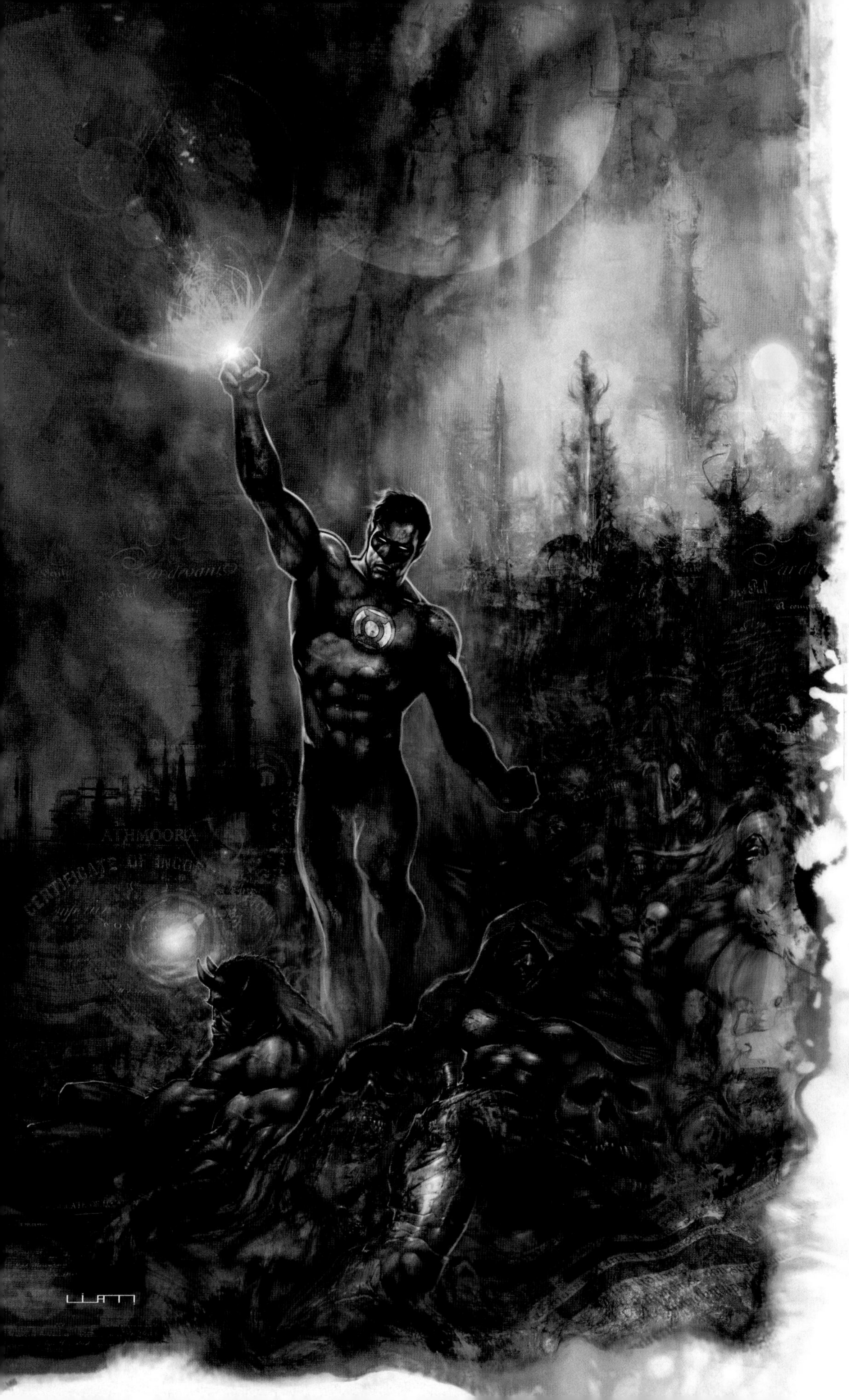

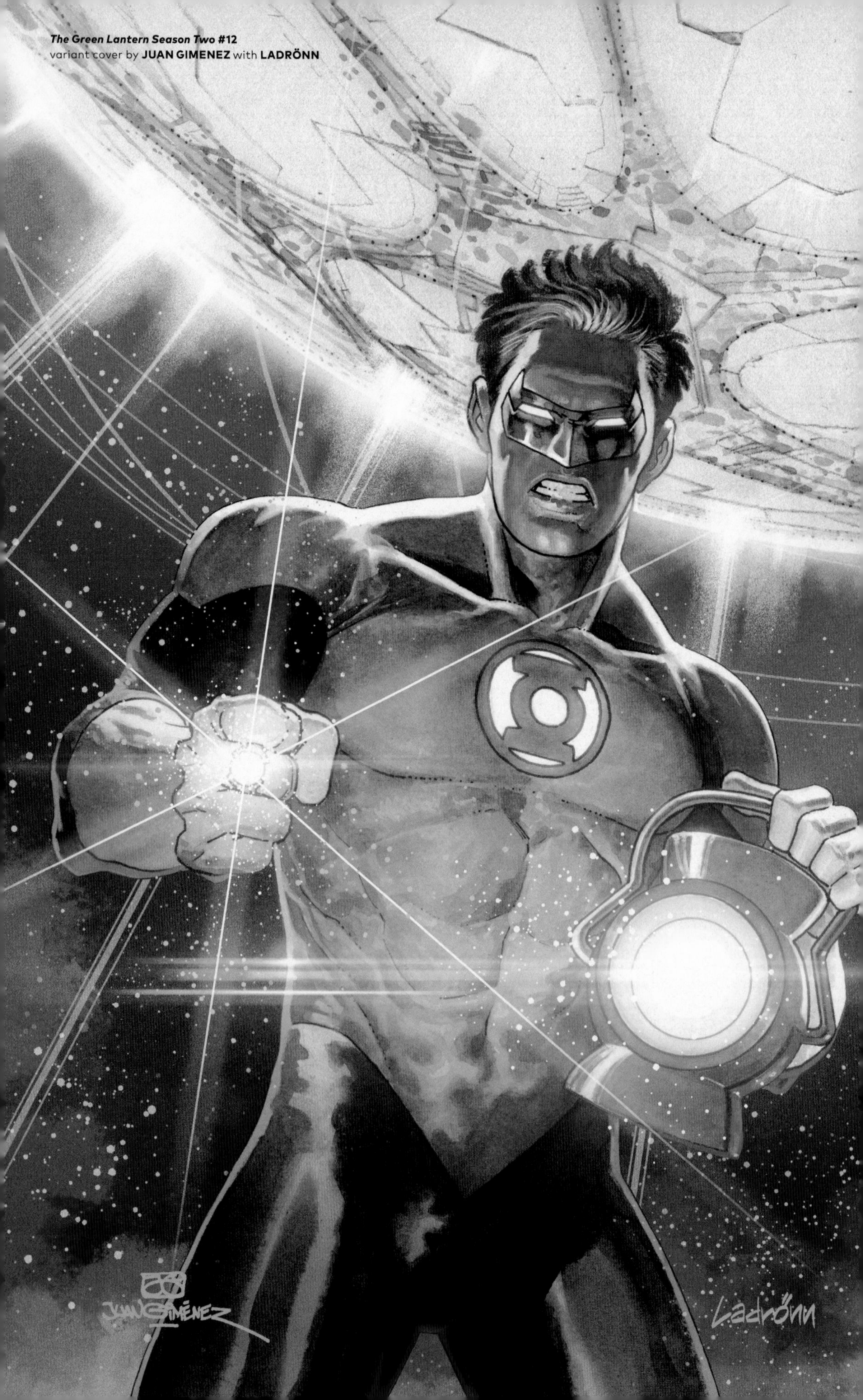
JUAN GIMÉNEZ
Ladrönn

The Green Lantern Season Two #12
variant cover by **JUAN GIMENEZ** with **LADRÖNN**

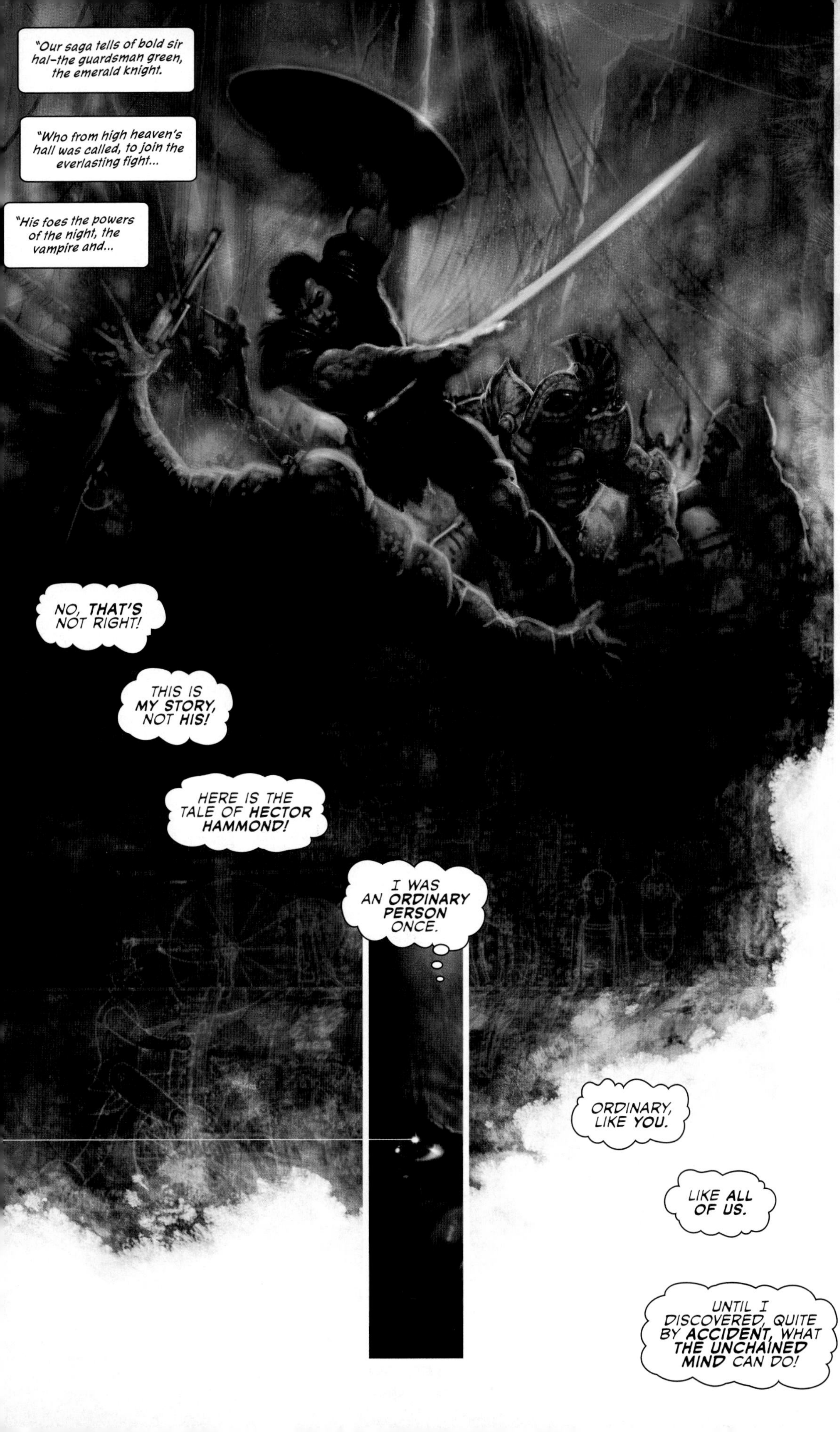
"Our saga tells of bold sir hal–the guardsman green, the emerald knight.
"Who from high heaven's hall was called, to join the everlasting fight...
"His foes the powers of the night, the vampire and...
NO, THAT'S NOT RIGHT!
THIS IS MY STORY, NOT HIS!
HERE IS THE TALE OF HECTOR HAMMOND!
I WAS AN ORDINARY PERSON ONCE.
ORDINARY, LIKE YOU.
LIKE ALL OF US.
UNTIL I DISCOVERED, QUITE BY ACCIDENT, WHAT THE UNCHAINED MIND CAN DO!

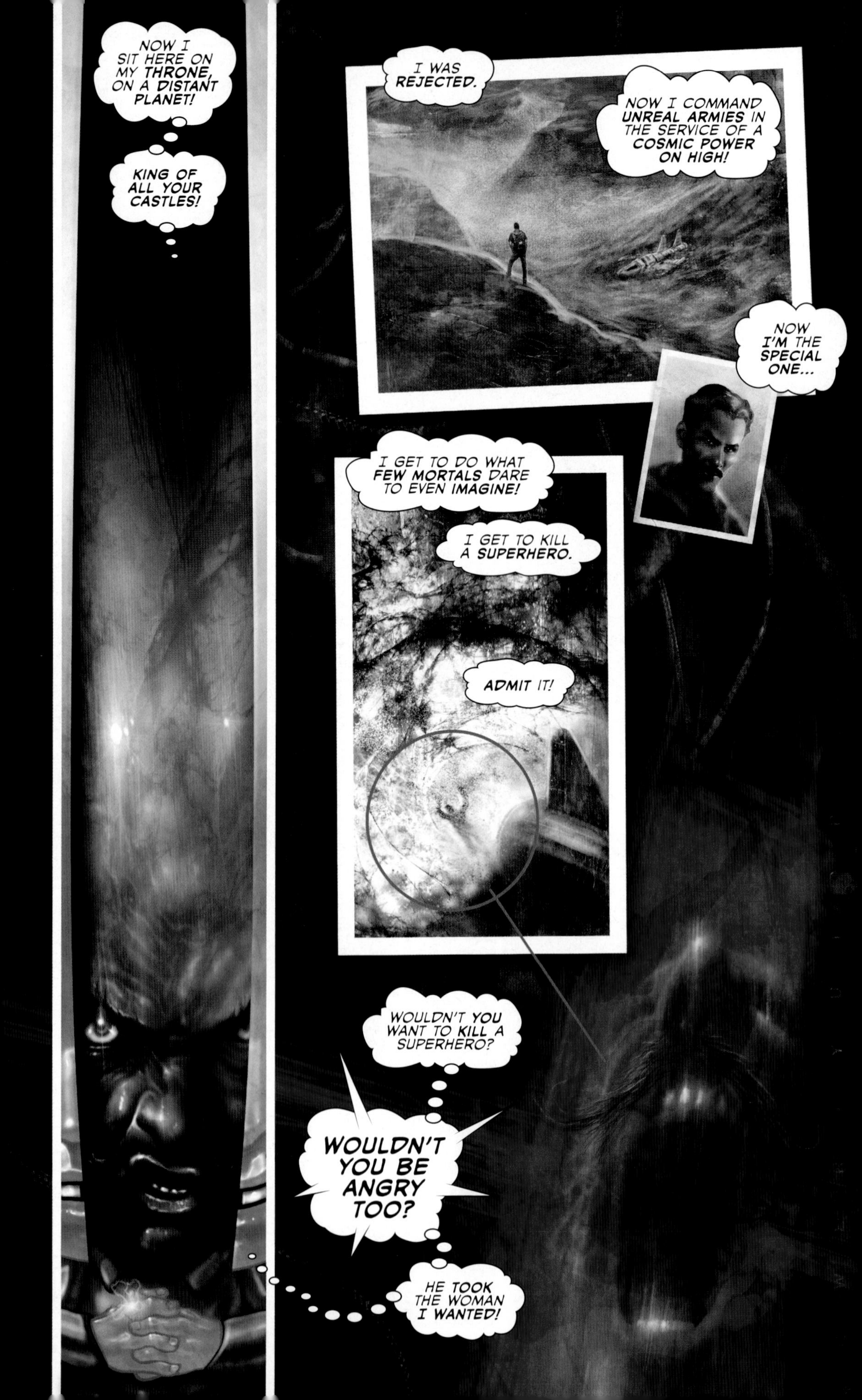
NOW I SIT HERE ON MY THRONE, ON A DISTANT PLANET!
KING OF ALL YOUR CASTLES!
I WAS REJECTED.
NOW I COMMAND UNREAL ARMIES IN THE SERVICE OF A COSMIC POWER ON HIGH!
NOW I'M THE SPECIAL ONE...
I GET TO DO WHAT FEW MORTALS DARE TO EVEN IMAGINE!
I GET TO KILL A SUPERHERO.
ADMIT IT!
WOULDN'T YOU WANT TO KILL A SUPERHERO?
WOULDN'T YOU BE ANGRY TOO?
HE TOOK THE WOMAN I WANTED!

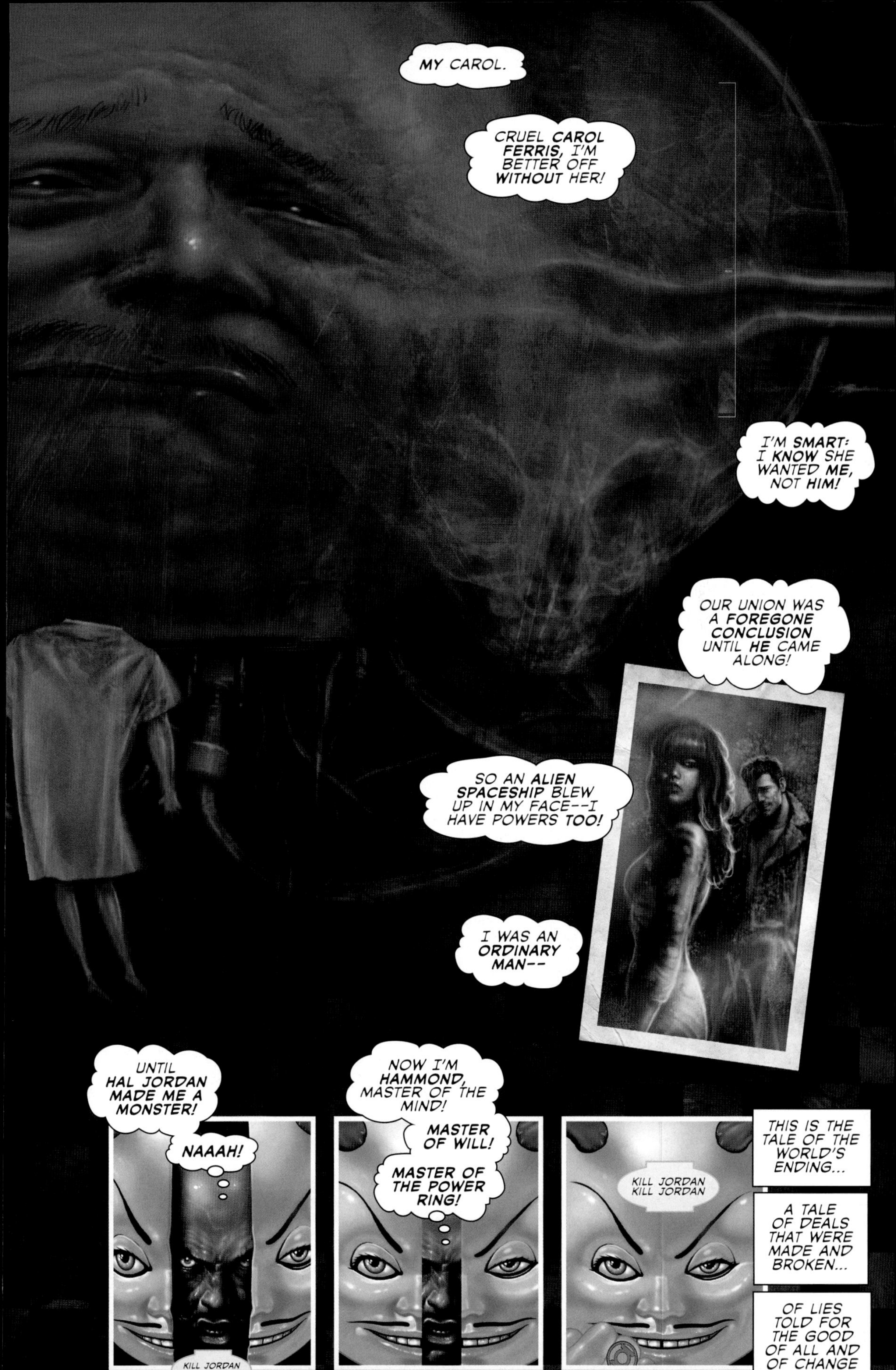
MY CAROL.
CRUEL CAROL FERRIS, I'M BETTER OFF WITHOUT HER!
I'M SMART: I KNOW SHE WANTED ME, NOT HIM!
OUR UNION WAS A FOREGONE CONCLUSION UNTIL HE CAME ALONG!
SO AN ALIEN SPACESHIP BLEW UP IN MY FACE--I HAVE POWERS TOO!
I WAS AN ORDINARY MAN--
UNTIL HAL JORDAN MADE ME A MONSTER!
NAAAH!
KILL JORDAN
NOW I'M HAMMOND, MASTER OF THE MIND!
MASTER OF WILL!
MASTER OF THE POWER RING!
KILL JORDAN KILL JORDAN
THIS IS THE TALE OF THE WORLD'S ENDING...
A TALE OF DEALS THAT WERE MADE AND BROKEN...
OF LIES TOLD FOR THE GOOD OF ALL AND OF CHANGE

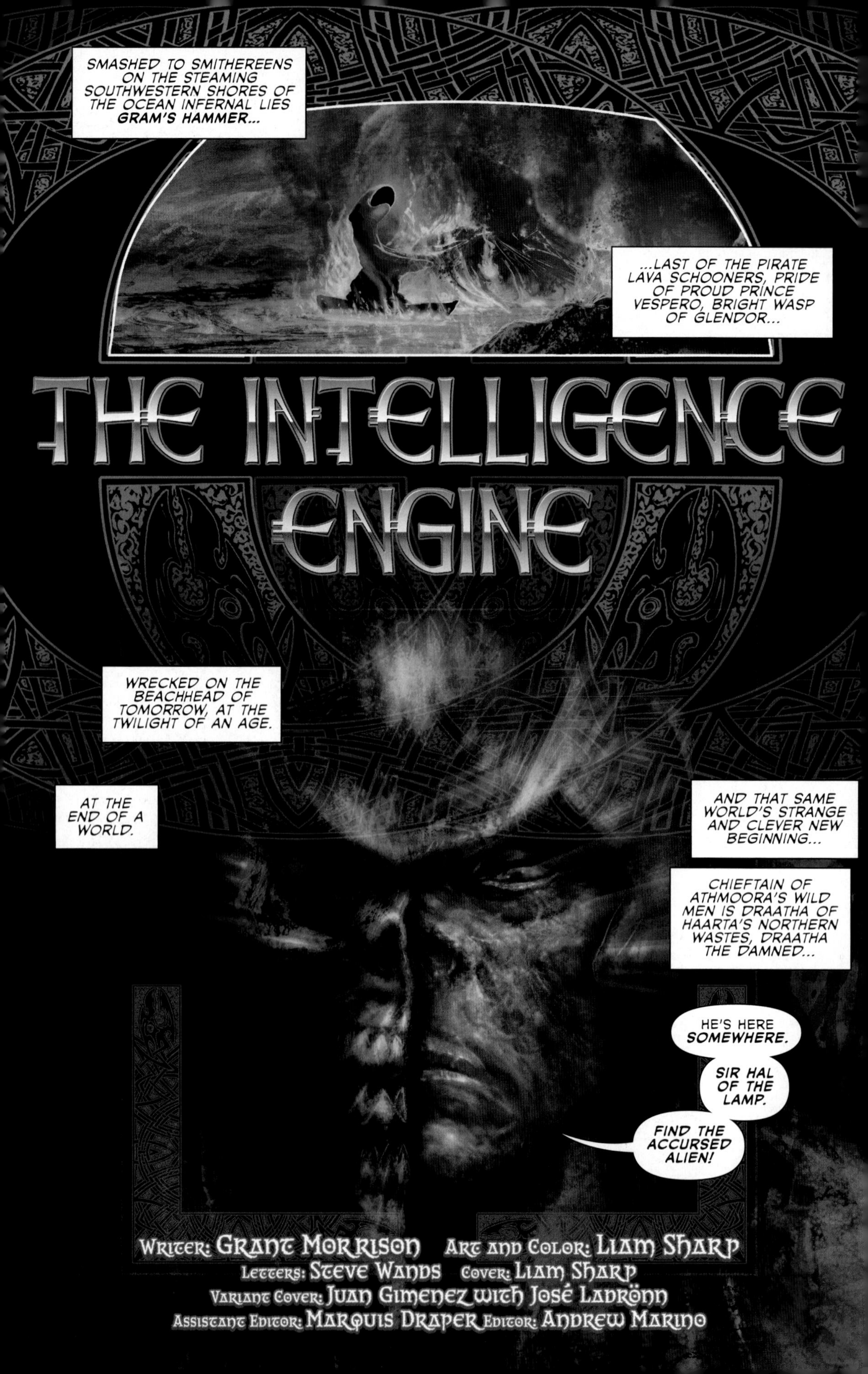
SMASHED TO SMITHEREENS ON THE STEAMING SOUTHWESTERN SHORES OF THE OCEAN INFERNAL LIES GRAM'S HAMMER...
...LAST OF THE PIRATE LAVA SCHOONERS, PRIDE OF PROUD PRINCE VESPERO, BRIGHT WASP OF GLENDOR...
THE INTELLIGENCE ENGINE
WRECKED ON THE BEACHHEAD OF TOMORROW, AT THE TWILIGHT OF AN AGE.
AT THE END OF A WORLD.
AND THAT SAME WORLD'S STRANGE AND CLEVER NEW BEGINNING...
CHIEFTAIN OF ATHMOORA'S WILD MEN IS DRAATHA OF HAARTA'S NORTHERN WASTES, DRAATHA THE DAMNED...
HE'S HERE SOMEWHERE.
SIR HAL OF THE LAMP.
FIND THE ACCURSED ALIEN!
Writer: GRANT MORRISON Art and Color: LIAM SHARP
Letters: STEVE WANDS Cover: LIAM SHARP
Variant Cover: JUAN GIMENEZ with JOSÉ LADRÖNN
Assistant Editor: MARQUIS DRAPER Editor: ANDREW MARINO

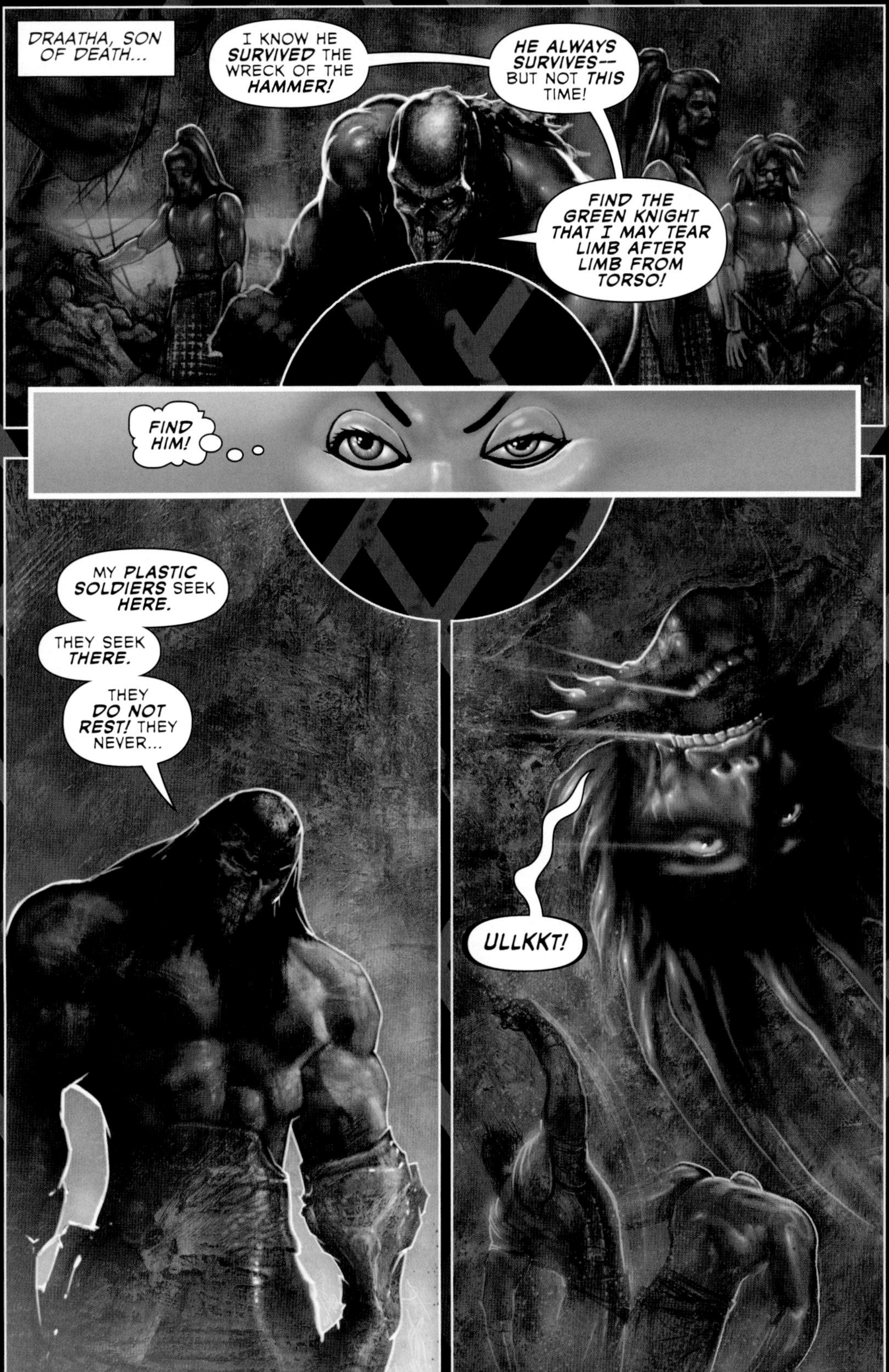

DRAATHA, SON OF DEATH...
I KNOW HE SURVIVED THE WRECK OF THE HAMMER!
HE ALWAYS SURVIVES-- BUT NOT THIS TIME!
FIND THE GREEN KNIGHT THAT I MAY TEAR LIMB AFTER LIMB FROM TORSO!
FIND HIM!
MY PLASTIC SOLDIERS SEEK HERE.
THEY SEEK THERE.
THEY DO NOT REST! THEY NEVER...
ULLKKT!

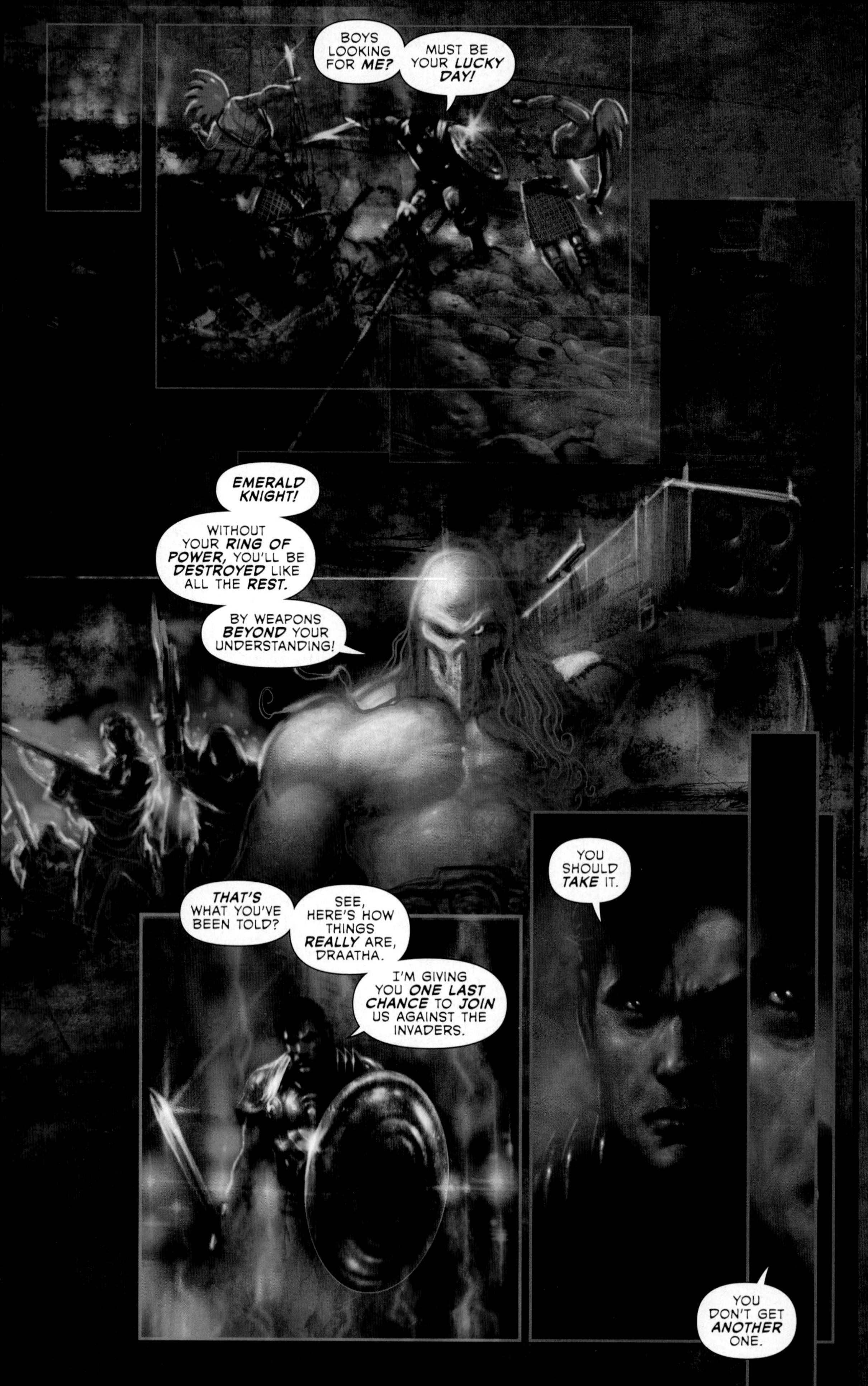
BOYS LOOKING FOR ME?
MUST BE YOUR LUCKY DAY!
EMERALD KNIGHT!
WITHOUT YOUR RING OF POWER, YOU'LL BE DESTROYED LIKE ALL THE REST.
BY WEAPONS BEYOND YOUR UNDERSTANDING!
THAT'S WHAT YOU'VE BEEN TOLD?
SEE, HERE'S HOW THINGS REALLY ARE, DRAATHA.
I'M GIVING YOU ONE LAST CHANCE TO JOIN US AGAINST THE INVADERS.
YOU SHOULD TAKE IT.
YOU DON'T GET ANOTHER ONE.

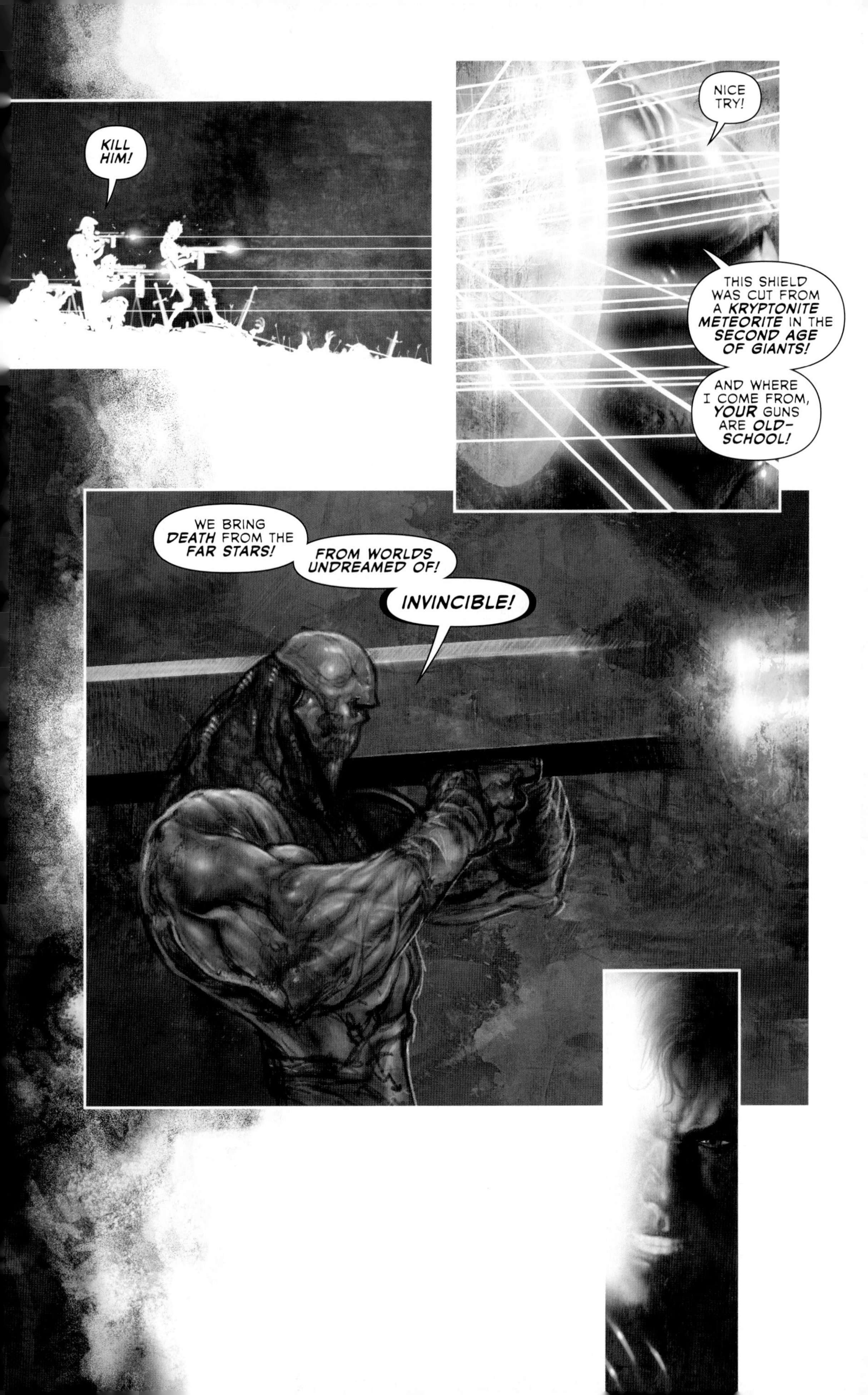
KILL HIM!
NICE TRY!
THIS SHIELD WAS CUT FROM A KRYPTONITE METEORITE IN THE SECOND AGE OF GIANTS!
AND WHERE I COME FROM, YOUR GUNS ARE OLD-SCHOOL!
WE BRING DEATH FROM THE FAR STARS!
FROM WORLDS UNDREAMED OF!
INVINCIBLE!

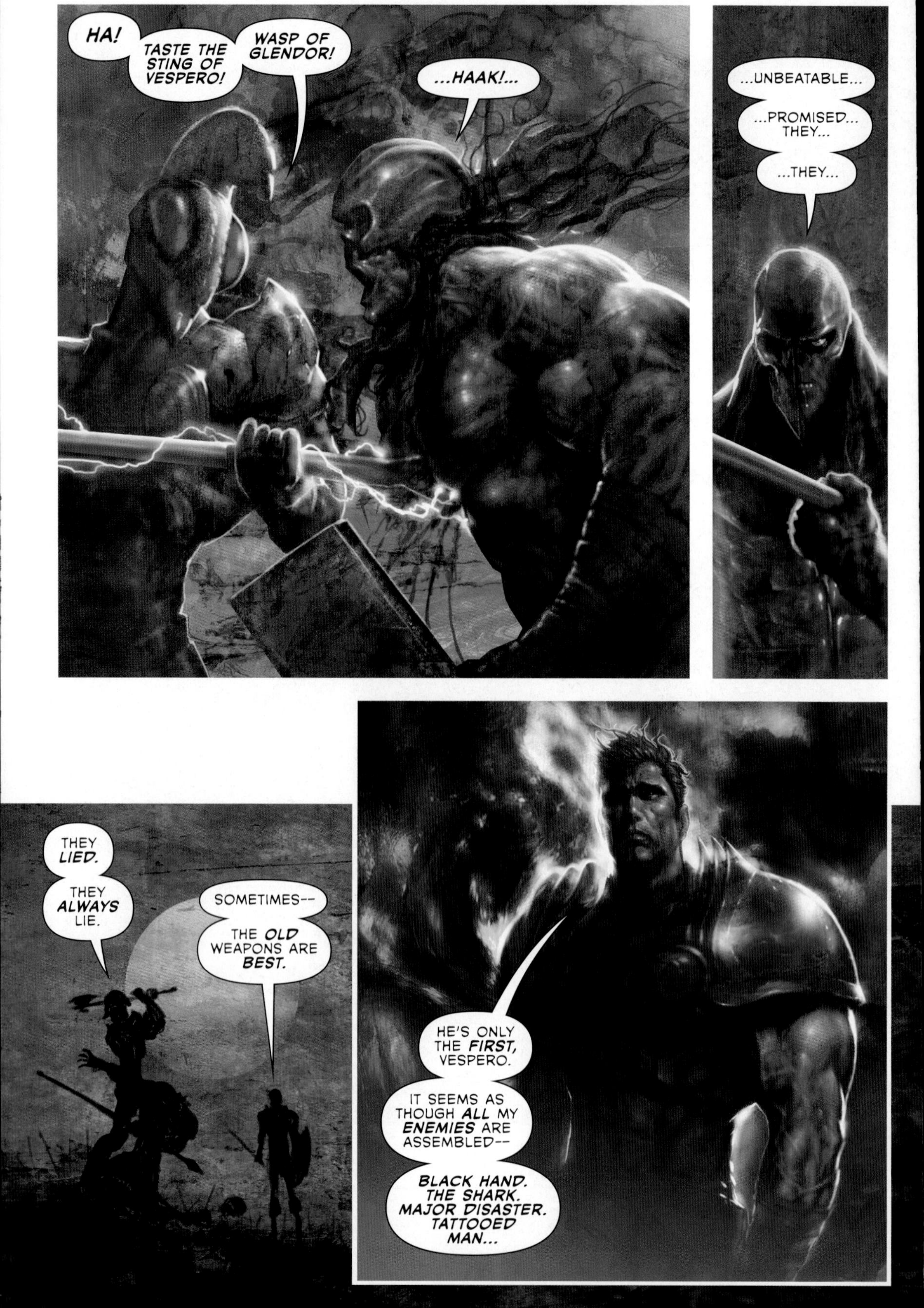
HA!
TASTE THE STING OF VESPERO!
WASP OF GLENDOR!
...HAAK!...
...UNBEATABLE...
...PROMISED... THEY...
...THEY...
THEY LIED.
THEY ALWAYS LIE.
SOMETIMES--
THE OLD WEAPONS ARE BEST.
HE'S ONLY THE FIRST, VESPERO.
IT SEEMS AS THOUGH ALL MY ENEMIES ARE ASSEMBLED--
BLACK HAND. THE SHARK. MAJOR DISASTER. TATTOOED MAN...

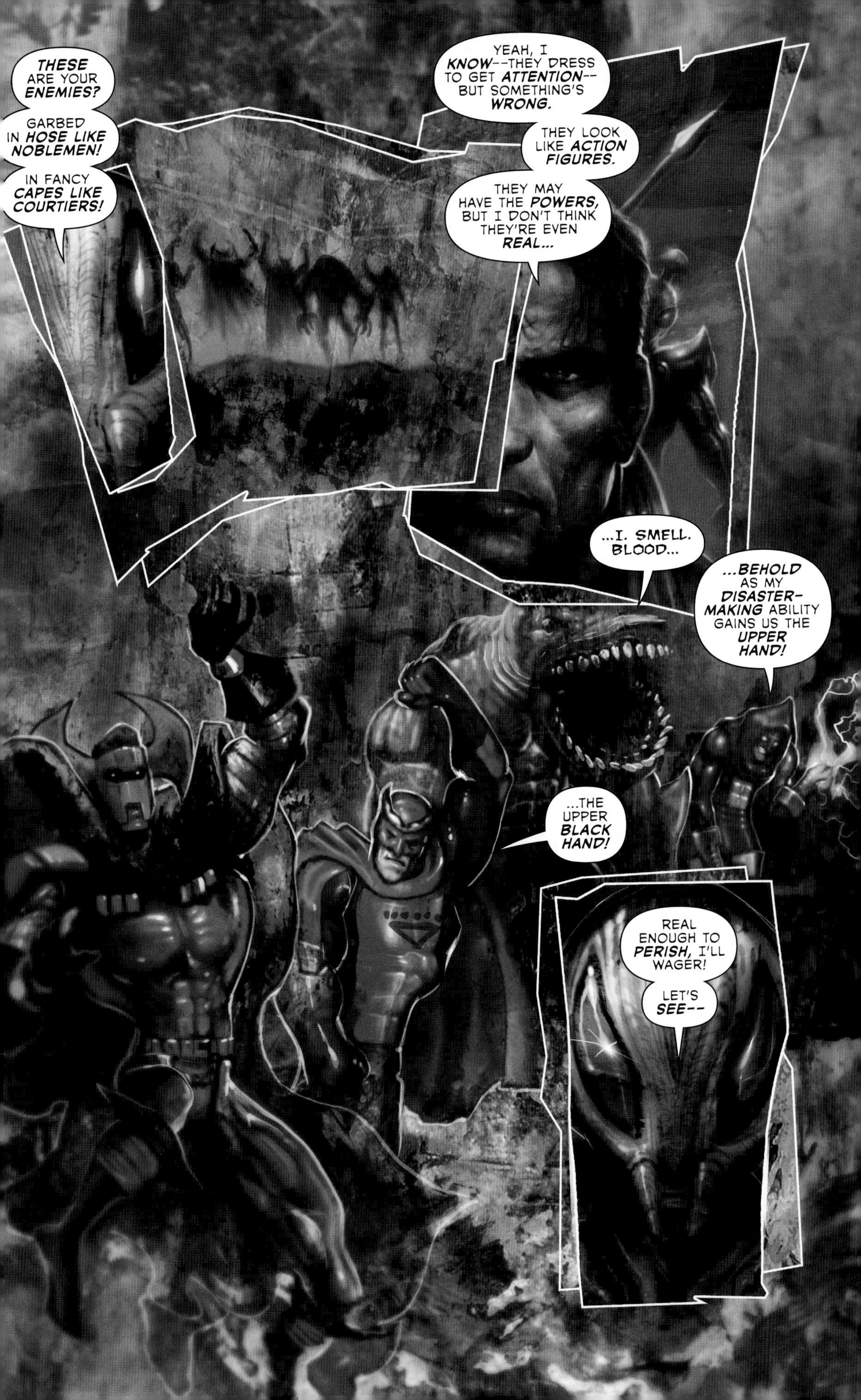
THESE ARE YOUR ENEMIES?
GARBED IN HOSE LIKE NOBLEMEN!
IN FANCY CAPES LIKE COURTIERS!
YEAH, I KNOW--THEY DRESS TO GET ATTENTION--BUT SOMETHING'S WRONG.
THEY LOOK LIKE ACTION FIGURES.
THEY MAY HAVE THE POWERS, BUT I DON'T THINK THEY'RE EVEN REAL...
...I. SMELL. BLOOD...
...BEHOLD AS MY DISASTER-MAKING ABILITY GAINS US THE UPPER HAND!
...THE UPPER BLACK HAND!
REAL ENOUGH TO PERISH, I'LL WAGER!
LET'S SEE--

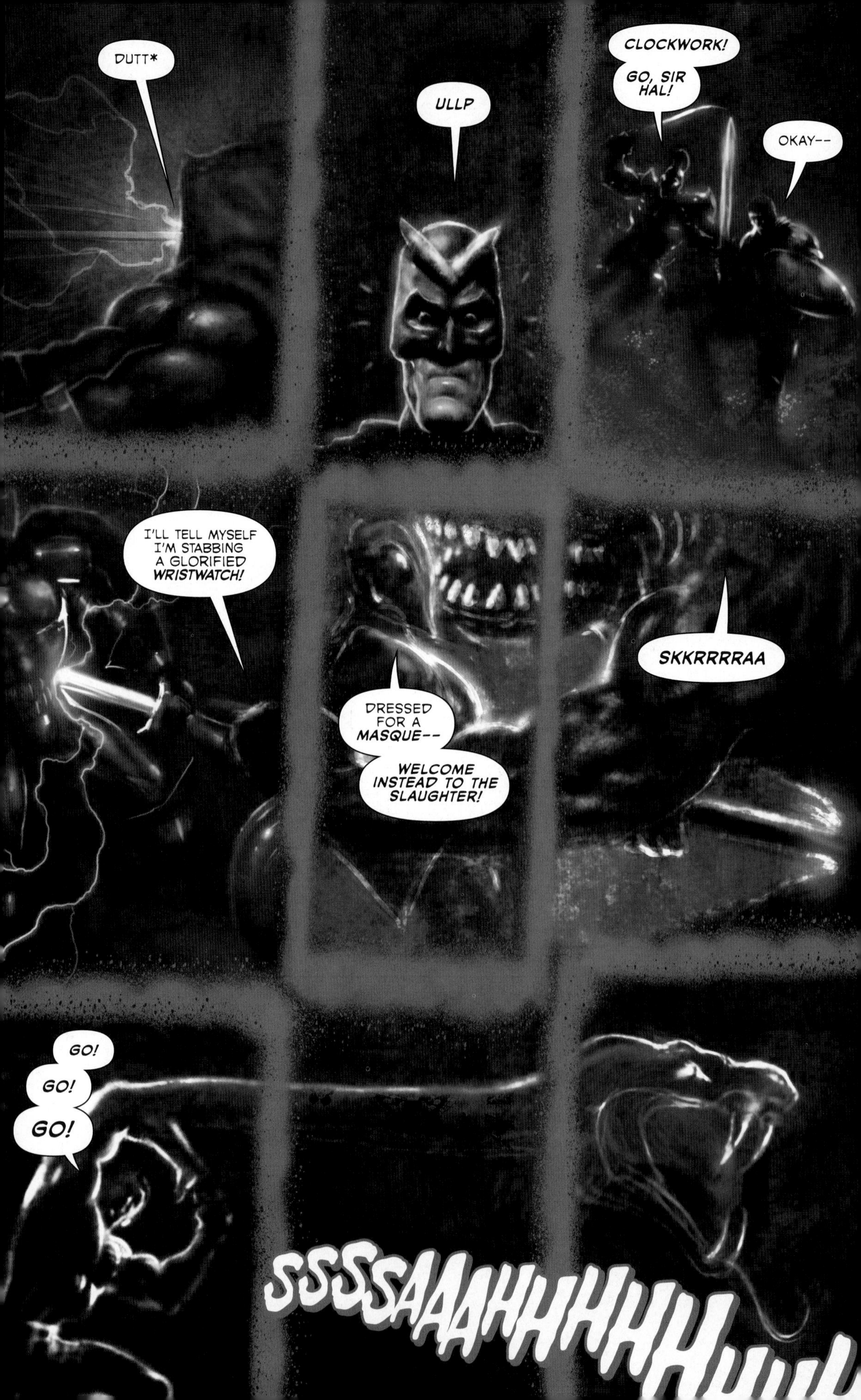
DUTT*
ULLP
CLOCKWORK!
GO, SIR HAL!
OKAY--
I'LL TELL MYSELF I'M STABBING A GLORIFIED WRISTWATCH!
DRESSED FOR A MASQUE--
WELCOME INSTEAD TO THE SLAUGHTER!
SKKRRRRAA
GO!
GO!
GO!
SSSSAAAHHHHHHuuul

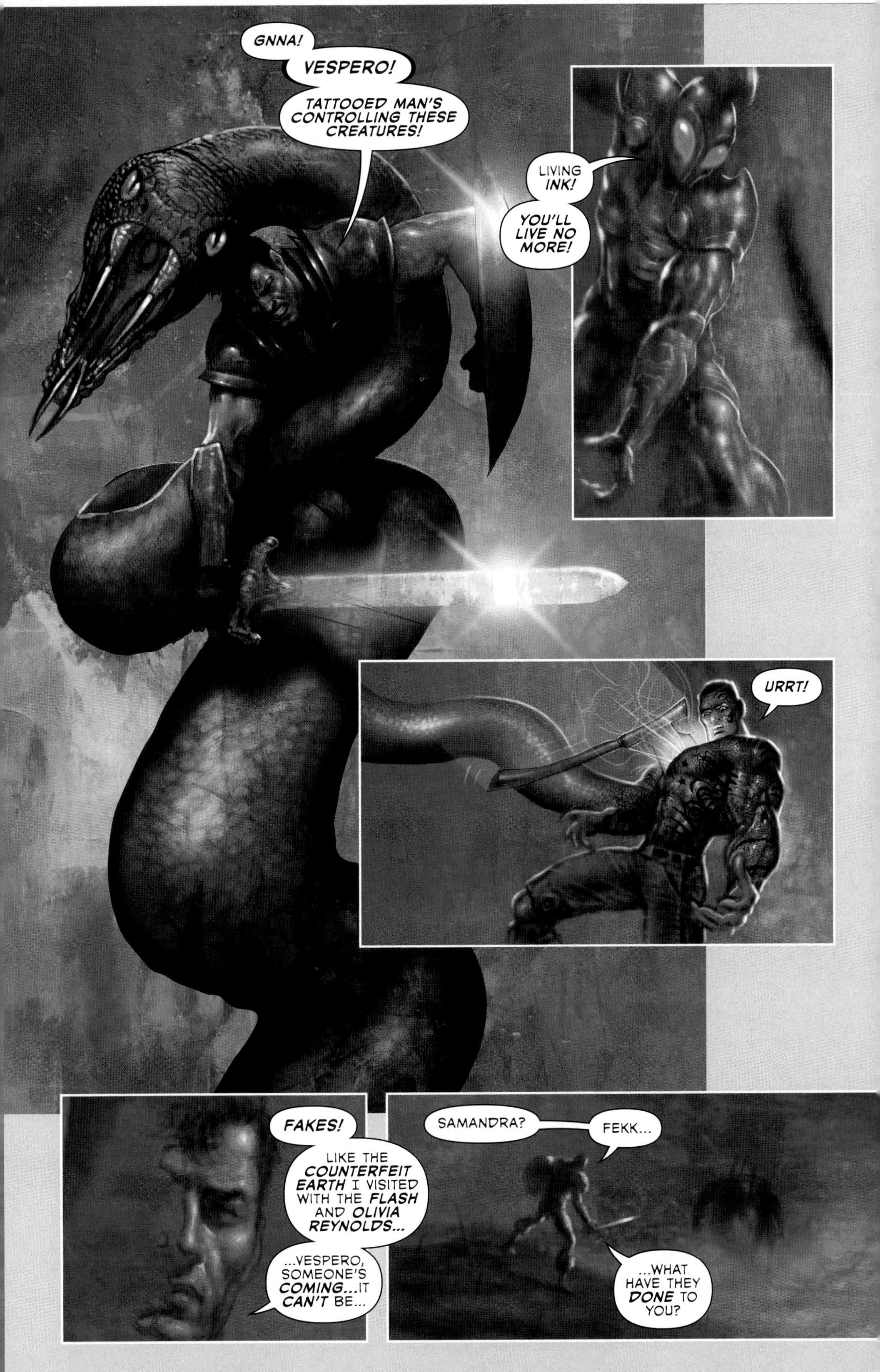
GNNA!
VESPERO!
TATTOOED MAN'S CONTROLLING THESE CREATURES!
LIVING INK!
YOU'LL LIVE NO MORE!
URRT!
FAKES!
LIKE THE COUNTERFEIT EARTH I VISITED WITH THE FLASH AND OLIVIA REYNOLDS...
...VESPERO, SOMEONE'S COMING...IT CAN'T BE...
SAMANDRA?
FEKK...
...WHAT HAVE THEY DONE TO YOU?

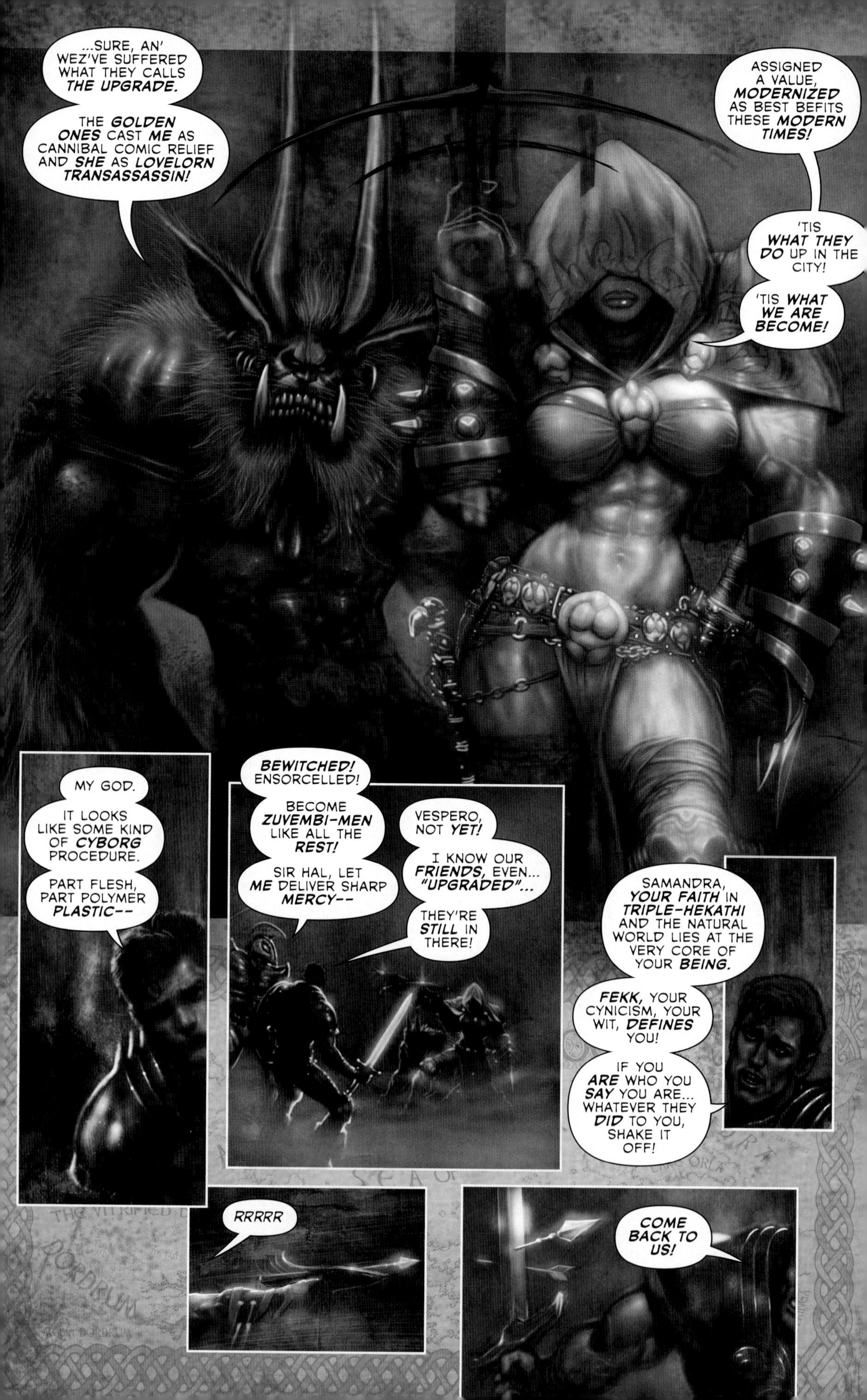

...SURE, AN' WEZ'VE SUFFERED WHAT THEY CALLS THE UPGRADE.
THE GOLDEN ONES CAST ME AS CANNIBAL COMIC RELIEF AND SHE AS LOVELORN TRANSASSASSIN!
ASSIGNED A VALUE, MODERNIZED AS BEST BEFITS THESE MODERN TIMES!
'TIS WHAT THEY DO UP IN THE CITY!
'TIS WHAT WE ARE BECOME!
MY GOD.
IT LOOKS LIKE SOME KIND OF CYBORG PROCEDURE.
PART FLESH, PART POLYMER PLASTIC--
BEWITCHED! ENSORCELLED!
BECOME ZUVEMBI-MEN LIKE ALL THE REST!
SIR HAL, LET ME DELIVER SHARP MERCY--
VESPERO, NOT YET!
I KNOW OUR FRIENDS, EVEN... "UPGRADED"...
THEY'RE STILL IN THERE!
SAMANDRA, YOUR FAITH IN TRIPLE-HEKATHI AND THE NATURAL WORLD LIES AT THE VERY CORE OF YOUR BEING.
FEKK, YOUR CYNICISM, YOUR WIT, DEFINES YOU!
IF YOU ARE WHO YOU SAY YOU ARE... WHATEVER THEY DID TO YOU, SHAKE IT OFF!
RRRRR
COME BACK TO US!

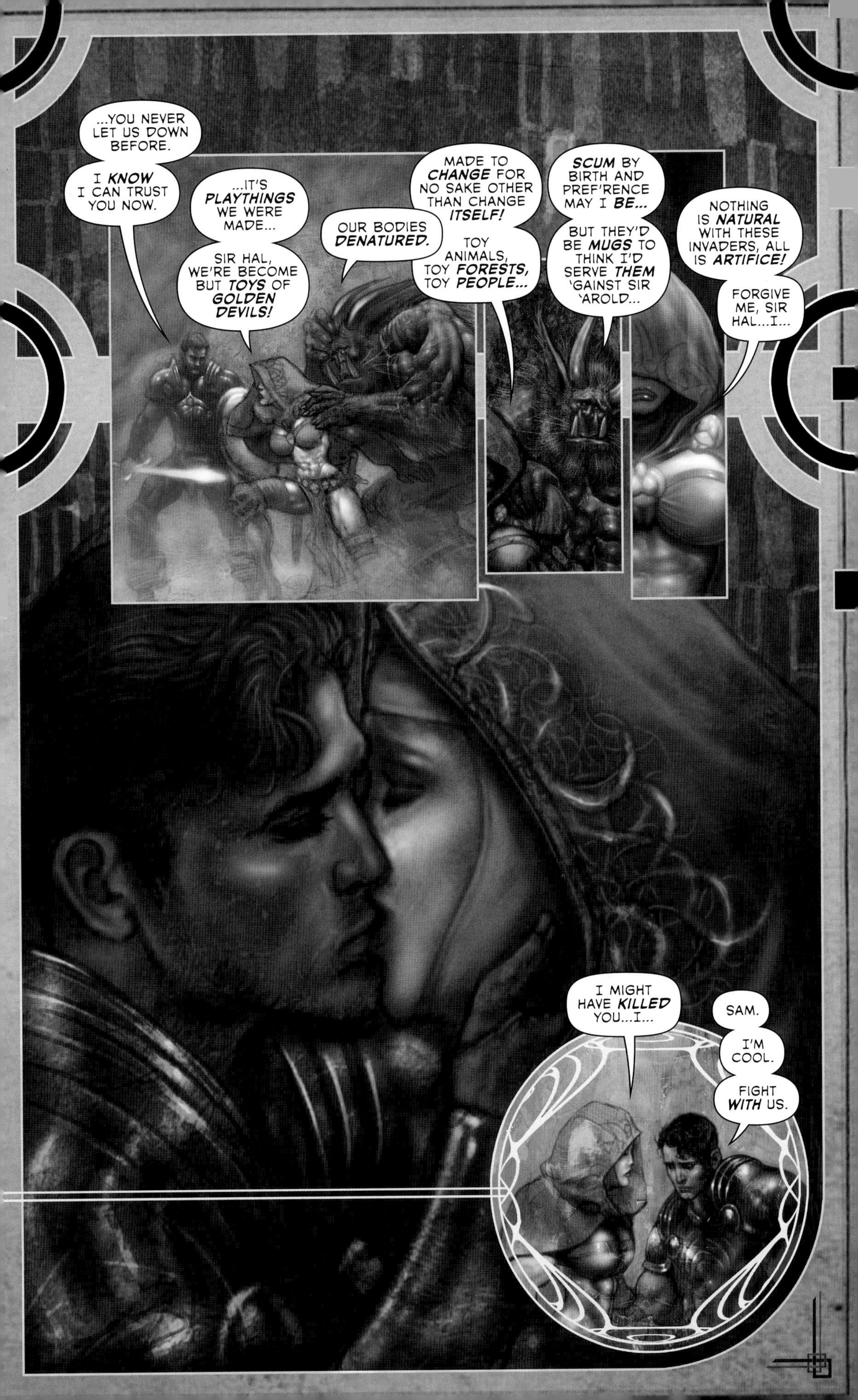
...YOU NEVER LET US DOWN BEFORE.
I KNOW I CAN TRUST YOU NOW.
...IT'S PLAYTHINGS WE WERE MADE...
SIR HAL, WE'RE BECOME BUT TOYS OF GOLDEN DEVILS!
OUR BODIES DENATURED.
MADE TO CHANGE FOR NO SAKE OTHER THAN CHANGE ITSELF!
TOY ANIMALS, TOY FORESTS, TOY PEOPLE...
SCUM BY BIRTH AND PREF'RENCE MAY I BE...
BUT THEY'D BE MUGS TO THINK I'D SERVE THEM 'GAINST SIR 'AROLD...
NOTHING IS NATURAL WITH THESE INVADERS, ALL IS ARTIFICE!
FORGIVE ME, SIR HAL...I...
I MIGHT HAVE KILLED YOU...I...
SAM.
I'M COOL.
FIGHT WITH US.

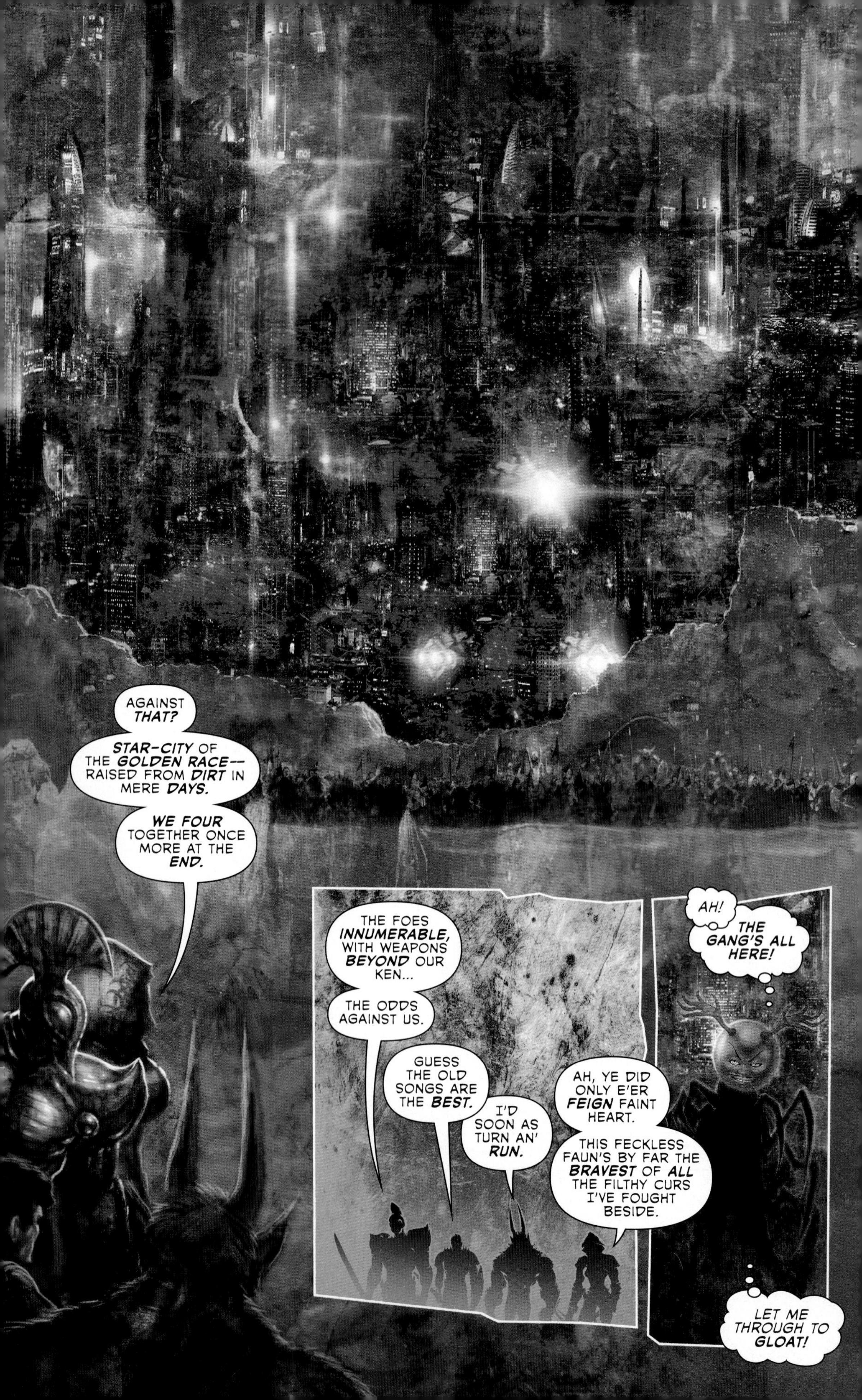
AGAINST *THAT?*
STAR-CITY OF THE ***GOLDEN RACE***-- RAISED FROM ***DIRT*** IN MERE ***DAYS.***
WE FOUR TOGETHER ONCE MORE AT THE ***END.***
THE FOES ***INNUMERABLE,*** WITH WEAPONS ***BEYOND*** OUR KEN...
THE ODDS AGAINST US.
GUESS THE OLD SONGS ARE THE ***BEST.***
I'D SOON AS TURN AN' ***RUN.***
AH, YE DID ONLY E'ER ***FEIGN*** FAINT HEART.
THIS FECKLESS FAUN'S BY FAR THE ***BRAVEST*** OF ***ALL*** THE FILTHY CURS I'VE FOUGHT BESIDE.
AH! ***THE GANG'S ALL HERE!***
LET ME THROUGH TO ***GLOAT!***

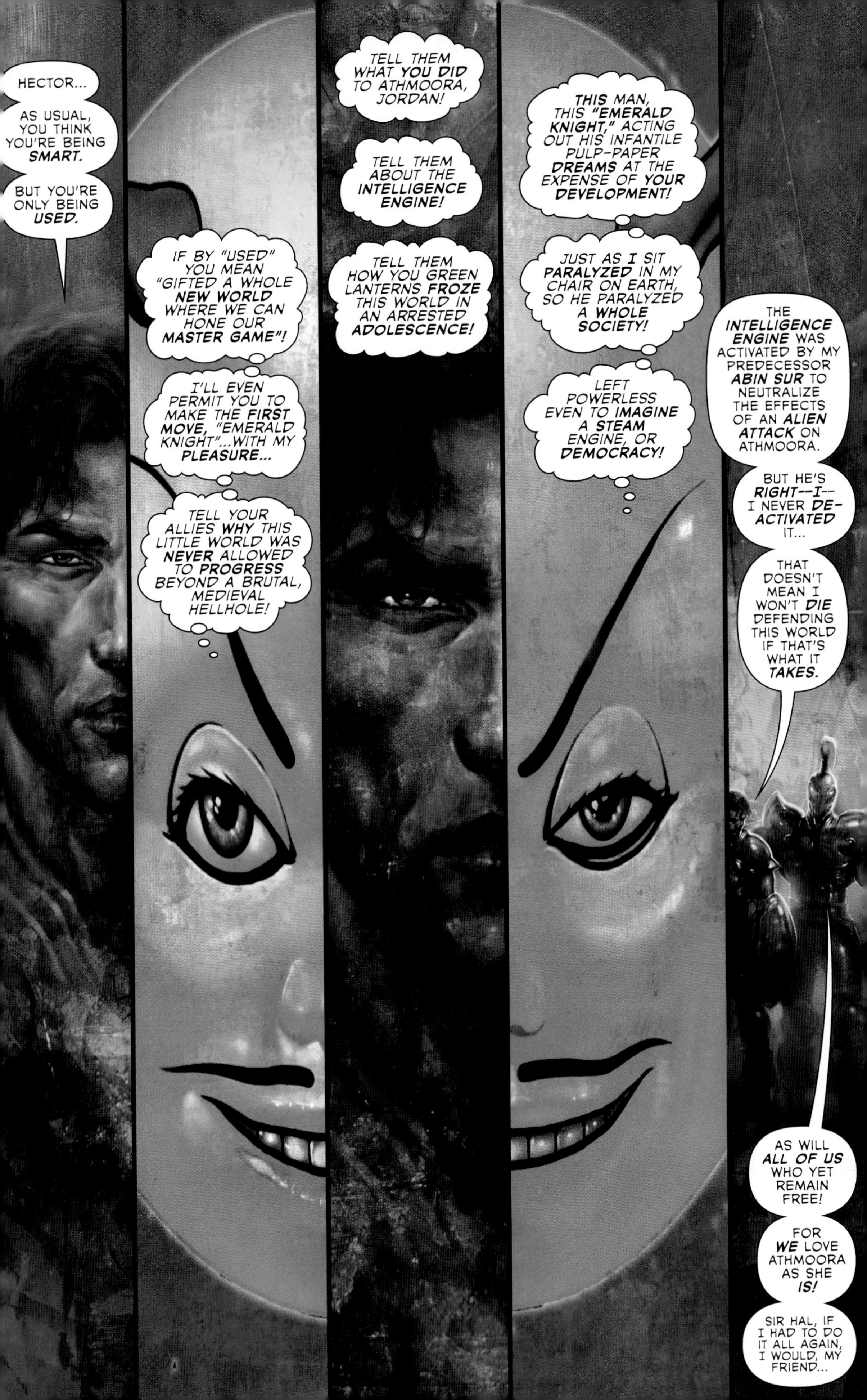
HECTOR...
AS USUAL, YOU THINK YOU'RE BEING SMART.
BUT YOU'RE ONLY BEING USED.
IF BY "USED" YOU MEAN "GIFTED A WHOLE NEW WORLD WHERE WE CAN HONE OUR MASTER GAME"!
I'LL EVEN PERMIT YOU TO MAKE THE FIRST MOVE, "EMERALD KNIGHT"...WITH MY PLEASURE...
TELL YOUR ALLIES WHY THIS LITTLE WORLD WAS NEVER ALLOWED TO PROGRESS BEYOND A BRUTAL, MEDIEVAL HELLHOLE!
TELL THEM WHAT YOU DID TO ATHMOORA, JORDAN!
TELL THEM ABOUT THE INTELLIGENCE ENGINE!
TELL THEM HOW YOU GREEN LANTERNS FROZE THIS WORLD IN AN ARRESTED ADOLESCENCE!
THIS MAN, THIS "EMERALD KNIGHT," ACTING OUT HIS INFANTILE PULP-PAPER DREAMS AT THE EXPENSE OF YOUR DEVELOPMENT!
JUST AS I SIT PARALYZED IN MY CHAIR ON EARTH, SO HE PARALYZED A WHOLE SOCIETY!
LEFT POWERLESS EVEN TO IMAGINE A STEAM ENGINE, OR DEMOCRACY!
THE INTELLIGENCE ENGINE WAS ACTIVATED BY MY PREDECESSOR ABIN SUR TO NEUTRALIZE THE EFFECTS OF AN ALIEN ATTACK ON ATHMOORA.
BUT HE'S RIGHT--I--I NEVER DE-ACTIVATED IT...
THAT DOESN'T MEAN I WON'T DIE DEFENDING THIS WORLD IF THAT'S WHAT IT TAKES.
AS WILL ALL OF US WHO YET REMAIN FREE!
FOR WE LOVE ATHMOORA AS SHE IS!
SIR HAL, IF I HAD TO DO IT ALL AGAIN, I WOULD, MY FRIEND...

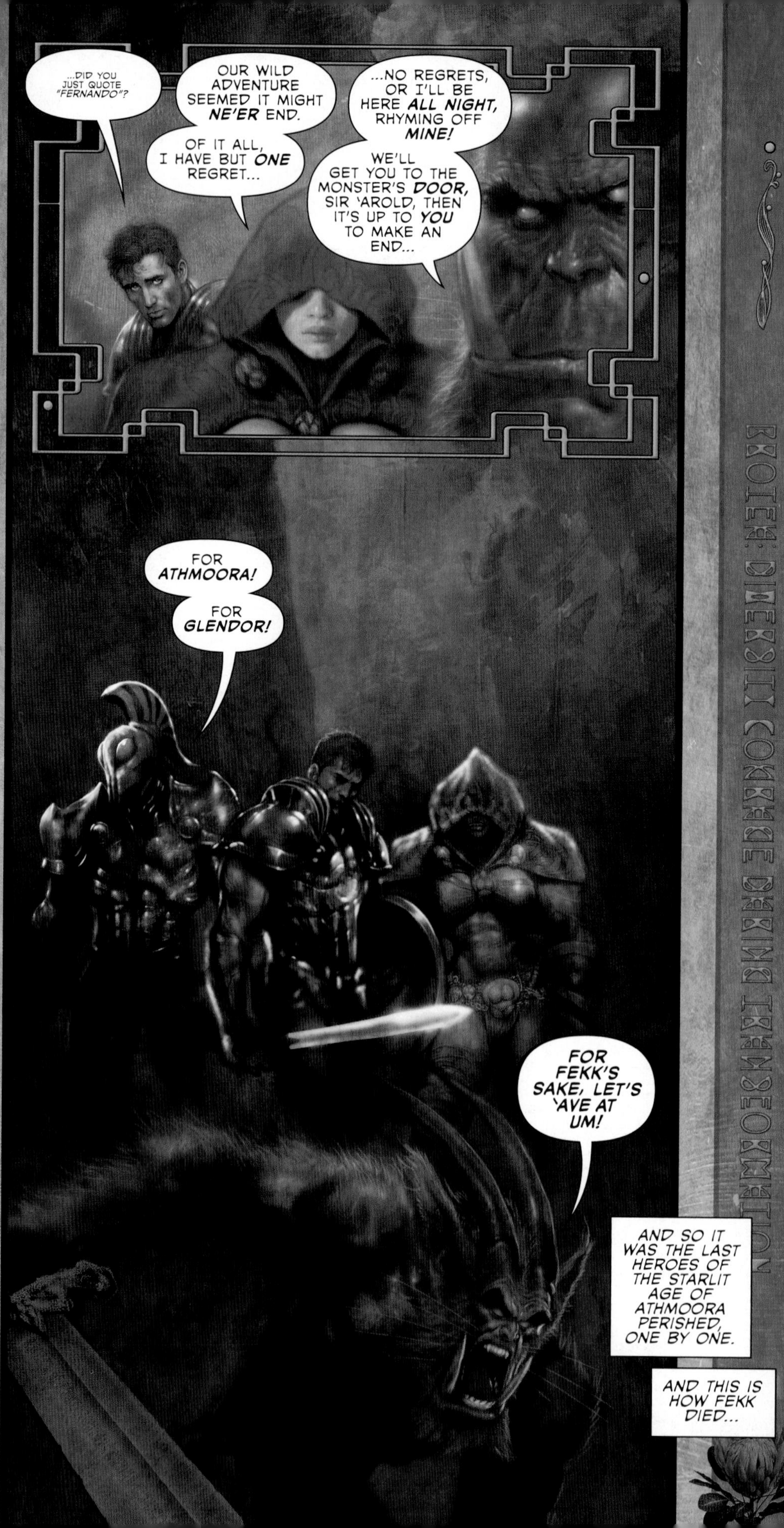

...DID YOU JUST QUOTE "FERNANDO"?
OUR WILD ADVENTURE SEEMED IT MIGHT NE'ER END.
OF IT ALL, I HAVE BUT ONE REGRET...
...NO REGRETS, OR I'LL BE HERE ALL NIGHT, RHYMING OFF MINE!
WE'LL GET YOU TO THE MONSTER'S DOOR, SIR 'AROLD, THEN IT'S UP TO YOU TO MAKE AN END...
FOR ATHMOORA!
FOR GLENDOR!
FOR FEKK'S SAKE, LET'S 'AVE AT UM!
AND SO IT WAS THE LAST HEROES OF THE STARLIT AGE OF ATHMOORA PERISHED, ONE BY ONE.
AND THIS IS HOW FEKK DIED...

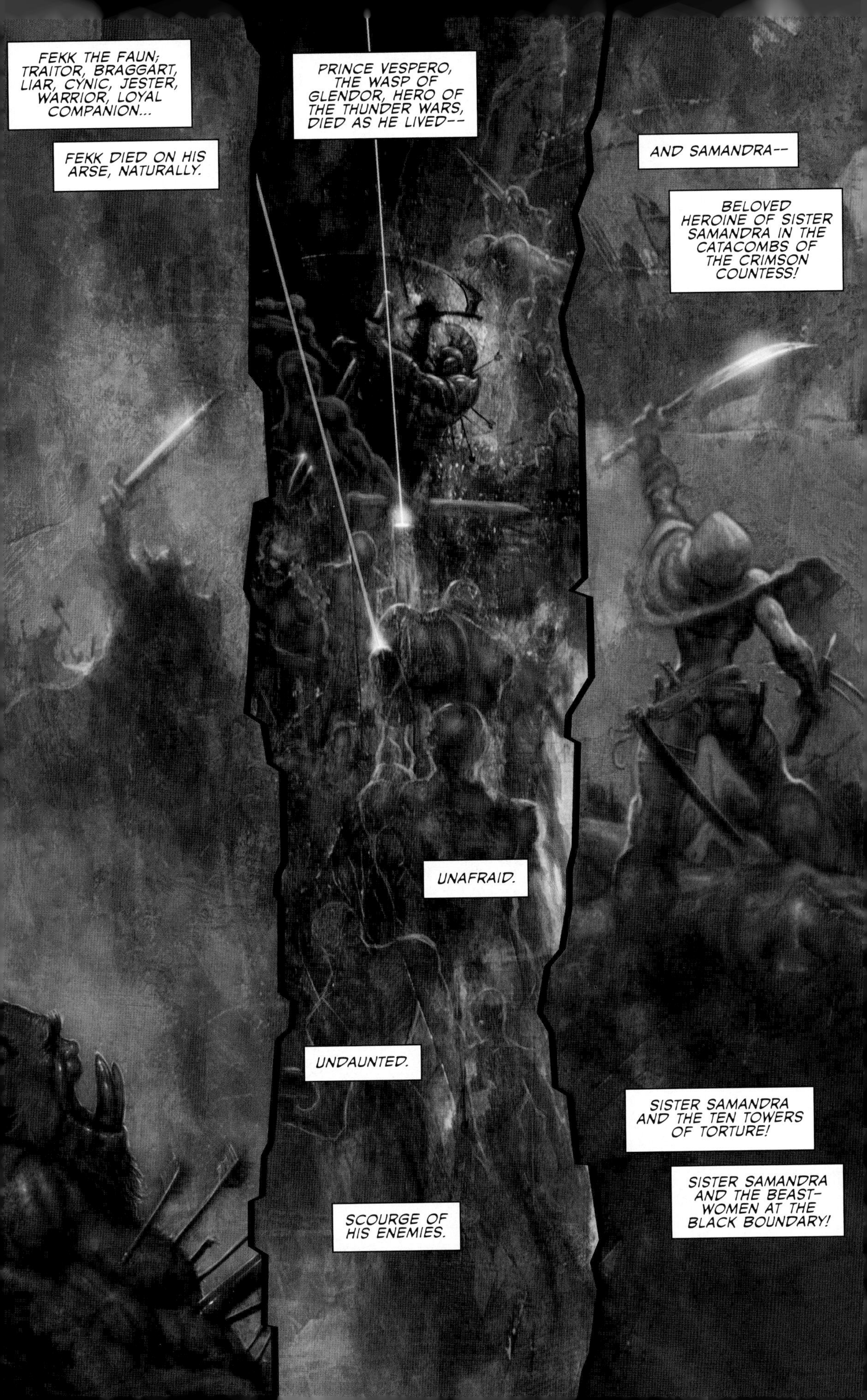
FEKK THE FAUN; TRAITOR, BRAGGART, LIAR, CYNIC, JESTER, WARRIOR, LOYAL COMPANION...
FEKK DIED ON HIS ARSE, NATURALLY.
PRINCE VESPERO, THE WASP OF GLENDOR, HERO OF THE THUNDER WARS, DIED AS HE LIVED--
UNAFRAID.
UNDAUNTED.
SCOURGE OF HIS ENEMIES.
AND SAMANDRA--
BELOVED HEROINE OF SISTER SAMANDRA IN THE CATACOMBS OF THE CRIMSON COUNTESS!
SISTER SAMANDRA AND THE TEN TOWERS OF TORTURE!
SISTER SAMANDRA AND THE BEAST-WOMEN AT THE BLACK BOUNDARY!

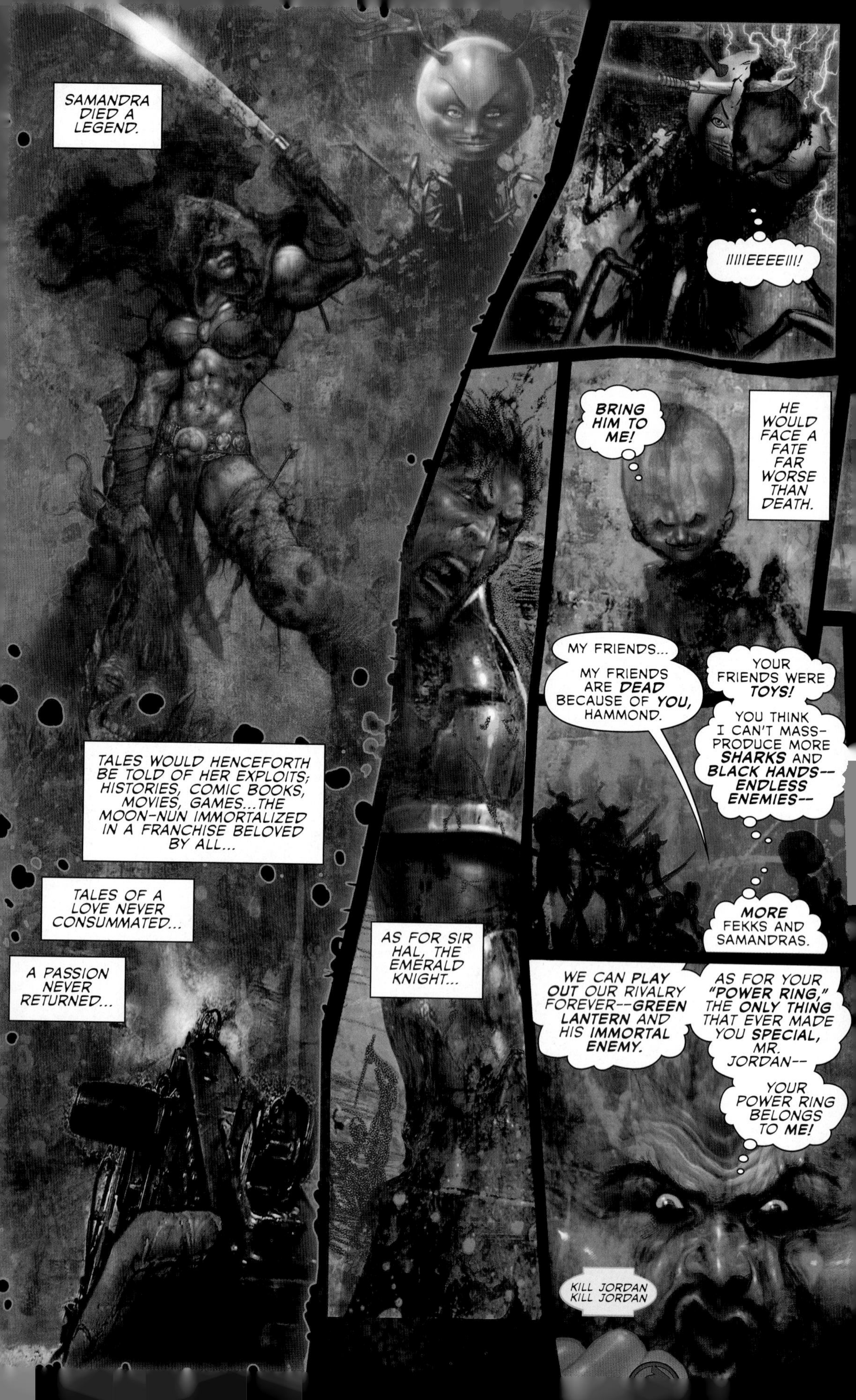
SAMANDRA DIED A LEGEND.
IIIIIEEEEIII!
TALES WOULD HENCEFORTH BE TOLD OF HER EXPLOITS; HISTORIES, COMIC BOOKS, MOVIES, GAMES...THE MOON-NUN IMMORTALIZED IN A FRANCHISE BELOVED BY ALL...
TALES OF A LOVE NEVER CONSUMMATED...
A PASSION NEVER RETURNED...
AS FOR SIR HAL, THE EMERALD KNIGHT...
BRING HIM TO ME!
HE WOULD FACE A FATE FAR WORSE THAN DEATH.
MY FRIENDS...
MY FRIENDS ARE DEAD BECAUSE OF YOU, HAMMOND.
YOUR FRIENDS WERE TOYS!
YOU THINK I CAN'T MASS-PRODUCE MORE SHARKS AND BLACK HANDS--ENDLESS ENEMIES--
MORE FEKKS AND SAMANDRAS.
WE CAN PLAY OUT OUR RIVALRY FOREVER--GREEN LANTERN AND HIS IMMORTAL ENEMY.
AS FOR YOUR "POWER RING," THE ONLY THING THAT EVER MADE YOU SPECIAL, MR. JORDAN--
YOUR POWER RING BELONGS TO ME!
KILL JORDAN KILL JORDAN

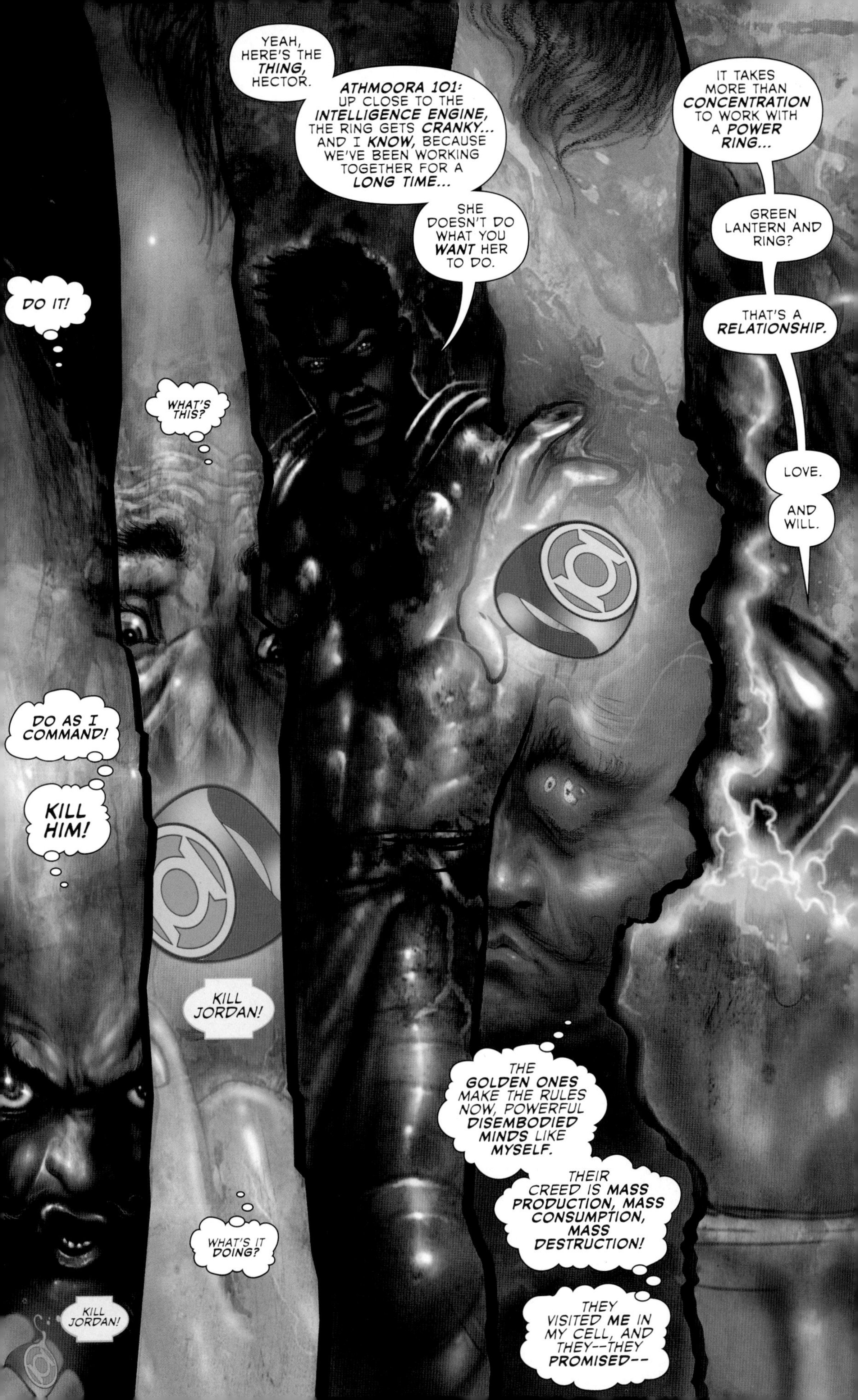
YEAH, HERE'S THE THING, HECTOR.
ATHMOORA 101: UP CLOSE TO THE INTELLIGENCE ENGINE, THE RING GETS CRANKY... AND I KNOW, BECAUSE WE'VE BEEN WORKING TOGETHER FOR A LONG TIME...
SHE DOESN'T DO WHAT YOU WANT HER TO DO.
IT TAKES MORE THAN CONCENTRATION TO WORK WITH A POWER RING...
GREEN LANTERN AND RING?
THAT'S A RELATIONSHIP.
LOVE.
AND WILL.
DO IT!
WHAT'S THIS?
DO AS I COMMAND!
KILL HIM!
KILL JORDAN!
WHAT'S IT DOING?
KILL JORDAN!
THE GOLDEN ONES MAKE THE RULES NOW, POWERFUL DISEMBODIED MINDS LIKE MYSELF.
THEIR CREED IS MASS PRODUCTION, MASS CONSUMPTION, MASS DESTRUCTION!
THEY VISITED ME IN MY CELL, AND THEY--THEY PROMISED--

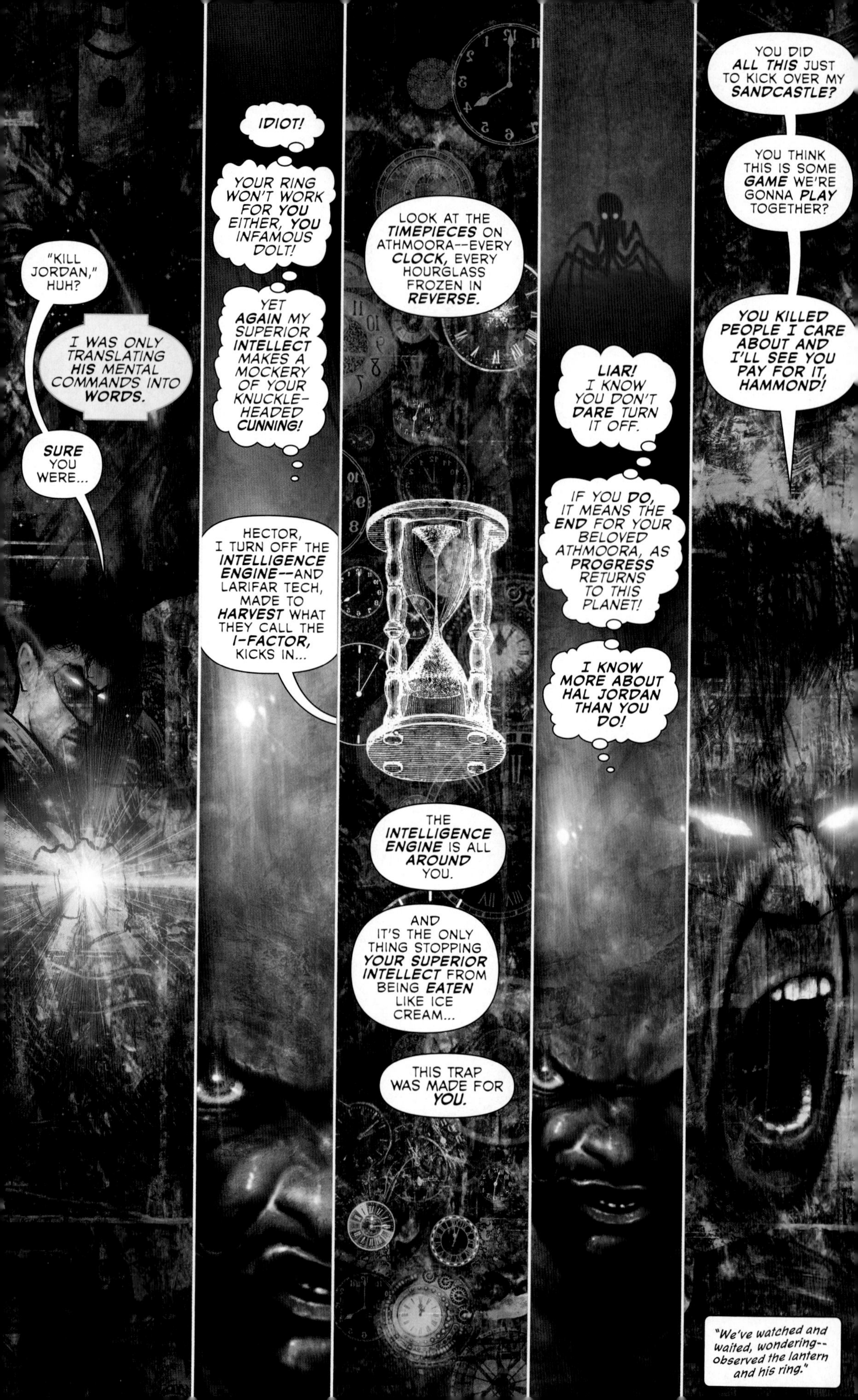

"KILL JORDAN," HUH?
I WAS ONLY TRANSLATING HIS MENTAL COMMANDS INTO WORDS.
SURE YOU WERE...
IDIOT!
YOUR RING WON'T WORK FOR YOU EITHER, YOU INFAMOUS DOLT!
YET AGAIN MY SUPERIOR INTELLECT MAKES A MOCKERY OF YOUR KNUCKLE-HEADED CUNNING!
HECTOR, I TURN OFF THE INTELLIGENCE ENGINE--AND LARIFAR TECH, MADE TO HARVEST WHAT THEY CALL THE I-FACTOR, KICKS IN...
LOOK AT THE TIMEPIECES ON ATHMOORA--EVERY CLOCK, EVERY HOURGLASS FROZEN IN REVERSE.
THE INTELLIGENCE ENGINE IS ALL AROUND YOU.
AND IT'S THE ONLY THING STOPPING YOUR SUPERIOR INTELLECT FROM BEING EATEN LIKE ICE CREAM...
THIS TRAP WAS MADE FOR YOU.
LIAR! I KNOW YOU DON'T DARE TURN IT OFF.
IF YOU DO, IT MEANS THE END FOR YOUR BELOVED ATHMOORA, AS PROGRESS RETURNS TO THIS PLANET!
I KNOW MORE ABOUT HAL JORDAN THAN YOU DO!
YOU DID ALL THIS JUST TO KICK OVER MY SANDCASTLE?
YOU THINK THIS IS SOME GAME WE'RE GONNA PLAY TOGETHER?
YOU KILLED PEOPLE I CARE ABOUT AND I'LL SEE YOU PAY FOR IT, HAMMOND!
"We've watched and waited, wondering--observed the lantern and his ring."

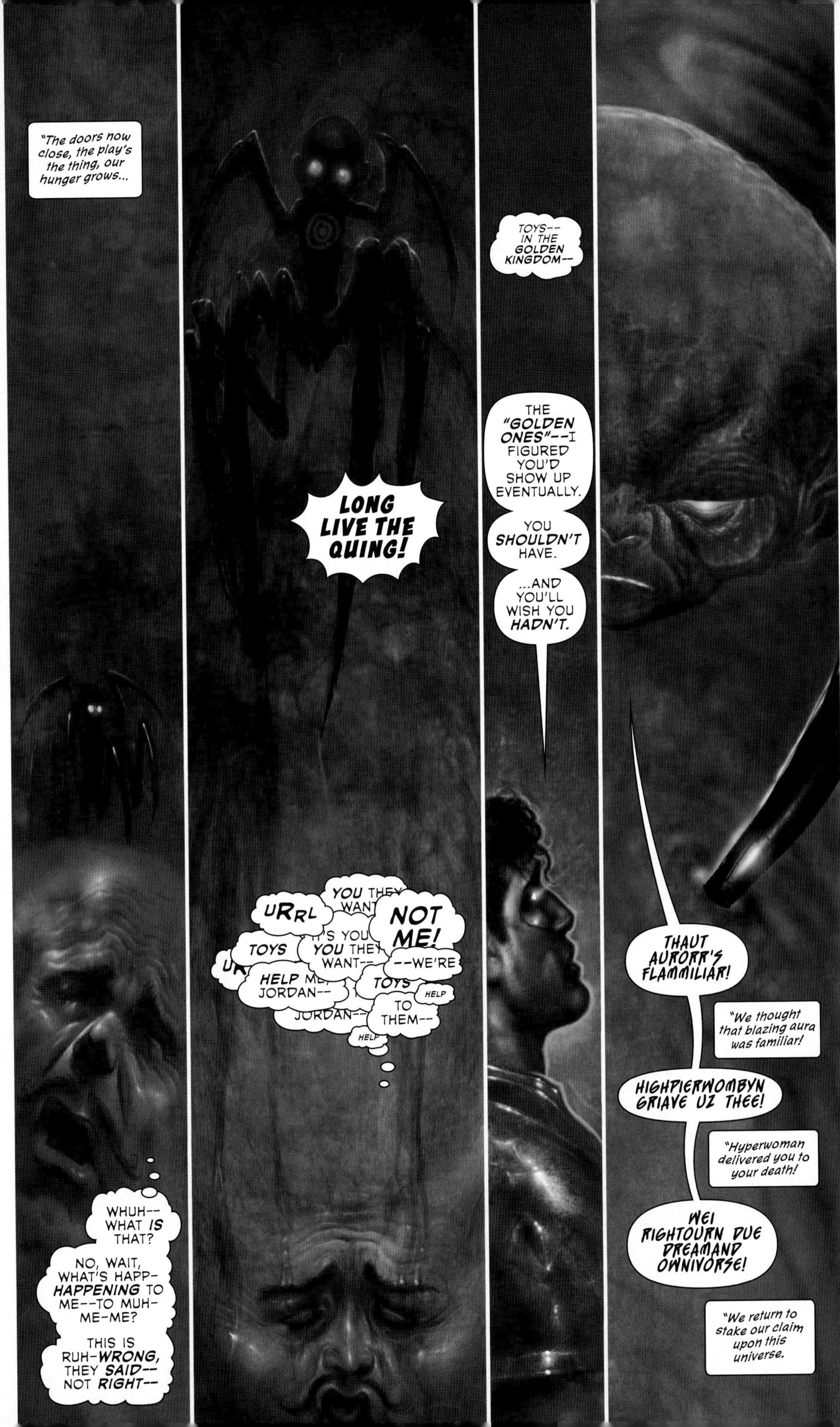
"The doors now close, the play's the thing, our hunger grows...
WHUH--WHAT *IS* THAT?
NO, WAIT, WHAT'S HAPP-*HAPPENING* TO ME--TO MUH-ME-ME?
THIS IS RUH-*WRONG,* THEY *SAID*-- NOT *RIGHT*--
LONG LIVE THE QUING!
URRL
NOT ME!
TOYS
YOU THEY WANT--
--WE'RE
HELP ME,
JORDAN--
TOYS
HELP
TO THEM--
JORDAN--
HELP
TOYS-- IN THE GOLDEN KINGDOM--
THE *"GOLDEN ONES"*--I FIGURED YOU'D SHOW UP EVENTUALLY.
YOU *SHOULDN'T* HAVE.
...AND YOU'LL WISH YOU *HADN'T.*
THAUT AURORR'S FLAMMILIAR!
"We thought that blazing aura was familiar!
HIGHPIERWOMBYN GRIAVE UZ THEE!
"Hyperwoman delivered you to your death!
WEI RIGHTOURN DUE DREAMAND OWNIVORSE!
"We return to stake our claim upon this universe.

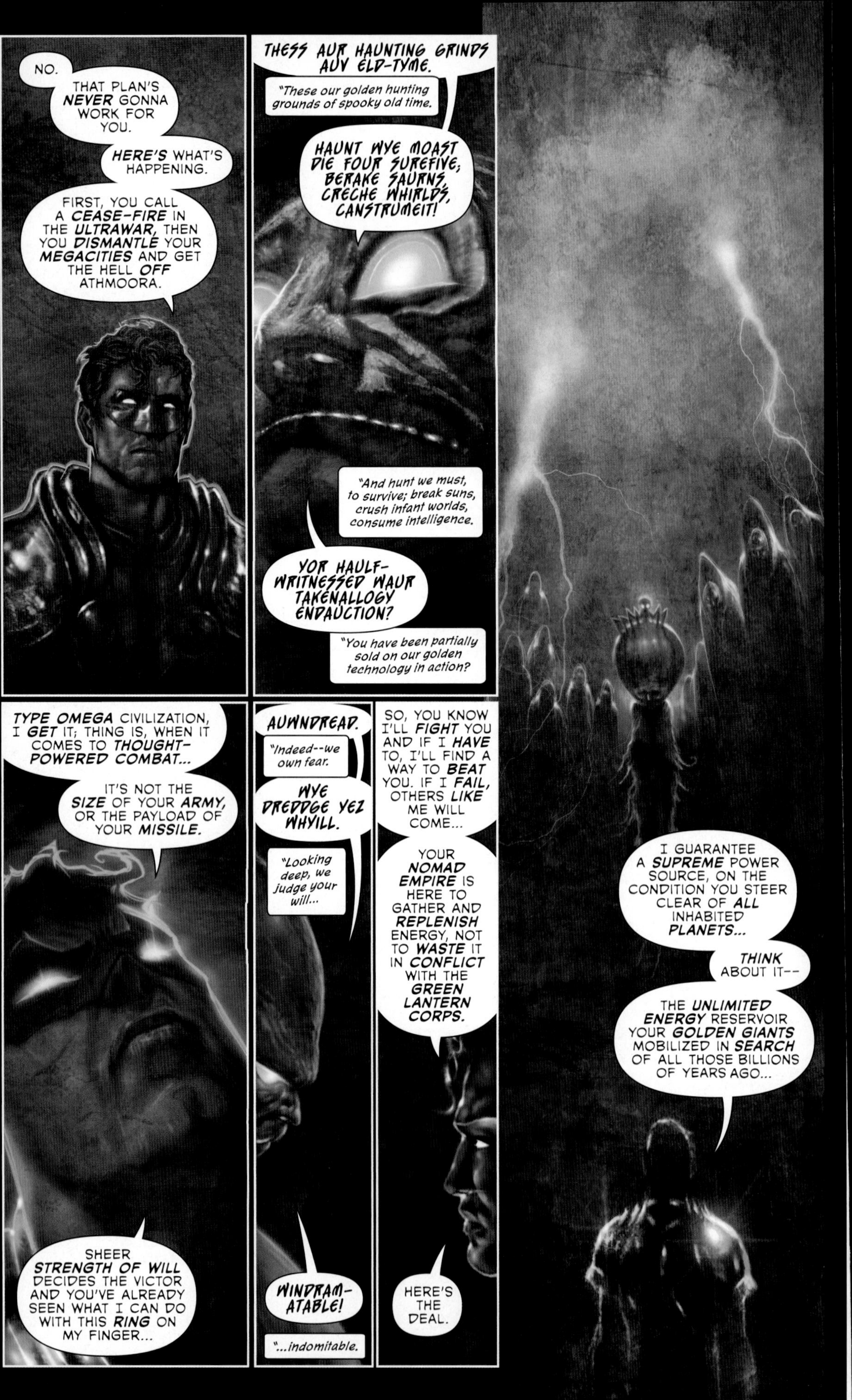

NO.
THAT PLAN'S NEVER GONNA WORK FOR YOU.
HERE'S WHAT'S HAPPENING.
FIRST, YOU CALL A CEASE-FIRE IN THE ULTRAWAR, THEN YOU DISMANTLE YOUR MEGACITIES AND GET THE HELL OFF ATHMOORA.
THESS AUR HAUNTING GRINDS AUV ELD-TYME.
"These our golden hunting grounds of spooky old time.
HAUNT WYE MOAST DIE FOUR SUREFIVE; BERAKE SAURNS, CRECHE WHIRLDS, CANSTRUMEIT!
"And hunt we must, to survive; break suns, crush infant worlds, consume intelligence.
YOR HAULF-WRITNESSED WAUR TAKENALLOGY ENDAUCTION?
"You have been partially sold on our golden technology in action?
TYPE OMEGA CIVILIZATION, I GET IT; THING IS, WHEN IT COMES TO THOUGHT-POWERED COMBAT...
IT'S NOT THE SIZE OF YOUR ARMY, OR THE PAYLOAD OF YOUR MISSILE.
SHEER STRENGTH OF WILL DECIDES THE VICTOR AND YOU'VE ALREADY SEEN WHAT I CAN DO WITH THIS RING ON MY FINGER...
AUWNDREAD.
"Indeed--we own fear.
WYE DREDDGE YEZ WHYILL.
"Looking deep, we judge your will...
WINDRAM-ATABLE!
"...indomitable.
SO, YOU KNOW I'LL FIGHT YOU AND IF I HAVE TO, I'LL FIND A WAY TO BEAT YOU. IF I FAIL, OTHERS LIKE ME WILL COME...
YOUR NOMAD EMPIRE IS HERE TO GATHER AND REPLENISH ENERGY, NOT TO WASTE IT IN CONFLICT WITH THE GREEN LANTERN CORPS.
HERE'S THE DEAL.
I GUARANTEE A SUPREME POWER SOURCE, ON THE CONDITION YOU STEER CLEAR OF ALL INHABITED PLANETS...
THINK ABOUT IT--
THE UNLIMITED ENERGY RESERVOIR YOUR GOLDEN GIANTS MOBILIZED IN SEARCH OF ALL THOSE BILLIONS OF YEARS AGO...

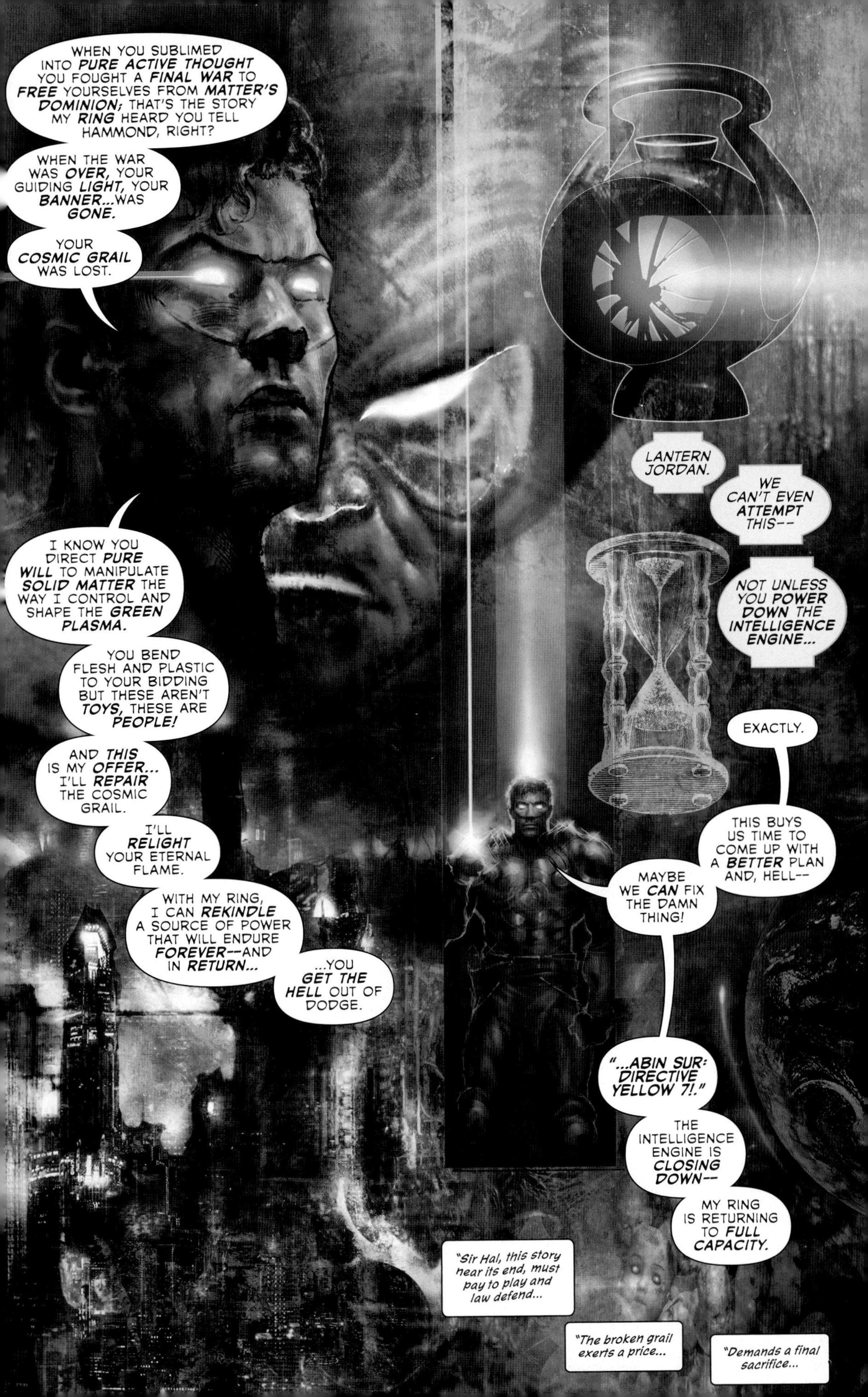
WHEN YOU SUBLIMED INTO PURE ACTIVE THOUGHT YOU FOUGHT A FINAL WAR TO FREE YOURSELVES FROM MATTER'S DOMINION; THAT'S THE STORY MY RING HEARD YOU TELL HAMMOND, RIGHT?
WHEN THE WAR WAS OVER, YOUR GUIDING LIGHT, YOUR BANNER...WAS GONE.
YOUR COSMIC GRAIL WAS LOST.
I KNOW YOU DIRECT PURE WILL TO MANIPULATE SOLID MATTER THE WAY I CONTROL AND SHAPE THE GREEN PLASMA.
YOU BEND FLESH AND PLASTIC TO YOUR BIDDING BUT THESE AREN'T TOYS, THESE ARE PEOPLE!
AND THIS IS MY OFFER... I'LL REPAIR THE COSMIC GRAIL.
I'LL RELIGHT YOUR ETERNAL FLAME.
WITH MY RING, I CAN REKINDLE A SOURCE OF POWER THAT WILL ENDURE FOREVER--AND IN RETURN...
...YOU GET THE HELL OUT OF DODGE.
LANTERN JORDAN.
WE CAN'T EVEN ATTEMPT THIS--
NOT UNLESS YOU POWER DOWN THE INTELLIGENCE ENGINE...
EXACTLY.
THIS BUYS US TIME TO COME UP WITH A BETTER PLAN AND, HELL--
MAYBE WE CAN FIX THE DAMN THING!
"...ABIN SUR: DIRECTIVE YELLOW 7!."
THE INTELLIGENCE ENGINE IS CLOSING DOWN--
MY RING IS RETURNING TO FULL CAPACITY.
"Sir Hal, this story near its end, must pay to play and law defend...
"The broken grail exerts a price...
"Demands a final sacrifice...

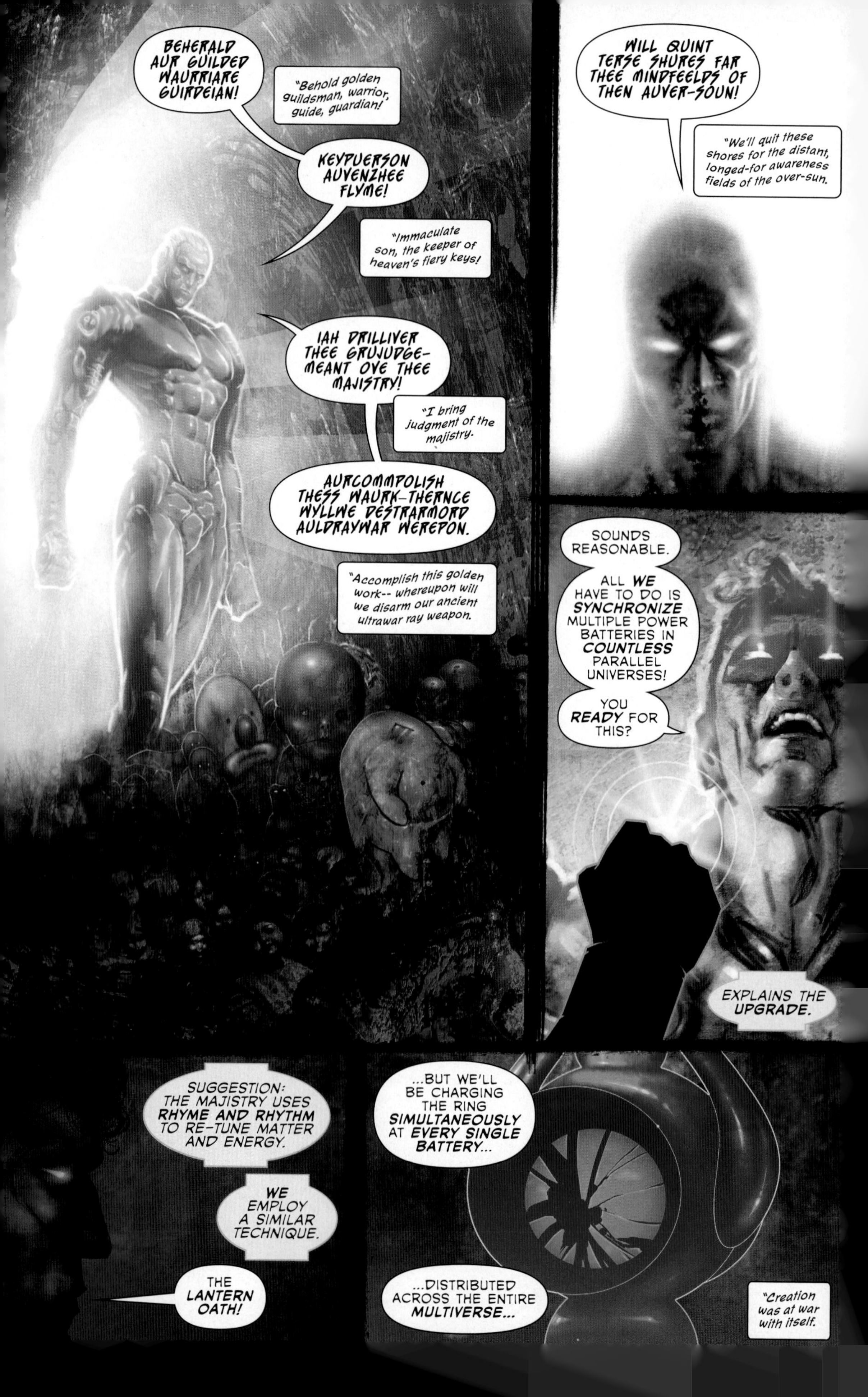

BEHERALD AUR GUILDED WAURRIARE GUIRDEIAN!
"Behold golden guildsman, warrior, guide, guardian!
KEYPUERSON AUVENZHEE FLYME!
"Immaculate son, the keeper of heaven's fiery keys!
IAH DRILLIVER THEE GRUJUDGE-MEANT OVE THEE MAJISTRY!
"I bring judgment of the majistry.
AURCOMMPOLISH THESS WAURK-THERNCE WYLLWE DESTRARMORD AULDRAYWAR WEREPON.
"Accomplish this golden work-- whereupon will we disarm our ancient ultrawar ray weapon.
WILL QUINT TERSE SHURES FAR THEE MINDFEELDS OF THEN AUVER-SOUN!
"We'll quit these shores for the distant, longed-for awareness fields of the over-sun.
SOUNDS REASONABLE.
ALL WE HAVE TO DO IS SYNCHRONIZE MULTIPLE POWER BATTERIES IN COUNTLESS PARALLEL UNIVERSES!
YOU READY FOR THIS?
EXPLAINS THE UPGRADE.
SUGGESTION: THE MAJISTRY USES RHYME AND RHYTHM TO RE-TUNE MATTER AND ENERGY.
WE EMPLOY A SIMILAR TECHNIQUE.
THE LANTERN OATH!
...BUT WE'LL BE CHARGING THE RING SIMULTANEOUSLY AT EVERY SINGLE BATTERY...
...DISTRIBUTED ACROSS THE ENTIRE MULTIVERSE...
"Creation was at war with itself.

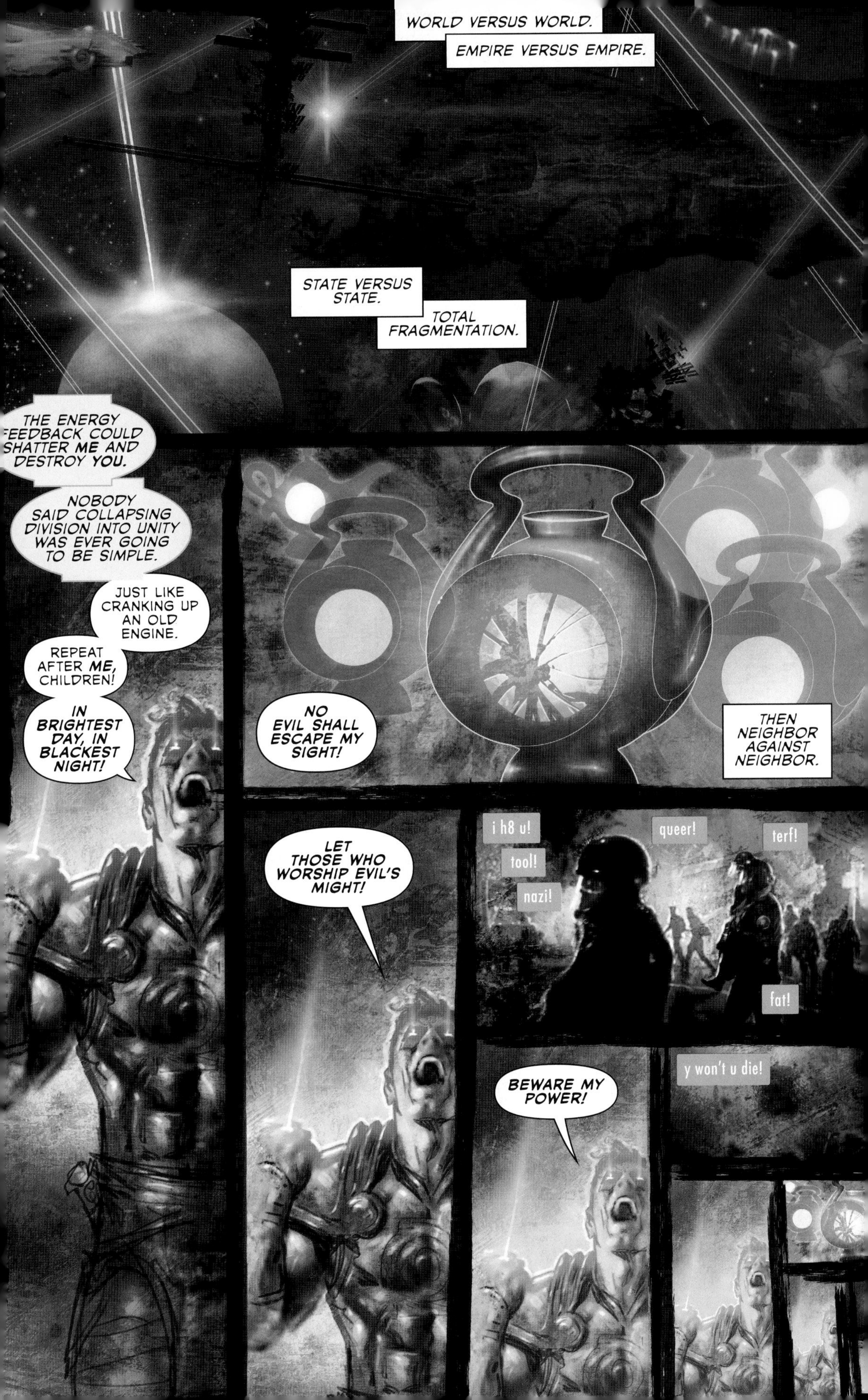
WORLD VERSUS WORLD.
EMPIRE VERSUS EMPIRE.
STATE VERSUS STATE.
TOTAL FRAGMENTATION.
THE ENERGY FEEDBACK COULD SHATTER ME AND DESTROY YOU.
NOBODY SAID COLLAPSING DIVISION INTO UNITY WAS EVER GOING TO BE SIMPLE.
JUST LIKE CRANKING UP AN OLD ENGINE.
REPEAT AFTER ME, CHILDREN!
IN BRIGHTEST DAY, IN BLACKEST NIGHT!
NO EVIL SHALL ESCAPE MY SIGHT!
THEN NEIGHBOR AGAINST NEIGHBOR.
LET THOSE WHO WORSHIP EVIL'S MIGHT!
i h8 u!
tool!
nazi!
queer!
terf!
fat!
BEWARE MY POWER!
y won't u die!

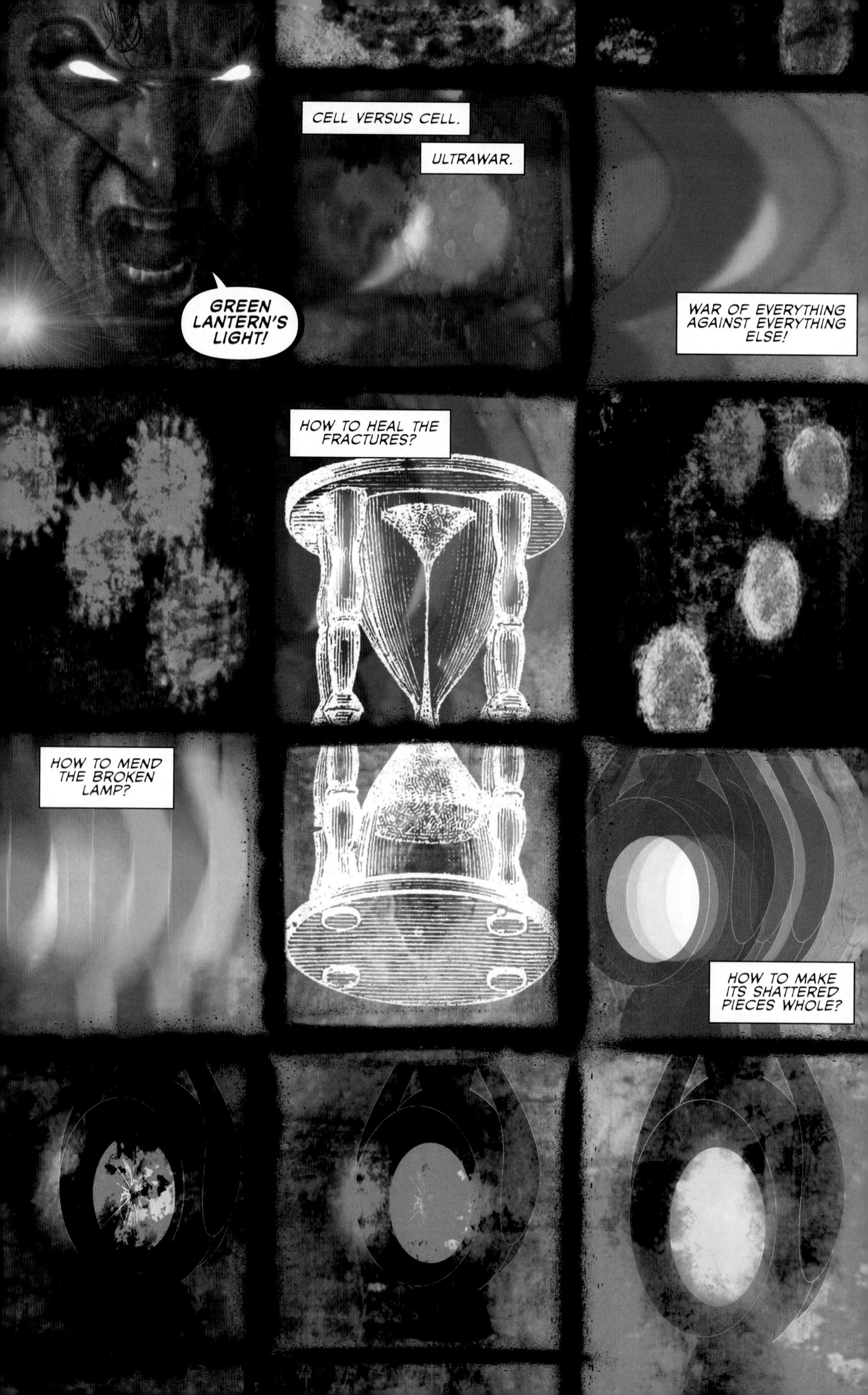
GREEN LANTERN'S LIGHT!
CELL VERSUS CELL.
ULTRAWAR.
WAR OF EVERYTHING AGAINST EVERYTHING ELSE!
HOW TO HEAL THE FRACTURES?
HOW TO MEND THE BROKEN LAMP?
HOW TO MAKE ITS SHATTERED PIECES WHOLE?

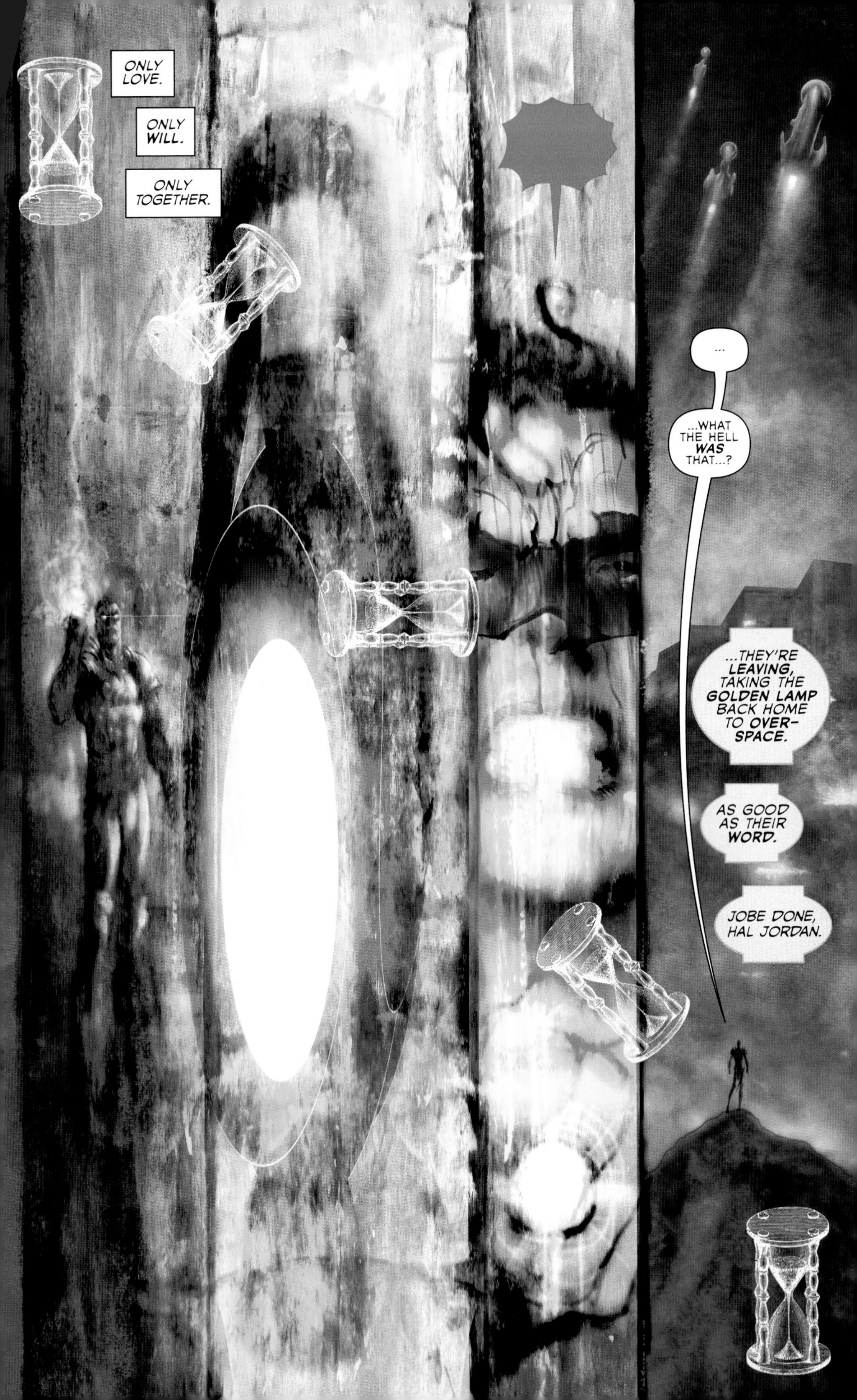
ONLY LOVE.
ONLY WILL.
ONLY TOGETHER.
...
...WHAT THE HELL WAS THAT...?
...THEY'RE LEAVING, TAKING THE GOLDEN LAMP BACK HOME TO OVER-SPACE.
AS GOOD AS THEIR WORD.
JOBE DONE, HAL JORDAN.

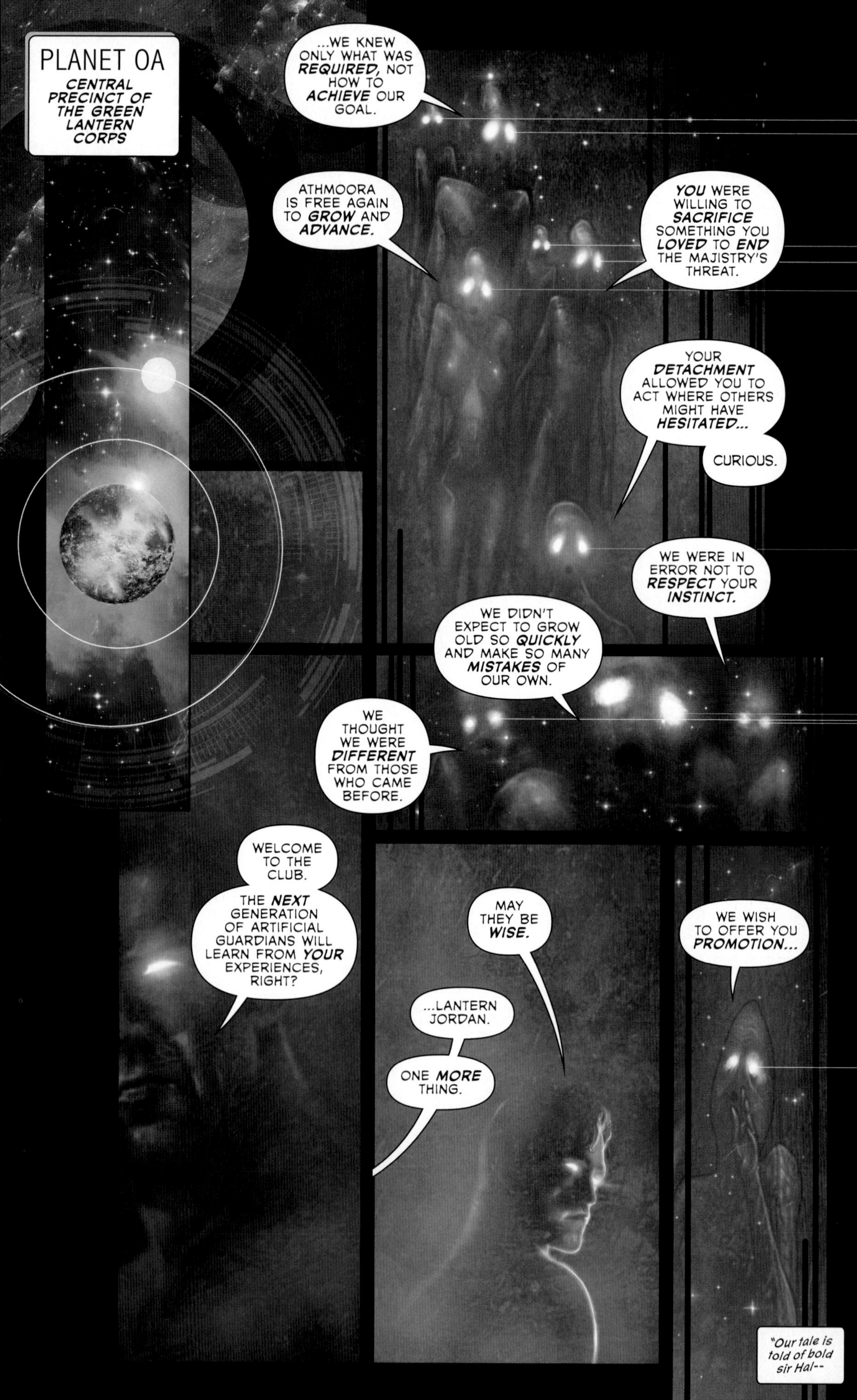
PLANET OA
CENTRAL PRECINCT OF THE GREEN LANTERN CORPS
...WE KNEW ONLY WHAT WAS REQUIRED, NOT HOW TO ACHIEVE OUR GOAL.
ATHMOORA IS FREE AGAIN TO GROW AND ADVANCE.
YOU WERE WILLING TO SACRIFICE SOMETHING YOU LOVED TO END THE MAJISTRY'S THREAT.
YOUR DETACHMENT ALLOWED YOU TO ACT WHERE OTHERS MIGHT HAVE HESITATED...
CURIOUS.
WE WERE IN ERROR NOT TO RESPECT YOUR INSTINCT.
WE DIDN'T EXPECT TO GROW OLD SO QUICKLY AND MAKE SO MANY MISTAKES OF OUR OWN.
WE THOUGHT WE WERE DIFFERENT FROM THOSE WHO CAME BEFORE.
WELCOME TO THE CLUB.
THE NEXT GENERATION OF ARTIFICIAL GUARDIANS WILL LEARN FROM YOUR EXPERIENCES, RIGHT?
MAY THEY BE WISE.
...LANTERN JORDAN.
ONE MORE THING.
WE WISH TO OFFER YOU PROMOTION...
"Our tale is told of bold sir Hal--

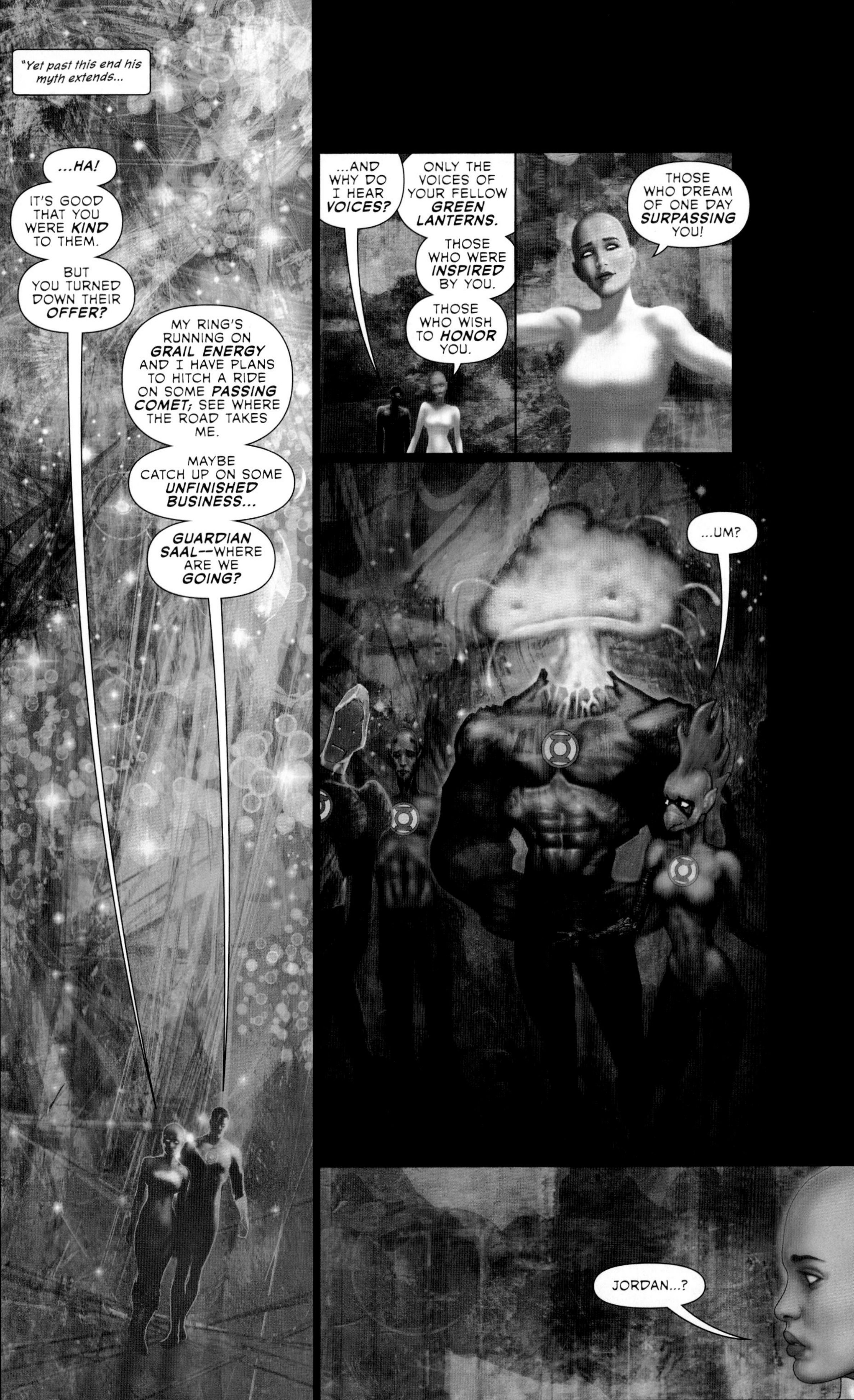
"Yet past this end his myth extends...
...HA!
IT'S GOOD THAT YOU WERE KIND TO THEM.
BUT YOU TURNED DOWN THEIR OFFER?
MY RING'S RUNNING ON GRAIL ENERGY AND I HAVE PLANS TO HITCH A RIDE ON SOME PASSING COMET; SEE WHERE THE ROAD TAKES ME.
MAYBE CATCH UP ON SOME UNFINISHED BUSINESS...
GUARDIAN SAAL--WHERE ARE WE GOING?
...AND WHY DO I HEAR VOICES?
ONLY THE VOICES OF YOUR FELLOW GREEN LANTERNS.
THOSE WHO WERE INSPIRED BY YOU.
THOSE WHO WISH TO HONOR YOU.
THOSE WHO DREAM OF ONE DAY SURPASSING YOU!
...UM?
JORDAN...?

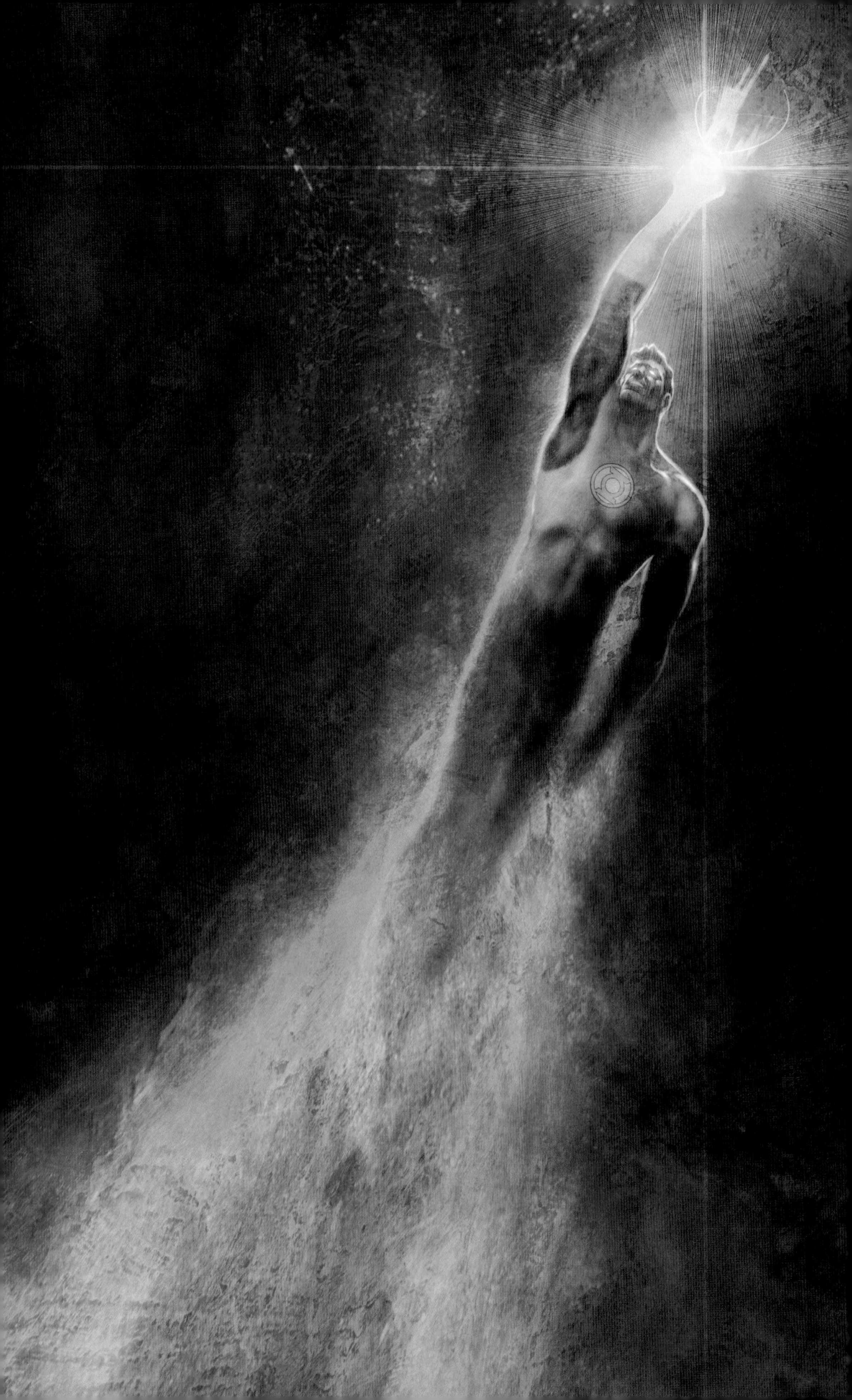

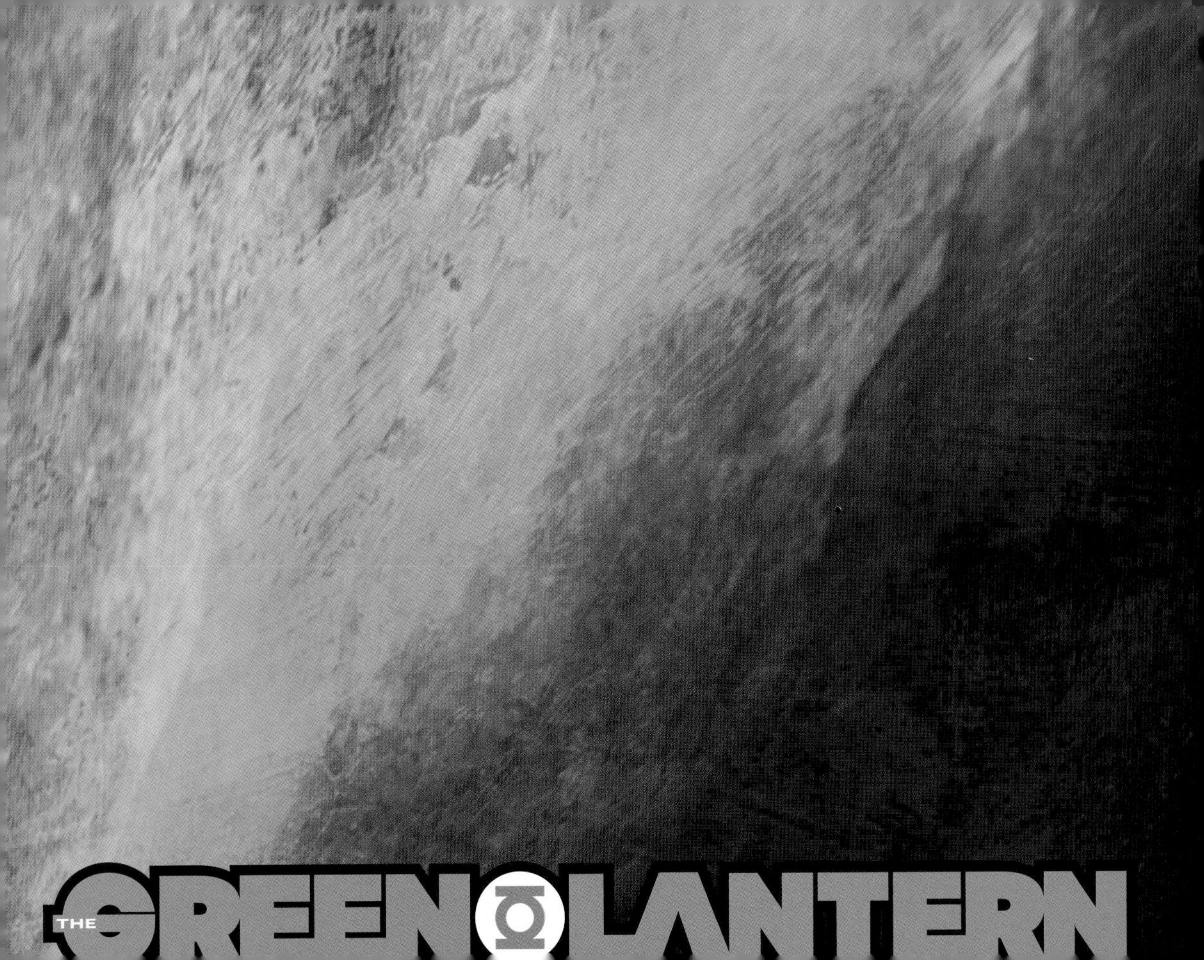
THE GREEN LANTERN

THE SPIRES

NORHAARTA

THE VARIAN STRAIGHTS

HAARTA

GRANT'S LEAP

LAKE HAARTA

NOR FEXXINGTON FEN

VARIAN

SE

THE VITRIFIED DESERT

THE FAE

THE SEA INFERNAL

THE VASTS

THE BOWL OF LORD COWL

DORDRUM

SHARPE ISLAND

MOUNT DORDRUM

Sea of Rathmoor

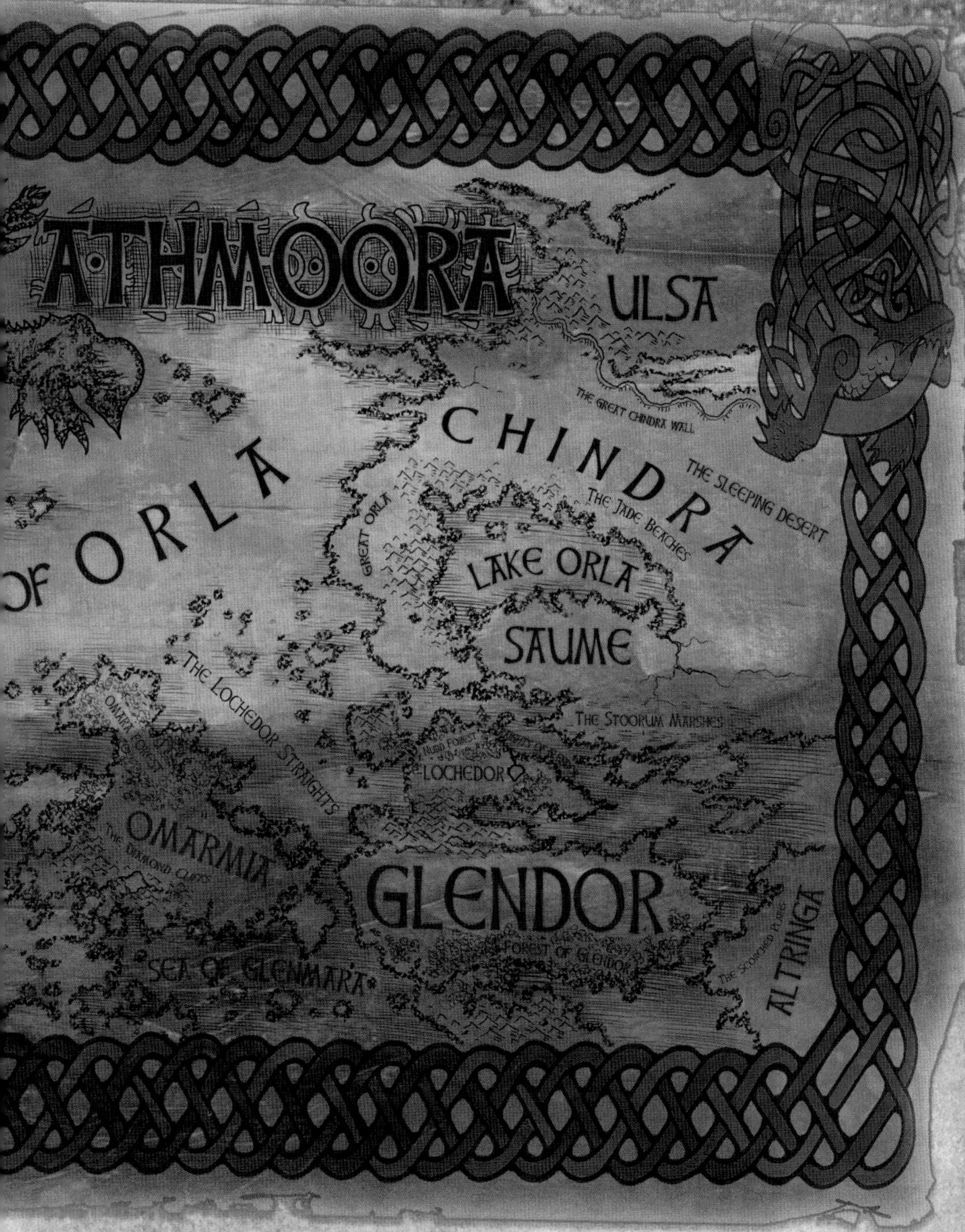

ATHMOORA
ULSA
THE GREAT CHINDRA WALL
CHINDRA
OF ORLA
THE SLEEPING DESERT
THE JADE BEACHES
GREAT ORLA
LAKE ORLA
SAUME
THE LOCHEDOR STRAIGHTS
THE STOORUM MARSHES
LOCHEDOR
OMARMIA
THE DIAMOND CLIFFS
GLENDOR
FOREST OF GLENDOR
SEA OF GLENMARA
THE SCORCHED PLAINS
ALTRINGA

Page 4 from *The Green Lantern Season Two #8*

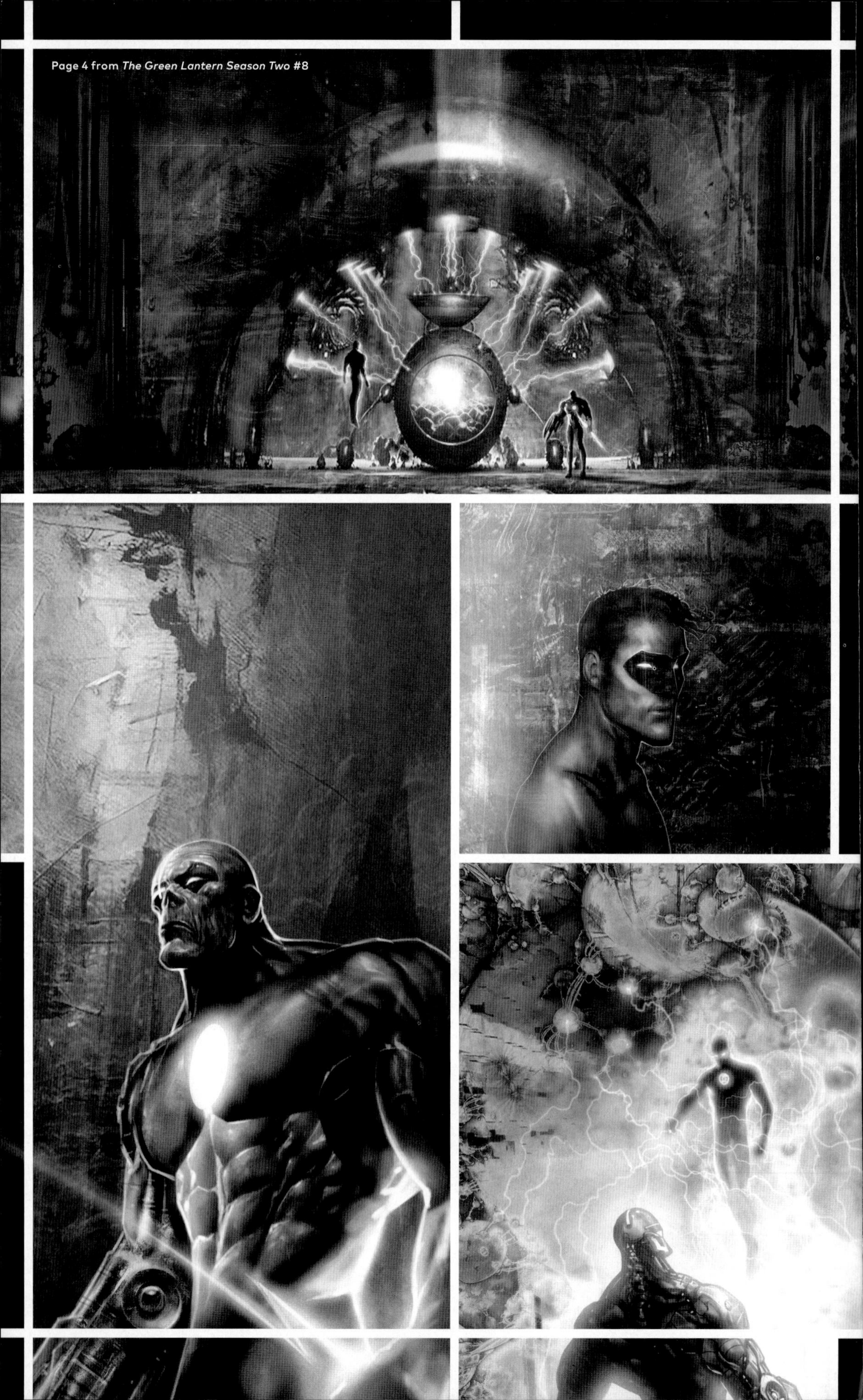

Page 6 from *The Green Lantern Season Two #8*

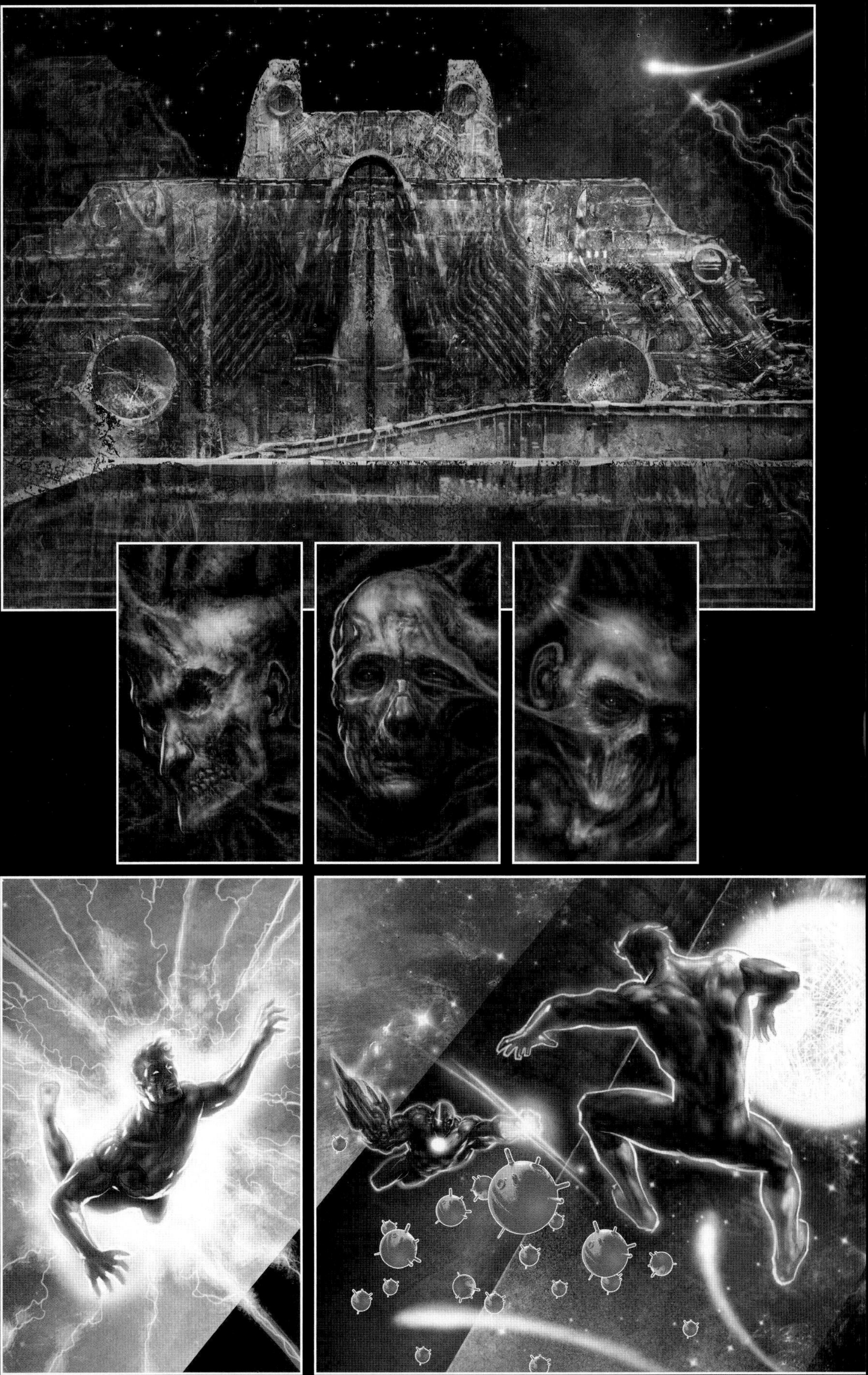

Page 11 from *The Green Lantern Season Two* #8

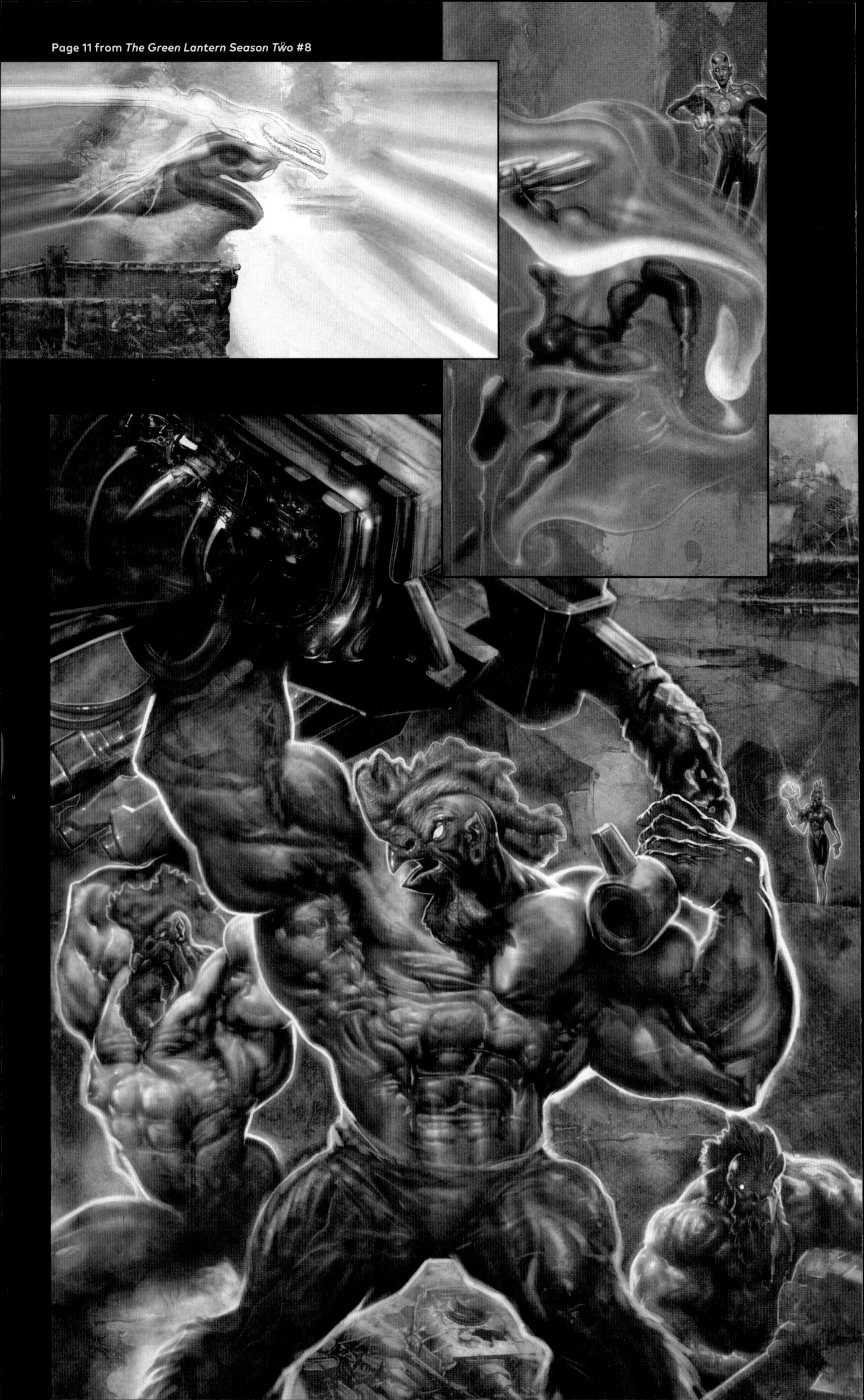

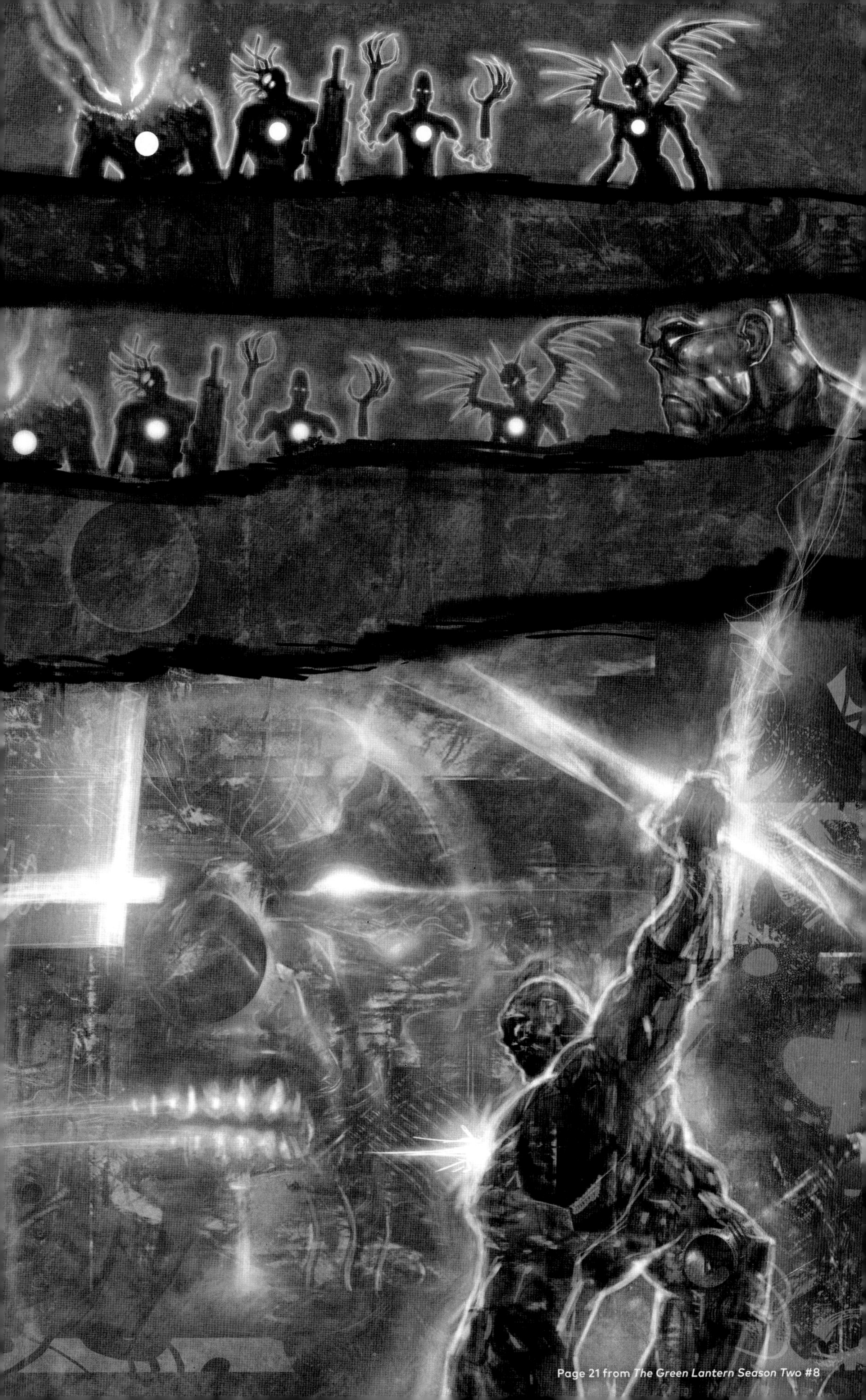

Page 21 from *The Green Lantern Season Two #8*

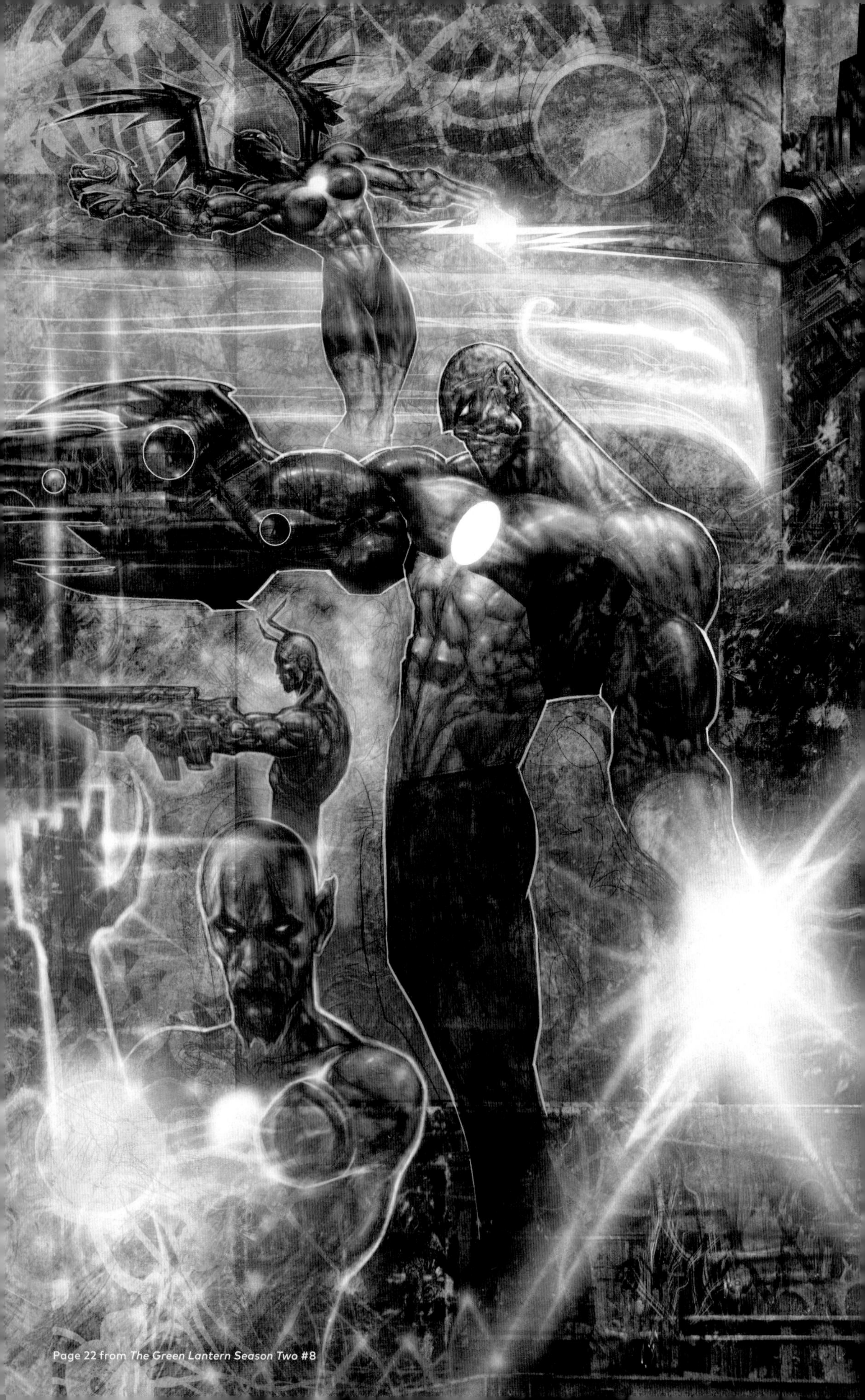

Page 22 from *The Green Lantern Season Two #8*